# Memories
## of the
# Future

# TAIWAN IN THE MODERN WORLD
Series Editor
Murray A. Rubinstein

# Memories
## of the
# Future

## National Identity Issues and the Search for a New Taiwan

Robert Edmondson

Kuang-chün Li

Chia-lung Lin

Tsong-Jyi Lin

Robert Marsh

Andrew Morris

Wei-Der Shu

Rwei-Ren Wu

## Stéphane Corcuff
### Editor

AN EAST GATE BOOK

*M.E.Sharpe*
Armonk, New York
London, England

An East Gate Book

Copyright © 2002 by M.E. Sharpe, Inc.

**Library of Congress Cataloging-in-Publication Data**

Memories of the future : national identity issues and the search for a new Taiwan /
Stéphane Corcuff, editor.
 p. cm.
 Includes bibliographical references and index.
 ISBN 0-7656-0791-3 (alk. paper); ISBN 0-7656-0792-1 (pbk.; alk. paper)
  1.  Taiwan—Politics and government—1895–1945.  2. Taiwan—Politics and
government—1945–  I. Corcuff, Stéphane, 1971–

DS799.716M45 2002
951.24'.904—dc21
2001049918

Printed in the United States of America

The paper used in this publication meets the minimum requirements of
American National Standard for Information Sciences
Permanence of Paper for Printed Library Materials,
ANSI Z 39.48-1984.

BM (c)  10   9   8   7   6   5   4   3   2   1
BM (p)  10   9   8   7   6   5   4   3   2   1

# Contents

# List of Tables and Figures

## Tables

**Figures**

# Acknowledgments

Through this book, the authors would like to express their gratitude to Mr. Huang Huang-hsiung, president of the Taiwan Research Fund, and to Mr. Lin Chia-lung, assistant professor at Chung-cheng University, for their strong commitment to Taiwan studies, which made possible the realization of this book project.

Paris, February 2002

# Introduction

## Taiwan, A Laboratory of Identities

### Stéphane Corcuff

This collection of essays addresses the question of national identity transition in Taiwan, the movement by which Taiwan explored its identity and the status quo in the Taiwan Strait imposed on the island since the 1970s. This question has fundamentally changed the political equilibrium in the Taiwan Strait in the 1990s. The idea of such a book appeared during one of the North American Taiwan Studies Association's annual conferences, and all the chapters in this book were first presented and discussed there as individual papers. However, the ideas expressed here only reflect the authors' views and do not represent any particular institutional position.

A transdisciplinary topic like national identity is hard to analyze exhaustively. When the content of a book depends on a pool of papers, each essay has to be adapted so that important dimensions are mentioned even if they cannot be the subjects of entire chapters. The essays published here have undergone revision and, in several cases, partial rewriting to update the data and analysis, as well as to better suit the constraints of a collective work.

In other words, this collection is not a mere compilation of conference papers presented in recent years. *Memories of the Future* is intended to be a contribution of its own to the study of the identity transition in Taiwan. It comprises ten chapters that explore the emergence of the sense of national belonging in Taiwan—its historical roots and its contemporary expressions. The earliest period evoked is the 1895 cession of Taiwan to Japan. Analysis in the chapters dealing with most contemporary issues stops at the political transition of the year 2000, only briefly evoking Chen Shui-bian's election to the presidency of the Republic. Its focus is mainly the transition in national identity experienced during the last years of Chen's predecessor, Lee Teng-hui.

## Historical Roots

The book is divided into three parts. The first part (chapters 1–3) presents some historical insights into the emergence of the identity question in Taiwan. The second part (chapters 4–7) analyzes some symbolic aspects of the transition, to show how people have reacted to this evolution in national identity. The third part (chapters 8–10) part offers perspectives on some new dimensions of the ethnic debate, on the national identity question in general, and about Taiwanese nationalism.

When Japan defeated China in 1895, the Qing court ceded Taiwan to Tokyo on April 17, in a treaty signed in the Japanese port of Shimonoseki. The cession was resented in Taiwan and helped nurture a feeling of abandonment, which was later turned into an argument illustrating the alleged lack of commitment by China in defending its insular and remote province of Taiwan. Crucial to understanding this is the question of the Qing modernization efforts in Taiwan before the war with Japan, and the true meaning of the short-lived Taiwan Republic established in May 1895, in an attempt to prevent a Japanese takeover. Previous works have viewed the Republic as a Chinese act of anti-imperialist heroism, and its failure, a consequence of its inappropriate or premature use of Western political thought. In chapter 1, Andrew Morris takes into account the modernizing and centralizing policies carried out on Taiwan from the 1870s to the 1890s as the Qing attempted finally to bring control over this peripheral territory. As Morris shows, during the last two decades of reform much had been done to impose Qing order on Taiwan, and there were great changes in Taipei, as the city was transformed from a fiercely contested settler frontier territory into a city thoroughly integrated into the Qing and international political economies. However, all on the island and in the court were aware that the process had not been completed, and that Taiwan was still vulnerable to the colonizing nations. Northern Taiwan was isolated and vulnerable by the time war arrived. China wished it could keep Taiwan during the Shimonoseki negotiation, or at least part of the island, but soon resigned itself to seeing it become Japanese territory. This chapter reveals that the continental origin of the troops in Taiwan probably played an important role in their lack of commitment to defending Taiwan. The same might well be said about some Qing officials sent to the island: Before accepting the presidency of the new Taiwanese Republic, the last Qing governor took the precaution of sending back to the continent most of the monetary reserves of the island.

China's attitude during the Shimonoseki negotiations is an often-debated point, subject to diverging and politicized interpretations. In fact, China has not ceded Taiwan without a fight, as attested by the preparatory documents of the treaty, now deposited in the National Palace Museum in Taipei. But

China had no illusion about the strategic importance of Taiwan for the court or about its capacity to keep the island as part of the Qing Empire. To understand this, we must resituate the event in the context of the expansion of China's frontier and of its real but late effort to modernize Taiwan after an attempted blockade of the island during the war with the French (1884–1885). Andrew Morris helps us understand this complex historical context by analyzing the strategies and identifying the actors. Nevertheless, one historical event had happened: China had ceded Taiwan to Japan, and the Qing court acknowledged that the island was "certainly important to [them], but obviously not as important as Beijing" (quoted by Morris). Under pressure from the Japanese in Shimonoseki, Li Hongzhang had to accept the fact that the Taiwanese who would not move to Mainland in the next two years would be considered Japanese subjects, according to a clause contained in the treaty. The ambiguity of the event is not foreign to the ambiguity of its interpretation today. Generally speaking, pro-independence activists consider that the Shimonoseki treaty symbolically and legally marks the original separation of Taiwan from China and that this separation dates back to more than a hundred years now. However, they rarely evoke the 1895 republic, because this event does not appear to be a point of departure for the Taiwan independence movement. The republic was founded with clear allegiance to the Qing court, and the declaration of independence was aimed at establishing sovereignty, with hope of international mobilization against what would then be seen as Japanese aggression against an independent country. It failed.

However, the symbolic importance of the event should not be underestimated. First, the Shimonoseki treaty remains important in the current discourse on Taiwanese identity. As Kuang-chün Li and I show in chapters five and eight, respectively, a 1995 Taipei march, touting the slogan "Farewell to China," commemorated the Shimonoseki treaty, prompting prounification forces to counterattack with a second march in the Taipei streets entitled "I am Chinese," a few days later. Second, the Taiwan Republic itself shows some important signs that an embryonic Taiwanese consciousness might have appeared then. If the first and only president of the Republic, Tang Jingsong, affirmed immediately to the Qing court that the use of his seal would be temporary, the initiative of founding and funding the first independent Taiwanese state, in 1895, was taken by the (North) Taiwan gentry, not by Qing officials, as shown in chapter one. And the political concepts that accompanied its creation show a great modernity for that time and place. In spite of its ambiguities, the 1895 experience, it seems, is a founding initiative in the history of the progressive emergence of Taiwan as a singular entity. Historian Hsu Chi-tun believes that it is during the 1895 Taiwan Republic that the notion of "Taiwanese," then expressed as *Taimin* or *Tairen,* first appeared (Hsu 1993, 41).

The Japanese colonization of the island lasted fifty years and had a tremendous impact on Taiwanese minds. Sociologist Chang Mau-kuei recently described the link between Japan's contempt for Han Taiwanese perceived backwardness and the island population's ethnic self-denial, which led to a desire for assimilation, at least among the elite. At the same time, this elite started to fight for home rule and in this process started to verbalize the idea of a Taiwanese self, a process facilitated by the fact that in Tokyo several young Taiwanese intellectuals found a window open on the world and new concepts that were beginning to be debated in the West: colonialism and the peoples' right of self-determination. According to Chang Mau-kuei, "It is clear that since the 1920s people had already begun to define Taiwanese people as a collectivity, as a distinct nation ruled by the Japanese colonial government. Taiwan, as a signifier for the place and the people as a whole, had been widely adopted." (Chang 2000, 54–62). But until the dramatic events following the 1945 Retrocession to China, these movements did not lead to an explicit call for a nation separated from China, except by the Taiwanese Communist Party (TCP), which had been founded in China itself. The TCP defended what appears clearly to be "the first political program that advocated an unequivocal Taiwanese nation and independence" (Chang 2000, 57).

Things changed brutally in less than two years, between October 1945 and February 1947. The so-called 2/28 Incident quickly became one of the most significant events (if not *the* most significant event) in this process of differentiation and boundary establishment between Taiwan and China. The February 1947 uprising was directed against the new government in Taipei, tarnished by corruption and incompetence after Taiwan was ceded back to (Nationalist) China. It led to weeks of violence throughout the island and implacable repression by the Nationalist forces. After describing the events of 2/28, Robert Edmondson shows in chapter 2 how the incident began to play the role of what could be called a founding massacre, perpetrated by what the Taiwanese now perceived as a new occupying force, a new ruthless colonizer. But this time, the new rulers were Han Chinese, which inevitably led Taiwanese to deeply question their Chinese belonging, the original start of a movement of Han introspection in contemporary Taiwan. So finally, the founding massacre and the oppressing power that arrived from outside were two important elements for the development of an independence movement. The core of Edmondson's analysis focuses on the symbolic importance of the event. As he shows, a political opposition of growing strength appealed in the 1980s to collective memory and to the 2/28 Incident to strengthen democracy, to hasten the transfer of power out of the hands of the Mainlanders, and to try to promote the independence movement. In recent years, however, the symbol has been recognized and courted by the Kuomintang (KMT) too, adding a new national interpretation to what the author considers as, in the past, an essentially ethnic symbol. Edmondson argues that new political and social realities require that new meanings be added to old symbols and that the emergence of a powerful nonethnic social cleavage has diminished the meaning and the market for 2/28 as an ethnically divisive memory and raised the demand for panethnic national symbols.

As everyone knows, the massacre never led to any apology from the regime under the two Chiangs. Furthermore, the regime was characterized by an authoritarian definition of political power combined with intense propaganda efforts to re-Sinicize Taiwan after a half-century of Japanese colonization. Intense political socialization, aimed at making the Taiwanese consider China as their only possible motherland, as well as the authoritarian character of the regime, had been the source of much acrimony and of numerous arguments for the proindependence activists. The ethnicity of the Taiwanese formed not only in response to "foreign" domination and early Nationalist misrule culminating in the 2/28 Incident, but also from a specific, exclusively Nationalist imagination of what it meant to be Chinese, and a rejection of an authoritarian rule viewed as being imposed from outside.

The severance of administrative and political links with China in 1895, the five decades-long Japanese rule, the dramatic events of 1947, the establishment of an autocratic political center in the 1950s, and the repression of suspected proindependence activists inside the island—all are reasons explaining the development of Taiwan independence movements outside of Taiwan. Wei-Der Shu argues that the Taiwan independence movement (TIM), the banner bearer of Taiwanese nationalism, originated in the mid-1940s when the KMT took over Taiwan at the end of World War II. He explains that due to the severe state repression, the TIM had to formulate its organizational infrastructure in political circles outside the island. From the late 1940s, activists began to organize clandestine political organizations in Japan and North America and to question the legitimacy of the KMT's rule over Taiwan. The focus of this third chapter is the political activism of the proindependence militants. Based on in-depth interviews Wei-Der Shu conducted in North America with twenty-two activists, chapter 3 deals with a fundamental aspect of activism in the clandestine political organizations: *Who* joined these organizations, and *why*? In the sociological literature of social movements, the studies regarding political activism can be divided into three approaches: the "macro structural determinants" point of view (people join the social movement organizations because of a particular sociohistorical context); the "micro socio-psychological determinants" point of view (people join the social movement because of the orientations, perceptions, and values of the participants themselves); the "meso micromobilization context" (whose fundamental concern is the group context for activists to deal with grievances, opportunities, or resources). Scholars in the last group explain activism from the intermediate level concerned with the processes by which activists evaluate and recognize what they have in common and decide to act together. Convincingly, this article argues that it is essential to use all three levels of analysis implied in all three approaches, if we are to enhance our ability to understand and explain the manifestation of political activism.

## The Psychological Impact of the Transition

In these first three chapters, we have made a simple presentation of the historical background, which helps us put into perspective the changes that occurred in the 1980s and 1990s. The second part of the book (chapters 4–7) deals with the current issue of national identity transition in Taiwan. There are analyses of some symbolic aspects of this identity transition, followed by demonstrations of how this evolution has affected people's perception of national identity. causing complex ethnic issues in electoral politics, as well as an identification problem among the former holders of political power, the Mainlanders. It starts with an analysis of the transition itself. In the 1980s and 1990s, Taiwan saw profound changes in term of national policies, national symbols, discourses concerning China and the reunification policy, the free expression of formerly banned proindependence discourses, and separatist definitions of Taiwan's identity. Much of Taiwan studies literature (in both English and Chinese) that deals with the recent transition has concentrated on the institutional changes, and the symbolic dimension of the transition in national identity during the Lee Teng-hui era has too often been forgotten. Chapter 4 is thus aimed at showing how national identity–related political symbols have been transformed. It also intends to show some of the mechanisms inside the party-state ensemble, through which political symbols in the broadest sense have changed and become Taiwanized in the last years before 2000, and to which extent they have changed. The analysis describes the key role of some administrative or political stakeholders inside this party-state apparatus in reforms, the pressure exerted from outside, and the loosening integration of this traditionally highly integrated ensemble after a decade of reforms. To give concrete examples, it focuses on four reform items, each of which concerns a certain type of political socialization tool: state doctrine, political commemorations, textbooks, and banknotes. In this chapter, I first discuss the near-disappearance of the official ideology of the Nationalist regime, the doctrine called the "Three Principles of the People"; second, the transition of the image of Chiang Kai-shek in today's Taiwan is presented, showing to what extent and within which limits references to the former strongman have disappeared from official discourse. Third, I analyze the reform of high school textbooks, which have been revised to make room for lessons on Taiwan's history after decades of deliberate obliteration; and fourth, we see that the reform of banknotes also occasioned important symbolic changes, closely linked to national identity. I try to show that different (transitional) symbolic fields show different stages of the process of indigenization of Taiwan's polity, and that the specific nature of each symbolic field naturally produces different patterns of change or political strategies to get them to change under the Lee Teng-hui presidency. This chapter tries, however, to show that all reform cases studied here do have one point in common: Each time, a total break with the past has been rejected—the accompanying historical movement is a process of reform, and not of revolution. This can be generalized to most of the reforms implemented during the Lee Teng-hui era. Rwei-Ren Wu comes back to this point in chapter 9.

The result is a complex mixture of symbols of different origins. In the process of differentiation from China, radical options have been rejected in favor of negotiated identity symbols, whether as a way to ensure a consensual support of the reforms or as a strategy to pull the rug out from under the then-opposition parties' feet. It also illustrates the acceptance, by Taiwanese or Taiwanized KMT stakeholders, of the necessary localization of the polity. Changes, in the end, have been numerous and far reaching. The four following chapters all deal with how the Taiwanese and the Mainlanders reacted to them. With a paradigm of "mirrors" and "masks," Kuang-chün Li proposes an interpretation of Taiwan's Mainlanders' identity dilemma, to which I return in chapter 8. Both Kuang-chün Li and I share a deep interest in the national identification of the civil war Chinese refugees and their offspring: How do the Mainlanders react to an increasing pressure for Taiwanization of the polity and of its symbols? What is the figuration of their national identification? How do different generations of Mainlanders deal with their apparent marginalization in the political system, the administration, and the army? Chapter 5 introduces, in its beginning, the notion of Mainlanders' "identity discomfort" in Taiwan, and explores closely the attitude of the Mainlanders, who traditionally view reunification with mainland China as a political objective that cannot be compromised. Through interviews Kuang-chün Li tries to answer the following question: "To what extent can Mainlanders adapt to the new reality, and to what extent can they identify with Taiwan?" I tried to do the same through a questionnaire, and our conclusions

converge: The very process of an identity crisis aroused the opposite phenomenon: their growing, though ambiguous, identification with Taiwan.
Kuang-chün Li thinks this Taiwanization is successful; I try to show that at
least it is undeniable—the movement is indeed constantly impeded by political factors.

Why do we have two chapters on the Mainlanders and none on the Aborigines? As the reader knows, the content of this book is drawn from papers
presented earlier. And certainly, a whole book should be devoted to the impact of the Aboriginal factor in the recent maturation of Taiwan's national
identity. But the presence of two chapters on the Mainlanders can also be
explained by the importance this minority still plays in Taiwan today—as
the beginning of chapter 8 tries to explain—and by the very meager academic literature available on this important topic.

Chapter 6 extends the analysis to native Taiwanese and puts in perspective statistical data on the way Taiwanese and Taiwan's Mainlanders redefine their national identification in the face of the threat from Mainland China,
and on their own evaluation of the democratic progress and prospects in
Taiwan. In this chapter, Tsong-jyi Lin argues that during the past several
years, the democratic values of the respective groups in Taiwan have been
stable; however, he says, the national identification schemes in both groups
have dramatically changed, particularly for the Mainlanders. He views the
most probable reason for the shift as intimidation from China. Second, he
argues that there is no significant relationship between ethnic division and
democratic attitude. In contrast, ethnic division has a significant association
with national identity and opinion about Taiwan's future. In addition, the
author finds that no significant relationship between ethnicity and evaluation of democratic progress or prospect consistently exists in any survey
data used. Third, he says that among several variables, only ethnicity, national identity, and democratic attitude have consistently exerted a significant impact on public opinion about Taiwan's future. And certainly analyzing
the national identity question requires addressing these two fundamental
questions: What is the will of the people of Taiwan concerning their future
national identification? And how do geopolitical constraints affect this area
of public opinion?

Chapter 7 shows that people in Taiwan who favor the establishment of
an independent Republic of Taiwan face the reality constraint that the PRC
says it would use force to prevent what Beijing would view as the loss of
Taiwan. Those who hold the opposite view and favor the reunification of
Taiwan with Mainland China face a different reality constraint: the nondemocratic, economically underdeveloped, and therefore unappealing, character
of the PRC. In the 1990s, Wu Nai-teh made a very significant advance by

incorporating these reality constraints into the way the questions were phrased in Taiwan surveys. Respondents were asked

1.  If, after Taiwan announces its independence, it could maintain peaceful relations with Communist China, should Taiwan become an independent country?
2.  If Mainland China and Taiwan become similar in economic, political, and social conditions, should the two sides of the strait be unified into one country?

Depending on how a person answered both these questions, he or she was categorized by Robert Marsh, in chapter 7, as one of the following four types: Taiwan nationalist, China nationalist, pragmatist, or conservative. Chapter 7 first analyzes the distribution of respondents in surveys conducted before and after the 1996 PRC firing of missiles into the waters near Taiwan's two largest seaports. The trend shows increasing support for Taiwan independence and declining support for unification with China. But in 1996, even after the PRC's military missile testing, only 21 percent favored Taiwan independence, even if this could be achieved without war with the PRC. The largest category were the pragmatists (39 percent), those who would support Taiwan independence, but would also support unification with China, depending upon which of the two ideal conditions—peaceful acceptance by the PRC of Taiwan's independence or China's "catching up" with Taiwan in democracy and economic development—occurs first in the future. This chapter next shows the effect of bureaucratically defined ethnicity (*Benshengren* vs. *Waishengren)* and subjective ethnicity (self-identification as "Taiwanese" or "Chinese" or "both") on national identification preferences. Ethnic self-identification as "Taiwanese" increases the probability that Minnan and Hakka people will be Taiwan nationalists, just as self-identification as "Chinese" increases the likelihood that *Waishengren* (usually, but wrongly, translated as Mainlanders) are China nationalists. Robert Marsh argues in his contribution that when these survey findings are combined with geopolitical considerations, surprising conclusions can be drawn: Even among ethnic Taiwanese and even after the PRC's 1996 missile firing, there are almost as many pragmatists as Taiwan nationalists. Pragmatists would accept unification rather than independence if China becomes as democratic and economically developed as Taiwan but does not become willing to accept Taiwan independence without a war. For Marsh, since even modern democratic states are unwilling to accept a loss of territory, if there is a departure from Taiwan's status quo in the future, both public opinion and geopolitics suggest that the change is more likely to be unification with China than Taiwan independence.

## Perspectives on Taiwanese Nationalism

The analysis developed in those three chapters, however, needed to be put into a larger context. The third part of this book, containing chapters 8 through 10, focuses on the political construction of Taiwanese nationalism and perspectives of maturation of the national identity question. Chapter 8 comes back to the Mainlanders. Using data from a large questionnaire distributed to them in Taiwan in 1997, this chapter aims to study how the national identification feelings of this politically salient group in Taiwan have adapted in the post–martial law era. Through this questionnaire, I tried to isolate variables able to measure the national identification phenomenon in general and to give precise statistics on the movement of Taiwanization of the Mainlanders in particular. The questionnaire was very detailed, containing 178 variables; so unfortunately, it was impossible here to give more than a glance at the results collected. But some of the most revealing data were chosen and first of all, the *order of priorities* in the Mainlanders' mind, when we put unification in perspective with domestic policy items (see the explanatory details in the chapter). The results are quite interesting, and they prove the Mainlanders' irrepressible Taiwanization. However, I try to show that the question is eminently political and that this undeniable movement, which can be measured in their day-to-day life, is instantly "disactivated" in a situation of political choice, whether expression of an opinion on Taiwan's identity or choice of a candidate in an election. This chapter also tries to draw the historical and political construction of the ethnic label *"Waishengren"* to show why it should be now abandoned and by what it could be replaced. For this, it was necessary to present some broader perspectives on new dimensions of the identity politics in Taiwan and Taiwanese nationalism, namely the famous debate on the "new Taiwanese." Finally, this chapter's contribution lies in some of the distinctions it tries to make between positions expressed in terms of principles, and positions perceived by the observer from the day-to-day habits of the respondents; between positions expressed in time of peace and possible attitudes in what is called, in French, *une situation-limite,* that is, when an essential choice is made necessary by an abnormal situation like a deep political crisis or war;[1] and last, between different dimensions of national identification—a work on the cognitive dimension of national identity. Distinguishing between these seems to me a *sine qua non* for understanding better the subtlety of the national identity question, which is most often impossible to render through the commonly used opinion polls.

The effort to question the validity of the *Waishengren* concept today, and to find a more suitable word to designate this settler population, is related to various attempts made in Taiwan to imagine the nation, and to, as Rwei-Ren Wu puts it in chapter 9, "reintegrate the settler group into this newly structured and nativized State" that emerged during the Lee Teng-hui era. In his chapter, Rwei-Ren Wu analyzes this era as a process of both decolonization and nation-building. Drawing a comparison with Gramsci's analysis of the late nineteenth century's *Risorgimento,* which enabled the formation of the modern Italian state, the author opposes a "passive revolution," which succeeded under Lee Teng-hui's nativized KMT, to more radical approaches held by opposition forces and militant proponents of Taiwan independence, such as the Democratic Progressive Party (DPP). Before showing the main differences between the two approaches in terms of political strategy and ideology, Wu asks the question of why Lee's gradualism won over the opposition's radicalism. His answers are convincing: the initial impulse given by Chiang Ching-kuo, who facilitated the transfer of power into Lee's hands; the Chinese threat: and the role played by the *Waishengren,* the eternal guardians of a political and conservative orthodoxy. One could add: the potency of the KMT's electoral machine, the effects of the past political socialization, and, as Chang Mau-kuei wrote, the fact that "the dignity of the Taiwanese has come from the improvement in economic conditions and material well-being over the last fifty years," which explains that "preserving these economic gains and democratic rights in Taiwan means that everyone has some stake in the status quo" in the Taiwan Straits (Chang 2000, 68). The impact of the victory of the gradualist approach, combined with the reforms achieved under Lee Teng-hui, has been such that the opposition DPP had to tone down its pro-independence rhetoric. For the author, Lee Teng-hui was "by temperament and by conviction . . . a gradualist reformer": one could ask if, as a reform-minded KMT official, he had the choice. Being a member of the KMT party-state apparatus, his only chance of success was very probably the gradualist approach. An important question that has been widely debated is: Was Lee Teng-hui determined to go that far from the very beginning (for example, when he started to feel that, Chiang Ching-kuo being ill, he might have to succeed him)? If he was, he certainly could not have known, until the highest point of his reforms (this moment being symbolized by his final "Two-states thesis" of July 1999), to what extent he could eventually go. His political mastery enabled him to go farther than anyone, probably including himself, would have expected him to be able to go. But we do not know yet, even with Lee's numerous writings, whether his plans had been established a long time ago, or whether he himself also *evolved* toward more radicalism, as China dramatically increased military and diplomatic pressure under his presidency. Probably, the answer is multiple. It is highly probable that this reform-minded politician evolved with the polity he was transforming, and that over time, dramatic events, such as the development of the Chinese military threat, persuaded him to go farther than he had originally planned.

As we see, Rwei-Ren Wu's paradigm is extremely fruitful and particularly relevant to understanding the extremely complex Taiwanese transition between 1988 and 2000. Finally, we can agree with the author when he shows that one of Lee's political successes was to formalize an equivalence that had long been visible, between the "Republic of China" and "Taiwan." This was a dramatic evolution, as it helped Taiwanese nationalists to partially solve one of their enduring problems: *Taiwan is de facto and de jure independent*, but not as a "Republic of Taiwan": constitutionally, politically, internationally, it is the "Republic of China," of which Taiwan is legally a province only, the other provinces on mainland being now ruled by the PRC. Verbalizing this equivalence was a bold step, and as Rwei-Ren says, "the popular President Chen [Shui-bian] . . . benefits tremendously from the pre-existing domestic consensus on Taiwan-ROC's sovereignty." Setting aside political passions (and before all, China's impressive hatred of Lee), and from a purely political science point of view, it can be said that Lee Teng-hui's political achievements are truly exceptional, and their dispassionate analysis has only just begun. This chapter is one of the first attempts at such an analysis, and we hope that this book will be a contribution in this direction. Let us hope that, for the sake of the study of political transitions, the Lee Teng-hui era in Taiwan will be viewed by more political scientists as one of the most interesting case studies in the contemporary world.

However, China is an additional important factor in the emergence of a modern Taiwanese nationalism, as mentioned already by Tsong-jyi Lin and Robert Marsh. In an analysis of the relations between state-making, democratization, and nation-building, Chia-lung Lin concludes that the Chinese threat has played as important a role as the process of democratization itself. In his chapter, the author concludes by discussing the political factors that explain how the ethnic nationalism in Taiwan has started to transform itself into a civic nationalism, serving more clearly the interests of the Taiwanese nation than those of individual ethnic groups. In his chapter, Chia-lung Lin adopts three approaches to present this transformation. He first puts the words "Taiwanese identity" and "Chinese identity" in perspective with each other, showing that three dimensions of identity can, theoretically, cohabit peacefully: an ethnic origin (the Han), a cultural identity (being Chinese), and a political identification (Taiwan). This is close to what is proposed in chapter 8 to analyze the different components of the *Waishengren*'s national identification. The problem is that in time of political tension, this neat disposition of feelings is quickly forgotten; and the transition analyzed by Chia-lung Lin, and more generally in the second and third parts of this book, is far from being complete. Lin then convincingly shows how the democratization process has produced a national consciousness in Taiwan, "transforming the term 'Taiwanese' from an ethnic term for 'native Taiwanese' to a civic term for 'citizens of Taiwan.'" The movement has been so strong that even the pro-unification New Party has been forced to localize its discourse, and view, with the rest of the Taiwanese, the elections, especially the presidential one, as an expression of "the people's sovereignty consciousness, . . . the government's ruling legitimacy, and [the] increase [in] international support for Taiwan." Cross-party issues and the KMT's nativization under Lee Teng-hui, he says, have also been very important in forcing or enabling parties to turn strategies of ethnic mobilization into discourses appealing to the nation. But, as said above, this chapter insists on the role China played, quite involuntarily, in fostering a community spirit in Taiwan. It states strongly the idea of a "sense of common suffering" resulting from China's attitude. But Chia-lung Lin recognizes also that the Taiwanese society is not homogeneously opposed to China: "not all Mainlanders lack Taiwanese consciousness and not all native Taiwanese embrace Taiwanese identity." He insists on the pluralistic nature of identities in Taiwan, as already exemplified by the *Waishengren* "case," and shows the diversity of the definitions of what makes someone "Taiwanese." Nevertheless, the awakening of Taiwanese consciousness under the impulse of China's regular menaces has been clearly measured on several occasions, reviewed by the author. As a result, even though PRC's regular menaces, whether verbal, diplomatic or military, have certainly intimidated Taiwanese minds and discouraged people from openly supporting a formal declaration of independence, it has nevertheless led to an increase in Taiwanese consciousness and nationalism, and the data used by Chia-lung Lin support such an analysis. But as it appeared in several chapters (Tsong-jyi Lin and Robert Marsh's analysis of national identification schemes, Rwei-Ren Wu's contribution on the form of revolution Taiwan experienced, and my chapter of the adaptation process experienced by the *Waishengren*), this tendency of replacing an ethnic discourse by mobilization strategies in favor of the nation is not subject only to Taiwan's domestic evolution and the internal factors of the maturation of its national identity. China remains a factor that is imponderable and that yet cannot be ignored. This certainly does not make things easy for the political leader, but it has made Taiwan a *laboratory of identities* that is particularly interesting for the researcher.

**Note**

1. *Une situation-limite,* in this case, would push people to make a dreadful choice that they would never have to make in a "normal" situation. It would force them to

redefine their identity, to mask and even try to forget a part of themselves, and it would crystallize a pluralistic identity by reducing it to its opposed, antagonist poles.

## Bibliography

Hsu, Chi-tun. 1993. *Xünzhao Taiwan xin zuobiao* (Searching for Taiwan's new marks). Taipei: Zili wanbao wenhua chuban bu.
Chang, Mau-kuei. 2000. "On the Origins and Transformation of Taiwanese National Identity." *China Perspectives*, no. 28, (March–April 2000) pp. 51–70.

# Note on Transcription

The debate in Taiwan on rationalizing the romanization of the Chinese has, since 1998, turned ideological. In the absence of consensus, and to avoid politicized debates, the present book will adopt different transcriptions depending on the context, following a logic that respects times and places. For every common word, such as book titles, transcription of a concept, an expression, a quotation, or an editor's name, the Mainland's *hanyu pinyin* transcription is used. For personal and place names on the Mainland, as for the names of Qing officials sent to Taiwan, pinyin is also used. For personal and place-names in Taiwan, the present book uses the Taiwanized Wade-Giles transcription, which remains, for the time being, the most familiar one used in Taiwan, in spite of its shortcomings. A list of characters is added at the end of the book.

# Part I

## Note on Transcription
### Historical Roots

# Part I

Historical Roots

—— 1 ——

# The Taiwan Republic of 1895 and the Failure of the Qing Modernizing Project

*Andrew Morris*

*"I've heard of the Republic [of Taiwan]. It came suddenly from above into the world of men."*
—Liang Qichao, 1911*

*"Frontiers are indeed the razor's edge on which are suspended the modern issues of war and peace, of life or death of the nations."*
—George Lord Curzon, 1907†

In the early morning of June 5, 1895, Tang Jingsong, president of the Taiwan Republic, collected his memorial drafts, official government seal, and a telescope case full of silver dollars, and stuffed them in a bag with his clothing. Paying ten bodyguards $100 each to protect him from the rioting troops outside his official residence, the presidential yamen, Tang was escorted out through the Taipei West Gate and one mile to the Tamsui River, just one hour before his yamen burst into flames behind him.[1] Tang boarded a small boat in Tamsui Harbor, and soon, along with several other officials, bankers, some two thousand Qing officers and soldiers, and a few European residents of

---

*Liang Qichao, 1911. *Yinbingshi he ji* (Collection from ice-drinking studio), volume 5. Shanghai: Zhonghua shuju, 1961 reprint, p. 205.

†George Lord Curzon of Kedleston, 1907, cited in Charles S. Maier, "Consigning the Twentieth Century to History: Alternative Narratives for the Modern Era," *American Historical Review* 106, no. 2 (June 2000), p. 817.

Taipei, boarded the German steamer *Arthur* bound for Xiamen. Taipei was now in a complete state of disorder, all its government yamens were in flames, and the treasury and arsenal had been emptied by rampaging soldiers. Tang's hasty exit would get no smoother. Tamsui garrison soldiers, who felt entitled to the eight crates of silver that their commanding officers hauled onto the *Arthur* that morning, fired on the ship. The German gunboat *Iltis* returned fire on the forts, and twenty men had been killed by the time Tang and company made their escape.[2]

This was the inglorious end of the Taipei-based Taiwan Republic (*Taiwan Minzhuguo*), inaugurated as Asia's first republic only eleven days earlier.[3] By the Treaty of Shimonoseki, signed on April 17, 1895, China ceded Taiwan and the Penghu Islands (Pescadores) to Japan. The Taiwan Republic was founded on May 25, as elites in Taiwan tried to stake their last claim to the forsaken island. Their appeal to the world was based on the idea that a sovereign republic could not be truly ceded by another nation (the Qing Empire), and the use of Western political principles illustrates the new government's faith in a quick Western response to the crisis Taiwan faced.

Previous Western scholarship devoted to the Taiwan Republic has treated it as a failure due to an inappropriate or premature use of Western political thought, a "sham affair" worthy of research only for the purpose of ascertaining "the degree of the republic's artificiality."[4] It is certainly true that this eleven-day republic did not realize the elites' objective of Western protection from Japan or their claims to represent the whole of Taiwan. However, there are other, more historically relevant ways to discuss the events in Republican Taipei. The fate of the Republic must be understood in the context of the preceding two decades, which saw great changes in the city. Taipei was transformed from a fiercely contested, settler frontier territory into an idealized symbol of a modern, united, and commercially flourishing Qing dynasty. Charles Maier has recently discussed the common modern drive to reinforce the frontier, especially in times of social upheaval and renewed international competition, describing how "national power and efficiency rested on the saturation of [national] space inside the frontier."[5] This describes precisely the late nineteenth-century administration of Taiwan, as the presence of Qing officials and Mainland Chinese and Western merchants reflected the image of a Taiwan thoroughly integrated into the Qing and international political economies. The Taiwan Republic was the final component of this pattern, as it was to be defended on the ground by mostly "Yue" armies (based in the southern Chinese province of Guangxi) and in the international political arena by the Western powers. However, it was precisely these nonsettler influences that left northern Taiwan even more isolated and vulnerable by the time war arrived.

## Anti-imperialist Policies of the Qing

As the mid-nineteenth century race among the imperialists heated up, the foreign powers began to formulate great designs on the strategically located island of Taiwan. British and American traders, officials, military men, and missionaries made many requests of their governments to occupy, colonize, or even purchase Taiwan. In the 1850s and 1860s, many Japanese elites hoped to expand northward into Manchuria and southward into Taiwan, which they believed was only a tributary state of the Qing.[6]

Japanese and French military expeditions on Taiwan in 1874 and 1884 marked important turning points in the way the Qing court saw Taiwan. Both nations—the Japanese explicitly in official negotiations and the French implicitly by offering Taiwan to Japan in exchange for military assistance against the Qing[7]—directly challenged Qing claims to sovereignty over part or all of Taiwan.

The Qing had done little, bureaucratically or militarily, since the late eighteenth century to truly administer Taiwan, quietly tolerating Taiwan's pattern of social unrest described by the saying "a small uprising every three years, and a large rebellion every five years." However, a foreign incursion every ten years was a much more serious problem. These brazen military forays convinced the court that they could no longer take its sovereignty over Taiwan for granted if no one else did. The threats of Western and Japanese imperialism dictated that the Taiwan frontier would have to be rationalized and clearly brought under Qing control, in order to demonstrate the Qing's unalterable authority in Taiwan.

These reforms were begun by Shen Baozhen, a Special Imperial Commissioner sent to Taiwan in June 1874. Shen worked to resolve conflict between Taiwan's Aborigine and Han settler populations, to redraw administrative boundaries,[8] to open mines, and to settle *youmin,* or wanderers. Shen procured modern troops for Taiwan, began work on installing telegraph lines, and even sent an envoy to Japan to learn more about the latest modernization strategies.[9]

This work was continued by Liu Mingchuan, in 1885 named the first governor of the new Taiwan Province. Liu was the main figure in the dual processes of modernization and centralization under Qing authority as he worked to make Taiwan a "foundation of national wealth and power." Administrative boundaries were further refined as Taiwan Province was now classified in to three prefectures, eleven counties, three subprefectures, and one independent department. Liu secured funding for an armaments factory outside Taipei's North Gate and for new cannon platforms in Keelung. A land survey begun in 1888 revealed that there was 20 percent more cultivated land on the island than previously believed. New telegraph lines criss-crossed the island and even the Taiwan Strait. Liu worked to open coal and sulfur mines in areas newly "opened" (i.e., cleared of their Aboriginal residents) by Chinese settlers. And in order to expedite the camphor and tea production so dependent on the appropriation of land belonging to these northern Aboriginal populations, Liu expended much effort to pacify these groups militarily and via the Qing educational system.[10]

Liu built the city of Taipei as a new center of power in Taiwan, distant from the provincial capital in Tainanfu. In Taipei, a new city with no entrenched elite class that could hinder his modernizing task, gentry-merchant elites proved very friendly to Liu's reforms, accompanied as they were by favorable taxation policies on Taiwan's northern tea lands.[11] From these groups Liu received valuable assistance in his construction efforts in nearby Tataocheng, which quickly became the commercial center of the north. With Liu's cooperation, an investment group from the wealthy lower Yangtze region formed the Taipei Urban Prosperity Company (Xingshi gongsi) to set up shops and fund modernization measures. The worries of other Mainland-run firms setting up operations in Tataocheng were quickly erased by Liu's repeated efforts to increase duties on goods handled by foreign merchants. This process of Qing centralization was evinced by the arrival of Anhui and Jiangsu officials taking provincial posts in what only a few years earlier was a lone outpost in the hardiest of hardy frontier lands.[12]

The Shen- and Liu-era reforms were China's answer to the late-nineteenth century trends of imperialism and colonialism, as the Qing finally moved to stake an unchallengeable claim to Taiwan, and to put an end to foreign efforts to conquer and colonize the island. The informal settling process carried out by Chinese migrants struck no fear in the hearts of imperialists, who still saw Taiwan as ripe for the taking. Governor Liu's project was meant to integrate this marginal area politically and economically into the workings of the entire empire—classifying new areas, drawing new boundaries, building new defenses, and subduing Aboriginal groups whose very presence mocked Qing claims to dominance. However, Liu's reforms proved to have their limits. The foreign and Tainan forces that Liu hoped to outmaneuver were still too strong, and the Qing recalled Liu in 1891.

Liu's replacement by Shao Youlian, with the court's blessings, promptly discontinued all the Liu-era reform policies and development projects. The foreign pressure being brought to bear on the Qing over Liu's trade restrictions made it impossible to maintain his anti-imperialist course. Shao served until 1894, when he was succeeded by the island's treasurer and lieutenant governor, Tang Jingsong, a rising star Qing official and veteran of nine years' service in Taiwan.

## The Western Presence in Taiwan

When Taiwan was ceded to Japan, a great cry came from the island's gentry, merchants, and officials: Taiwan had to be saved from Japan and occupied by one or more of the Western powers. But what did the Taiwanese know of the West? European merchants, who began arriving in the north in the 1860s, were often attacked or harassed by disgruntled urban residents.[13] Presbyterian missionaries began to work in 1865, and unified Chinese resistance to them began immediately, coming to a head just three years later. When British missionaries protested the Fujian provincial camphor monopoly, officials spread rumors of missionaries poisoning wells and food, and mobs sacked and burned two chapels in the Pingtung area.[14]

However, violent attacks on Europeans were punished with the help of "gunboat diplomacy." The Tamsui prefectural government issued (and even carved into a stone monument) warnings against harassing Westerners. Civil treatment of foreign merchants and missionaries in the Taipei area was recorded after the early 1870s, as officials began to enforce foreign treaty "rights."[15] However, this was not true of the rest of the island, as attacks on missionaries in the south continued through the 1880s. While no violence was reported against the foreign community in Taipei during the Sino-French War, a Canadian missionary wrote of the "violent persecution" of missionaries in other areas of the north at this time.[16]

The accompanying graphs (see page 19), illustrating the rapid expansion of foreign trade in Taipei-area ports, can give us a clue as to the role of foreign commerce in the north. Northern trade grew explosively through the 1870s and 1880s, as foreign merchants, drawn by the tea trade, flooded into Taipei. The leveling off of trade shown in 1886–1891 mirrors exactly the period of Liu Ming-chuan's harsh taxation of foreign traders; the spikes before and after his tenure show the extent to which growth depended on uninhibited foreign capital. Newly arriving Chinese merchants with previous experience in the Mainland treaty ports profited from Liu's taxation policies. However, Taiwan merchants served largely as middlemen in the tea trade and thus profited more from a strong *foreign* presence. It was recorded that officials in Taipei became "generally prompt in giving satisfaction" to the Westerners when conflicts arose and that the Chinese were eventually "taught to respect foreigners."[17] Urban elites were clearly behind this new atmosphere of international cooperation, as their ties to foreign capital now took precedent over a united northern opposition to the economic disruptions that had accompanied the Western merchants' arrival.

However, these elite ties to foreign capital meant very little to the average Taipei resident. For twenty years, commoners had been forced to accept quietly the presence of Westerners who dominated Taipei trade and exhibited arrogant disregard for the people of Taiwan. Where financial and political elites would find it logical to turn to the West for assistance in 1895, the average urbanite would likely feel no reason to spring into the arms of a foreign protector in the face of Japanese invasion.

## Japanese Landing

In July 1894, Japanese armies took over Seoul, and the Sino-Japanese War began. The Qing court promptly sent some 8,500 troops from Guangdong and Xiamen to defend Taiwan and the Penghu (Pescadores) Islands.[18] Hubei-Hunan governor-general Zhang Zhidong wired Treasurer Tang, offering to send troops from Guangdong and guns and bullets to Taiwan; he added that "if munitions were sent now on government or commercial ships, Japan would not dare to stop them."[19] In Taipei, outgoing governor Shao ordered gentry leader Lin Wei-yuan to organize anti-Japanese militia units.[20] The last two decades of reform had done much to impose Qing order on Taiwan, but all were aware that the island was still vulnerable. In November Zhang expressed to Senior Grand Secretary Li Hongzhang that Taiwan must not be ceded to the Japanese; the court would have to approach England or Russia to help prevent this "incalculable loss."[21]

On March 23, 1895, the Japanese landed in the Penghu Islands, the strategic gateway to Taiwan. This symbolism was lost on the Qing troops stationed there, however, and they did nothing to resist the Japanese. Morale among the Yue troops was less than electrifying at the time; Penghu brigadier-general Zhou Zhenbang was attacked by soldiers and arrested in Takou (Kaohsiung) for leaving with his troops' pay. Many of the troops did not even bother to fight. Boats of Qing soldiers were reported weaving unmolested through the approaching Japanese fleet.[22]

March 31 brought more bad news. The three-week cease-fire signed the day before was limited in scope to the three Qing provinces Fengtian, Zhili, and Shandong, and excluded Taiwan. This news only exacerbated Taipei tensions. Food prices increased, business was demoralized, and the once bustling streets of the commercial center Tataocheng were now silent. Rumors about the Japanese enemy began to sweep the city. One told of Japanese soldiers who descended in balloons and landed in the middle of Penghu forts armed with invulnerable shields. Others told of how the legendary commander Liu Yongfu and his Black Flag troops were already engaged in battle with the Japanese at Takou, or of impending Japanese attacks on the Taipeifu north or south gates. Some concerned residents congregated at the governor's yamen, asking if Taiwan was no longer part of China.[23] These discussions taking place among the common people of Taipei allow us to get at least a tiny glimpse of how they saw the unfolding crisis—their concern and their lack of confidence that Taiwan would be effectively protected by the Qing against these invincible Japanese invaders.

Li Hongzhang soon was put in the unenviable position of negotiating a settlement with Count Itō Hirobumi, representing a very eager Japanese Empire-to-be. Li warned Itō about malaria, about the British who pushed opium into Taiwan, and about the dangerous rebels who rose up from time to time to kill officials; to which Itō merely answered: "We have not swallowed [Taiwan] yet and we are very hungry."[24] On April 13, the court wired Li that he could cede the south of Taiwan if the Qing could keep the north, but Li knew that Itō would not be swayed.[25] The second provision of the Treaty of Shimonoseki, signed April 17, gave the Qing just two months to hand over Taiwan and all other islands under provincial jurisdiction.

That day, Zhang Zhidong wired Governor Tang with news of the cession.[26] This at least ended the suspense for Tang, who had been pleading with the court for a hint as to Taiwan's status. On April 14, he wired the court, "The nation makes these great plans; it is unforgivable that a lone official across the sea should have to pin his hopes on these rumors and wild predictions."[27] Official notice of the cession reached the city only on April 19, when Tang was notified with a simple telegram. The court apologized to Tang for the cession, but reminded him that "Taiwan is certainly important to us, but obviously not as important as Beijing. . . . Since Taiwan is by itself there in the ocean, we would not be able to help defend Taiwan anyway." The Qing also announced that day that anyone who did not leave Taiwan for the Mainland within two years would become a Japanese subject.[28]

On April 20, a strike was held in Taipei, as people closed shops and shouted and banged gongs in protest. Others gathered at the governor's yamen to learn more news. Still others showed their displeasure by attempting (unsuccessfully) to break into the provincial treasury and armory.[29] There was a rumor in Taipei that Western firms were being used to channel funds from the Japanese government to Qing officials.[30] Some Taipei resident's notified the Qing officials that they were expected to stay in Taiwan to resist the Japanese.[31]

Seemingly permanent chaos erupted in Taipei on April 22, when armed conflict broke out between Yue soldiers under Tang's aide-de-camp Colonel Fang Yuanliang and Fujian Admiral-in-Chief Yang Qizhen's Huai Army troops. During a pitched battle on the grounds of the governor's yamen, Li Wenkui, a disgruntled officer under Fang, killed his colonel, then led the troops in firing on the milling crowds outside the yamen, killing eighteen and wounding twenty-five civilians.[32] On April 26, Tang told the court of his efforts to "capture the murderers." However, in the chaos that was now Taipei, Tang was already powerless to arrest any of these troops. This violent episode, plus the fact that many Qing officials had been leaving Taipei before the cession had even been signed,[33] contributed to the public's quickly fading confidence.

When Tang was promoted to governor in October 1894, he had moved to solidify his authority over the northern military forces. Tang transferred the Sino-French war hero Liu Yongfu and his Black Flag armies south to Tainan and spent 200,000 taels to recruit irregular Hakka troops from his home province of Guangxi to replace them in the north. These were armies notorious for their bandit activities back home, but Tang counted on his fellow Guangxi provincials to fall under his command.[34] These "Yue" troops commanded by Tang's Guangxi cronies made up the great majority of northern forces. It was an odd selection of forces to count on to save the people of Taiwan from the Japanese. Their sullied reputations and Yue/Hakka heritage could only have exacerbated the problems; it had been exactly fifty years since the last remnants of the Hakka population had been removed from Taipei in fierce ethnic feuding there.[35] This sudden occupation of Taipei by Yue troops made it unlikely that this reunion would go smoothly, and incidents like that of April 22 did nothing to inspire trust in these armies among the residents of Taipei.

**Elite Maneuvers in the Face of Invasion**

By 1895, Western merchants had become an integral part of the Taipei social and political elite. It is natural that it was the foreigners to whom the Taipei gentry first turned. On April 20, gentry members approached the British consul with an offer: In return for protecting Taiwan from the Japanese, the British would have full use of Taiwan's coal, gold, tea, camphor, and sulfer resources.[36] Western merchants, for decades able to summon gunboats at the slightest conflict with Chinese officials, seemed to have great influence over their nations' foreign policies, and Taipei elites were confident that these partners in modernity would not let them down in this time of danger. Indeed, envoy Kung Chao-yuan reported on March 22 that the British government would follow the wishes of the trading companies with regards to the protection of Taiwan.[37] By April 22, gentry members were reassuring the people that they had seen "confidential telegrams" that indicated the West would save Taiwan. A series of meetings this same week between the Taipei gentry and Governor Tang confirmed this confidence the elites had in their abilities to control the resistance efforts. In one meeting, the gentry discussed the Russian-French-German Triple Intervention that saved the Liaodong Peninsula from Japanese occupation and expressed their confidence that their influence with the foreigners would save Taiwan as well.[38]

An April 25 meeting at Tang's yamen attracted a large crowd of Taipei residents, who in past days had shown their displeasure threateningly enough to warrant a doubling of the yamen guard. The crowd outside the yamen filled the Taipei streets with shouts of "Down with the traitors!" and "Drive out the Anhui cowards!" Interestingly, the crowd was not directing their anger towards the Yue troops now occupying the city, but rather toward a less specific Qing/Mainland scapegoat. Most of Liu's reform personnel had been Anhui natives. Anhui was also associated with Li Hongzhang, vilified in Taiwan for signing the cession of the island. Was the crowd perhaps giving voice to their suspicion that Taiwan had been consistently undermined by a vague Anhui (or Qing) element? Midway through the meeting, more than half the gentry stood up and left in protest. In the riot that ensued, the yamen guards came under attack, and dozens were killed before the uprising was silenced.[39]

Tang's telegrams to the court in late April show the evolution of his decision to throw in his lot with the gentry's plan. Before this time, Tang had often voiced his opposition to appealing to the untrustworthy Western powers for help. He originally planned to organize the resistance using money collected from wealthy elites. In late March, Tang started collecting donations and secured the court's permission to force a million-tael "loan" from leading elite Lin Wei-yuan.[40] However, Tang's mentor and patron Zhang Zhidong had been in contact with the Western powers for months. On March 1, he outlined a plan for the court whereby the British could "open up" the mountainous areas of Taiwan, install roads, and wipe out malaria in exchange for full mining rights. As early as March 7, Zhang asked French officials for a commitment to help Taiwan. On April 20, he secured a £1 million loan from a British merchant, and on April 25, he even offered land in Xinjiang and Tibet to the British and Russians in exchange for help.[41] However, Zhang's initiatives never convinced Tang to consider foreign assistance.

The Taipei gentry's pressure did win Tang over, on the other hand, as his April 27 telegram to the court indicates:

Taiwan has much coal, but the government hasn't sufficient funds to develop and mine it. We cannot build harbors; the road is long and hard and requires much capital. . . . There is much gold in Keelung and Chuanlan, much more than just gold dust. We would like to open this up to private investors as well. The important thing is not to do the job merely halfway; we need a party who will do the job well. One way is to divide all of Taiwan into foreign concessions. Each nation would have its own distinctly marked concession. They would develop the mines, and our government would collect a tax on their work. This way, everyone will share in the wealth. Taiwan will truly flourish. Only when each country has its own concession, will capital accumulate here. Of course, these nations will also prevent any foreign invasion or disturbance. . . .[42]

Despite these plans, however, Taipei simply was falling apart. The riots had Tang worried about the very troops he had brought to Taiwan; on April 26 he ended a wire to the court, "I fear that I might be taken hostage by the military; alas, that I might die in this place!"[43] The next day, Tang reported to the court that "imperial law has already vanished . . . civil officials and military officers are not even waiting for the Japanese to arrive before they leave their posts [for the Mainland] . . . the departure of all the secretaries, clerks, and runners has left the yamens empty."[44] Disorder provoked by Yue troops continued to shock locals. On May 7, in a trading establishment that housed gambling facilities, several Taipei residents beat up a Yue soldier who allegedly tried to cheat a local. Later that day, fifteen of his compatriots returned to the scene, and fired at random from the street into the gambling house, killing one gamester and wounding several others. The soldier originally involved in the dispute was arrested, but later that night was rescued again by his friends in another shoot-out that killed a young boy. That same week, locals in Mengchia (Bangka) attacked a band of Yue soldiers with knives, killing one. It was also reported that Yue soldiers had forcefully driven all the men out of Palipen Village, taking their wives and occupying their homes.[45]

This disorder did not escape the notice of the foreign powers, which bolstered their presence in Taipei. Within one week, the *HMS Spartan,* the *HMS Redbreast,* the *USS Concord,* and a French steamer arrived in Tamsui Harbor.[46] These naval reinforcements eased the spirits of the merchants, who were now "buying tea wildly" while they still could.[47] During the seven weeks from April 21 to June 8 that foreign troops were stationed in the city, Taipei firms exported 6.9 million pounds of tea (worth 2.1 million taels, 35 percent of 1894 total tea exports) and 1.3 million pounds of camphor (worth some 700,000 taels, 43 percent of the 1894 total).[48] Indeed, the situation was relaxed enough for foreigners that the German and British guards could join a "sing-song" on May 17, reported as the largest gathering of foreigners in Taipei in recent memory.[49]

Besides the elites' daily planning meetings, which reverberated with talk of inaugurating a republic and appointing a Taiwan *"bo-li-xi-tian-de"* ("president"), there was one more important aspect of the Taipei elites' plans. The northern mountain Aborigine populations posed concerns, as it was not known whether their allegiances would lie with those who had tried so hard to Sinicize and "civilize" them. When news of the cession hit Taiwan, Aborigine uprisings were reported in the "camphor districts" to the east and south of Taipei.[50] A Western commentator pondered, "There is also the possibility that the Aborigines . . . who are bitterly hostile to the Chinese colonists, may side with the invader."[51] The gentry sought to remedy these worries with a new alliance between the Han and Aboriginal peoples. Three thousand Remington rifles were given to Aborigine representatives, and leaders of all sides drank wine and blood from animal skulls to ritually cement the relationship.[52]

On May 16, a group of these gentry elites paid a visit to the governor. They told Tang of their plans for an autonomous (zizhu) republic, but Tang refused their request to serve as president (now called zongtong).[53] Despite this setback, the gentry used Tang's telegraph office the same day to wire the Qing court. The message relates some of the confidence they felt with regards to their relations with the Western nations and even as to their political strength vis-à-vis the court:

> All we can do is to declare ourselves an island republic, independent of the mainland . . . on the strength of the people's will we are keeping Governor Tang here with us temporarily to lead Taiwan. . . . We are asking other nations to help locate international legal precedents of situations where land was ceded against the wishes of the gentry. Then, an international tribunal would decide how to handle Taiwan's situation. At this time we would send Tang back to the capital. . . . This undertaking by the people of Taiwan is not without its changes in our relation to the Qing. . . .[54]

Meanwhile, people in Taipei discussed their own predictions for their island; one rumor had France and Germany acting to divide Taiwan into two territories, the western half to be ruled by the Chinese and the east under Japanese control.[55]

Despite this talk of forthcoming Western aid, events suggested that these foreign trump cards had taken themselves out of the game. The Taiwan gentry's best hope was Great Britain, but the Crown was content to let Japan have the island as long as the French did not get involved.[56] The French, despite earlier guarantees to help Tang, now told Zhang Zhidong that their participation in the Triple Intervention made it impossible for them again to interfere in Japan's sphere. The Russians and Germans were unavailable; both fearing that the British might take advantage of their intervention in Taiwan to side with Japan against them. The Germans, concerned about their chances in Jiaozhou, feared renewed Japanese attacks that might endanger their designs on this valuable North China harbor and warned the Qing of the dangers of a Taiwan resistance.[57] Thus, the talk of republican principles and parliaments, thought to be a foolproof way of winning Western support, was hardly enough to outweigh the great powers' geopolitical concerns.

While many still hoped to secure funds from abroad, Taiwan's own financial and administrative assets were being routed back to the mainland. By mid-May, Tang had succeeded in quietly transferring most of Taiwan's silver to Shanghai in two shipments of 220,000 and 280,000 taels.[58] On May 20, Tang received an imperial edict dismissing him from the Taiwan governorship and ordering him to proceed immediately to Beijing for an audience with the court. Qing civil and military officials in Taiwan were also ordered to cross the Taiwan Straits and return to the Mainland immediately.[59] Even though President Tang remained in Taipei, the Taiwan treasurer, circuit military attendant (*daotai*), and the magistrates of Taipei, Taiwan, and Tainan prefectures all left the island,[60] further endangering a population threatened by bandits and unruly armies. The Qing court also hammered its own nails into Taiwan's coffin. Worried that Japan would get the wrong idea about the resistance being organized, the court declared publicly that it was "certainly not unwilling to cede" Taiwan.[61]

On May 21, gentry leaders again visited Tang, this time receiving the governor's word that he would serve as president of a Taiwan Republic. On May 23, invitations were issued to Western merchants and envoys in Taiwan, and the following proclamation was made:

> The Qing court has not heard the mandate of the people; in ceding Taiwan they totally ignored our anger. A united Taiwan gentry telegraphed our appeals and telegraphed our advice, but nothing was done. The public is flush with grief and fury; a call for autonomy (*zizhu*) will arouse the people. . . . We must unite the people and gentry of Taiwan and establish a Taiwan Republic. Together we will push forward a constitutional draft, taking the good points of the American and French models; establish a legal system; inaugurate a Parliament; establish an administration; use a banner of a golden tiger on a blue background as our national flag; and take the reign title "Everlasting Qing." This will be Asia's first republic.[62]

These modern national symbols—the people, autonomy, a republic, a constitution, a Parliament, a national flag—were exactly those which captured the imaginations of Qing reformers from the mid-1890s on. However, the events taking place outside the governor's residence were more representative of popular feelings in Taipei at the moment. That day, three soldiers brought the freshly severed head of an Aborigine into the city and allowed residents to examine it. When it was discarded by the soldiers, locals picked it up and took it to the front of Tang's yamen, leaving it there for others to spit on and kick around.[63] Taipei residents, who only weeks before took steps to intimately involve themselves in the resistance and guard against the departure of Qing officials, already saw little in the resistance worth saving and turned to grotesque behavior to register their condemnation of Tang.

## Birth of a Republic

The Taiwan Republic was inaugurated on the drizzly morning of May 25. A grand procession was headed by the new golden tiger flag of the Republic, sixteen licentiate (*xiucai*) degree-holders bearing a silver seal of the president of the Taiwan Republic, several gong bearers, several officials, and 100 members of the Taipei gentry community. A jubilant gathering with many foreign traders in attendance followed at the presidential yamen. However, the general Taipei population showed little interest in the public ceremony and Tang's dramatic kowtowing on his reception of the presidential seal. The only other interested parties were Japanese naval forces in Tamsui harbor, who boarded a British steamer leaving with several Qing officials and demanded information about the day's developments.[64]

Now, the Taipei population, in the words of Customs General Hosea Morse, "noticeably apathetic, and even reluctant,"[65] simply had no interest in their new government. On May 27 a gentry-sponsored public meeting to discuss the new Republic attracted exactly zero interested "citizens."[66] The political terminology used by the Republicans may have been new to Taipei residents, but this was not the problem with this enterprise. The problem was not a "premature" arrival of Western principles of republicanism and constitutionalism that precluded any public support, as has been argued.[67] Popular support for and participation in the resistance efforts had been killed off long before the new government was inaugurated. Yue troops' violence and Qing officials' neglect were the main factors at work here, turning the people against Tang's resistance efforts and leaving novel ideas of "citizenship" hollow and meaningless.

Despite its constituents' apathy, the new government proceeded to set up its republican institutions. The Parliament, consisting of an upper house of twenty-four members and a lower house of sixty, was established. Lin Wei-yuan was unanimously named as parliament speaker as a gesture of thanks for his one-million-tael "loan."[68] This nomination posed a problem, however. When plans for the Republic were announced on May 23, Lin declared the next day that he would have nothing to do with the Republic and took the next boat to the Mainland.[69] The Parliament was left without an effective leader, and representatives were so worried about possible Japanese reprisal that none were willing to commit themselves to policies of any consequence. The misplaced trust in foreign assistance was also evident among the republican personnel. Stationed at Keelung were Taiwan Republic chief artillery instructor Billy Waters and his two assistants, Prebble and Christie. Waters had been a champion boxer in Montana, a barkeeper in Shanghai, and proprietor of the Stag Hotel in Hong Kong; Hosea Morse described these men simply as "irresponsible adventurers."[70]

If the Republic cost Speaker Lin 1 million taels, President Tang was now concerned about the chance that it might cost him his head. He was quick to reassure the court of republican intentions, wiring on May 26, "I am staying on temporarily to protect the people . . . the [presidential] seal is only for temporary use; it was designed only for dealing with the foreign nations."[71] Tang wired the court again on May 28, "The people of Taiwan are not submitting to Japanese rule; this is because they are subjects of the sacred empire. The autonomy announced recently is only a measure with which to resist Japan; we are not trying to be flippant towards China. When we have the chance Taiwan will revert back to Chinese rule."[72]

## A Quick Demise

On May 29, 15,000 Japanese troops landed at Aoti, forty kilometers east of Taipei.[73] The first several battles, from Aoti west to Keelung, were fought solely by Tang's Yue armies, who were hardly up to the task of defending Taiwan. Zeng Xizhao, in command of three battalions at Aoti, deserted when the Japanese landed, and the encampment was taken in one and a half hours.[74] Tang then ordered Wu Guohua, his trusted recruiter in Guangxi, to take 700 men to Santiaoling, ten kilometers inland from Aoti. Not eager to face the Japanese, Wu waited until the next day and took only 400 men; then another insubordinate Yue commander, Bao Ganchen, ignored Tang's orders to take full command there. When fighting began on May 30, a Japanese tactical retreat resulted in Bao and Wu racing back to headquarters to take credit for the "victory," while the Japanese proceeded to take the point easily.[75] Interior Minister Yu Mingzhen hoped to provoke more earnest participation from Wu in the next day's battle at Juifang with this message: "Three deserters have already been beheaded. This battle is for the survival of Taiwan. . . . If you go back to camp and do not fight to the death with us, I am willing to have you beheaded."[76] Thus inspired, Wu helped give the Japanese their only real fight on June 1, but Juifang was also quickly taken, with Chinese losses of 130 men.

On June 1, Tang's yamen was again the site of a large gathering of Taipei locals. The crowd did not represent the great surge of popular support that the republicans had been hoping for; rather, the crowd assembled to look at a display of three Japanese heads stuck on bamboo poles and a bloodstained Japanese tunic.[77] This was another, and most convincing, statement of the popular withdrawal from the resistance effort. Taipei residents had been let down on the international stage; the Western support the gentry promised never materialized. Qing officials and troops were no better, forfeiting their end of the bargain by either deserting or degenerating into brutality once crisis hit. The merchant community was no help either; those with the resources to contribute to the resistance instead left Taiwan for friendlier ports. Even local elites like Lin Wei-yuan were gone, alienated by the republican leadership.

The events of June 3 finally doomed the Republic. Tang had four Yue commanders at Keelung ready to battle the Japanese, but sent Huang Yide as well to make sure that the fight went smoothly.[78] Huang was in Patu, just three kilometers from Keelung, when he heard that the port city had already fallen and promptly returned his troops to Taipei. Huang reported that he had returned only to protect Tang from Japanese assassins seeking the 600,000 tael gold reward that was on the president's head. His noble motives were soon betrayed by his troops, however, who began rioting. Other troops defeated that day at Keelung tore up the railroad tracks as they made their way to the city, and in the riot they started upon their arrival, killed and wounded 150 locals. Reports came in from all over the city of great battles between Taipei residents and these Yue troops, as well as between different Yue units.[79]

June 4 provided no relief for the people of the city. Shichiuling fell that day in a three-hour battle in the rain, and the troops defeated there also headed back to Taipei. Civilian and military corpses started to pile up in the streets, as many wounded soldiers who made it back to Taipei soon died there. Soldiers continued their burning and looting of the city, and residents of the city continued to protect their neighborhoods and attack the Yue soldiers. In rural areas farther away from the capital, soldiers abandoning their arms and hoping to pose as peasants were attacked and killed by real Taiwan farmers taking this rare chance to register their rejection of the Republican resistance.[80]

On June 5, as most of the republican government, led by President Tang, was heading for Xiamen, Taipei was the site of pure mayhem. All of Taipei's yamens and the powder mill were burnt. What was not yet in flames was looted by troops and locals alike. Soldiers, armed to the teeth with their booty from the arsenal, were selling Krupp mountain guns for two dollars, and Winchesters for twenty cents. Others experimented with dynamite. Hosea Morse estimated that ten thousand soldiers were on the streets firing rifle shots.[81] On June 6, dozens were trampled as the powder magazine was looted, and its explosion killed more than 100 people. Hundreds were also reported beaten and shot to death around Taipei.[82]

As Taipei was going up in smoke, the merchants and gentry at the heart of the original resistance met to decide their next step. They decided to invite Japanese armies to occupy the city, suppress the bandits, and put a stop to "the howls of the mob and the lamentful cries of the city residents."[83] Koo Hsien-jung, owner of a Mengchia general store, was selected to be the gentry representative on this mission. No violence toward foreigners had been reported,[84] but the foreign population was probably terrified by the chaos.

On June 7, *New York Daily News* reporter James W. Davidson, British merchant G.M.T. Thomson, German merchant R.N. Ohly, and Danish electrical engineer E. Hansen accompanied Koo in approaching the Japanese troops in Keelung. There, Koo communicated the group's intentions, supposedly using his umbrella handle to write in the dirt, "We come to invite the Great Japanese Army to enter Taipei and pacify the people" (*yaoqing da Riben jun ru Taibei anmin*). Koo also expressed to the officers that the gentry would be willing to pay for soldiers' provisions if they occupied the city.[85]

The Japanese army, originally hoping to attack Taipei twenty days later, sent a small force back with Koo that same day, and city residents greeting the group were "most enthusiastic" about their arrival.[86] On June 8, two infantry divisions and one cavalry division approached the north gate, and Japanese troops faced some slight resistance from Chinese guerrillas concealed in roadside bamboo.[87] The great majority of the people were grateful for Koo's diplomacy, however, and "poured out to welcome the former enemy" troops into Taipei.[88] A woman named Chen Fa took a ladder to the city wall to help troops enter (and later was honored with an official Japanese military award for her efforts).[89] Residents showed their gratitude by hanging homemade Japanese flags, "inscribed to indicate that the residents within were 'peaceful subjects of the Empire of Japan.'"[90] Household doorways were draped in red with large banners proclaiming "We welcome you as friends." Laborers were hired to clean streets according to Japanese specifications, and people brought food to Japanese guards stationed on the streets. On his arrival on June 14, the new governor of Taiwan, Kabayama Sukenori, reported a "warm welcome" from the people.[91]

The Taipei gentry were quick to adapt to and assert their leadership in this new situation; eighty-three gentry members joined twenty-four foreign envoys and 550 Japanese officials and naval officers in a welcoming ceremony on June 17.[92] Gentry collaboration, led by Lin Wei-yuan's Panchiao clan, with the Japanese began almost instantly. In exchange for the guarantee of a peaceful surrender of the villages around Panchiao, eight kilometers southwest of Taipei, these gentry secured the right to direct and assist Japanese units in conducting raids of retaliation, even receiving permission to use weapons to "maintain order" during the rice harvesting season.[93]

### The Fate of Qing Rule in Taiwan

The policies of economic and political modernization pursued by the Qing state in Taiwan over the previous two decades had tremendous implications for the general population. Parallel efforts by reformers to rationalize Qing borders and centralize Taiwan under firm Qing control and by local elites to

Figure 1.1 **Foreign Trade, Northern and Southern Ports, 1863–1893**

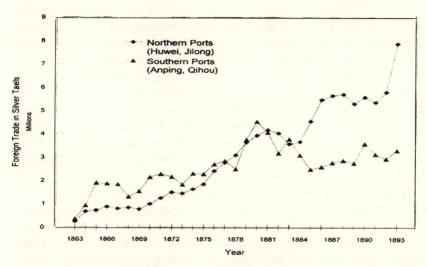

*Source:* Lian Heng, *Taiwan tongshi* (A general history of Taiwan) (Tainan, 1918; Taibei: Youshi wenhua shiye gongsi, 1978 reprint), pp. 491–493.

Figure 1.2 **Tamsui Tea Exports, 1866–1895**

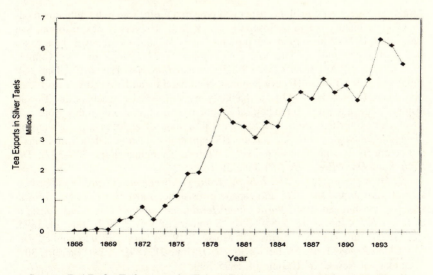

*Source:* Dai Defa, *Taibei xianzhi* (Taipei County gazetteer), Volume 23 (Banqiao: Taibei xian wenxian weiyuanhui, 1960), pp. 3, 73–74.

share control of Taipei with Western and Mainland elites, distorted former networks of reliance. Appropriation of control by these nonsettler groups was surprisingly smooth in this hardiest of frontier regions. Feuding among Quanzhou, Zhangzhou, and Hakka groups precluded any truly united power structure by the 1870s, when nonsettler elites from the Mainland and from the West were able to move in without the threat of any organized resistance.

Yet when crisis came in the form of the Japanese invasion, those outside groups that could easily transfer their governmental or financial influence elsewhere did so. The colonial manner of the Qing modernizers and well-connected merchant elites and the violence of the wild and unaccountable Yue troops left the alienated settler population without any means, or indeed, any desire to resist the invading Japanese.

Qing reform in Taiwan had been undertaken with the assumption that Qing centralization was an acceptable option, as opposed to Western or Japanese colonialism, as the island was technically Chinese territory and the majority of its inhabitants were ethnic Chinese. The events of 1895 Taipei suggest otherwise, as the people of the city stood up, in a manner more democratic than the Taiwan republicans had ever dreamed, to veto this final stage of Qing centralization, even at the price of an uncertain future under the Japanese.

## Notes

An earlier, longer version of this paper was prepared for the research seminar in modern Chinese history taught by Joseph Esherick at the University of California, San Diego, Fall 1993–Winter 1994, and presented at the Western Conference of the Association of Asian Studies, Claremont, CA, October 21–22, 1994; at the 1995 Conference of the North American Taiwan Studies Association, New Haven, CT, June 2–4, 1995; and at the Taiwan History Seminar, National Taiwan University, Taipei, Taiwan, May 24, 1996. I would like to thank my many classmates, teachers, and Taiwan history colleagues who offered helpful comments and suggestions on this project.

1. Yu Mingzhen, 1966, "Taiwan ba ri ji" (Diary of eight days in Taiwan), in *Zhongguo jin bainian shi ziliao chubian* (Compilation of historical data from China's last century), ed. Zuo Shunsheng, vol. 2 (Taibei: Zhonghua shuju, 306–307); *The Hong Kong Daily Press* (*HKDP*), June 21, 1895, 2.

2. Huang Xiuzheng, 1992, *Taiwan gerang yu yiwei kang Ri yundong* (The cession of Taiwan and the 1895 anti-Japanese resistance movement) (Taibei: Taiwan shangwu yinshuguan, 164); *North China Herald and Supreme Court and Consular Gazette* (*NCH*), June 7, 1895, 850–851; "Summary of News," *NCH*, June 14, 1895, 899; *HKDP*, June 12, 1895, 2; Hosea B. Morse, 1919, "A Short-Lived Republic," *The New China Review* 1, no. 1 (March): 30; *HKDP*, June 21, 1895, 2; Yu, "Ba ri ji," 307; "Summary of News," *NCH*, June 14, 1895, 899.

3. The Taiwan Republic was revived in Tainan in late June, and this incarnation endured until October 21, when Tainan was taken after eight days of fierce fighting.

However, in this paper I will deal only with the Taipei-based original, if shorter-lived, Republic.

4. Harry Lamley, 1968, "The 1895 Taiwan Republic: A Significant Episode in Modern Chinese History," *Journal of Asian Studies* 27, no. 4 (August): 739–762; A.B. Woodside, 1963, "T'ang Ching-sung and the Rise of the 1895 Taiwan Republic," *Papers on China* 17 (December): 160–191.

5. Maier, "Consigning," pp. 817–819.

6. Huang Xiuzheng, 1986, "Maguan yihe de ge Tai jiaoshe" (The treaty of Shimonoseki and negotiations over the cession of Taiwan), *Jindai Zhongguo* (Contemporary China) 55 (October 31): 240–241.

7. Leonard H. D. Gordon, 1976, "The Cession of Taiwan—A Second Look," *Pacific Historical Review* 45, no. 4 (November): 544–552.

8. The area previously covered by one prefecture (*fu*), four counties (*xian*), and two subprefectures (*ting*) now became partitioned into two prefectures, eight counties, and three subprefectures. Perhaps the most important of these administrative changes was to finally bring that great portion (roughly the eastern third) of the island previously quarantined as savage territory under Qing jurisdiction, as the new Taidong subprefecture.

9. Ting-yee Kuo, 1973, "The Internal Development and Modernization of Taiwan, 1863–1891," in *Taiwan in Modern Times*, ed. Paul K.T. Sih (New York: St John's University Press, 194–198); Guo Tingyi, 1954, *Taiwan shishi gaishuo* (Outline of historical events in Taiwan) (Taibei: Zhengzhong shuju, 178–184); Samuel C. Chu, 1980, "China's Attitudes Toward Japan at the Time of the Sino-Japanese War," in *The Chinese and the Japanese: Essays in Political and Cultural Interactions*, ed. Akira Iriye (Princeton, NJ: Princeton University Press, 87); Lian Heng, 1978 [1918], *Taiwan tongshi* (A general history of Taiwan), reprint (Tainan, 1918; Taibei: Youshi wenhua shiye gongsi, 697).

10. Ramon H. Myers and Adrienne Ching, 1964, "Agricultural Development in Taiwan under Japanese Colonial Rule," *Journal of Asian Studies* 23, no. 4 (August): 561; William G. Goddard, 1966, *Formosa: A Study in Chinese History* (Michigan State University Press, 131); Liu Mingchuan, n.d., *Liu Zhuangsu gong (sheng san) zouyi* (The imperial memorials of Sir Liu Mingchuan [Zhuangsu]) (Taibei: Wenhai chubanshe, *juan* 4: 1–34); Kuo, "Internal Development," 222–224; William M. Speidel, 1976, "The Administrative and Fiscal Reforms of Liu Ming-ch'uan in Taiwan, 1884–1891: Foundation for Self-Strengthening," *Journal of Asian Studies* 35, no. 3 (May): 457.

11. Speidel, "Reforms," 453–454.

12. Zhang Zhidong, 1961, *Zhang Wenxiang Gong xuanji* (Selected writings of Sir Zhang Zhidong [Wenxiang]), vol. 1, (Taibei: Taiwan yinhang jingji yamjiushi, 9–17); Wang Ermin, 1978, *Qingji bing gongye de xingqi* (The Qing-era rise of military industry) (Taibei: Zhongyang yanjiuyuan jindaishi yanjiusuo, 119–120); Harry J. Lamley, 1977, "The Formation of Cities: Initiative and Motivation in Building Three Walled Cities in Taiwan," in *The City in Late Imperial China*, ed. G. William Skinner (Stanford University Press, 201); Speidel, "Reforms," 455.

13. James W. Davidson, 1903, *The Island of Formosa: Historical View from 1430 to 1900* (Yokohama, 188–189).

14. Edward Band, 1936, *Barclay of Formosa* (Tokyo: Christian Literature Society, 23–24); Reverend James Johnston, 1972, *China and Formosa: The Story of the Mission of the Presbyterian Church of England*, (Taipei: Ch'eng Wen Publishing Company, 173).

15. Davidson, *Formosa*, 199–206.

16. Davidson, *Formosa*, 204–205; Band, *Barclay*, 61–65; Duncan MacLeod, 1923, *The Island Beautiful: The Story of Fifty Years in North Formosa*, (Toronto: Presbyterian Church in Canada, xi-xii).

17. Davidson, *Formosa*, 198.

18. Sitongzi ("The one pained by longing"), 1959, *Tai hai si tong lu* (A record of longing and sorrow from the Taiwan Straits) (Taibei: Taiwan yinhang jingji yanjiushi, 20.

19. Zhang Zhidong, *Xuanji*, vol. 2, 131–132.

20. Wu Micha, 1981, "Yibajiuwu nian 'Taiwan minzhuguo' de chengli jingguo" (The course of establishing the 1895 "Taiwan Republic"), *Guoli Taiwan daxue lishixi xuebao* (Journal of the history department of National Taiwan University) no. 8 (December): 85.

21. Wu Micha, "Yibajiuwu," 85.

22. *NCH*, May 3, 1895, 648; "Japanese Attack and Occupation of the Pescadores," *NCH*, April 11, 1895, 562.

23. "The China-Japan War," *China Mail* (*CM*), April 13, 1895, 3; *NCH*, April 19, 1895, 576–577.

24. "The Shimonoseki Negotiation," *NCH*, June 28, 1895, 982; *NCH*, July 5, 1895.

25. Wu Micha, "Yibajiuwu," 88.

26. Zhang Zhidong, *Xuanji*, vol. 2, 171.

27. Zhang Xiongchao, 1965, "Tang Jingsong kang Ri zhi xinji ji qi zoudian cungao" (Tang Jingsong's innermost thoughts on resisting Japan and his imperial memorial telegram drafts), *Taiwan wenxian* 16, no. 1 (March 27): 85.

28. Lishi jiaoxue yuekanshe (*Historical Education Monthly* publishing house), ed., 1954, *Zhong-Ri jiawu zhanzheng lunji* (Collected essays on the 1894 Sino-Japanese War), (Beijing: Wushi niandai chubanshe, 51).

29. *Qingji waijiao shiliao (Guangxu chao)* (Historical materials from Qing-era foreign diplomacy (Guangxu period)), vol. 4, (Taibei: Wenhai chubanshe, 1969), *juan* 110, 6.

30. This rumor did touch on several truths: On April 19 Tang asked British merchants if he could send 600,000 taels, all of Taiwan's assets, to the Mainland on their *SS Formosa*. Tang never acted to discontinue trade with Japan during this time, and he soon began requesting that Western diplomats and Japanese merchants jointly pacify the Taiwan population. Wu Micha, "Yibajiuwu," 91; Qian Chongshi, 1971, "Zhong-Ri jiawu zhanzheng hou de geguo andou" (The clandestine struggles between several nations after the 1894 Sino-Japanese War), *Dongfang zazhi* (Dongfang magazine) 5, no. 5 (November): 82; Guo Tingyi, 1963, *Jindai Zhongguo shishi rizhi* (Daily record of historical events in modern China), vol. 2, (Taibei: Zhongyang yanjiuyuan).

31. Morse, "Republic," 25.

32. Yang Jialuo, ed., 1976, *Zhong-Ri zhanzheng wenxian huibian* (Compiled documents on the Sino-Japanese War), vol. 1, (Taibei: Dingwen shuju, 92); Wu Micha, "Yibajiuwu," 92; "Report from Taipehfu, Formosa," *NCH*, May 10, 1895, 700.

33. *NCH*, April 19, 1895, 579.

34. Yang Yinting, ed., 1982, *Kanqiting zaju shiliuzhong* (Sixteen farces from the Chess-Viewing Pavilion) (N.P.: Guangxi xiju yanjiushi, 5).

35. Lamley, "Formation of Cities," 179.

36. Wu Micha, "Yibajiuwu," 92; F.Q. Quo, 1968, "British Diplomacy and the Cession of Formosa, 1894–95," *Modern Asian Studies* 2, no. 2 (April): 153.

37. Wu Micha, "Yibajiuwu," 87.

38. Xu Bodong and Huang Zhiping, 1987, *Qiu Fengjia zhuan* (A biography of Qiu Fengjia) (Beijing: Shishi chubanshe, 70).

39. "Riot at Tamsui," *NCH*, May 3, 1895, 671; *HKDP*, May 6, 1895, 2.

40. Zhang Zhidong, *Xuanji*, vol. 2, 171–172; Zhang Xiongchao, "Tang Jingsong," 85–86; "The China-Japan War," *CM*, March 27, 1895, 3.

41. Yang Jialuo, *Zhanzheng*, vol. 3, 483; Qian, "Geguo andou," 79; Guo Tingyi, *Rizhi*.

42. *Qingji waijiao shiliao*, vol. 4, *juan* 110, 7.

43. Ibid., 6.

44. Yu, "Ba ri ji," 316–317.

45. "The China-Japan War," *CM*, May 17, 1895, 3; "Report from Taipehfu, Formosa," *NCH*, May 24, 1895, 779.

46. Morse, "Republic," 25; "Report from Taipehfu, Formosa," *NCH*, May 17, 1895, 741; *CM*, ship schedules, pp. 2–4 daily.

47. H.B. Morse letter to Sir Robert Hart, April 13, 1895.

48. H.B. Morse, 1960, *The International Relations of the Chinese Empire*, vol. 3 (New York: Paragon Book Gallery, 48; Dai Defa, 1960, *Taibei xianzhi* (Taipei County gazetteer), vol. 23 (Banqiao: Taibei xian wenxian weiyuanhui, 3–5, 73–74).

49. "Report from Taipehfu, Formosa," *NCH*, May 24, 1895, 779.

50. "The China-Japan War," *CM*, April 29, 1895, 3.

51. "The Dregs in the Victor's Cup," *Peking and Tientsin Times* (*PTT*), May 11, 1895, 246.

52. *NCH*, May 17, 1895, 724; *HKDP*, May 22, 1895, 2.

53. Yang Jialuo, *Zhanzheng*, vol. 6, 454–455.

54. 1965, *Qing Guangxu chao Zhong-Ri jiaoshe shiliao xuanji* (Selected materials from Sino-Japanese negotiations during the Guangxu reign, Qing dynasty), vol. 3 (Taibei: Taiwan yinhang jingji yanjiushi, 393–394).

55. "The China-Japan War," *CM*, May 27, 1895, 3.

56. "Les Bras Croisés," *PTT*, March 30, 1895, 222–223; "Much Ado About Nothing," *NCH*, May 10, 1895, 681; Quo, "British Diplomacy," 151.

57. Wu Micha, "Yibajiuwu," 98–103; Qian, "Geguo andou," 81–83.

58. Yang Jialuo, *Zhanzheng*, vol. 1, 93.

59. 1964, *Qing Dezong shilu xuanji* (Selections from the Veritable Records of the Guangxu reign, Qing dynasty), vol. 2 (Taibei: Taiwan yinhang jingji yanjiushi, 300–301).

60. Zhong Xiaoshang, 1982, *Taiwan xianmin fendou shi* (The history of struggle of our Taiwan forebears) (Taibei: Zili wanbao she wenhua chubanbu, 247).

61. Wu Micha, "Yibajiuwu," 103.

62. The tiger flag was designed to acknowledge the Qing dynasty, the tiger symbolizing the prince to the Qing's imperial dragon. Zheng Xifu, ed.,1981, *Minguo Qiu Canghai xiansheng Fengjia nianpu* (A chronological biography of Mr. Qiu Canghai [Fengjia] of the Republic) (Taibei: Taiwan shangwu yinshuguan, 81); Chen Shuoyi, 1957, *Qiu Fengjia* (Qiu Fengjia) (Taibei: Haiwai wenku chubanshe, 10).

63. "The Crisis in Formosa," *CM*, May 30, 1895, 3.

64. Huang Xiuzheng, *Taiwan gerang*, 131; Yang Jialuo, *Zhanzheng*, vol. 1, 94; *Shenbao*, June 10, 1895, 1.

65. H. B. Morse letter to Sir Robert Hart, May 27, 1895.

66. "The Crisis in Formosa," *CM*, June 1, 1895, 3.

67. Lamley, "The 1895 Taiwan Republic."

68. Huang Xiuzheng, *Taiwan gerang*, 134–136.

69. "Report from Formosa," *NCH*, July 26, 1895, 140.

70. "Report from Taipehfu, Formosa," *NCH*, May 10, 1895, 700; H.B. Morse letter to Sir Robert Hart, April 20, 1895.

71. *Qing Guangxu chao Zhong-Ri jiaoshe shiliao xuanji,* vol. 3, 409–410.

72. Ibid., 411–412.

73. These Japanese troops were much better armed than the Chinese. Japanese soldiers carried new Murata .815 rifles with smokeless powder, while the average Chinese soldier had only secondhand Mausers and Winchesters that fired black powder. Huang Xiuzheng, *Taiwan gerang,* 146–150; Morse, *International Relations,* vol. 3, 49.

74. Mao Yibo, 1954, "Taiwan yiwei kang Ri shimo" (The entire history of the 1895 anti-Japanese resistance in Taiwan), in *Taiwan wenhua lunji* (Collected essays on Taiwan culture), ed. Lin Xiongxiang, vol. 2 (Taibei: Zhonghua wenhua chuban shiye weiyuanhui, 192).

75. Qiu Shiru, 1975, "Qiu Fengjia zai Tai kang Ri shilue" (An historical outline of Qiu Fengjia's resistance against the Japanese in Taiwan), in *Qiu Fengjia de yi sheng* (The life of Qiu Fengjia), ed. Jiang Junzhang (Taibei: Zhongwai tushu chubanshe, 95).

76. Yu, "Ba ri ji," 303–304.

77. "The Crisis in Formosa," *CM*, June 11, 1895, 3.

78. Yang Jialuo, *Zhanzheng,* vol. 1, p. 95; Mao, "Kang Ri," 192.

79. Luo Dunrong, "Ge Tai ji" (A record of the severance of Taiwan), in Zuo, *Jin bainian shi,* 392; Mao, "Kang Ri," 192; Wu Degong, 1959, "Rang Tai ji" (A record of the cession of Taiwan), in *Ge Tai san ji* (Three records of the severance of Taiwan) (Taibei: Taiwan yinhang jingji yanjiushi, 37–38).

80. Mao, "Kang Ri," 192; Yu, "Ba ri ji," 307; Morse, "Republic," 29; Morse, *International Relations,* vol. 3, 52.

81. *NCH,* June 7, 1895, 851; Morse, *International Relations,* vol. 3, 52; "The Crisis in Formosa," *CM,* June 13, 1895, 3.

82. Wu Degong, "Rang tai ji," 39.

83. Huang Xiuzheng, *Taiwan gerang,* p. 165.

84. *NCH,* June 7, 1895, 850–851.

85. Sheng Qingyi, 1956, "Guangxu yiwei Taibei xian dashiji" (Record of great historical events in Taipei County, 1895, Guangxu reign), *Taibei xian wenxian congji* (Collection of archives from Taipei county) 2 (April): 448; Zhong, *Fendou shi,* 258.

86. Xu and Huang, *Qiu Fengjia,* 87; "The Crisis in Formosa," *CM,* June 24, 1895, 3.

87. Sheng, "Guangxu yiwei," 448.

88. H. B. Morse letter to Sir Robert Hart, June 10, 1895.

89. Zheng Tiankai, 1995, *Gong Tai tulu: Taiwan shi shang zui da yi chang zhanzheng* (The invasion of Taiwan, an illustrated record: The greatest war in the history of Taiwan) (Taibei: Yuanliu chuban gongsi, 66).

90. Morse, "Republic," 30.

91. "The Crisis in Formosa," *CM,* June 24, 1895, 3; *HKDP,* June 27, 1895, 2.

92. Huang Xiuzheng, *Taiwan gerang,* 171.

93. Harry J. Lamley, 1964, "The Taiwan Literati and Early Japanese Rule, 1895–1915: A Study of Their Reactions to the Japanese Occupation and Subsequent Responses to Colonial Rule and Modernization," Ph.D. diss, Seattle, University of Washington.

# ——— 2 ———

# The February 28 Incident and National Identity

*Robert Edmondson*

The 1945 Retrocession to China ended fifty years of Japanese rule, soon followed by the February 28 Incident of 1947. This event is perhaps the most important single event in Taiwanese history because it made Taiwanese history thinkable.[1] The betrayal and violence of the Chinese Nationalist government made the boundaries of a distinct historical subject, "the Taiwanese people," clear and compelling. This collective imagination would ultimately write the exiled Mainlanders into its own story, (over)turning their Chinese nationalism into a chapter of Taiwanese history. This discursive inversion, however, was neither sudden nor inevitable. The relationship between the February 28 Incident and the solidification of Taiwanese identity and national sentiment should not be thought of as cause and effect, because this kind of mechanical historical sufficiency masks the connection between the event and its interpretation and narrative production. I would like to offer an expanded sense of the event that draws these processes into the fold of its own history, a telling of the February 28 Incident history that shifts our attention from seemingly permanent things to "the processes whereby permanence and thingness are achieved" (Herzfeld 1997, 57).

The February 28 Incident made Taiwanese history knowable not through its sufficiency as a historical cause per se, but through a much more complex, drawn-out process of meaning-making, iconization, deployment, and ritualization. Attending to this kind of "narratological causality" (White 1987, 194) challenges us to think about the intricate and intimate relationship between what we think of as the "facts" of history and the process of their performative and narrative construction. The issue becomes not so much a "true account" of the past, but rather a treatment of the past and its accounting, search for strands of power and interest revealed only by embracing the "irreducible distinction and yet . . . equally irreducible overlap between what happened and that which is said to have happened" (Trouillot 1995, 2).

I am interested in exploring moments of dynamic interaction between historical events and their representation because the past is one of the key grammars of identity. Werbner argues that what Nora (1989) and others have identified as our modern "crisis of memory" finds a particularly salient expression in the new nation-states, and locates issues of memory and the past at the heart of postcolonial studies. In the case of Taiwan, the February 28 Incident is important because it has become "historically relevant" at several critical moments. As an event, a memory, a silence, a protest, and a history, this seemingly singular moment in time is, through representation, interpretation, and performance, repeatedly drawn into the contingent present and projected onto the unwritten pages of the future. Agency, generally thought of as working forward in time, operates through the past as well; we arrange our histories to make the present a fulfillment of past necessity and a promise toward a particular future. The narration of the February 28 Incident, as we shall see, has indeed been harnessed as just this kind of historical agency, and may serve as a window into the contemporary multivalent negotiations of Taiwanese national identity.

The Japanese considered Taiwan their model colony. In addition to a rapid modernization project, which included "unifying weights, measures, and currency; guaranteeing private property rights; building a modern infrastructure; mobilizing natural resources; increased agricultural productivity; [and] making investment capital available" (Gold 1986, 44), the Japanese also invested in Taiwanese society for its "human capital" potential, establishing a stable rule of law, providing comprehensive public education, introducing local-level democratic institutions, and training an intellectual elite in both Taiwan and Japan. Heavily influenced by the liberal political philosophy current between 1910 and 1930 in Japan, a number of organizations were established by Taiwanese advocating greater rights and a political voice within the Japanese Empire (Chen 1972).

Following an agreement made at the Cairo Conference in 1943, Taiwan was given to Chiang Kai-shek's Nationalist (KMT) government upon Japanese surrender in 1945. Under Chen Yi's brief administrative tenure on Taiwan (October 1945–April 1947), the island's economy progressively deteriorated due to mismanagement, corruption, and the heavy drain of resources siphoned into the war effort on the Mainland. Lai, Meyers, and Wou (1991, 170) estimate that around 17 percent of Taiwan's gross domestic product (GDP) was nationalized and disposed of and that as many as 36,000 Taiwanese were forced out of public sector jobs. Mandarin Chinese, which few Taiwanese spoke, was eventually imposed as a "national language" to replace Japanese, the language of the educated under the previous colonial administration. Philips (1999) draws our attention to the power of the collective memory of the Japanese era to provide the social frames through which Taiwanese elites interpreted their new context and developed political strategies. In his nuanced and insightful account of the negotiations and conflicts between the Mainlanders and the Taiwanese, however, Philips maintains a decolonization/reintegration framework, and leaves unquestioned the master historical narrative of the KMT state. By doing so, he presents a "victor's history"—and misses one of the key issues at stake at the time.

The polity into which the Taiwanese were to be reintegrated was in fact a novel entity, a newly imagined community. Duara's work (1997) detailing how early Chinese nationalists sought to define clearly and "harden" an exclusively Chinese national identity highlights for us the fact that for the Taiwanese, who had not been exposed to these new discourses, Chineseness carried no political or national register. A "soft" cultural identity, Chineseness on Taiwan was one of several nonexclusive modes of identification. Incorporation into a new Chinese nation, in this sense, involved the imposition of a very new kind of Chineseness, one that rejected or sublimated all other identities in order to create subjects whose primary sense of self was tied to the nation. The term "reintegration" masks the radically alienating effects of this process and was challenged by Taiwanese elites who preferred a more autonomous position within the Nationalist regime. Ultimately, the bloodshed in 1947 came because the KMT state was losing ground in this soft war of historical interpretation. Victory would come not by mastering the illusions of *nation*, hardening a Chinese identity among Taiwanese, but by silencing those who would articulate an alternative vision.

As Su (1986) and Chen (1972) have suggested, an alternative narrative positioned the KMT as yet another "colonial" regime: recolonization rather than decolonization. In many significant ways, the Nationalists were unable to distance themselves from the Japanese who had ruled before them. They moved into Japanese residences, filled the most important administrative posts, replaced the Japanese as the police force, nationalized the largest industries previously owned by the Japanese, and imposed Mandarin Chinese, a foreign language to the Taiwanese, as the national dialect. Portraits of the Japanese emperor in public schools and offices were replaced by pictures of Sun Yat-sen and Chiang Kai-shek as the new objects of mandatory ritualized state-worship, and urban spaces were reordered with place-names evoking a "motherland" that few living Taiwanese had ever seen.

For many Taiwanese, the "pigs" (Mainlanders) had simply replaced the "dogs" (Japanese). Cholera and other public health risks appeared on the island for the first time in decades, fueling images of the Mainlanders as dirty, diseased, and backward. In addition to the "othering" generated through language policies, employment segregation, and the appropriation of colonial architecture and practice, both the Taiwanese and Mainlanders used rhetorical metaphors of pollution and violation, creating a shared subtext of difference and distance. For the Taiwanese, however, this was generally limited to references to personal habits, education, and moral character, whereas Nationalist stereotypes operated on a political and cultural level. Although the KMT held that the Taiwanese were racially Chinese, both Chen Yi and Chiang had publicly expressed concern that the Taiwanese had been tainted by long exposure to the Japanese ways and ideas, and were in need of reeducation. With guidance and discipline, the Taiwanese would have to learn how to be Chinese citizens.

In February 1947, the tensions caused by "inflation, grain shortages, corruption, lack of military discipline, unemployment, industrial collapse, and cultural conflict,"—whether understood as issues of "reintegration" or recolonization—were becoming critical. Social order was strained, and outbursts of violence were increasing. At dusk on the 27th, Taipei Wine & Tobacco Monopoly Bureau agents wounded a street peddler while confiscating her cash and untaxed cigarettes, and a bystander was shot as the agents fled an angry pressing crowd. A group of Taiwanese marched on the police station that evening demanding that the shooter be handed over. When they were refused, a petition was drafted overnight asking for the execution of the agent responsible for the shooting death and for reforms in the monopoly laws. The petition was taken to the Monopoly Bureau, where no one would emerge to receive it. The crowd marched on Chen Yi's headquarters to present the petition; several Taiwanese were killed when they were fired upon from the top of the building (Kerr 1965, 254–300).

A band of protesters stormed the Taiwan Radio building and broadcast these events across the island, sparking violent demonstrations in all the major cities. Chen Yi later declared martial law on national radio and denied that any deaths had occurred, but he was unable to defuse the situation. On March 2, Taiwanese elites persuaded Chen Yi to agree to a short list of "temporary demands" that allowed a local student police force to keep order in the cities, provided for the release of emergency food supplies, and required Chen Yi to meet with Taiwanese leaders to discuss further reforms. The scope and meaning of the event had expanded and generalized from anger toward a few agents and targeted attacks on Monopoly Bureau buildings to the broadest social fissure at that time, between the Taiwanese people and the Mainland state. This was rapidly becoming a powerful division, with congruent ethnic, political, and class dimensions (Gates 1981).

This temporary redress opened a window of creativity for the Taiwanese community. As Kerr describes it, "Once a formal Settlement Committee was established, the spontaneous outbursts of anger gave way to a new public mood and a rather remarkable show of public cooperation with Formosan leaders who, for nearly a week, formed the effective government" (1965, 270). The "thirty-two demands" presented to Chen Yi on the 7th suggested a complete overhaul of the KMT administration on Taiwan, from a civilian Taiwanese police force, rather than the Mainlander military, to open elections as provided for under the Republic of China (ROC) constitution.[2] On Saturday, March 8, rumors began to circulate about a convoy of troop ships approaching Taiwan's shores. The KMT army arrived the following day and strafed the docks with gunfire before disembarking. The weeks of bloody chaos that followed destroyed any progress that had been made through the settlement committees, whose members, as well as the student police force, were now specifically targeted for execution (Kerr 1965, 299–300). Governor Chen Yi had been negotiating in bad faith, aware that the troops he had secretly asked Chiang Kai-shek to send were on their way.

A KMT investigation immediately after the Incident interpreted the event within the broad themes of Nationalist history, the struggle against Japanese aggression, and the civil war against Mao Zedong:

> Background causes: The Taiwanese people have received a sordid, evil education from the Japanese, and had been misled by depraved propagandists.

> Proximate causes: The Communist Party and mad, ambitious leaders had used the case of an arrested smuggler to launch their uprising. (Lai, Myers, and Wou 1991, 5)

After this initial investigation, martial law was lifted briefly and later reimposed on May 20, 1949, in anticipation of the mass exodus to Taiwan of the Nationalist administrative and military apparatus in August. On May 23, 1950, the Nationalist government announced that the investigations and trials of those responsible for the February 28 Incident had been completed. The case was closed. The official state of "civil war" continued until changes such as the lifting of martial law in 1987 and the termination of the Period of National Mobilization for the Suppression of Communist Rebellion in 1991 restructured the political landscape. In the long decades between, public discussion of the February 28 Incident was outlawed and the fear of death loomed over the collective memory, reinforced by a program of state-sponsored terrorism which claimed the lives of untold thousands of Taiwanese and Mainlanders. The "White Terror," as it came to be called in the 1950s and 1960s, evoked the February 28 Incident through the silences it created. As we try to understand the relationship between historical narratives and their sociohistorical contexts, it becomes clear that not all silences are created equal. Michael Taussig points out that

> Scaring people into saying nothing in public that could be construed as critical of the armed forces . . . is more than the production of silence. It is silencing, which is quite different. For now the not said acquires significance and a specific confusion befogs the spaces of the public sphere, which is where the action is. . . . The point about silencing and the fear behind silencing is not to erase memory. Far from it. The point is to drive the memory deep within the fastness of the individual so as to create more fear and uncertainty in which dream and reality commingle. (1992, 27)

After a resounding military defeat and enforced exile to Taiwan in 1949, the discursive perpetuation of Chinese nationalism and "civil war" were the only tools available to the KMT to legitimate their continued monopoly of power. They were in possession of neither the land nor the people of China, Fernando Coronil's two "bodies" of nation (1997). They did have an army and a state apparatus, Taiwan (including the land, resources, and a well-trained population), and the "encompassment" of the cold war Western will to create a "Free China" on Taiwan.[3] In this historical frame, the Taiwanese were due only the political rights of a single Chinese province, rights that were to be suspended until the successful conclusion of the anti-Communist civil war. The February 28 Incident disappeared, becoming a lost footnote of Chinese history. The "invisibility of Taiwan" perpetuated by the KMT and United States foreign policy was also reproduced in Western and local social science discourse, an increasingly important arena as political struggles moved toward the language and tropes of identity (Murray and Hong 1994).

Taussig's "unforgettability" generated by state terrorism conflicted with the government's efforts toward erasure. The Taiwanese were presented with what Homi K. Bhabha (1990b, 310) calls "the obligation to forget," which is inherent in nationalist discourse. In order to conceive and remember the nation, subjects must "forget to remember. . . . The violence involved in establishing the nation's writ." For most Taiwanese, however, the coercive silencing of Chinese nationalism and its obligations to forget reinforced its own antithesis, that the KMT was in fact another foreign regime. The deepening divide between Mainlanders and Taiwanese after the February 28 Incident was intensified by the imposition of a Chinese nationalist discourse that rejected rather than incorporated Taiwanese local identity, language, culture, and perhaps most important, Taiwanese collective memory of the February 28 Incident. The radical incongruity between KMT national history and Taiwanese local memory produced what Werbner calls "unfinished narratives":

Popular history in which the past is perceived to be unfinished, festering in the present—these are narratives which motivate people to call again and again for a public resolution to their predicament. Subjected to buried memory, people do not so much forget as recognize—and often ever more forcefully—that they have not been allowed to remember. Though not always obviously or immediately, such situations are potentially explosive, when people feel compelled to unbury the memory and reject their past submission. (1998, 9)

Narratives of the Incident remained locked in private spaces, with many of those who directly experienced the Incident hesitant to tell the story to the next generation. Three important histories written overseas, however, came to play a crucial role in the formulation of a February 28 Incident counterhistory. In *Formosa Betrayed* (1965) George Kerr tells a story of the Incident based on his own and others' eyewitness accounts, and he estimates that between 10,000 and 20,000 Taiwanese were killed. In addition to random violence, Kerr describes a pattern of targeting the intellectual elites; specifically, the members of the Settlement Committees, teachers, lawyers, newspaper editors, and other well-educated Taiwanese (1965, 310). His strong indictment of the Nationalist government leadership and detailed account of the Incident became a critical source of historical ballast for a growing overseas Taiwanese Independence Movement. Peng Ming-min, an influential leader in this overseas mobilization, published his widely read English-language biography, *A Taste of Freedom: Memoirs of a Formosan Independence Leader* (1972), which also provided a firsthand narration of the Incident.

A most influential piece of historiography was written by Su Bing (Shi Ming), a staunch opponent of the Nationalist government since the early 1940s. His massive *Taiwan's 400 Year History*—published in Japanese (1962), Chinese (1979), and English (1986)—provides a Marxist anticolonial ethnonationalist account of Taiwanese subjugation and resistance to successive foreign regimes. Su's presentation of the Nationalist government as a colonizing aggressor frames a graphically detailed narrative of the February 28 Incident:

> The soldiers of the 21st Army in Shanghai also arrived. These soldiers seemed to have an even more hostile feeling toward Taiwanese. As soon as they landed at Keelung, they shouted, "The Taiwanese are not Chinese! Kill them! Kill them!" They fired and rushed into the city. Letting the policemen lead the way, they searched every home, arrested any person they found on the street. Cutting off ears and noses of the arrested, amputating arm and legs, or pushing their victims off roofs, the Chinese soldiers went

through the catalogue of massacres. Some people, bound together with several other people by wires piercing through their palms and ankles, were tied in a row, and were thrown into the Keelung Harbor. Some port laborers were pressed into jute sacks individually, and then, after the sacks were tied, were thrown into the sea. (1986, 127)

The importance of these interpretations of the past—now classics in an ever-broadening genre of Taiwanese historiography—should not be underestimated. The Taiwanese independence movement, kept alive in Japan and the United States, was firmly rooted in a particular reading of history that challenged the legitimacy of KMT rule over Taiwan. For a new generation of returning university students, activists working overseas, and local leaders, the February 28 Incident story—whether recounted by a family member, Su Bing, or by George Kerr—had a powerful eye-opening impact, shaping their subjectivities, rhetoric, and agendas.

The decade of the 1970s saw the illusion of nation stretched to its thinnest veneer. In 1971 the ROC was forced to give up its United Nations seat to the People's Republic of China (PRC). The following year, Japan switched recognition to the PRC, and Nixon made his famous trip to the Mainland. President Carter officially recognized the PRC as the legitimate regime governing of China in 1978, three years after Chiang's death. The announcement came only eight months after his son, Chiang Ching-kuo (CCK), assumed the presidency of Taiwan. Official histories today present CCK as a reformer responsible for beginning the "Taiwanization" of the KMT and the lifting of martial law. In the late 1970s, however, CCK was known best as the mastermind behind his father's extensive and dangerous security operation. For many Taiwanese who had long awaited Chiang Kai-shek's death, CCK's rise to power was a bitter disappointment.[4] The legitimacy of the ROC, as either the true government of China or a democracy, was at its weakest hour since the rout of 1949.

The political opposition in Taiwan began to mobilize in public in 1979, when disparate groups crystallized into an "integrated political force around the magazine *Meilidao* (Formosa)." This became the propaganda machine for the *dangwai* (literally "outside the [Nationalist] party") opposition leaders, "while its local distribution centers served as 'party' branches and its subscribers were treated as potential members" (Wu 1995, 35). The movement, after staging a number of illegal demonstrations across the island, was nearly crushed by KMT forces at a march in Kaohsiung. The Kaohsiung Incident and the events of 1947 share a protest praxis, a repertoire of strategies, subjectivities, and positions informed and adapted to contemporary issues, collapsing the two events into a single economy of meaning for the

Taiwanese people. Ironically, this connection would be made most explicit not by the opposition but by the machinations of the KMT security forces.

Lin Yi-hsiung (now a well-respected Democratic Progressive Party legislator) had been arrested during the Kaohsiung Incident, and during a brief prison visit in February he told his wife of his torture in jail. Her phone call revealing these details to a human rights activist in Japan caused the security agencies to retaliate. On the morning of February 28, 1980, an unknown assailant murdered Lin's mother and twin daughters at home.[5] Following Coronil's insights into a similar murder in Venezuela, my purpose in bringing this to light is to "render the murder intelligible not by pointing out the trigger, or who gave the order, but why and how it worked structurally" (Coronil 1997, 325). The Kaohsiung Incident in December and the Lin family murders are intelligible by logic condensed within February 28 Incident memory and silence, a register of oppression and opposition in which the very roles and scripts of resistance and subjugation trace their lineage back to 1947, collapsing the past into the performance of history in the present.

The performance of the February 28 Incident as a moment of terror or a moment of resistance—whether implicitly through protest practice and ideological positioning or explicitly through commemoration—would often be replayed as various oppositions regrouped to force open the public sphere. The continuing annual pilgrimages to the Lin family graves on February 28 provide for us an excellent example of how personal loss, through public commemoration, becomes woven into the tapestry of a national narrative. It draws on and contributes new meaning to the events of 1947 by connecting them directly to the Kaohsiung Incident and its aftermath in a rich, multivalent, symbolic metonymy. This historical dialogue is in turn drawn into the contingent commemorative present, shaping and being shaped by issues of the hour and imaginations of the future.

As the opposition reconstructed itself after the Kaohsiung Incident, activists continued to develop their agenda of democratization and independence by focusing on ethnic inequality between Mainlanders and Taiwanese. Friedman describes one aspect of "modernist politics" as a shift toward the tropes of cultural identity, where "an increased number of social and political projects are recognized in the public sphere," including ethnic, nationalist, religious/fundamentalist, and indigenous discourse (1994, 234). Lin Chia-lung (1999) explains that in the early stages of democratization in Taiwan, nationalist mobilization based on Taiwanese ethnicity was the most effective strategy available to the opposition, despite the problems it would eventually present for a more complete democratic consolidation. This political mobilization of Taiwanese ethnicity was part of a broad movement involving language, literature, art, and religion:

As the opposition party carried out greater resistance against the KMT and the "outsider regime," more and more cultural symbols and cultural forms were infused with new political meaning. The ethnic mobilization movement calling for "Taiwanese self-promotion" relied more and more on cultural activities to bring about self-affirmation and brought about a new Taiwanese cultural restoration movement. This effort led . . . Taiwanese intellectuals to try and "search out their roots" and discover the meaning and origins of what it meant to be "Taiwanese." University students, despite the opposition of school administrations, set up their own "Taiwan Research Society" and attempted to seek out the "essence" of Taiwan history, cultural meaning, and life. Taiwan studies also became a hot topic. Studies of the February 28 Incident, the local dialect, Taiwanese literature, aesthetics, biographies of famous Taiwanese, and Taiwan folk art all became popular in what can be described as a rediscovery or re-creation of Taiwanese "self-consciousness." (Chang 1995, 83)

Anthony Smith has called this kind of cultural and historical reconstruction "retrospective nationalism" (1995, 68), and Maurice Meisner has noted that "like other modern nationalists, the Formosan nationalist is inclined to look as far back into the past as possible for signs of a distinctive national existence" (1963, 92). Niu (1962) and Su (1985), for example, locate an ethnic "awakening" as early as the native revolt against the Dutch in 1652. Cultural authenticity and essentialism—the epistemological foundations of both Chinese nationalism and Taiwanese ethnic mobilization—are based on a sense of continuity that, ironically, assumes a radical dichotomy between past and present, leaving unexamined the relationship between the "objective truth" of history and the politically charged process of historical interpretation. Legitimacy adheres in a fetishization of things past at the expense of a contingent performative present. Activists tend to overemphasize the determining power of roots in what is essentially a mutually constitutive dynamic between past and present.[6] Peng Ming-min framed Taiwanese resistance in precisely these ideal historical terms, not merely power politics:

The movement for Formosan self-determination has not been conceived as a political party movement, but has grown out of universal protest against the exploitation experienced by one and all since 1945. As an organization it has become a symbol of the aspirations of the great majority of Formosans since the tragic experience of February and March 1947. That experience destroyed popular trust in the continental Chinese and revived the old antagonisms of the eighteenth and nineteenth centuries. (1972, 255)

Conversely, "uncovering" the inherently contingent aspects of such discourse becomes the key to delegitimization. Folding the February 28 Incident into a contemporary ethnonationalist narrative, for example, would become part of the deconstruction of Chinese nationalism in Taiwan, derailing the historical legitimacy of the KMT by revealing the violent process of its fabrication. In turn, as we shall see, the legitimacy of the February 28 Incident commemorations would be challenged by accusations that they were "politically motivated."

Five months before martial law was lifted in July 1987, members of the newly formed Democratic Progressive Party (DPP), under the name of the Organization for Promoting the Consolation of the February 28 Incident, sponsored seventeen commemorative activities across Taiwan. Chang Shenglin's research on Incident memorial design describes these early events as "virtually an extension of the opposition movement—[they] basically consisted of speeches and demonstration parades at the traditional political rally locations. . . . The mere breaking of the silence was a triumph for the organizers" (1994, 26). These first activities openly introduced the Incident to the broader public, strengthening support for the political opposition by historicizing current ethnic tensions and antigovernment sentiment. The DPP used the issue to drive open the public sphere, and linked demands specific to the memory of the Incident—such as an apology, financial compensation for victims and families, official pardons, a memorial, and the release of certain documents—to the DPP's broader program for liberal democratization and Taiwanese independence. The participation of survivors and witnesses in these commemorations reinforced the image of a historically grounded popular mandate. For one moment, the opposition appeared both unified and in command of a coherent meaningful past: Remember February 28—Vote for the DPP.

Early activities to commemorate the February 28 Incident were often answered with violence from the state. They were treated as potential riots, a posture by the government that only fueled the opposition, confirming and actualizing their master narrative of political and ethnic oppression, and dramatically reenacting the events of 1947. Riot police, news blackouts, water cannons, and razor wire reinforced the incongruency between the "Free China" myth held up both at home and abroad, and the reality of postwar Taiwan. President Lee Teng-hui was in a precarious position between older KMT hard-liners and a growing DPP opposition. His initial strategy was to try and remove the Incident from the public sphere by challenging the motives of those who would commemorate it. Consider, for example, the view expressed in 1988 in his first interview as president of Taiwan:

I am really curious why nowadays it is always those under the age of forty who talk about the "2/28 Incident." When the "2/28 Incident" happened, I was only a senior at National Taiwan University. *Wouldn't it be more appropriate to leave what happened then to future historians?* Why should we be so obsessed with this incident at this juncture? Why do some people want to use it to incite the public, telling them "Don't forget 2/28" or "Let's make a 2/28 Peace Day"? Historically, the incident was a tragedy that happened right after Taiwan's retrocession. Isn't it against the principle of love to repeatedly make this tragedy a topic to be rehashed every year and keep telling people not to forget "2/28"? If we persist in repaying evil with evil, our society will never enjoy one single restful day. *And I am opposed to this incident being exploited by some people for subversive purposes from a completely political stance.* (Lee 1989, 33–34; emphasis added)

Clearly, however, the issue would not be left to "future historians"; the Incident as deployed by the DPP was undermining KMT legitimacy, despite the rapid "Taiwanization" of the party. This left no alternative but to try and contain its impact by actively engaging in the negotiations of its meaning and historical mandate. Lee ordered a full investigation of the Incident in 1991, and in February 1992 sponsored the first official state commemoration, a symphony concert for survivors and victims' families. This provided Lee and others in the KMT with an opportunity to address the grief and pain of the Incident while avoiding the risk of political confrontation, disruption by protest, and the charge that they were ignoring the issue entirely. Their strategy conferred commemorative legitimacy only to those personally connected to the Incident, whereas the DPP worked to make the Incident part of an ethnonational narrative. Even these limited gestures caused dissent within the KMT, as evinced by reports issued that year by prominent members of Lee's own cabinet downplaying the importance of the event. One report listed only 398 deaths and once again cited "Communist instigation" as the cause of the uprising, ultimately concluding that the 1947 government dealt with the Incident "under the principles of peace and magnanimity" (Central News Agency [Taiwan], 24 February 1992).

To meet other specific commemorative demands, the KMT published the findings of their investigation in 1992, proposed in 1994 and completed in 1995 the February 28 Incident Memorial in downtown Taipei, and passed a bill that provided NT$6 million (US$750,000) to "compensate" victims' families.[7] The same year, President Lee apologized for the Incident, and recognized it as "Taiwan's most significant historical event" (UPI [Taiwan], 28 February 1995). The following year, President Lee went as far as to say that he, too, was a victim of the February 28 Incident, recalling that as a college student he was almost arrested (China Economic News Service, 29 February, 1996).

Official rhetoric continued to focus on the sorrow and tragedy (*beitong, beiju*) of the Incident, circumventing the issue of responsibility. Conversely, opposition groups used terms like "massacre" (*datusha*) and, in English, "holocaust," pushing for more accountability for those involved. The KMT commemorative interpretation of the February 28 Incident follows a pattern outlined by Maier in his work on the Holocaust and German national identity, which he calls Bitburg history after Ronald Reagan's controversial visit to an SS cemetery on the fortieth anniversary of V-E day. "Bitburg history" is designed to unite oppressors and victims in a "common dialectic" that avoids the idea of collective responsibility. It is a narrative that contextualizes the event by comparing it to similar incidents during the same era, or among the same people, and suggests that "further efforts to encourage collective memory are obsessive" (Maier 1988, 14–15).

"Bitburg history" has clearly been the KMT strategy since the early 1990s. President Lee, for example, has often called the Incident a "bitter memory [for] all compatriots, no matter which province of China they are from" (Central News Agency [Taiwan], 4 March, 1991). In addition to the ambiguous language of the compensation legislation, many felt that an apology by President Lee, a Taiwanese, on behalf of the "central government" rather than the KMT, fell far short of accepting responsibility. Others have voiced concern over the KMT's nonnegotiable stance toward war crimes trials or amnesty hearings. In *A Tragic Beginning,* a book based on an official investigation report, Lai, Myers, and Wou, (1991, 1) described the Incident as "the kind of mass urban violence that has often accompanied the evolution of Chinese regimes." In this same line of reasoning, others have pressed for a more explicit accounting of Japanese violence against both Chinese and Taiwanese as a relativizing historical frame.

By the fiftieth anniversary of the February 28 Incident in 1997, however, the salience of the local Mainlander/Taiwanese ethnic distinction was giving way to a more ethnically inclusive "new Taiwanese" identity in counterpoise to the Chinese Mainland. This discourse integrates indigenous groups, Taiwanese of Fujian descent, Hakka, and Chinese war-era immigrants into a "community of common fate" and emphasizes Taiwan's strategic geohistorical Pacific Rim positionality (Taiwaner 1996; Cumings 1993). Understood by Taiwanese scholars variously as oceanic nationalism (Li 1999), civic nationalism (Lin Chia-lung 1999), or state identity (Chiang 1999), this de-essentialization of Taiwaneseness merged with a series of state-sponsored reforms targeting key aspects of Chinese nationalist ideology and iconography in Taiwan, producing a more syncretic reading of Taiwanese history and identity.

This "new Taiwanese" identity formulation based on ethnic harmony, while key to mature democratic consolidation (Lin Chia-lung 1999), is at times in tension with the ethnonational Taiwaneseness based on opposition and political reform. Some have gone as far as to argue that because oppositional Taiwaneseness has historically been linked to other political issues, including labor, the environment, women's rights, indigenous rights, and democratization, the "new Taiwanese" identity, which seems to resolve a "fundamental" ethnic fissure in Taiwanese society, cannot provide the same kind of discursive political terrain upon which other social contradictions might be mapped. In other words, "new Taiwanese" discourse may take the postcolonial anti-imperialist critique out of Taiwanese subjectivity (Taiwaner 1996). What is important to remember in this comparison, however, is that these two formulations (ethnic oppositional Taiwaneseness and the more syncretic "new Taiwanese" perspective) are not mutually exclusive or totalizing. Like all narratives of identification, they are incomplete, contradictory, and contextually deployed.

We must therefore be cautious in our discussions of contemporary February 28 Incident collective memory. Although the KMT commemorative strategy clearly conforms to a "Bitburg" revisionist model, we must also recognize that the promotion of a "common dialectic" between Mainlanders and Taiwanese resonates with a public worn down by ethnic tension and a decade of confrontational, protest-style February 28 Incident commemoration. For both the increasingly centrist DPP and the "new" KMT, the formulation of a less disturbing, more politically neutral narration and performance of the Incident in public memory dovetails with other efforts toward democratic consolidation. Official fiftieth anniversary commemorations that stressed ethnic harmony and a shared destiny for all the people of Taiwan should be read as more than an attempt to salvage KMT legitimacy. They also reflect a new formulation of Taiwanese national identity and its search for a usable past.

It was in this spirit that the February 28 Incident Peace and Reconciliation Committee, after years of impasse on the precise tone and wording, produced a text to accompany the Incident memorial in Taipei. On the morning of the fiftieth anniversary, speaking in front of the February 28 Memorial and the newly unveiled plaque text, then vice president Lien Chan listed each official gesture and site dealing with the February 28 Incident public memory: the investigation, the published report, the compensation, the memorial, the renaming of New Park the February 28 Peace Park, the new plaque text, the February 28 national holiday (passed into law two days prior to his speech), and finally the February 28 Memorial Museum. The KMT refrain to "let bygones be bygones," which had only a decade earlier infuriated many Taiwanese and fueled the opposition's support, sounded more reasonable after an account of such a thorough public-memory portfolio. Lien Chan, addressing a select audience of victims' families, notables from across the political spectrum, and press, called the Incident a "historic mistake," and asked Taiwan to move beyond the "sorrowful, nebulous, and old era" with "grace and understanding." Taiwan should "tender the truth unto history, clear the victims of their unjust charges, clarify misunderstandings and wipe out the hidden concern for ethnic tension." He asked that the people use "forgiveness and retrospection to promote unity and cooperation."

Tight security ensured that the dedication would not become a stage for protesters, but would instead carry all the weight of a popular mandate and the sobriety of an official state ritual. The image produced was the consecration of a piece of national history, an accounting of the past that was to be not one version among many, but the real story recorded in bronze and stone. The text itself was a careful mediation: conciliatory, unifying, reflective, pedagogical, and neutralizing. It *mentioned* Chiang Kai-shek, but whether he sent troops magnanimously to keep peace, or, as one account suggests, instructed them to "Kill them all, keep it secret," is left for the reader of the plaque to decide.[8]

In the 1990s, KMT leaders tended to blame the Incident on the excesses of untrained soldiers and the incompetence of Chen Yi in order to protect the public memory of Chiang Kai-shek. Like the February 28 Incident, the memory of the generalissimo condenses and crystallizes a range of political and social issues into a single site of memory, and the KMT strategy has been one of gradual change, to protect the core while reforming the cult (Corcuff 1997, 125). The Incident memory threatens to destabilize this process. There is a disconnect between the February 28 Incident monument and museum in Peace Park, and the massive Chiang Kai-shek memorial only blocks away; they are fissures in the landscape of memory. New syncretic constructions of Taiwanese national identity must navigate between different contradictory historical narratives and weave Chiang the Chinese Nationalist hero, liberator of Taiwan, and his son the great democratizer, into the same fabric of the past that would authentically represent the February 28 Incident, the White Terror, the Kaohsiung Incident, and the Lin family murders. The memorial text was unable either to lay blame or absolve Chiang, caught as it was between the empirical risks of historical detail and the subjective risks imposed by the traces and tropes of Chinese nationalism.

Just after noon that same day, only hours after the bronze disc had been unveiled, a cluster of protesters from the Taiwan Independence Army attacked it with a sledgehammer, knocking it off its stand. Protesters and members of the crowd that gathered took turns hitting it with the hammer before throwing it into a nearby pond. Soon after, park workers waded into the murky water and retrieved the dented plaque, storing it indefinitely in the newly opened February 28th Memorial Museum—not a relic from the past but a refugee from the present. Although this pedagogical narrative crumbled under the weight of its own silences, unable in a few short paragraphs to bridge the spaces within Taiwan's heterogeneous historicity, the attempt nevertheless highlights collective memory as a creative space for political reformulations and negotiations. Certainly the text was intended to represent a new vision of Taiwan's ethnically harmonious future—a goal most in Taiwan share—but was unable to short-circuit the multilayered oppositional genealogy of meanings shaping the memory of the Incident.

Within this cacophonous and fragmented field of commemoration, the anniversary of February 28 has been adopted by Taiwan independence supporters and a range of interest groups that continue to define the authenticity and legitimacy of Incident commemoration by the metaphors of resistance and struggle. Authenticity to the past, for Trouillot, requires more than historical accuracy, education, or reparations:

> Authenticity implies a relation with what is known that duplicates the two sides of historicity: it engages us both as actors and narrators. Thus, authenticity cannot reside in attitudes toward a discrete past kept alive through narratives. Whether it invokes, claims, or rejects The Past, authenticity obtains only in regard to current practices that engage us as witnesses, actors, and commentators—including practices of historical narration. That the foundations of such practices were set by our precursors with the added value of their respective power is an inherent effect of the historicity of the human condition: none of us starts with a clean slate. But the historicity of the human condition also requires that practices of power and domination be renewed. It is that renewal that should concern us most, even if in the name of our pasts. The so-called legacies of past horrors—slavery, colonialism, or the holocaust—are possible only because of that renewal. And that renewal occurs only in the present. Thus, even in relation to The Past our authenticity resides in the struggles of our present. Only in that present can we be true or false to the past we choose to acknowledge. (1995, 151)

The 1997 Nation-Building Forum (held by the Taiwan Association of University Professors, or TAUP) February 28 Incident commemoration serves as an instructive example, as it effectively combined commemorative authenticity based both on oppositional Taiwaneseness *and* "new Taiwanese" identity. Held on the night of the 27th, the lengthy procession traced a route of significant Incident locations through the heart of old Taipei and included a powerful street theater reenactment of the Incident itself at the *Yuan huan* market, where the initial events of the 1967 uprising had taken place. Participating sponsors included a wide range of social interest groups, including the Presbyterian Church of Taiwan, the Taiwan Writers' Association, the Union of Taiwan Medical Professionals, the Taiwan Environmental Protection Union (antinuclear), the Goa-seng-lang (Mainlanders) Association for Taiwan Independence, the Wan Buddha Association, the Voice of Ocean Radio, the Ocean Taiwan Association, Taiwan Teachers' Union, the Green Peace Radio, Society for Promotion of Indigenous Rights, the Union of Native Taiwanese Villages, and the Society for Taiwan Hakka Public Affairs. In this case of coalition commemoration, the diversity of the interests represented suggests a broad antiestablishment interpretation of the February 28 Incident.[9] Lin Yi-hsiung explains this link between social activism and the memory of the Incident:

> The February 28th [protests] cannot be simply seen as a confrontation between the natives and Mainlanders, or conflict between people with different provincial backgrounds, it was an uprising by the people against the corrupt and tyrannical authorities. . . . Memorial activities held by the authorities—the gold commemorative coins, the monuments—cannot create the genuine touching power of social reforms." (Agence France-Presse, 27 February 1997)

Lin suggests that the Incident represents the abstraction of struggle against corruption and tyranny, a battle in which most social groups believe they are embroiled. This interpretation implicates the KMT, not only as the party responsible for the bloodshed in 1947, but also as the contemporary conservative majority party considered indifferent or hostile to liberal social reform.[10] In addition to these issues, however, the commemoration also resonated with "new Taiwanese" discourses that place more emphasis on Taiwan's antagonistic relationship with Mainland China rather than internal tensions. The central theme of the march was "Remember February 28th, Don't Become Chinese" (*jinian er-er-ba, bu zuo Zhongguoren*). Slogans on banners and literature included:

> Wake up from the dream of the motherland, be independent and be reborn.
> Cut the umbilical cord, be independent and be reborn.
> Besides Taiwan, there is no motherland.
> Taiwan, our eternal motherland.
> Remember the sites where our ancestors spilled their blood, commit to our ancestors to build a new nation.
> We can forgive, but should never forget.
> Refuse to let February 28 happen again. (TAUP 1997)

Admonitions to "never let it happen again" refer not to a resurgence of KMT-led oppression, but to the dangers of unification. Peng Ming-min, the DPP's presidential candidate in 1996, made this clear: "The February 28 Incident only proves that Taiwan must not unify with China, otherwise an even worse historical disaster would take place" (UPI [Taiwan], 26 February 1996). It should be further noted that neither the oppositional interpretations emphasizing social reforms nor the "new Taiwanese" narrative concerned with the Mainland play on ethnic tension between Mainlander Taiwanese and those of Fujianese descent, a fact evinced by the prominent participation of the Mainlanders for Taiwanese Independence group in the march.[11]

In like measure, February 28 Incident narratives found in the seventh grade social studies and history texts first introduced in 1997 stand true to both the social reform legacy of the event and a national unity interpretation. The texts are based on a "new Taiwanese" sense of civic nationalism and ethnic harmony, and their publication is a tribute to what is now a very broad-based social reform effort. As Corcuff (2001) explains, the overall impact of these books is revolutionary, as they "start to complete with an official historiography the already *de facto* existing independence of Taiwan." Inasmuch as Taiwan might be considered a post-national space, where traditional definitions of the nation-state based on a single ethnic group are being renegotiated, so we might also revisit the concept of historical truth to accommodate multiple authenticities within narratives of the past. We should expect an adequate Taiwanese national history to reflect its complex social order, highlighting rather than glossing over its tensions and contradictions. That the Incident has been key to the formation of Taiwanese identity is incontrovertible, but inasmuch as the negotiations of that identity are multivocal and constantly adapted to new social and political contexts, so we must also expect to see the importance and meanings of the Incident to shift. The February 28 Incident continues to be variously interpreted and accounted for as the people of Taiwan assume the powerful agency of historical narrative production in the always unfinished process of nation-building.

## Notes

1. For more extensive histories of the Incident, and its influence on Taiwanese society, see Chang (1994), February 28 Peace and Reconciliation Committee (1997), Historical Research Commission of Taiwan Province (1991), Kerr (1965), Lai, Meyers, and Wou (1991), Liao (1993), Meisner (1963), Niu (1962), Peng (1972), Philips (1999), Su (1986), and Wang and Wang (1990).

2. Chiang Kai-shek, only weeks before the Incident, had decided the new ROC constitution, adopted on December 25, 1946, would not apply to Taiwan due to their Japanese "contamination." Denial of the civil rights promised by the new constitution was a critical blow to KMT legitimacy on Taiwan prior to the Incident.

3. During the two decades after Japan's surrender in 1945—a piece of the past in

Taiwan overshadowed by the memory of the February 28 Incident and the White Terror—the United States transferred as much as US$4 billion in military aid and economic assistance to the Nationalist government, amounting to 85 percent of the Nationalist's total expenditures (Gold 1986, 53; Su 1986, 74). Compare this to the US$13 billion to rebuild all of war-torn Western Europe under the Marshall Plan.

4. In 1970, when it became clear that Chiang was grooming his son to be his successor, Huang Wen-hsiung attempted to assassinate him (Chiang Ching-kuo) on a visit to the United States. Huang hoped the action would draw international attention to the plight of the Taiwanese people and create an opening for political participation at home. After twenty-five years of living in secret abroad, Huang returned to Taiwan in May 1996, around the time of the Chinese missile tests. He now heads a human rights organization in Taipei.

5. Interview with Linda Arrigo, 1 March, 1997. Arrigo, who had lived in the Lin residence prior to the murders, points out that because the activist's home was under constant government surveillance, the search for an "unknown red-bearded assailant" and the arrest of Bruce Jacobs were simply diversionary tactics.

6. It is indeed this assertion of historical necessity that evinces the kind of narrative agency at work in the political process.

7. The wording of the bill was changed at the last minute, from *peichang* (compensation implying responsibility or guilt) to *buchang,* which simply means a financial debt. Similarly, the original wording of the plaque to be displayed at the memorial referred to the government's actions during the Incident as *suijing,* or "pacification" and was considered by many survivors to be too ambiguous. In the end, the memorial was simply left without a text until 1997.

8. A former bodyguard of Governor Chen Yi, Shu Tao, implicated Chiang Kaishek by describing a telegram from Chiang to Chen Yi ordering him to suppress any opposition. According to Shu, the message was chillingly concise: "Kill them all, keep it secret." Shu was then ordered to pass the telegram on to General Ke Yuan-fen, then chief of the Command of State Security, the forerunner of the infamous Taiwan Garrison Command. Ke is considered one of the people primarily responsible for the atrocities during and after the 1947 Incident. Historians in Taiwan believe the document could be among the personal papers of General Ke, who lived in retirement in Monterey Park in Southern California until his death in 1995 (*Far Eastern Economic Review,* March 23, 1995).

9. Huang Chung-hsien (1997) asserts that the early opposition's strategy of pitting "civil society" as a whole against the state is no longer effective. Secondary associations, particularly social interest groups, are now the key to understanding political mobilization in Taiwan, and as such have come to play a greater role in defining the terms of authenticity in historical interpretation, once monopolized by the KMT and DPP.

10. A focus on social issues such as indigenous rights, environmental conservation, and nuclear power regulation as a primary legacy (and commemorative theme) of the February 28 Incident, a spin developed by the DPP during the democracy movement, has ironically left the "new" DPP in an awkward situation as they try to shift their image away from that of a party whose militants are disruptive street protestors.

11. This group held a number of small commemorations and activities, including a series of discussion meetings dealing with the Incident. These were broken down into three sessions, with programs designed to meet the specific concerns and interests of three generations of Taiwanese and Mainlanders.

# Bibliography

Bhabha, Homi K. 1990a. "Introduction: Narrating the Nation." In *Nation and Narration.* Ed. Homi K. Bhabha. New York: Routledge.
——. 1990b. "DissemiNation: Time, Narrative, and the Margins of the Modern Nation." In *Nation and Narration.* Ed. Homi K. Bhabha. New York: Routledge.
Chang, Sheng-lin. 1994. "Memorial Space and Commemorative Behavior: A Case Study of the 2/28 Massacre Memorials in Taiwan." Ph.D. diss., Cornell University.
Chang, Mau-kuei. 1995. "Provincialism and Nationalization." *Taiwan Studies* 1, no. 2 (summer): 67–96.
Chen, Edward I-te. 1972. "Formosan Political Movements Under Japanese Colonial Rule, 1914–1937." *The Journal of Asian Studies* 31, no. 3 (May).
Chiang, Yi-hua. 1999. "The Identity Problem of an Emerging Nation." Paper presented at the Third Annual Conference on Democracy on Both Sides of the Taiwan Straits: Nationalism and Cross-Straits Relations, Harvard University, November 16–17.
Chiu, Hungdah, ed. 1973. *China and the Question of Taiwan: Documents and Analysis.* New York: Praeger.
Corcuff, Stéphane. 1997. "What Remains of Chiang Kai-shek? Ritualization of a Political Commemoration in Taiwan (1988–1997)." *Études chinoises* 16, no. 2 (fall) (in French).
Corcuff, Stéphane. 2001. "*Han* Introspection in Formosa. The Question of the 'Knowing Taiwan' Textbooks (1994–1997). *Études chinoises* 20, no. 1–2 (spring–autumn) (in French).
Coronil, Fernando. 1997. *The Magical State: Nature, Money, and Modernity in Venezuela.* Chicago: University of Chicago Press.
Cumings, Bruce. 1993. "Rimspeak; or, the Discourse of the 'Pacific Rim.'" In *What is in a Rim? Critical Perspectives of the Pacific Region Idea,* ed. Arif Dirlik, ed. Boulder: Westview Press.
Duara, Prasenjit. 1997. "Nationalists Among Transnationals: Overseas Chinese and the Idea of China, 1900–1911." In *Ungrounded Empires: The Cultural Politics of Modern Chinese Transnationalism.* Ed. Aihwa Ong and Donald M. Nonini. New York: Routledge.
Foucault, Michel. 1994 [1966]. *The Order of Things: An Archaeology of the Human Sciences.* New York: Vintage Books.
Friedman, Jonathan. 1994. "Order and disorder in global systems." In *Cultural Identity and Global Process.* Ed. Jonathan Friedman. London: Sage, 233–253.
Gates, Hill. 1981. "Ethnicity and social class." In *The Anthropology of Taiwanese Society.* Ed. Emily Martin Ahern and Hill Gates. Stanford: Stanford University Press.
Gold, Thomas. 1986. *State and Society in the Taiwan Miracle.* Armonk, NY: M.E. Sharpe.
Herzfeld, Michael. 1997. *Cultural Intimacy: Social Poetics in the Nation-State.* New York: Routledge.
Historical Research Commission of Taiwan Province. 1991. *Er er ba shijian wenxian jilu (The historigraphical records of the Taiwan event of February 28, 1947).* Taichung: Taiwan Provincial Government.

Huang Chung-Hsien. 1997. "My Utopia or Yours? Steering Between a Course of National Identity Formation and Welfare State Making by Reinventing Social Citizenship in Taiwan." Paper presented at the Third Annual North American Taiwanese Studies Conference, May 30–June 1, University of California, Berkeley.

Kerr, George H. 1965. *Formosa Betrayed*. Boston: Houghton Mifflin.

Lai Tse-han, Ramon H. Myers, Wei Wou. 1991. *A Tragic Beginning: The Taiwan Uprising of February 28, 1947*. Stanford: Stanford University Press.

Lee, Teng-hui. 1989. *Selected Addresses and Messages: 1988*. Taipei: Government Information Office.

Li, Kuang-Chun. 1999. "Some Reflections on the Social Orientation of Post-war Taiwanese Nationalism." Paper presented at the Third Annual Conference on Democracy on Both Sides of the Taiwan Straits: Nationalism and Cross-Straits Relations, Harvard University, November 16–17.

Liao, Ping-hui. 1993. "Rewriting Taiwanese National History: The February 28 Incident As Spectacle." *Public Culture* 5:281–296.

Lin, Chia-lung. 1999. "Taiwan's Democratization and Nation-Formation." Paper presented at the Third Annual Conference on Democracy on Both Sides of the Taiwan Straits: Nationalism and Cross-Straits Relations, Harvard University, November 16–17.

Lin, Tsung-yi. 1997. "Confrontation or conflict resolution? Part 1: Violent Oppressors versus Miserable Survivors." Paper presented at the February 28th Incident 50th Anniversary International Academic Research Conference, February 24–27, Taipei. Photocopied.

Maier, Charles S. 1988. *The Unmasterable Past: A History, Holocaust, and German National Identity*. Cambridge: Harvard University Press.

Meisner, Maurice. 1963. "The Development of Formosan Nationalism." *China Quarterly* 15 (July–September): 91–106.

Murray, Stephen O., and Keelung Hong. 1994. *Taiwanese Culture, Taiwanese Society: A Critical Review of Social Science Research Done on Taiwan*. New York: Lanham.

Niu, Cionghai. 1962. "The Formation of the Formosan Nation." *Formosan Quarterly* 1, no. 2 (October)46.

Nora, Pierre. 1989. "Between Memory and History: *Les lieux de mémoire*" (Loci of memory). *Representations* 26 (spring): 7–25.

Peng, Ming-min. 1972. *A Taste of Freedom: Memoirs of a Formosan Independence Leader*. New York: Holt, Rinehart and Winston.

Philips, Steven. 1999. "Between Assimilation and Independence: Taiwanese Political Aspirations Under Nationalist Chinese Rule, 1945–1948." In *Taiwan: A New History*. Ed. Murray A. Rubinstein. Armonk, NY: M.E. Sharpe.

Shu, Wei-der. 1995. "The Emergence of Taiwanese Nationalism: A Preliminary Work on the Approach of Interactive Episode Discourse." Paper presented at the First Annual North America Taiwan Studies Conference, Yale University, June 2–4.

Smith, Anthony D. 1995. *Nations and Nationalism in the Global Era*. Cambridge, UK: Polity.

Su, Bing (Shih Ming). 1986. *Taiwan's 400 Year History: The Origins and Continuing Development of the Taiwanese Society and People* (English). Washington, DC: Taiwanese Cultural Grassroots Association. Original edition (Japanese), Tokyo, 1962. Chinese edition, San Jose, 1972, CA: Paradise Culture Associates.

TAUP (Taiwan Association of University Professors). 1997. *Jinian er-er-ba, wu-shi zhounian:* *'Zhuisi yehsheng' zhuguang youxing* (February 28th 50th anniversary commemoration: Candlelight parade in remembrance of victims). Program. Photocopied.

Taiwan Peace and Reconciliation Committee. 1997. *Er er ba wu shi guo nian: Er Er Ba hui bu hui zai fasheng?* (February 28 50th Anniversary: Can 2–28 Happen Again?) Taipei: Taiwan Peace and Reconciliation Committee.

Taiwaner, A. 1996. "Pseudo-Taiwanese: *Isle Margin* Editorials-Alter-Native-Taiwanese: Taiwan's Fifth Major Ethnic Group." *Positions* 4:1.

Taussig, Michael. 1992. *The Nervous System.* New York: Routledge.

Trouillot, Michel-Rolph. 1995. *Silencing the Past: Power and the Production of History.* Boston: Beacon.

Wu, Jaushieh Joseph. 1995. *Taiwan's Democratization: Forces Behind the New Momentum.* New York: Oxford University Press.

# —— 3 ——

# Who Joined the Clandestine Political Organization?

Some Preliminary Evidence from the Overseas Taiwan Independence Movement

*Wei-der Shu*

The Taiwan Independence Movement (TIM), the vanguard of Taiwanese nationalism, originated in the mid-1940s, when the Kuomintang (KMT) took over Taiwan at the end of World War II. However, due to severe state repression, the TIM had to formulate its organizational infrastructure in political circles away from the island. From the late 1940s, activists began to organize clandestine political organizations in Hong Kong and Japan to question the legitimacy of the KMT's rule over Taiwan. Starting in the mid-1950s, the idea of Taiwanese nationalism gradually found some resonance among Taiwanese students who were studying in North America. It can be said that of all the phenomena that characterized the history of Taiwan in the 1990s, the emergence of Taiwanese nationalism has had the most dramatic impact on its political landscape (Shu 1998).

Indeed, since World War II, U.S. universities have become the training ground of elites from the Third World countries, particularly those who had not been subject to European colonial rule. Taiwan is no exception. In the United States, a territory far beyond the sovereignty of Taiwan, the KMT government has still maintained a strong network that can infiltrate the college and university campuses across the New World. According to Michael Glennon, who helped conduct a study of KMT's agents in America for the Senate Foreign Relations Committee, the KMT intelligence agencies "have conducted extended harassment, intimidation, and surveillance of the United States residents here on American soil" (quoted in Cohen, 1991, 25). Without a doubt, the presence and activities of the KMT's agents on U.S. campuses and in other community organizations have created a chilling atmosphere for overseas Taiwanese who might otherwise have been eager to test the more open political environment they found in America.

In spite of repression and the KMT's campaigns against the Taiwanese national culture, the Taiwanese nationalist movement still blossomed and became an overseas political force in the 1960s. In January 1970, the World United Formosans for Independence (WUFI), an ally of various overseas organizations advocating Taiwan independence, was formed in New York City. On April 24, 1970, the vice premier of the Republic of China. Chiang Ching-Kuo, Chiang Kai-shek's eldest son, was nearly assassinated by two WUFI members. As a counterblow to the KMT's arbitrary arrest of Taiwanese dissidents in the Kaohsiung Incident, a large protest demonstration organized by the oppoisition force, in December 1979, the overseas TIM also launched a series of activities targeting KMT representative offices in the United States. In other words, a number of Taiwanese joined the clandestine political organizations and played the role of political exiles in the struggle against the KMT dictatorship and in the development of Taiwanese nationalism.

The focus of this chapter is the political activism of these overseas TIM activists. Based on in-depth interviews with fourteen TIM activists' life histories, the chapter deals with a very fundamental aspect of activism in the clandestine political organizations: Who joined these organizations? The central questions I will address in this study are: Who are those individuals engaging in clandestine political activities such as the overseas TIM? What are their social origins? Until recently, these questions have remained unanswered, as discussion of Taiwanese nationalism was taboo for ordinary Taiwanese people as well as social scientists conducting Taiwan studies under the KMT's authoritarian rule. It is only recently, with the change in the political climate and the availability of new sources of information, that it has become possible to analyze the phenomenon. Even in this situation, compared to other subjects in the field of Taiwan studies, the TIM, especially the postwar overseas TIM, is a relatively ignored research subject.[1] This research is a preliminary attempt to bridge this gap.

## Activism in Clandestine Political Organizations

Within the literature on clandestine political organizations, researchers often explain the most radical forms of collective action by the assumed pathology of the activists. Eric Hoffer's (1951) notion of the "true believer" can be seen as a representative of this tendency, which describes activists as frustrated individuals, blindly obedient to a leader or following the mass, content to lose their "unwanted" selves. In the case of clandestine political groups, participation has been related to low self-esteem, impatience, uncompromising attitudes, a tendency to blame others, relative deprivation, social uprootedness, personality dependence, egocentrism, and frustrated attempts to build positive identities (e.g., Crenshaw 1986; Kornhauser 1959; Livingstone 1982). Following the tradition of collective behavior studies, these researchers emphasize the discontinuities between "normal" political behavior and deviant political behavior.

One of the main critiques of this trend of studies addresses their empirical validity. As Donatolla della Porta contends (1988, 156), these aforementioned interpretations, however, "have never been proven by empirical research." Even in the few cases in which militants have been given personality tests, the subjects were individuals who had passed through two "total institutions"—the clandestine organization and the prison system (della Porta 1992, 7). As the research of Richard G. Braungart and Margaret M. Braungart (1992, 60) demonstrates, "personality, rather than a prior given, changed as a result of affiliation with the group." Thus, this "pathology" offers little help for this research in the case of overseas TIM activists. In order to conduct the following empirical investigation, we have to look for some other route to solve the puzzle.

Considering terrorist groups as forms of political organization, albeit with particular characteristics, may suggest alternative hypotheses about individual participation. In investigating these alternatives, we can draw insights from the general literature about social movement organizations. In other words, rather than focusing on the discontinuities between clandestine political organizations and social movement organizations,[2] we can take into account the continuities between different forms of political activism. We can see della Porta's argument in the following:

> [T]he motivation to join terrorist groups can be understood within the framework of categories used for *other types of political organizations,* especially those which are less well-equipped with institutional resources [emphasis added]. (1988, 156)

Following this argument about the continuity between the clandestine political organizations and other types of political organizations, I will assume that the general literature on social movements provides the valuable analytical tools for the explanatory model of activism in clandestine political organizations.

As far as the social movement literature is concerned, a diversity of opinion also exists there about the "best" theoretical framework to employ regarding the origins of political activism. Confronting the immense variety of writings on social movements, two approaches can be seen as direct approaches of political activism: marginality thesis and the privilege thesis.[3]

On the one hand, some researchers hold that the behavior of the less institutionalized forms of political participation is accepted more readily in the marginal strata of the population than in any others. Vulnerability to social-movement participation is in part a function of being weakly attached or peripheral to existing social networks. Readiness to participate comes from an absence of those conditions that integrate people into the system. With this emphasis on the cohesive functions of movements, movements are viewed as surrogate families and primary groups that meet previously isolated participants' needs for social affiliation, a sense of belongingness, and group identity (Kornhauser 1959). I label this position the "marginality thesis." From this perspective, activists tend to be marginal people in their societies—that is, they deviate in significant and perceptible ways from accepted norms, whether social, psychological, or physical. This thesis is supported by Peter Waldmann's empirical research (1922). In his study of several ethnic underground organizations like the Irish Republican Army (IRA) and *Euskadi ta-Askatun* (ETA),[4] he finds that the militants are mainly from the lower or lower-middle classes.

On the other hand, some scholars propose a second, quite opposite thesis focusing on the middle class. This maintains that the radicalization of a working-class ideology in a middle class is a psychological device to "compensate" for bourgeois origins (Braungart and Braungart 1992; Keniston 1968). I label this position the "privilege thesis." Klaus Wasmund (1986, 201), after analyzing 227 life histories of leftist terrorists from West Germany, concludes that the terrorists "come mostly from the upper middle classes." Nearly every other terrorist (47 percent) has a father who holds a so-called higher position. The level of education of the terrorists is correspondingly of an above-average standard (Wasmund, 1986, 202). From this perspective, activists could be individuals who are very strongly rooted in the social system. High social status could be considered conducive to collective action since it implies that an individual has specific skills as well as great probability of success. Furthermore, more free time and a small risk of social sanction have also been mentioned to account for the higher propensity of young people to mobilize. I will try to solve the contention between the marginality thesis and the privilege thesis by presenting my original data on the social origins of fourteen interviewees.

## Fourteen Life Histories

In many respects, the data obtained from the open-ended interviews serves as the main sources of information for this study. Fourteen life histories of the overseas TIM activists are presented in this paper.[5] Ideally, an analysis of the personal backgrounds of the overseas TIM rank-and-file activists would require data on a random sample of all activists. Unfortunately, in clandestine political organizations like the overseas TIM, it is difficult, if not impossible, to access this kind of information. Secret organizations, of course, do not provide public access to their membership files. No comprehensive or even partial listing of overseas TIM activists exists. Therefore, I relied instead on three indirect methods to identify these TIM activists in North America and conduct my interview. First, the initial set of respondents came from the public accounts about overseas TIM activists, that is, those activists who used their names publicly as leaders or spokesmen for the overseas TIM.[6] Then, other respondents were identified and recommended to me through my personal networks. The remainder of the respondents came as the result of referrals from the first and second groups of respondents.

The interview questions were designed to examine the role of the participants in overseas TIM to document the history of their involvement with the organizations, their motivations for joining, and how they fit into the organizational structure. The interviewers also gathered biographical data, examined participants' perceptions regarding their role in overseas TIM, and investigated what influence involvement in the organization had on the participants' personal development. Interviews took place between September 1995 and February 1997.

## The Blacklists

These fourteen case studies of activists' life histories have been supplemented by two other data sets, one derived from Dang (1991, 172–179), the other originated from Kwei-Ch'üan Wang (1991). I refer to the first list as "blacklist record I." This is a list of seventy-six people on the "Taiwanese-American Homeland Visit Group Member's Roster" as of April 1991. This group was organized by the Federation of Taiwanese in Southern California and the Taiwanese Association of America in December 1990. The principle purpose of this group was to challenge the KMT government's "notorious and ridiculous so-called "blacklist policy" (Dang 1991, 171)," which barred thousands of people from entering or returning to Taiwan.[7] After some serious arguments with the KMT government, more than sixty members out of the original seventy-six members of this group were still denied visas to visit

Taiwan. To some degree, we could treat members of this group as activists of the overseas TIM, at least from the perspective of the KMT government.

I term the second list "blacklist record II." It is a report on seventy-four blacklisted people around the world (most of them residing in the United States) compiled and written in Chinese by a journalist from Taiwan in 1991. Based upon the location of the interview, this book is divided into four parts: the western United States, the eastern United States, the Central United States, and Japan. It is notable that there is some membership overlap between the two lists.

Both lists provide only the activists' name, year of birth, native place, educational background, professional experience, and community involvement. In Wang's book, there is also an extracted short statement describing the interviewee's rationale for joining the TIM. I will use these blacklist records, together with my fourteen case studies, to illustrate several important characteristics of overseas TIM activists.[8]

**The Genesis of the Taiwan Independence Movement**

The genesis of the overseas TIM can be traced back to the February 28 Incident, as chapter two has shown.[9] The suppression of the February 28 Incident proved to the Taiwanese the dictatorial nature of the KMT regime in Taiwan, a rule that was characterized by the oppression of one group of people, the Taiwanese, by another, the Mainlanders. However, as most of the Taiwanese elite had been jailed or executed in the Incident, the opposition movement was virtually in the hands of a few surviving members of the Taiwanese elite in exile or other overseas dissidents. The Incident crystallized the development of Taiwanese nationalist feelings. As these feelings developed, the overseas Taiwanese living in Japan started the TIM in the early 1950s (Ong 1964, 167; Mendel 1970, 147). In the United States, because Taiwanese students came to this country after the late 1950s, the TIM also blossomed in the 1960s.

In 1956, Wen-I Liao (Thomas Liao) and his associates set up the *Taiwan gongheguo linshi zhengfu* (Provisional Government of the Republic of Formosa) in Japan, the chief intellectual and political center for overseas anti-KMT activities in the 1950s and 1960s. In February 1960, some younger Taiwanese students in Japan founded another TIM organization, *Taiwan qingnian she* (Taiwan chinglian [youth] associates), which was renamed the *Taiwan qingnian hui* (Formosan Association) in 1963. Believing that propaganda work and clandestine organizations were the most critical activities at that time, the association began to publish *Taiwan chinglian* in Japanese and the *Formosan Quarterly* in English (Ong 1964, 169–170). In 1965, the formal name of this organization was again changed to the *Taiwan qingnian duli lianmeng* (United Young Formosans for Independence) (Ming-Cheng Chen, 1992) (see Figure 3.1).

In the United States, up to 1965 no unified, nationwide organization for Taiwan independence had been founded, though a number of local groups were actively engaged in the movement, notably those in New York, Philadelphia, Kansas, Oklahoma, Wisconsin, and California. Among these local groups, Formosans' Free Formosa (3F)[10] (*Taiwanren de ziyou Taiwan*) was the first as well as the most significant organization advocating Taiwan independence in North America. This organization was founded by Jung-Hsün Lin (John Lin), I-Te Chen (Edward Chen), and Chu-I Loo (Jay Loo) in Philadelphia in 1956. Later, 3F was restructured and renamed the United Formosans for Independence (UFI) (*Taiwan duli lianmeng*) in 1958.

In Madison, Wisconsin, there was also another well-organized group called the Formosan Affairs Study Group (*Taiwan wenti yanjiu hui*), actively conducting political campaigns under the leadership of Shebing Ciu, a medical doctor. In October 1965, a meeting called the Formosan Leadership Unity Congress was held in Madison, Wisconsin, where leading figures of the independence movement from all over the country gathered and agreed to make preparations for a unified organization. In the following year, a new organization, the United Formosans in America for Independence (UFAI) (*Quan-Mei Taiwan duli lianmeng*) was born (King 1974, 22).

In Canada, Yi-Ming Huang (Robert Y. M. Huang) and Che-fu Lin (Albert Lin) founded the League for Self-determination of Formosans (*Taiwan zhumin zijue lianmeng*) in 1963. Two years later, this organization was renamed the Committee for Human Rights in Formosa (*Taiwan renquan weiyuanhui*). This title was based on the task of rescuing Peng Ming-min[11] in the name of human rights (Nan-Fang Shuo 1980, 64). In Europe, the Union for Formosa's Independence in Europe (UFIE) was founded in 1965 through the effort of Sekun Kang (King 1974, 22). In 1968, the UYFI in Japan, the UFAI in the United States, the UFIE in Europe, and the Committee for Human Rights in Formosa in Canada made a joint declaration, announcing that two magazines—*Taiwan Chinglian* and *The Independent Formosa*[12]—were to be their joint organs. This was to be the first step toward a complete amalgamation of the TIM organizations throughout the world. In 1970, the expected worldwide organization was started under the name of the World United Formosans for Independence (WUFI) (*Taiwan duli jianguo lianmeng*).

In addition to WUFI, there also existed some other, smaller organizations, most of them located in Japan and North America, advocating the ideas of both socialism and Taiwan independence. They labeled themselves the

Figure 3.1

## The Evolution of World United Formosans for Independence, 1956–1970

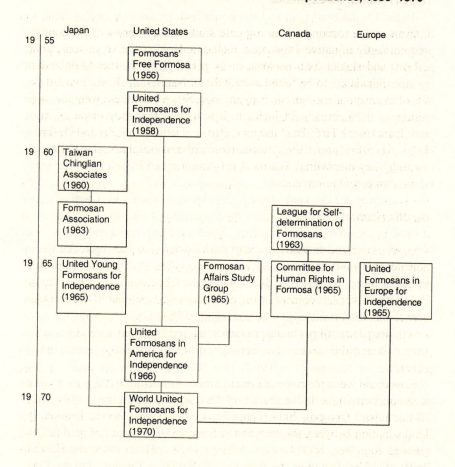

*Source:* Wei-der Shu

"Taiwan Left," as they rejected not only the KMT and the Chinese Communist Party's claim to Taiwan, but also the WUFI's ignorance of welfare programs for the needy and the poor (Shu 1996a). Most of my informants in this study were activists in WUFI-related organizations, though some of them partly shared the ideological position of the Taiwan Left. There is no "great" reason for excluding the Taiwan Left activists in this study. The only explanation is that I had great difficulty in accessing those activists, albeit I spent a lot of time in trying to locate those people.

## Biographical Roots of Activism

### Activists' Ethnic Background

In terms of the respondents in my case studies, the overseas TIM consists predominantly of native Taiwanese, including Hoklo (twelve persons, or 86 percent) and Hakka (two persons, or 14 percent), but neither Mainlanders nor Aboriginals are to be found among them. Neither blacklist provided details of the respondents' ethnic backgrounds. Since Taiwanese were the main victims of the February 28 Incident, it is natural that they made up most participants in the TIM. This finding is also very similar to Rejai and Phillips's (1983, 51) work about the characteristics of revolutionary elites. In their research, they discovered that most revolutionary elites belong to the *main ethnic groups in their societies.*

### Age Distribution

Next, let us explore data on the age of the TIM activists (see Table 3.1). This indicates that most of them were born in the 1930s (43 percent of my case studies, 33 percent of the blacklist record I, and 42 percent of blacklist record II) and the 1940s (36 percent of the case studies, 55 percent of the blacklist record, and 39 percent of blacklist record II). Only a few respondents were born in the 1950s (14 percent of my informants, 12 percent of record I, and 9 percent of record II) and even fewer in the 1960s (7 percent, 0 percent, and 1 percent).

How could we explain the uneven age distribution of those activists? Why do people born in the 1930s and the 1940s compose the majority of overseas TIM activists? One possible explanation, the "publicity" thesis, is based on the distinction between the first and successive generations of activists, or between founders and followers. While the generations of the 1930s and 1940s could be treated as the founders of this second-wave overseas TIM, the generations of the 1950s and 1960s are definitely the followers of this movement. It could be said that the founders occupy the highest ranks in the organizations already when followers join. To a certain extent, the founders also control the organization's resources, information, and money. Furthermore, the founders have created the group's rules and are likely to have a higher emotional involvement with the organization than the followers. Accordingly, the generations of the 1950s and the 1960s, compared to the latter generations, tended to occupy the more publicized position in the overseas TIM. The "overrepresentation" of generations of the 1930s and the 1940s in the TIM could be understood from this logic of "publicity." During my inter-

Table 3.1  **Age Distribution of Overseas TIM Activists**

| Sample | 1910– 1919 | 1920– 1929 | 1930– 1939 | 1940– 1949 | 1950– 1959 | 1960 or later | Unknown | N |
|---|---|---|---|---|---|---|---|---|
| Case Studies | 0 (0%) | 0 (0%) | 6 (43%) | 5 (36%) | 2 (14%) | 1 (7%) | 0 (0%) | 14 (100%) |
| Blacklist Record I | 0 (0%) | 0 (0%) | 25 (33%) | 42 (55%) | 9 (12%) | 0 (0%) | 0 (0%) | 76 (100%) |
| Blacklist Record II | 1 (1%) | 2 (3%) | 31 (42%) | 29 (39%) | 7 (9%) | 1 (1%) | 3 (4%) | 74 (99%) |

*Source:* Wei-der Shu

view with him, one informant born after 1950 made similar comments about the phenomenon, when I mentioned that the number of TIM activists born after 1950 was relatively small. He expressed that

> It does not make sense to say that there are so few people born after 1950 participating in the Taiwan Independence Movement. Maybe they are just not as famous as those old guys. But they are really right there, based on my own understanding. (Life history no. M3: 31)[13]

In other words, the "publicity" thesis interprets the dominance of the 1930s and the 1940s generations in the TIM as the result of their "louder voices." Therefore, it treats this dominance as a "superficial" phenomenon, rather than a "factual" reality. However, there is an alternative hypothesis, which takes this dominance as a reality. This alternative thesis tries to illustrate the dominance of the 1930s and the 1940s generations in the overseas TIM through the concept of "1960s historical generation."[14] This concept is developed by Braungart (1993) in his ambitious project of explaining the rise of youth-movement activity over the last 170 years throughout the world. To him, youth movements around the world have not been random political behavior but have clustered around four periods in world time. These periods can be identified as the "Young Europe, Post-Victorian, Great Depression, and 1960s Historical Generations" (Braungart 1993, 118). These historical generations represent "unique patterns of social and political behavior that converge on the exposure or experience of historical events, the age-conscious interpretation of these events, and the dynamic models of responses to these events" (Braungart 1993, 114). In this sense, the 1960s represent a watershed in post–World War II youth-movement activity that occurred on every continent around the world.

It is notable that most of the 1930s and 1940s generations of TIM activists came to North America for advanced studies in the 1960s (50 percent of my case studies and 58 percent of blacklist record II, see Table 3.2). In the relatively liberal environment, with the stimuli of the civil rights movement and the Vietnam War, those Taiwanese were exposed to various liberal, or even radical, ideologies. The influence was reinforced by contemporary global nationalism and the new political culture made possible by modern technology and communications systems. Furthermore, most of the 1930s and 1940s generation were in their early childhood during the 1947 massacre. In terms of the emotional attachment to the February 28 Incident, their personal experience during childhood makes this generation very different from the generations born after the 1950s. While considering the 1947 incident as the origin of the Taiwan independence movement, it is understandable that the generations of the 1930s and 1940s figure prominently among these overseas TIM activists.

Due to the impossibility of finding a comprehensive list of overseas TIM activists at this stage, it is very difficult to evaluate the relative strength and weakness of the "publicity" thesis and the "1960s historical generation" thesis. I suggest that the reader treat these two hypotheses as complementary rather than competing, since I believe both theses could explain *part* of this phenomenon.

## Age at Enrolling in the TIM

Most of my informants came to North America as graduate students, and after earning their degree, took jobs and stayed here.[15] Furthermore, most of them tended to be in their middle to late twenties when they came to North America for graduate studies. This specific "life course" can be understood through the following dimensions. First, since the KMT government did not allow students to study abroad for an undergraduate degree, most of the Taiwanese students came to North America as graduate students. After finishing sixteen years of schooling, the normal age of graduate students tends to be at least twenty-two. Second, in Taiwan, every male citizen has to fulfill the military service obligation for at least one year. Finally, before attending graduate school abroad, most students worked several years to accumulate the professional experience and raise the necessary tuition. Therefore, these TIM activists' typical career beyond the sea began at around their middle to late twenties. Almost all my informants fit this observation, the only exceptions are D3 and I1. D3 did not arrive in the United States through the graduate student route but, instead, came through kinship ties at the age of forty-three. I1 spent several years in Europe for graduate study before attending the Ph.D. program of an American university at the age of thirty-five.

Table 3.2    **Year Overseas TIM Activists Went to North America**

| Sample | 1950–1959 | 1960–1969 | 1970–1979 | 1980 or later | Unknown | N |
|---|---|---|---|---|---|---|
| Case Studies | 0 (0%) | 7 (50%) | 4 (28.6%) | 3 (21.4%) | 0 (0%) | 14 (100.0%) |
| Blacklist Record II | 2 (4%) | 33 (58%)* | 15 (26%)† | 6 (11%) | 1 (2%) | 57 (100%)‡ |

*Source:* Wei-der Shu

*Includes one activist who went to the United States for advanced study twice; once in 1967 and once in 1974. After finishing the first study, he went back to Taiwan in 1969.

†Includes one activist who went to the United States for master's degree in 1973. After returning to Taiwan for several years, he went to the United States again for Ph.D. study in 1981.

‡Seventeen activists are excluded in this table because their overseas destination after leaving Taiwan was other than North America (e.x., Japan, Europe, or Latin America).

After coming to North America, most of my informants almost immediately entered the overseas TIM network. Then, among all respondents, at least half of them (i.e., D4, I1, I2, M3, M5, U1, and Z2) made the decision to join the movement within one or two years. In other words, most of the TIM members were under thirty years of age when they joined the organization. We can say that the overseas TIM was a typical youth movement. This finding coincides fairly closely with researches about other clandestine political organizations. For instance, both Robert P. Clark's (1986) project on the lives of ETA members and Peter Waldmann's (1986) work on guerrilla movements in Argentina, Guatemala, Nicaragua, and Uruguay demonstrate that activists of these movements tend to be very young.

*Gender Profile*

The data on sexual composition reflects that the overseas TIM is dominated by male activists. In terms of the respondents of my case studies, almost all activists are male, except Z1. As far as both blacklist records are concerned, only twenty-one female activists (or 28 percent among all respondents) are listed in record I, and fifteen (or 20 percent among all respondents) are listed in record II. It is not unfair to describe the overseas TIM as "a predominantly male movement." Even though there are female members, who are, based on Friedhelm Neidhardt's (1992, 218) description of right-wing terrorist groups in Germany, "clear patriarchal annexations as girlfriends, fiancées, daughters, or wives of male members." For instance, even though Z1's husband was a member of WUFI, she did not join this organization until 1985, fifteen years after she arrived in the United States. She made the following statement to explain this situation:

> I don't know why. . . . When my husband served as head of the local [WUFI] chapter, I made phone calls to contact comrades about the monthly meeting for him. Whenever George [then the chairperson of WUFI] came here for financial campaigning, I took him to visit the potential supporters. I participated in every activity sponsored by WUFI, even though I was not a formal member at that time. In 1985, *someone happened to find* that I was not a member of WUFI yet, so he asked me to file the application (emphasis added). (Life History no. Z1: 5)

*Native Place*

Where do the overseas TIM activists come from? Based upon the information about native place derived from my case studies, both blacklist records, and Taiwan's total population, we can encounter two interesting and seemingly significant observations (see Table 3.3). First, while taking "region" as the unit of analysis, almost half of the respondents (42.9 percent of my case studies, 47.4 percent of record I, and 45.9 percent of record II) come from the southern region of Taiwan. As far as the total population in Taiwan is concerned, the proportion of people living in the southern region is only 29.7 percent. Accordingly, it is reasonable to claim that people from southern Taiwan were more likely to participate in the overseas TIM.

Second, while taking "county" rather than region as the unit of analysis, the three largest pools of activists are from Tainan (35.7 percent of my case studies, 30.3 percent of blacklist record I, and 28.4 percent of blacklist record II), Taichung (21.4 percent, 19.7 percent, and 12.2 percent, respectively), and Taipei (7.1 percent, 11.8 percent, and 9.5 percent, respectively).[16] Residents of Tainan and Taichung make up only 8.4 percent and 9.8 percent of Taiwan's population, respectively. And Taipei has the highest share of the population, with 28.1 percent. People from Tainan and Taichung, especially those from Tainan, are more likely to engage in the overseas TIM, as their proportion among the activists is much larger than their proportion of Taiwan's total population. Furthermore, people from Taipei are less likely to join the overseas TIM, as their percentage of the activists is much smaller than the percentage of their total population of Taiwan.

To summarize, people from southern Taiwan, especially those from Tainan, are more likely to engage in the overseas TIM. This phenomenon is not found only by me (the researcher), but also discovered by some informants of my case studies, the subjects. During the interview, when I asked

Table 3.3 **Native Place of Overseas TIM Activists**

| Native Place | Case Studies | Blacklist Record I | Blacklist Record II | People Living in Taiwan, 1989* |
|---|---|---|---|---|
| Northern Region | 5 (35.7%) | 18 (23.7%) | 16 (21.6%) | 8,450 (42.1%) |
| Taipei | 1 (7.1%) | 9 (11.8%) | 7 (9.5%) | 5,653 (28.1%) |
| Keelung | 1 (7.1%) | 1 (1.3%) | 1 (1.4%) | 348 (1.7%) |
| Ilan | 2 (14.3%) | 5 (6.6%) | 7 (9.5%) | 448 (2.2%) |
| Hsinchu | 1 (7.1%) | 3 (3.9%) | 1 (1.4%) | 688 (3.4%) |
| Taoyuan | 0 | 0 | 0 | 1,313 (6.5%) |
| Central Region | 3 (21.4%) | 21 (27.6%) | 18 (24.3%) | 5,043 (25.2%) |
| Taichung | 3 (21.4%) | 15 (19.7%) | 9 (12.2%) | 1,973 (9.8%) |
| Nantou | 0 | 3 (3.9%) | 1 (1.4%) | 533 (2.7%) |
| Changhua | 0 | 2 (2.6%) | 5 (6.7%) | 1,234 (6.2%) |
| Yunlin | 0 | 1 (1.3%) | 1 (1.4%) | 758 (3.8%) |
| Miaoli | 0 | 0 | 2 (2.7%) | 545 (2.7%) |
| Southern Region | 6 (42.9%) | 36 (47.4%) | 34 (45.9%) | 5,949 (29.7%) |
| Tainan | 5 (35.7%) | 23 (30.3%) | 21 (28.4%) | 1,688 (8.4%) |
| Kaohsiung | 0 | 2 (2.6%) | 3 (4.1%) | 2,468 (12.3%) |
| Chiayi | 1 (7.1%) | 8 (10.5%) | 7 (9.5%) | 808 (4.0%) |
| Pingtung | 0 | 3 (3.9%) | 3 (4.1%) | 889 (4.4%) |
| Penghu | 0 | 0 | 0 | 96 (0.5%) |
| Eastern Region | 0 | 0 | 0 | 607 (3.0%) |
| Other Than Taiwan | 0 | 1 (1.3%) | 2 (2.7%) | N.A. |
| China | 0 | 1 (1.3%) | 1 (1.4%) | |
| Japan | 0 | 0 | 1 (1.4%) | |
| Unknown | 0 | 0 | 4 (5.4%) | N.A. |
| N | 14 (100%) | 76 (100%) | 74 (100%) | 20,048 (100%) |

*Source:* Wei-der Shu

*In thousands. Furthermore, the information is based on people's "registered place" rather than "native place." The original source is *Social Indicators in Taiwan Area of the Republic of China, 1989,* Table 9, published by Director-General of Budget, Accounting and Statistics, Executive Yuan, Republic of China, 1990.

D4 to explain the phenomenon that "many overseas TIM activists are from Tainan," he said,

I don't know. Maybe it is just an incident. Maybe there is some geographical connection or cultural connection. I don't know. While Hsu Hsin-liang just arrived in the United States, his relationship with WUFI was not bad. However, he broke the relationship and looked down the Taiwan independence movement later on. Someone asked him about the content of the Taiwanese consciousness of the Taiwan independence movement, he said "Their Taiwanese consciousness is nothing special, it is only the consciousness of the Chia-Nan Plain."[17] So, he [Hsu] looked down the Taiwan independence movement (Life history no. D4: 2). . . . So, in the mind of Hsu Hsin-liang, he felt that it is the "Tainan Gang" playing a critical role in the Taiwan independence movement. The reason was that there were too many activists who had graduated from Tainan First High School. At that time, there was a teacher called Ong Joktik at that school. He was teaching Chinese. Later on, he lived in exile in Japan and began to organize the Taiwan independence movement. Due to his *influence in terms of ideas,* many accepted the idea of Taiwan independence on coming to the United States and Japan (emphasis added). (Life history no. D4: 3)

### Educational Level

Perhaps the most striking characteristic of the attributes of these activists in this study is their high level of education (see Table 3.4). While taking my case studies into consideration, among 14 interviewees, 8 (57 percent) hold a doctorate, 4 (29 percent) have a master's degree, and only 2 (14 percent) have a bachelor's degree. As far as both data sets are concerned, 37 percent of record I and 46 percent of record II have a doctorate, 34 percent in both records hold a master's degree, 20 percent of record I and 12 percent of record II have a bachelor's degree, and only 5 percent in both sets have a high school education or less.

Several observations are of interest here. First, the educational level of activists derived from both records is quite *similar* to that of the interviewees in my case studies. Second, all data sets demonstrate that *over seven-tenths* of the activists were awarded at least a master's degree. Third, while considering the possible "sampling" problem, I do not think these figures are unreliable indicators, even if the sampling procedures in both data sets are not really "scientific." According to WUFI's open statement, "75 percent of their [WUFI's] members in the United States held a Ph.D. degree or at least a master's degree. To many people, WUFI might look more like an academic and intellectually oriented organization rather than a revolutionary group such as the PLO or the ANC in South Africa" (Chang 1991, 318). Finally, compared with other reference populations like Taiwanese living in the United States, people living in Taiwan, and people living in the United States, these TIM activists are still surprisingly well educated.

### Occupation of Overseas TIM Activists

In order to round out the demographic profile of overseas TIM activists and thereby move closer to a more precise understanding of who has joined the movement, one further question calls for examination: From what social classes or socioeconomic categories within the larger social structure has the movement drawn the majority of its adherents? Since I had difficulty securing data pertaining directly to those activists' income levels, however, the only available information regarding the matter is the occupational composition

Table 3.4   **Educational Level of Overseas TIM Activists**

| Sample | Doctorate | Master | Bachelor | High School or Less | Unknown | N |
|---|---|---|---|---|---|---|
| Case Studies | 8 (57%) | 4 (29%) | 2 (14%) | 0 (0%) | 0 (0%) | 14 (100%) |
| Blacklist Record I | 28 (37%) | 26 (34%) | 15 (20%) | 4 (5%) | 3 (4%) | 76 (100%) |
| Blacklist Record II | 34 (46%) | 25 (34%) | 9 (12%) | 4 (5%) | 2 (3%) | 74 (100%) |
| Taiwanese Living in the United States, 1990* | 3,658 (8.3%) | 9,549 (21.7%) | 11,090 (25.2%) | 19, 637 (44.7%) | 0 (0%) | 43,934 (99.9%) |
| People Living in Taiwan, 1990† | 98,000§ (0.7%) | | 2,240,000" (15.1%) | 12,473,000 (84.2%) | 0 (0%) | 14,811,000 (100.0%) |
| People Living in the United States,1990‡ | 1,205,426 (0.8%) | 7,520,469 (4.7%) | 20,832,567 (13.1%) | 129,309,974 (81.3%) | 0 (0%) | 158,868,436 (99.9%) |

*Source:* Wei-der Shu

*Based on Taiwanese population aged twenty-five and over living in the United States. The original source is *1990 Census of Population (Asian and Pacific Islanders in the United States), 1990 CP-3-5,* Table 3, published by U.S. Census Bureau, 1993.

†Based on Taiwanese population aged fifteen and over only. The original source is *An Extract Report on the 1990 Census of Population and Housing, Taiwan-Fukien Area, Republic of China, Part I,* Table 6-4 and Table 6-6, published by Census Office of the Executive Yuan, Republic of China, 1992.

‡Based on people aged twenty-five and over living in the United States. The original source is *1990 Census of Population (Asian and Pacific Islanders in the United States), 1990 CP-3-5,* Table 3, published by U.S. Census Bureau, 1993.

§Original data does not separate people with doctorate and master's degree; data is combined here.

"Includes people with university and college education (986,000) and from junior college (1,254,000).

of those activists. Accordingly, I will try to shed some light on the above question by inferring the movement's socioeconomic base from its occupational profile, which is provided in Table 3.5.

First, given the fact that all my data sets indicate that at least half of the activists were employed in professional occupations (64.3 percent, 51.3 percent, and 62.2 percent, respectively), and given the fact that around 30 percent of overseas TIM activists worked for managerial specialty occupations (28.6 percent, 27.6 percent, and 18.9 percent, respectively), it seems fair to

Table 3.5  **Occupation of Overseas TIM Activists**

| Case | Professional specialty occupations | Managerial specialty occupations | Technical, sales, and administrative support occupations | Service Occupations | Others or Unknown | N |
|---|---|---|---|---|---|---|
| Case Studies | 9 (64.3%) | 4† (28.6%) | 0 (0%) | 1 (7.1%) | 0 (0%) | 14 (100.0%) |
| Blacklist Record I | 39 (51.3%) | 21‡ (27.6%) | 2 (2.6%) | 3 (3.9%) | 11 (14.5%) | 76 (99.9%) |
| Blacklist Record II | 46 (62.2%) | 14**** (18.9%) | 1 (1.4%) | 0 (0%) | 13 (17.6%) | 74 (100.1%) |
| Taiwanese living in the United States, 1990* | 9,241 (29.4%) | 5,940 (18.9%) | 10,727 (34.1%) | 2,885 (9.2%) | 2,658 (8.5%) | 31,451 (100.1%) |

*Source:* Wei-der Shu.

*Based on Taiwanese population aged sixteen and over living in the United States. The original source is *1990 Census of Population (Asian and Pacific Islanders in the United States), 1990 CP-3-5*, Table 4, published by U.S. Census Bureau, 1993.

†Includes two business owners.

‡Includes thirteen business owners/partners. The typical businesses run by these activists include motels (four persons), engineering consultant firms (two persons), and other small business. I assume that all these business owners also work as management staff, which is common for Taiwanese residing in the United States.

§Includes nine business owners/partners.

conclude that overseas TIM has drawn the majority of its adherents from the occupational categories of the broad "professional middle class." This is not surprising given their astonishing high level of educational attainment.

Second, a comparison of figures in the column "Taiwanese living in the United States, 1990," shows that the proportion of professional and managerial occupations among the activists (almost 80 percent) is much larger than for Taiwanese in general (only about 50 percent). And while very few activists worked for nonprofessional/managerial occupations, a certain proportion of Taiwanese made their living in either technical, sales, and administrative support occupations (34.1 percent) or service occupations (9.2 percent).

## Conclusion

To summarize, overseas TIM activists typically are *native Taiwanese*, the main ethnic group in Taiwan. They were born in *the 1930s and 1940s*, and joined the movement in their mid to late twenties. They were predominantly *male* and from *southern Taiwan*, especially *Tainan*. They constitute a *well-educated group*, many of them having obtained a doctoral or master's degree from universities in North America. Accordingly, they are concentrated in the *professional and managerial specialty occupations*.

What, in the light of the foregoing, can we conclude regarding our understanding about the contention between the "marginality" thesis and the "privilege" thesis in terms of the social origins of overseas TIM activists? To begin with, it seems that the empirical data are more likely to fit the prediction of the privilege thesis, since most of the activists could be broadly categorized as middle class in origin. Why is the middle class more susceptible to joining the overseas TIM? Why do people from non-middle-class backgrounds have difficulty joining the overseas TIM? We have to understand this phenomenon from the perspective of a *"student movement."* Most of the activists in this study came to North America as graduate students first. Then, after earning their degree, they found jobs and stayed there. Accordingly, most of them began to participate in the overseas TIM under the status of "students." Given students' privileged access to *free time* compared with employees of similar age, their articulateness, and the natural tendency of young people toward *rebellious idealism*, student politics tend to be activistic and radical.

However, it seems that the marginality thesis is not totally irrelevant to our empirical result. First, one can argue that all native Taiwanese are almost by definition marginal, as the Mainlander-led KMT government systematically and consciously infused them with a deep sense of inferiority. Second, after coming to North America for advanced studies, many of the young Taiwanese also underwent a painful process of what psychologists call "marginalization," both intellectually and emotionally. They were torn between the values of the two cultures. Many became activists of the TIM after being exposed to liberal professors, who more often than not criticized the KMT's record on the Mainland and attributed the debacle of 1949 to the corruption and ineffectual leadership of the KMT.

Conclusively, if we defined "marginality" by socioeconomic indicators, then the overwhelmingly middle-class activists of the TIM are a challenge to the marginality thesis. However, if we expanded the referred scope of the definition of marginality to include the psychological dimension, we have to acknowledge that most of the activists share the characteristics of marginality to some extent.

Why does the empirical evidence of this study support two competing theses at the same time? Probably this paper asks the wrong question, since the contention between the marginality thesis and the privilege thesis is not really an interesting puzzle waiting for the researcher's continuous quest. To me, there are at least two reasons for this. First, the concepts like the marginality and privilege themselves are troublesome to some degree. For instance, if the notion of marginality was so broadly defined as to apply to the virtually diversified dimensions in the social, psychological, economic, or even historical sense, it may be that marginality is a *human* characteristic and not an attribute of political activists. Should this be the case, all findings concerning marginality, this study included, are no findings at all. Second, but probably more important than the truth or falsity of both theses, is their insufficiency. Even if the activists' privileged background does contribute to political activism, a much larger number of people exhibited the same characteristics, but did not join the movement. In other words, rather than the social background, we have to consider some other factors, besides social background, influencing people's decision to join social movements.

I have just focused on my fourteen life histories and Dang's (1991) blacklist record. The themes detailed here may or may not be evident when covering other, more comprehensive data sets. It would be useful to look at some other data sets to conduct a more systematic analysis in the future. I have also focused only on one social movement organization (i.e., WUFI) within the overseas TIM. The information about all other major organizations like the Formosan Association for Public Affairs (FAPA) obviously deserve future attention.

## Notes

1. To my best knowledge, the only relatively comprehensive accounts of this subject published in English are by Douglas Mendel (1970) and Mei-Ling Wang (1999).

The best Chinese work in this field is by Ming-Cheng Chen, though this is written in a journalistic style. Similarly, other recent works (Chia-shu Huang 1994; Geoffroy 1997) provide only the chronological description, rather than an explanation of the TIM. None of these works offers a thorough sociological analysis of the emergence of the TIM.

2. The implication of this "discontinuity" is that there are "normal," legitimate, conventional actors on the one hand and there are "abnormal," illegitimate, and unconventional actors on the other. Of course, clandestine political organizations are seen as a kind of "abnormal" collective action in this approach.

3. It is difficult to categorize the fruitful and diversified literature on political activism in the sociological field of social movements. Furthermore, categorizing theories into broad groups is necessarily a "reductionist" task, since no individual theory may be justly treated in such an exercise. Nonetheless, the categorization is heuristic in that it gives researchers a starting point from which we can approach a synthesis.

4. ETA is a Basque underground organization advocating Basque nationalism.

5. I am being deliberately vague by not attaching a table here with the profiles of my interviewees. It would have provided the readers with greater understanding, but it would also have made it easier to identify the interviewees.

6. I acknowledge that this kind of information meets the problem of "representation," since there probably emerges an overrepresentation of the especially "bold and enterprising leading forces in the underground organizations" (Waldmann 1986, 264). However, this was the only source of interviews at the initial stage.

7. The KMT government used this "blacklist policy" as a vehicle for political control from the 1950s until the early 1990s.

8. I also obtained TIM-related information from some other published sources, which include (1) the biographies of individual activists; (2) written material from the activists themselves—pamphlets, papers, essay selections, newspaper articles, or interviews; (3) overseas TIM publications; and (4) secondary data relevant to the overseas TIM. For the more comprehensive lists about published sources of the overseas TIM, refer to Shu (1996b, Appendix).

9. It is notable that the first call for Taiwan Independence came long before the Incident. In 1928, the Taiwanese Communist Party (Taiwan gongchandang), which existed as the national branch (minzu zhi bu) of the Japanese Communist Party (Riben gongchandang) then, had advocated the idea already (Chen Fang-ming 1994, 290–295). However, since the nature of "Taiwan independence" before World War II, at the time Taiwan was ruled by the Japanese colonial government, is quite different from that after World War II, when Taiwan was ruled by the KMT government, I will ignore the former in this paper.

10. There are different versions about the exact wording of these "3 Fs" in the existing literature. For instance, 3F is described as Free Formosans' Formosa by Chen Fang-ming (1992, 81), as Free Formosan's Formosa by Huang (1994, 27, 296), as Formosans for Free Formosa by Copper (2000, 90). In this paper, I follow Cheng-san Li's work (1998) to describe the 3F as Formosans' Free Formosa, since this project is based upon Li's newly conducted interviews with the original founders of 3F.

11. Peng, then a professor of political science at National Taiwan University, was arrested for drafting "A Declaration of Formosan Self-salvation," in 1964. This advocated the ideal of "One China, One Taiwan" as the final resolution to the so-called China question. For Peng's biography, refer to Peng (1972) and Sung (1996).

12. For the detailed description of the evolution of publications by overseas TIM, refer to Shu (1996b).

13. All names used in this paper are pseudonyms. The quotations from "Life History #XX," which appear throughout this paper, refer to the transcription of the interviews conducted for this study.

14. There can be some confusion here. While my previous term the "1930s and 1940s generations" refers to people born in the 1930s and 1940s, the current term "1960s historical generation" means people, most of whom were youth, actively participating in the various movements of the 1960s. Accordingly, these two terms probably indicate the same group of people.

15. The discussion in this paragraph is based on the data from my case studies only, since neither blacklist record includes information about the exact year when the respondent joined the TIM.

16. The fourth and fifth pools are Chiayi (7.1 percent, 10.5 percent, and 9.5 percent, respectively) and Ilan (14.3 percent, 6.6 percent, and 9.5 percent, respectively). The phenomena also deserve further attention because the opposition force in both Chiayi and Ilan is relatively strong, when compared with that in some other counties in Taiwan.

17. The "Chia (Chiayi)-Nan (Tainan) Plain," located in southern Taiwan, is the major and largest plain in Taiwan. Tainan County is part of the Chia-Nan Plain.

## Bibliography

Braungart, Richard G. 1993. "Historical Generations and Generation Units: A Global Pattern of Youth Movements." In *Life Course and Generational Politics*. Ed. Richard G. Braungart and Margaret M. Braungart. Lanham, MD: University Press of America, 113–135.

Braungart, Richard G., and Margaret M. Braungart. "From Protest to Terrorism: The Case of SDS and the Weathermen." *International Social Movement Research* 4: 45–78.

Chang, George T. "What is WUFI?" In *Taiwangate: Blacklist Policy and Human Rights*. Ed. Winston T. Dang. Washington, DC: Center for Taiwan International Relations, 318–319.

Chen Fang-ming. 1994. "*Zhimindi geming yu Taiwan minzu lun—Taiwan gongchandang de 1928 nian gangling yu 1931 nian gangling*" (Colonial revolution and the thesis of the Taiwanese nation—The 1928 programme and the 1931 programme of the Taiwanese Communist Party). *Jiaoshou luntan quankan* (Professor forum journal)) (Taipei) 2: 287–320.

Chen Ming-cheng. 1992. *Haiwai Taidu yundong sishi nian* (Forty years of overseas Taiwan Independence Movement). Taipei: Zili.

Er-er-ba minjian yanjiu xiaozu et al. (Civil Research Group of 228 et al.) 1992. *Er-er-ba xueshu taolunhui lunwenhui lunwenji* (Symposium of 228 academic conference). Taipei: Zili.

Clark, Robert P. 1986. "Patterns in the Lives of ETA Members." In *Political Violence and Terror: Motifs and Motivations*. Ed. Peter H. Herkl. Berkeley: University of California Press, 283–309.

Copper, John F. 2000. *Historical Dictionary of Taiwan*. 2d ed. Metuchen, NJ: Scarecrow.

Crenshaw, Martha. "The Psychology of Political Terrorism." In *Political Psychology*. Ed. M. G. Hermann. San Francisco: Jossey-Bass, 379–413.

Dang, Winston T., ed. 1991. *Taiwangate: Blacklist Policy and Human Rights*. Washington, DC: Center for Taiwan International Relations.

Della Porta, Donatella. 1988. "Recruitment Processes in Clandestine Political Organizations: Italian Left-wing Terrorism." *International Social Movement Research* 1: 155–169.

Geoffroy, Claude. 1997. *Taiwan duli yundong: qiyuan qi 1945 nian yihou de fazhan* (Taiwan Independence Movement: Origin and the Development after 1945) (). Trans. Huang Fa-tien. Taipei: Qianwei, (original in French).

Hoffer, Eric. 1951. *The True Believer: Thoughts on the Nature of Mass Movement*, New York: Harper.

Huang, Jiashu. *Taiwan neng duli ma? Toushi Taidu* (Can Taiwan be independent? Analyzing Taiwan Independence). Haikou (Hainan, China): Hainan.

Keniston, Kenneth. *Young Radicals: Notes on Committed Youth*. New York: Harcourt, Brace and World.

King, Alice M. 1974. "A Short History of Formosan Independence Movement," *The Independent Taiwan* (Kearny, NJ) 34 (December 28): 16–22.

Kornhauser, Arthur. *The Politics of Mass Society*. Glencoe, IL: Free Press.

Lai Tse-han et al. 1994. *Er-er-ba shijian yanjiu baokao* (Research report on the 228 incident). Taipei: Shibao wenhua.

Lai Tse-han, Ramon H. Myers, and Wou Wei. 1991. *A Tragic Beginning: The Taiwan Uprising of February 28, 1947*. Stanford, CA: Stanford University Press.

Li Cheng-san. 1998. "The Profile of New York 228 Memorial Lecture—Happy Reunion of 'The Philadelphia Three' (Section 3)," *Taiwan gonglun bao* (Taiwan tribune*)*, no. 1635 (March 25) (in Chinese).

Li Feng-chun et al. 1985. *Fengqi yunyong–bei Meizhou Taiwan duli yundong zhi fazhan* (The Raging Wind and Stormy Cloud—The Development of the Taiwan Independence Movement in North America). Kearny, NJ: World United Formosans for Independence (*Taiwan duli jianguo lianmeng*) (in Chinese).

Livingstone, Neil C. 1982. *The War against Terrorism*. Lexington, MA: Lexington Books.

Mendel, Douglas. 1970. *The Politics of Formosan Nationalism*. Berkeley: University of California Press.

Ministry of Education, Republic of China. 1996. *Education Statistics of the Republic of China*. Taipei, Taiwan: Ministry of Education, Republic of China.

Shuo Nan-fang. 1980. *Diguo zhuyi yu Taiwan duli yundong* (Imperialism and the Taiwan Independence Movement). Taipei: Siji.

Neidhardt, Friedhelm. 1992. "Left-wing and Right-wing Terrorist Groups: A Comparison for the German Case." *International Social Movement Research* 4: 215–235.

Ong Joktik. 1964. "A Formosan's View of the Formosan Independence Movement." In *Formosa Today*. Ed. Mark Mancall. New York: Frederick A. Praeger, 163–170.

Peng Ming-min. 1972. *A Taste of Freedom: Memories of a Formosan Independence Leader*. New York: Holt, Rinehart and Winston.

Shu Wei-der. 1996a. "Zhanhou haiwai 'Taiwan zuopai' yundong de yishi xingtai fenxi—yi 'Taiwan minzu zhuyi lunchang' (1979–1982) weili shuoming" (Analyzing the ideologies of the postwar overseas "Taiwan Left" movement—A case study of the "debate on Taiwanese nationalism" [1979–1982]). Paper presented at

the First Annual Meeting of Taiwanese History and Culture Conference, August 9–12, University of Texas–Austin.
——. 1996b. "Haiwai Taiwan duli yundong de yanjiu—yi ke shehui yundong quxiang de fenxi" (A study of the Overseas Taiwan Independence movement, 1947–1992—A perspective from social movements). Unpublished research proposal.
——. 1998. "The Emergence of Taiwanese Nationalism—A Preliminary Work on an Approach to Interactive Episodic Discourse," *Berkeley Journal of Sociology* 42.
Sung Chung-yang. 1996. *Taiwan duli yundong siji san shi wu nian zhi meng* (The backstage story of the Taiwan Independence Movement—A dream of thirty-five years). Taipei: Zili.
Waldmann, Peter. 1986. "Guerrilla Movements in Argentina, Guatemala, Nicaragua, and Uruguay." Trans. Michael R. Deverell and Richard Fleischauer. In *Political Violence and Terror: Motifs and Motivations.* Ed. Peter H. Herkl. Berkeley: University of California Press, 257–281.
——. 1992. "Ethnic and Sociorevolutionary Terrorism: A Comparison of Structures," *International Social Movement Research* 4: 237–257.
Wang Kwei-chüan. 1991. *[Te] heimingdan xianchang baogao,* ([Special] The live report on the blacklist). Taipei: Zili.
Wang Mei-ling T. 1999. *The Dust that Never Settles: The Taiwan Independence Campaign and U.S.-China Relations.* Lanham, MD: University Press of America.
Wasmund, Klaus. 1986. "The Political Socialization of West German Terrorists." In *Political Violence and Terror: Motifs and Motivations.* Ed. Peter H. Merkl. Berkeley: University of California Press, 191–228.
Zurcher, Louis A. and David A. Snow. 1981. "Collective Behavior: Social Movements." In *Social Psychology: Sociological Perspectives.* Ed. M. Rosenberg and R. Turner. New York: Basic, 447–482.

# Part II

The Transition of National Identity

# 4

# The Symbolic Dimension of Democratization and the Transition of National Identity Under Lee Teng-hui

*Stéphane Corcuff*

The proindependence militants, whose backgrounds were analyzed in chapter 3, would have to react to a new situation in Taiwan after Lee Teng-hui replaced Chiang Ching-kuo in January 1988. The president would start to reform the political system and the symbolic environment, and this new situation was potentially leading the opposition to a conflict of positions: The new leader, of Taiwanese origin, was doing much, but he was still the leader of the Nationalist Party. He became what Rwei-ren Wu calls in chapter 9 "a dexterous political enemy-friend." Would he merely adjust Taiwan's polity to the Kuomintang's (KMT) new needs, or would he push the Nationalist Party toward an entirely new direction, even if it was against the will of prominent members of the party?

Analysts of institutional change have studied the democratization of the regime in Taipei in detail. However, the deep transition Taiwan has experienced since the critical years of 1987–1988 could also be approached by a study of symbolic change. A political regime functions with a wide range of political symbols acting as sources of legitimacy, indications of policy directions, tools of political socialization, or objects of national identification. Among these symbols, we commonly find the myths built around the founding fathers and their doctrine, stories of dynastic origins, the Constitution and the political philosophy it refers to, the founding texts or declarations they refer to, the country's official map, the national anthem, the history textbooks, the national flag, even the banknotes or a national flower. Perhaps more than in any other country, most of these symbols are, in Taiwan, related in one way or another to the debate on national identity, and we know that this debate is particularly acute on the island.

In this realm, changes have been tremendously important in Taiwan between the lifting of martial law (1987) and the KMT's defeat at the 2000 presidential election. This fourth chapter in our enquiry into the island's national identity question will try to present some important changes in national identity–related symbols under the former president Lee Teng-hui, who held office from 1988 to 2000. Intentionally, I chose very different types of symbols, hoping to show with four examples, among many other possible ones, that the transition to national identity was already proceeding at a fast pace under Lee's presidency. Changes have been far-reaching, and were not achieved easily. In 1988, Lee Teng-hui inherited a political, administrative, and military apparatus that was still tightly controlled by Taiwan's Mainlanders (see chapters 4 and 8), and which was operating within the framework of a legal system and a set of political symbols established during the authoritarian era of the KMT regime. During that period, everything was done to ban any discourse tending to promote the idea of a separate Taiwanese nation.

A decade after Lee Teng-hui came to power, an important ruling by Taiwan's Council of Grand Justices surprisingly went unnoticed, in a way showing how far in everyone's mind the transition in national identity had gone already. In February 1999, the council ruled that it was no longer necessary to include the words "Republic of China" in the name of island-wide organizations registering at the Ministry of Interior, even though it remained the name of the regime and was still enshrined in the Constitution. To understand the meaning of such a decision, we must remember that using the words "Republic of China" had been a legal obligation for decades in Taiwan, thus preventing new organizations, even though they were operating in the island only, to use the word "Taiwan" in their official name. The Grand Justices' ruling was taken after Taiwan, in the 1980s and 1990s, experienced dramatic changes in term of national policies, national symbols, the discourse concerning China, the unification policy, independence, and separatist definitions of the insular identity. Such changes have deeply affected people's perception of national identity issues, the focus of the second part of this book.

The present chapter is intended to provide a glance at the actual extent of this transition and to introduce the reader to some mechanisms that made this transition possible and viable. The main focus of this chapter is the nexus of relationships between the inside of the KMT's party-state system and the progressive opposition forces, during the last years before the 2000 election, and to try to assess the dynamic created by it by measuring the evolution of the national identity–related symbols it facilitated. It will try to briefly analyze the role that some key stakeholders inside this party-state apparatus played in reforms; the pressure exerted on them from outside; and finally the loosening of this traditionally highly integrated ensemble after a decade of reforms. Innumerable examples can illustrate this great transition, and it would be impossible to make an extensive list of them. I have chosen, for their particular relevance to this study, to focus on four political social-ization tools of very different type: political doctrine, official commemora-tions, history textbooks, and banknotes.

We will see first how the official ideology of the Nationalist regime, the doctrine called The Three Principles of the People, has been progressively pushed into the background. Second, we will learn about the change in Chiang Kai-shek's image in Lee Teng-hui's Taiwan, showing to what extent refer-ences to the former strongman have disappeared from official discourse. Third, we will see that the reform of high school textbooks was designed to make room for lessons on Taiwanese history after decades of deliberate oblitera-tion. Last, we will see that the reform of banknotes resulted in a compro-mise-style mix of different national identity symbols, some inherited from the Nationalist past, some insisting on Taiwan's specificity, showing both the impetus for change and the numerous barriers that still hampered the free expression of a separate national identity in Taiwan under Lee Teng-hui.

**The Demise of a State Doctrine**

Important elements of the thought of Sun Yat-sen, founder of the Republic of China (ROC), on what he envisioned for the new republican China, were presented in a series of speeches delivered in Guangzhou in 1924 and later published as the *Three Principles of the People* (which are: Nationalism, Democracy, and People's Welfare). For decades, the Nationalists on Taiwan constantly referred to this corpus of ideas, using it as a counter-ideology of political identity, and as a counter-model of economic and social development, in its ideological, political, and territorial fight against the competing Chi-nese Communist regime established in Beijing in October 1949. However, when the Nationalists lost power in 2000, *tridemism*, as we shall call the Principles,[1] had nearly totally vanished from Taiwan's symbolic scene. What could explain such a change? Which mechanisms made it possible?

Taiwan has now achieved political freedom and a high degree of popula-tion welfare, and the gradual extinction of references to the tridemism was at least partially permitted by the implementation of these two important goals of Sun Yat-sen's thought. However, a few other reasons probably played a larger role. Tridemism had been systematically used as a tool of ideological

Figure 4.1  **The Bronze Map in the National Assembly Secretariat, Taipei**
*(Photograph by Stéphane Corcuff, 1999)*

mobilization. Questions on tridemism were part of every civil service ex-amination[2] and of school curricula at several levels.[3] It was constantly bran-dished in political discourses, and implementing it was presented as the *raison d'être* of the Nationalist regime. In the 1980s, a large bronze map of China was inaugurated in the National Assembly's secretariat in downtown Taipei. It represented Taiwan with a huge lighthouse on it, lighting China with tridemism (see Figure 4.1). Clearly, for decades, Taiwan was ideologically presented as "The model province of tridemism" *(Sanmin zhuyi de mofan sheng).* .

Several factors have stimulated reforms since 1987. The liberalization of the regime was making it urgent to reduce the place of ideology in examina-tions and school curricula, an idea expressed as early as 1990 in the Exami-nation Yuan, the administrative body in charge of organizing civil service examinations.[4] The tridemism was Sun Yat-sen's answer to the problems China faced in the 1920s; thus, it is not surprising that students and teachers found it increasingly irrelevant to the Taiwan of the 1990s. The archaic meth-ods of teaching the tridemism in schools (such as examinations with mul-tiple-choice questions on a corpus of *thought*) also made it uninteresting for both students and teachers. Everyone who has lived in Taiwan until the recent reforms could remember how much Taiwanese students considered it a truly unbearable burden to learn the details of Sun Yat-sen's doctrine. Many professors earned a living by teaching the tridemism while silently wondering how long they would have to do that. However interesting the tridemism can be for the history of China's modern political development, the course had become dated in Taiwan in a fast-changing political, social, and intellectual environment; its place in the curriculum was too prominent, as it had become merely a reminder of an era now rapidly disappearing.

At the beginning of its eighth session (1990–1996), the Examination Yuan decided to include the suppression of obsolete examination topics from every civil service examination in the session's platform. On September 8, 1994, the Yuan suppressed tridemism from its "superior examination" and its "ordinary examination."[5] Though the Yuan considers them its two most important exams, there was no apparent reaction from the then-ruling Nationalist Party. The daily press had published the information two days before the announcement by the Yuan, and the KMT could not have been unaware of the imminent reform. Then, in December, the Yuan moved further, announcing its intention to abolish the tests on tridemism from *every* state examination. The Presidential Office called Chiu Chuang-huan, then the Yuan's head, to talk about the decision. According to an inner source in the Yuan, Lee Teng-hui did not seek to reverse the decision but only wished to have it delayed. He was indeed about to make a speech on the role of tridemism in Taiwan's development, the source said; it would have been embarrassing if such a move had been announced just days before. Notwithstanding the presidential request, the Yuan decided on December 29, 1994, to adopt the reform. An open debate followed in Taiwan's press about the relevance of Sun Yat-sen's thought to today's Taiwan and about the attachment of the now Taiwanized Nationalist Party to its doctrine.

That was an important step in what could be called the process of "de-Kuomintangizing" Taiwan. Tridemism is the Nationalist Party's official ideology, and the confusion between the ROC state and the Nationalist Party that presided over Taiwan's postwar development enabled the KMT to make it the national ideology. The head of the Examination Yuan was an old KMT member, present at the party's weekly central standing committee meeting (held on Wednesday mornings), and thus closely associated with central policy making in Taiwan. The move illustrated the progress made in the separation of state and party and the breaches in the state-party ensemble in Taiwan. It was also the result of global changes that may have finally surpassed the KMT's own expected and desired reforms. But it could also be interpreted as the result of connivance between reformist elements in the party to accelerate the party's changes. Undoubtedly, most of the members who voted for the reform in the Examination Yuan were KMT members. Still, though an important reform, this was not a revolution. Contrary to what the spokesmen of the Examination Yuan declared to the press, the December 1994 decision was not taken unanimously and followed heated debates. And tests on tridemism were replaced with questions on the ROC constitution, with explicit reference to Sun Yat-sen's doctrine. A Yuan member told me then in an interview that the aim was to "reorganize the content of the test and suppress obsolete parts, to save what was essential and avoid suppressing the whole doctrine."[6]

Another important point is the example the Yuan's decision gave of the psychological impact a particular reform can have on the general transition process. It is mentioned above that the reform was widely discussed in the press. What had been decided inside the state-party ensemble was immediately echoed outside. A few days later, on January 10, 1995, the Taipei Association of Film Industry (Taibei dianying xiehui) decided to suspend the tradition of playing the national anthem before each film showing in Taipei theaters. The mechanism by which this tradition was suddenly abolished is highly interesting: The event revealed that there had been no law, during the previous forty years, that specifically required theaters to play the anthem. It was purely a tradition that had developed under the martial law era, when social control helped collective self-discipline make legislative intervention unnecessary to implement certain political socialization policies. Later, this collective self-discipline was progressively transformed into a wait-and-see attitude, like the attitude of the teachers wondering when they would stop teaching Sun Yat-sen's outdated 1920s programs for China's railroad development. Once a signal had come from a powerful, official institution or stakeholder—here the Examination Yuan—it became easier to change the custom.[7]

At the same time, this reform was an official acknowledgment of what could be called a progressive "ritualization" of references to Sun Yat-sen's doctrine in the post–martial law era. The society had since long lost its interest in Sun. Sun is linked to the Continental era of the ROC, and for the island's youngest generation, this sounds a bit like prehistory. After the deep changes that affected Taiwan, the symbolic environment in which young people grow up today has nothing to do with what the elders have known. It was interesting to hear, in 1995, even the chair of the Institute of Tridemism of a Taipei university qualifying Sun as the "only original thinker of the nineteenth [sic] century." And even inside the ruling KMT, one cannot but feel the ritualization of the references to Sun. Each month, at the "Commemorative Meeting of the Director-General,"[8] topics presented by keynote speakers have nothing to do with a commemoration of Sun Yat-sen; only the name is kept.

Another important conclusion is that the 1994–1995 reform preceded a change in the mode of political legitimization in Taiwan. In 1995, it was still not possible for Lee Teng-hui to support such a move openly. It was one year before the March 23, 1996, presidential election, which radically transformed the political legitimacy of the head of the Republic. In his previously mentioned speech on tridemism, which was made in February 7, 1995, Lee Teng-hui did not appear very convincing about what he was saying concerning the relevance of tridemism:

> If our efforts to democratize Taiwan and transfer power into the hand of the people are not the Principle of Democracy, what are they? If promoting the universal health protection system and the establishment of an Asia-Pacific Regional Operation Center [APROC] in Taiwan are not the principle of people's livelihood, what are they? And if our efforts in favor of ethnic harmony and the return of Taiwan to the international society are not the Principle of Nationalism, what are they?

The link between the APROC and Sun's principle of people's livelihood is quite tenuous, not to mention the irony of declaring an application of Sun's (pan-Chinese) nationalism his efforts to bring Taiwan back on the world stage. It seems rather that before the ultimate implementation of the new political legitimization system, Lee Teng-hui was still obliged to refer, as had been done for decades, to tridemism to legitimize the power of the party and his power in the party. At that time, the so-called nonmainstream faction of the KMT had already clashed openly with Lee Teng-hui.

This first example has underlined some interesting mechanisms of the symbolic transition. First, the reform was decided inside the state-party system by members of the KMT and nominated by the KMT, but without the explicit consent of the KMT, and most likely against the party's will (the question of knowing Lee Teng-hui's personal position is certainly a distinct one). Second, outside the state-party ensemble, society was eager to see things change, and once a signal had been launched from above, a spillover effect immediately occurred. Interestingly, as we have noticed, the KMT itself was also experimenting with a process of ritualization of the references to Sun's doctrine. Last, the reform accompanied a deep refoundation of political legitimacy in Taiwan, in place by the March 23, 1996, election. This profound change was the sunset of Sun's thought. After this direct popular election, the tridemism was no longer necessary to legitimize a head of state that had, until then, suffered from an uncertain political legitimacy with regards to democratic canons. By the end of the 1987–1997 decade, references to the founder of the Republic of China and his doctrine had totally vanished from Taiwan's political speeches.

## Farewell to a Strongman: Ritualization and Disappearance of the Cult of Chiang Kai-shek

One of the consequences of the liberalization and the reinforced legitimacy of the political institutions was the diminishing appeal of the old helmsmen. Another observation point that can give us a good view of the transition in political symbols unfolding in Taiwan in the 1990s is the image of Free China's central icon and former Taiwan strongman, Chiang Kai-shek. In this area too, changes have been radical. Through this example, I will try to show how a few opposition politicians accelerated the demise of Chiang's cult and how the Nationalist Party, which Chiang Kai-shek served and ruled for sixty-three years, has dealt, under Lee Teng-hui, with such a complex and delicate heritage.

The KMT began to build the cult of Chiang Kai-shek in Taiwan almost as soon as the Japanese left the island. It started in Taipei with the elevation of the first statue of Chiang on May 5, 1946. This was only 192 days after the retrocession to (Republican) China on October 25, 1945. A street was first renamed after Chiang in November 1945. Then, little by little, the cult was built through raising many other statues, naming of roads or buildings, songs, portraits, a day off on Chiang's birthday, praise of his military abilities in the army's textbooks, and so on. In the past, commemorations of Chiang's birthday could be lively events observed either by conviction or by constraint.[9]

After Chiang's death on April 5, 1975, however, things started to change, but rather slowly. Chiang Ching-kuo, Chiang's alleged son,[10] authorized the Bank of Taiwan to print Chiang Kai-shek's image on banknotes (starting in 1976) and had an immense memorial built in Taipei in his memory (finished in 1981). But he also stopped the practice of the cult of personality for himself; time and men did the rest for his adoptive father's image.[11] A few months after taking over the presidency in 1988, following the death of Chiang Ching-kuo, Lee Teng-hui presided over his first Double-Ten (National Day) celebrations as head of state. For the festivities, he reinstituted something that had disappeared seven years before, the military parades.[12] In his speech, he talked about the military achievements of his illustrious predecessor. But the following year, all references to Chiang except the portraits had disappeared for good. As far as I know, portraits of Chiang were brandished in the parades for the last time in 1990. In 1992, the presidential office stopped a tradition, dating back to 1958, of opening the building to the population on each October 31, to let people show their respect and bow in front of the bronze of Chiang Kai-shek. And for the first time, during the 1996 Double-Ten celebrations, the portrait of the former president was not hung on the west side of the Ching-fu Gate, in front of the presidential building. It was replaced by the portrait of Lee Teng-hui, the new president, for whom each commemoration of Chiang Kai-shek's death was obviously a burden, if we can judge from the grim face he showed during this political ritual when going to Chiang's mausoleum in Tz'u-hu and bowing before his coffin, in the last years of his mandate.[13]

Of all the activities linked to the cult of Chiang Kai-shek, few had survived ten years of dramatic symbolic changes. Among the survivors were some bronze statues, the traditional visit by high-level KMT government officials to the memorial and the mausoleum, and the characters written on the cities' sky-walks and official buildings: "commemoration of the birthday of President Chiang" on October 31. But people had long stopped noticing these colorful characters. With the passing of time, every Chiang-related commemoration had become ritualized and had turned into a set of conventional, lifeless, compulsory activities. Needless to say, even fewer commemorations have survived since Chen Shui-bian was elected president.

The former opposition Democratic Progressive Party has indeed helped hasten the end of a cult that had ossified and long since lost its vitality. Chen Shui-bian was elected mayor of Taipei in December 1994. One of his first actions was to decide, on February 15, 1995, that every portrait of Chiang Kai-shek and Chiang Ching-kuo should be taken down from the walls of all offices and schools under the jurisdiction of the city government. The KMT tried to oppose the decision by publishing an "Open letter to Mayor Chen" in the party's *Central Daily News*. But instead of talking of "the KMT," we should ask: "Which stakeholder inside the KMT?" Due to the fact that Taipei is a city administrated directly under central government supervision, the Nationalist Party might have had the leverage to force Chen Shui-bian to abandon this decision. The Ministry of Interior lobbied the premier's office to this end. Chen Shui-bian nevertheless implemented his decision, and the affair was not commented on afterward. A year later, in June 1996, Chen Shui-bian decided to change the name of Taipei's Chieshou Road (Jieshou lu) (literally: Road [wishing] long life to Chiang Kai-shek). This time, the decision drew no protest except for a discreet complaint from the Ministry of Foreign Affairs, which was located at number 2 Chieshou Road. Interestingly, the idea was initially proposed to Chen Shui-bian by two KMT city councillors.[14] Then, in the summer of 1996, Chen Shui-bian opened to the public the park of the famous Shilin Mansion, the former residence of Chiang Kai-shek and his wife, Soong Mei-ling. Until then the whole estate had remained under the control of the army. But this time, Chen's plan was too bold. His attempt to open the house to the general public as a museum was opposed a number of times by the military: Intending to create a museum about Chiang Kai-shek, he would have been able to turn the page. He

Figure 4.2  **Statues of Chiang Kai-shek are disappearing one after another, but still remain in many military schools. Here, a school in Ta-Chih, Taipei.** *(Photograph by Stéphane Corcuff, 1997)*

failed to create it, but the page has been turned anyway, and in the DPP camp other militants helped accelerate Chiang's definitive fall into history, among them the now-vice president Lu Hsiu-lien,[15] a sharp-tongued political activist, Chen Wan-chen,[16] and Kaohsiung county commissioner Yu Cheng-hsien, whose policy of removing statues of Chiang Kai-shek drew the media's attention.[17]

Though many statues islandwide are still in place, the changes have been evident everywhere. In this movement, the ruling KMT has not only been unable to stop the trend, but it is even likely that at the local level, native Taiwanese KMT officials themselves have pushed for change. In the end, the strategy of the KMT has been to protect the core, while accepting the disappearance of the cult. For the KMT, what has to be protected is respect for Chiang (especially his remains), the memory of his past actions, and secrecy about in his role certain events. For instance, when Chiang's archives at the Institute of National History (Guo shi guan) were partially opened in 1996 (Chiang's personal documents during his Continental era), documents concerning the 1947 events were reported to have been transferred elsewhere. Nevertheless, the Kuomintang was forced to accept the progressive abandonment of an already desiccated cult. When the cabinet invented the system of a "second weekly day off every two weeks" (*gezhou zhouxiu er ri*) on February 28, 1997, to alleviate the burden on productivity induced by too many holidays, one of the first holidays to be "transferred" to the following Saturday was the October 31 commemoration of Chiang's birthday. When the move was proposed in a cabinet meeting, no KMT minister protested except Chang Hsiao-yen (then minister of foreign affairs), Chiang Ching-kuo's son.

This second example has shown other mechanisms of the symbolic transition that accompanied and permitted at the same time the institutional transition. Both abrupt decisions and a slow tendency toward ritualization have led to the final disappearance of the cult of a former strongman, a natural trend in a democratic regime. This movement has, of course, irritated old KMT stalwarts. The conservative faction of the KMT, which hated Lee Teng-hui even more than they hated the opposition DPP, were left voiceless between 1996 (the date of their resounding defeat at the 1996 presidential election) and 2000 (when Lee Teng-hui was forced out of the KMT presidency). However, even with this "nonmainstream faction" (*fei zhuliu pai*) muzzled, Lee Teng-hui could not abandon until January 1999 the ritual visits to both of Chiang's mausoleums. He needed to maintain a minimal cohesion of a divided party in order to keep the KMT oriented toward reform and Taiwanization—this is precisely what has been endangered with his forced resignation from the KMT leadership in 2000. We see here a combination of personal decisions and a historic trend. We saw that the KMT accepted the change rather than initiated it, which is a difference from the first example I analyzed. What we have noted here is the role played by the pressure exerted from outside the KMT state-party apparatus. This pressure had an echo inside, and in this respect, the fact that KMT members asked Chen Shui-bian to take down Chiang's portrait is a clear indication of the relations between "the inside" and "the outside," in what was less and less a monolithic apparatus.

## Promoting Taiwan-Centered School Textbooks

Chiang Kai-shek certainly would have been the last wishing to see Taiwanese history in Taiwanese textbooks. Under his rule, the history programs were those used during the pre-1949 Mainland era of the Republic of China, that had been transferred to Taiwan with the relocation of the Nationalist government. Between 1948 and 1975, changes to the history curriculum had been minor. After the generalissimo's death in April 1975, no more changes had been made in the Ministry of Education's history curriculum guidelines.

Nineteenth-century French historian Jules Michelet explained that the first part of politics was education and that education had to help the population develop a democratic feeling and avoid being manipulated by antirepublican forces. Intellectuals have also long criticized school textbooks in Taiwan, especially proindependence scholars, for being a political socialization tool helping to propagate the grand-Han ideology. As Roberta Martin wrote, "Textbooks . . . are one medium extremely susceptible to centralized political control and to the uniformity of message, particularly when they are published by government printing houses and circulated through many if not all of the nation's schools, as they are in both Taiwan and China" (Martin, 1975, 243). Article 158 of the 1947 Chinese republican constitution, still in effect in Taiwan, even states clearly that education has a political goal: "Education culture must develop the nationalist spirit of the citizens."[18] One logical consequence of this was a state monopoly of textbook edition and printing, decided during a 1968 reform, and implemented by a National Institute of Editions and Translations (Guoli bianyi guan) (NIET). For decades the NIET had served the ruling KMT in its aim of imprinting in Taiwanese hearts the nationalist view of what it meant to be Chinese, until the institution began to change at the end of the 1990s. Taiwan's textbooks and the NIET itself had logically become a target of opposition militants. For instance, still unaware of the reform being prepared under the supervision of the Ministry of Education (MOE), or to put pressure on it, some National Taiwan University students gathered in April 1996 at the front gate of Taipei's 2.28 Peace Park to stage a two-week protest against the NIET and the MOE. While organizing a textbook *auto-da-fé,* they distributed tracts calling on the minister and his personnel "not to be History's criminals." One year later, while the announcement of the *Knowing Taiwan* textbook reform was triggering huge protests from the conservative camp, a proindependence member of the Legislative Yuan (Chen Chi-mai, DPP, Kaohsiung), declared that "For more than forty years of martial law in our country . . . national education has constantly fallen into the state of a brainwashing tool serving institutions governing us." His opinion can be considered as quite representative of what most opposition politicians and intellectuals thought about Taiwan's educational system.[19] Furthermore, the obsolescence of some parts of the programs was obvious after ten years of domestic and international changes such as the termination of the cold war, the end of the Soviet Union, and the lifting of the martial law in Taiwan. As one can imagine, everyone now is much more concerned with Taiwan's daily reality than with the regime's continental era or the exhaustive (and exhausting) list of China's emperors. Reforming history textbooks had become a matter of the credibility of the whole educational system.[20] All the arguments in favor of a reform—the political use of education, the state's monopoly in printing textbooks, the obsolescence of history programs—had been regularly asserted by Taiwanese professors through opinion columns in newspapers. Discussions in research institutions and academic circles had led to a kind of consensus among progressive intellectuals, which was to bear fruit discreetly once they were given power to reform the programs.

The reform announced in June 1997, discreetly prepared for years, was a new junior high school curriculum, called *Knowing Taiwan* (Renshi Taiwan). The boldness of the reform provoked a panic reaction in the conservative camp, leading to one of the hottest ideological tempests of the decade—and, in many respects, one of the most important steps in Taiwan's recent transition. Yet few people actually spoke against the reform, which took place amid the general indifference of the population. This second example will help us to see the forces behind the evolution, as we detail when the reform started, who initiated it, what was at stake, who fought against it, and, ultimately, what was the attitude of the ruling KMT. I hope here that the reader will pardon me for being a bit longer on this third example, for the 1997 textbook reform is clearly a milestone in Taiwan's evolution. This next example will again show the importance of completing institutional change analysis by a study of symbolism and symbolic change to understand better Taiwan's democratization process.

Outside the state-party ensemble, the necessity of a reform was advocated by both the antiunification Democratic Progressive Party and the prounification New Party, though in different terms and with different aims. Inside, four institutions seem to have been pushing for reforms. President Lee Teng-hui, who gave the official green light and pressured the minister of education, played a key role.[21] At the Executive Yuan, Premier Lien Chan launched the educational reform plan in 1994. At the Ministry of Education, Minister Kuo Wei-fan launched the reform of the programs by asking scholars of different political sensibilities to get together and work on the content, defending the audacious reform policy in an inner meeting of the ruling party. The fourth key institution was the National Institute of Editions and Translations itself, which seemed to have matured in recent years and to have been aware of the necessary changes. Its role became more important as the new program was taking shape, and it staunchly defended it against the attacks launched by the prounification New Party when the reform was announced in June 1997. The initial stimulus originated outside the state-party nexus, with early parliamentary pressure soon after the lifting of the martial law. Proindependence members of Parliament repeatedly asked for early revision of textbooks. As early as 1989, the MOE reacted timidly and instituted a reform committee.[22] After renewed pressure from the Legislative Yuan, the committee was replaced on September 21, 1994, by a bigger Commission of Deliberation on the Educational Reform, which was granted a more substantial budget by Lien Chan. Shortly afterward, in October, the new *High Schools Curricula Reference* was promulgated (Ministry of Education 1995). It contained the basic guidelines that were to be developed into the program *Knowing Taiwan*. Obviously the conservative New Party was unaware of its existence at the time of the June 1997 event, even though the document had been published two years before.[23]

Historians had time to work quietly on their new program, with a degree of freedom from political interference unknown until then. At the immediate border of the state-party ensemble was situated a government-appointed commission composed of scholars under the supervision of Taiwan's most respected intellectual authority, the head of Academia Sinica, Lee Yuan-tse. The Commission of Deliberation on the Educational Reform soon established a subcommission for editing new textbooks in charge of writing the three textbooks (*History, Geography, Society*) of the new program. *Knowing Taiwan's* first revolution was there: The composition of this new body showed a clear decision to give back to educators the duty of deciding educational content.[24] Meetings started in June 1995 and ended in February 1997. The writing of the *History* textbook was directed by Huang Hsiu-cheng, professor of history at Taiwan's Chung-hsing University. The one on society questions was directed by Tu Cheng-sheng, then director of Academia Sinica's research center on history and languages.[25] Four fundamental ideas have emerged from their work.

The team intended first to sweep ideology away from schoolbooks. In particular, with regard to what is often called the Greater China ideology, the Greater Han ideology, or the Greater Han chauvinism, a radical change of perspective was decided. The second idea was to evaluate with greater objectivity Taiwan's Japanese colonial period (1895–1945), traditionally darkened by the Nationalist vulgate as Mainlanders had experienced the trauma of the war against Japan. Considering the extreme sensitivity of conservative politicians and scholars on this precise point, it became the hottest topic during the June 1997 storm. Another important idea was to state, for the first time, what had been a political taboo in Nationalist education for decades: the plurality of Taiwan's historical experiences. The first and most urgent step was to give back to the island's Aboriginal population groups their due status in historiography, after hundreds of years of contempt by Han Chinese settlers and Qing officials.[26] Emphasizing the diversity of historical experiences was a direct attempt to overthrow the classical linear Chinese historiography that viewed Taiwan as a historical place only from the time Han Chinese had begun settling the frontier island. It was also a severe blow to post-1949 politicized history, which sought to silence dissenting historical narratives that could give the impression that the Chinese had not been the only source of cultural influence in Taiwan. The spirit of the reform was clear. As Huang Hsiu-cheng wrote in defense of the collective work:

> I personally consider that the use of the history manual *Knowing Taiwan* will necessarily help the development of our students' international vision. Taiwan's historical development shows complex international relations with Holland, Spain and Japan, countries that all occupied Taiwan, and that gave, to a certain extent, the island's culture the colors of a foreign country [foreign to China, needless to say].[27]

Last, the ministry and the working team seem to have agreed to express, at least indirectly, the idea that national identification in Taiwan is pluralistic. The preparative work developed the new idea of "concentric circles," an expression that can also be read literally as "circles of shared concern." This idea, expressed by the words *tongxin yuan*, designates a three-step plan to expose Taiwanese youth to outside reality by letting them "stand on Taiwan, have consideration for China, open their eyes to the world." Inside the state-party ensemble, an important role might have been played here by Kuo Wei-fan. After launching the reform in 1994, the Taiwan-born minister revealed to the party decision makers this new idea in an April 8, 1996, speech, at an inner meeting of the ruling KMT. After openly criticizing the "Greater China ideology" that prevailed in Nationalist education, he opined that

> If we look at things from the point of view of the textbook structure, a student book must start learning from the immediate environment, then extend the scope step by step to local culture and the main ethnic groups of the society, extending it then to the knowledge of the culture of all ethnic groups that compose the territory and the nation. Only then can one understand the world's culture. Consequently, primary and secondary programs are being reformed following a strategy consisting of standing on Taiwan, having consideration for China, opening eyes on the world.[28]

At the margin of the state-party ensemble, Tu Cheng-sheng, leader of the government-recruited team of professors working on the heatedly debated *Society* manual, defended this collective work with a similar theory, only employing stronger words:

This new thinking is the hope that our children can stand on Taiwan, have consideration for China, open their eyes to the world; consequently, we must first emphasize Taiwan, the land on which all of us depend to survive, and assert that this has a meaning indeed. Taiwan was not developed only by Han Chinese clearings [of Taiwanese forests], and history started with Aborigines. Giving this back to them is not to put them on a pedestal, it is merely being more fair toward Han Chinese themselves.[29]

*Knowing Taiwan* was the first step of a new three-year high school program: The second year would have courses on China, and the third, courses on the rest of the world. By conviction or precaution, the Commission of Deliberation on the Educational Reform decided not to forget China in the new courses, and instead reduce it to one part only, the scope of which was clearly defined, of the new high school curricula. This is exactly the conclusion of Voltaire's philosophical novel, *Candide, ou l'optimisme: "Ceci est bien dit, répondit Candide. Mais il faut cultiver notre jardin."*[30] Starting first with their immediate location was acknowledged as being the safest way to educate Taiwan's children.

Yet, the interpretation and implementation of this theory differed noticeably between the *History* and the *Society* manuals. The first one can be considered as having a cautious point of view, whereas topics of the manual on society were much bolder. Claiming "We are all Taiwanese," the second manual insisted that Taiwan's "ethnic pluralism" had produced a "Taiwanese consciousness," and that Formosans inherited from past generations a "Taiwanese soul" (an expression coming from the Japanese colonial period and which particularly angered the New Party). There followed a romantic description of the Taiwanese nation and a discourse on the inhabitants' heroic defying of authoritarian rulers from abroad. Indeed, the manual used the well-known rhetoric of tragic history, saying that Taiwanese could be their own masters. The end of the manual, dealing with Taiwan's future, did not mention eventual reunification with China, and said that on the eve of the twenty-first century, the word "Taiwanese" had already become a "nationality name" for all Formosans going abroad. Calling upon Taiwanese to think with "our own point of view," it said, "no spirit nor any hero can decide the destiny of the New Taiwan" in place of the Taiwanese people themselves.

This manual had been prepared with the full knowledge, acceptance, and support of the National Institute of Editions and Translations, and perhaps from Kuo Wei-fan. It had thus every possible reason to provoke an unprecedented crisis among prounification hard-liners. That was *Knowing Taiwan's* second revolution. The *Shankei Shimbun,* a Tokyo newspaper, was quicker than any other paper to say, not without exaggeration, that "vis-à-vis its co-

Figure 4.3  **The Guoli bianyi guan's internal copy of the *Knowing Taiwan* textbooks, which produced the 1997 ideological tempest.** *(Photograph by Stéphane Corcuff, 1997)*

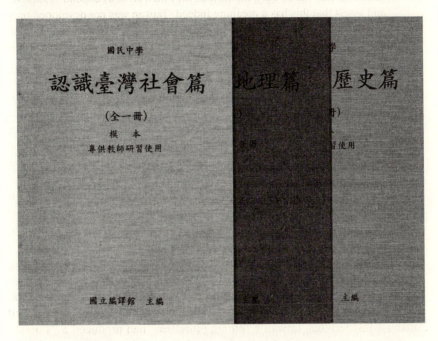

lonial past, Taiwan has switched from total rejection to approval" of the Japanese rule, further convincing conservative politicians in Taipei that a landslide change had occurred.[31] Lee Ching-hua, then a member of the New Party, himself a university-level history professor, took the lead of the counter-reform movement and produced a pamphlet against reform (Lee 1997). Criticisms of the manual were directed mainly at the treatment of the colonial period, the conservatives being upset by what they saw as a pro-Japanese reform. Concerning links with China, opponents viewed the text as a denial that Taiwanese were Chinese. As far as Taiwan's "national character" was concerned, they dismissed the notion with arguments embedded in paradoxes. Lastly, on the topic of Lee Teng-hui, the New Party's bugbear, the conservative camp read the last part of the *Society* manual as an official consecration of Lee Teng-hui's Taiwanese nationalism (see chapter 9). When he visited the new minister of education, Wu Ching, on June 6, 1997, Lee Ching-hua called the reform a *heixiang zuoye,* an equivalent in Chinese for what we call a conspiracy, declaring that the reform was a plot by Lee Teng-hui and the illustrious Japanese author Shiba Ryotaro, with whom Lee Teng-hui once had, in the spring of 1994, a long and controversial interview about the sadness of being Taiwanese.[32] Reacting to that, inside the apparatus, at the heart of a technical institution, the head of the NIET strongly, openly, and courageously defended reform, even after receiving personal threats. Chao Li-yun was no KMT stalwart, and very far from the political decision center of the KMT party-state system.

A few important conclusions may be drawn from this third example of symbolic change. The most important one seems to be that after ten years of reform, prounification hard-liners' ideas were then totally marginalized. During three weeks of huge protests from a surprisingly small number of conservative personalities in June 1997, many professors, known and unknown; thinkers; Legislative Yuan and National Assembly members and even their assistants, wrote numerous opinion columns in the press to defend reform.[33] Numerous elements of Taiwan's intellectual scene sided with elements inside the apparatus to barrage the antireform movement. This was a reform process very particular to the 1996–1999 period of Lee Teng-hui's rule, when the conservative opposition inside the party seemed voiceless, when the prounification opposition was attacking mainly from outside, and when his reformist faction could work with progressive elements outside the KMT and KMT-controlled government. Facing this movement in favor of reform, Lee Ching-hua had no support, except from his party's silent supporters. One scholar, from Taipei's University of World Journalism, contributed an opinion column to support the antireform crusade;[34] and a conservative historical study association wrote a collective book.[35] On June 24, after minor changes that were not, as the press quickly said, concessions to the conservative camp, the Institute officially adopted the new textbooks.

Like the reform of the tridemism doctrine, the reform came from inside the state-party apparatus. This is not to deny that during the whole process the opposition forces played a crucial role, which was obviously determinant at several stages. This is to say that the former integrated ensemble formed by the state and the party had evolved, and the liberalization helped non-KMT members and Taiwanese or Taiwanized reformist KMT members to assert their point of view inside administrative units, and by the end of the decade 1987–1997 gave them much larger scope to operate than they had immediately after the lifting of the martial law. The MOE had been influenced by scholars during numerous meetings held during the process of writing the official *Curricula Reference*. The influence of academics on the reform commission that followed was strong. Several key players within the party-state apparatus had agreed to reform the system. They called scholars from opposition ranks to collaborate and, in a way, temporarily enter the system and cooperate from inside or at the margin to reform it. This resembled the way Chiang Ching-kuo had called on scholars in 1986 to help him draw up the guidelines for political reform.

The reform illustrates the decade-long movement of localization of the polity. The three manuals focus exclusively on the "Tai-Peng-Kin-Ma" area (Taiwan, Penghu, Kinmen, Matsu, the main components of what the Republic of China government actually controls of its former territory). This goal was set in the program guidelines for high school written by the MOE (Ministry of Education, 1995). Its guidelines for writing the *Society* textbook could not be more explicit. The goals to achieve were "One: to increase the knowledge of the societies of Taiwan, Penghu, Kinmen, and Matsu. Two: to develop a vision that corresponds to a pluralistic culture and to nurture love for one's local land that enables an even stronger love for the nation" (Ministry of Education 1995, 133). Authors of the *Society* manual, who have been under heavy attack, did not do much more than follow the MOE recommendations, and indeed a member of the institute in charge of supervising the reform confirmed in private that "everything was already written clearly in the Ministry curricula reference."[36] This reform was not the proindependence manifesto the prounification camp had described. But since independence has been a *de facto* reality since 1949, the reform started to complete with historiography the already existing independence of Taiwan. What this program may change is important: The new generation will learn Taiwan's past and its geography, and more important, *before* starting courses on Chinese history, will first be taught that Taiwan forms a community of destiny.

Last, it may be a generalization and a superficial analysis to speak today of "the role of the KMT" in certain reforms. What we saw in the last years before 2000 was a general evolution toward localization of KMT's policies, but with a key role played by certain persons who had their own convictions and who tried to accelerate or, on the contrary, slow down the party's evolution.

In conclusion, it appears that reforms have been neither always hierarchic nor always linear. It is likely that the authors of the manuals pushed the MOE and the KMT to accept a reform leading to a radical change that was probably well beyond what many KMT members saw as the limits. In this sense, the reform has been antihierarchic. Kuo Wei-fan was replaced one year before the adoption of the reform, in 1996. His successor seemed to be much less enthusiastic about the reform. During the June 1997 tempest over the textbook reform, Wu Ching suggested that the reform committee review the text one more time and eventually make necessary changes. He cautiously added that they should do so only if they considered it necessary,[37] but the second edition of the manuals, published in 1998, contained fewer innovations that the first edition, adopted after the June 1997 tempest.

If the fate of the reforms can evolve with the change of stakeholders, then it means the reforms are not linear either. Clearly, the destiny of reforms were in the hands of persons rather than of the party, at that stage of the democratization process, and their fate was heavily linked to key stakeholders in decision-making bodies. But this is not denying that deep historical trends do exist. Stakeholders only delay or accelerate their materialization in actual events. It is my feeling that the transition of national identity on Taiwan is a historical necessity, not the mere result of political contingencies, and even a good number of Mainlanders now accept this idea. If ever Wu Ching was really opposed to reform, he proved nevertheless that the ROC's education minister was finally unable to prevent history books from turning into a defense of Taiwan's pride and Taiwan's point of view. This third example has given us some new insights about the mechanisms behind the transition of national-identity symbols: the connection between opposition intellectuals and a state-party apparatus in a process of reforming the polity; voices expressed from inside the apparatus, by non-KMT members with technical responsibilities, supporting the evolution, and eventually leading to a reform that contradicts completely the party's historiography; and the role played by key individuals who accompany or resist historical trends.

## Patchworking Symbols of National Identity in the Banknotes

The reform of the banknotes was presented to the public a year and a half later. The March 2, 1999, announcement ended years of discussion: The political implications of reforming Taiwan's banknotes were obvious as Taiwan's metal and paper money traditionally bore portraits of only Chiang Kai-shek and Sun Yat-sen. A change would mean not only potentially making a decision to abandon their pictures, but it would also imply that new figures were to be found, not an easy task in an island torn by different visions of its identity. In this process, reforming the coins proved much easier than reforming the paper money. Two new coins had indeed already been put into circulation in 1992 and 1996 without the portraits of Chiang Kai-shek and Sun Yat-sen. But the reform of banknotes took years.

Prior to the emission of the new paper money, starting in July 2000, Taiwan had banknotes of NT$50, NT$100, NT$500, and NT$1,000. For the old banknotes, Sun Yat-sen's portrait was chosen for the two most widely used by the population: NT$50 and NT$100. Chiang Kai-shek's portrait was chosen for the two others. The new notes feature two more bills (NT$200 and NT$2,000) and every note's two sides have been entirely redrawn. The first political dimension of the 1999 reform is that it was decided to keep portraits of the two leaders. The press in Taipei reported that at first the

Central Bank moved to suppress the portraits, but that pressures from unnamed "civil organizations"—which may have included the KMT—finally persuaded the board of directors of the Central Bank to keep the portraits for the NT$100 and NT$200 bills.[38] This, obviously, prompted antiunification newspapers to interpret the reform as an illusionary change, and newspapers like Kaohsiung's *Commons Daily* and *Taiwan Times* did not even deem it necessary to report the change, whereas more conservative newspapers like the *China Times* and *United Daily News* made it a front-page story. Another reason could have dissatisfied the antiunification camp: Traditional Chinese vegetal ornaments were used as the banknotes' watermarks. The plum flower (NT$100), orchid (NT$200), bamboo (NT$500), chrysanthemum (NT$1,000), and pine (NT$2,000) all have a strong Chinese identity. From these two characteristics, it is clear that it was decided to avoid any rupture with the ROC's official Chinese identity.

Every major newspaper, however, noticed the undeniable localization of the new banknotes. The NT$500 bill features Taiwan's Red Leaf baseball team on one side, reminding people of the pride this sport restored to Taiwanese after the disappointment of successive diplomatic setbacks in the 1970s. On the other side, a group of deer (the Formosan sika or *cervus nippon taiouanus*) stands behind Tapachien Mountain in Kenting National Park. The deer is on the verge of extinction, and it reminds us of the time when Aborigines were the only masters of the island and when the delicate Formosan sikas roamed freely in plains that are now human conurbations. The NT$1,000 bill on one side features a group of primary students, symbolizing education, one of the keys to the successful post-1949 transformation of the natural resources–poor island. It emphasizes the recent history of Taiwan, which had been, as seen earlier, systematically obliterated from history books. On the back is a mikado pheasant, an endangered species in Taiwan, behind Mount Morrison (Yu mountain), the highest peak in Taiwan and in the region. As for the NT$2,000 banknote, it takes technological developments as its main theme, while the other side features the landlocked Formosan salmon, which Taiwan is trying to save from extinction. In the back is the main Nanhu peak. As we can see, features of today's Taiwanese achievements and the environmental concerns they raise, the choice of animals symbolizing Taiwan, the most illustrious Formosan mountains all give a very strong Taiwanese identity to the new banknotes. The strong local flavor of these new banknotes was probably germane to the decision of the *China Times* and the *United Daily News*, sensitive to any change in national identity, to make a front-page story of it.

The second layer of the 1999 reform was the decision to transfer the responsibility for printing the banknotes to the Central Bank. Before, banknotes

Figure 4.4  **The New NT$500 and NT$1,000 Banknotes** *(Photograph by Stéphane Corcuff, 2000)*

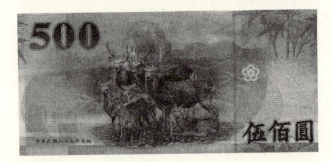

were printed by the Bank of Taiwan, so that the myth could be perpetrated that the New Taiwan Dollar was only the currency of the Taiwan Province of the ROC. Since its adoption, after the ROC central government moved to Taiwan, the New Taiwan Dollar was officially considered by the authorities as the money used in the Taiwan Province of the ROC, or the "free area of the ROC" only. When the banking law was amended in 1979, the new article 14 stipulated that the New Taiwan Dollar was now the national currency, but it was not perceived in that way, due to the political context of that time. With the 1999 reform, the status of the New Taiwan Dollar as the national currency of the *Republic of China on Taiwan* was now official, as the two above-mentioned newspapers immediately pointed out; the symbolic change was considerable.

What this last example shows best is the result of Taiwan's search for national identity after a decade of reform by the ruling KMT under pressure from a strong historical movement toward localization of the polity: a combination of different symbols—old icons and new realities—images that, until recently, would have been thought of as being totally antagonistic. Depending on the point of view adopted, this could be interpreted as an attempt by a sort of catchall party, patchworking together different symbols to get support from everywhere.

## Conclusion

Refusing a total break with the past, but trying to input as much of Taiwan as they could within the limits set by the party's legacy, can represent quite faithfully one aspect of Lee Teng-hui and his followers' attitude toward the change in symbolism during the last years before 2000. Clearly, Lee Teng-hui has done his best, as expressed by his important July 1999 declaration on the "special state-to-state [or country-to-country] relations" (*liangguo lun*). The *liangguo lun* was quickly abandoned by the KMT after Lee Teng-hui's inauspicious fall from the party leadership in 2000. Under his leadership and against elements in his own party, the regime went quite far in a compromise-style of reform to adopt negotiated identity symbols, as the result of an unfinished, ongoing, yet already deeply advanced, national identity maturation in Taiwan, heading toward the birth of a full-fledged Taiwanese nation. But the KMT itself could not go much further, and had Lee Teng-hui remained in power, he might soon have faced this contradiction. Interestingly, the new president elected in 2000 himself might have less leverage than Lee Teng-hui to pursue the reform of national identity symbols, precisely because his defense of an independent Taiwan is well known. Lee Teng-hui, though a constant target of prounification forces both in China and in Taiwan, could play on the ambiguities and deny having intentions to go that far. However, Chen Shuibian, like Lee Teng-hui, knows how to reform discreetly, a necessary skill for reformers confronting a still extremely conservative political establishment. At the same time, the compromise both presidents had and have to make between two figurations of national identity must also take into consideration the fact that the Formosan identity is *eminently plural*. Any political discourse trying to silence voices diverging from a single historical narrative and identity would be a genuine manipulation, which is precisely what had been done in the Nationalist education until the 1997 textbooks.

Each of these transitional symbolic fields shows a different stage of the political indigenization. The reform of the banknotes shows a juxtaposition of Republic of China founders; Taiwan's economic, technological and educational development; Chinese traditional floral ornaments; and indigenous Formosan animals. This patchwork does not tend toward the affirmation of a Taiwan nation, yet the same reform has officially turned the New Taiwan Dollar into the official "national currency" of the regime. The disappearance of Sun Yat-sen's doctrine is near total, and though it has not officially been replaced by any other ideology, the switch is *de facto* operated amid a relatively consensual new ideology of "soft" Taiwanese nationalism, which encompasses the defense of Taiwan's democracy, appeals to its consolidation and common defense of Taiwan's sovereignty, the necessity to put aside the question of the national title in the face of the PRC's diplomatic pressure and military build-up. Chiang Kai-shek's image has been fading away for nearly two decades and it is rare today to hear any mention of his achievements. The reform of the schoolbooks has until now concerned primary and secondary school. It is far from finished, but it is one of the fields in which reform has been the boldest. The specific nature of those four elements produces different patterns of change. The banknotes, the textbooks, and ideology have led to explicit decisions, whereas the cult of Chiang Kai-shek did not. In this respect, the way chosen was to reduce references to the former leader, to accompany his image's natural fading away from people's minds. Yet the four cases have one strong common point: Each time, a total break with the past has been rejected—the accompanying historical movement is a process of reform, not revolution. The result is a complex mixture of symbols of different origins.

In the process of differentiation from China, radical options have been rejected in favor of more negotiated identity symbols. Several interpretations can be made here. This may be a way to ensure a consensual support of the reforms. It could also be analyzed as a way for the KMT under Lee Teng-hui to pull the rug out from under the then–opposition parties' feet. It could be, too, the result and illustration of the Taiwanese or Taiwanized KMT stakeholders' accepting of the necessary localization of the polity, under constant pressure of opposition movements. A last way to interpret such a policy is to view it as the result of a voluntarist policy by members of Lee Teng-hui's Taiwan Faction inside the KMT to reform the established order while nevertheless being conscious of the limits to what they could do. This reminds us of what happened to South Africa after 1994, when Nelson Mandela's cornerstone policy of "Reconciliation," as well as the necessity to obtain allegiance from the army, the administration, and the business community, prevented the new government from suppressing symbols of the former apartheid regime and led to a new configuration in which the old and the new are now side by side, although in a somewhat chaotic way.

Taiwan has seen numerous political symbols, ideologies, institutions, and national policies reformed at different paces, to various degrees, by a negotiated process between the now defunct state-party ensemble and social movements, opposition politicians, the press, and scholars. As a result, in only ten years since the lifting of martial law in 1987 there have been very big changes in many other fields besides the often-mentioned democratized electoral system, and the process is not yet finished. Since the beginning of the 1990s, says professor Lu Fei-yi of National Cheng-chi University, national identity debates have drawn numerous resources and finally invested every possibility of expression, whether artistic, social, scholarly, or political. "Whatever the point of view [defended], any way of seeing things will always necessarily be confronted by the challenge of other ways of seeing things. The kind of feeling that things are never fixed has led to an identity crisis of the overall society" (Lu 1998, 337). People still need to realize the strength this pluralism gives to Taiwan instead of viewing it as a source of destabilization. Such is the new Taiwan, and in this short period its people have been confronted with numerous symbolic changes and political upheavals. In the following chapters we will see how they reacted to them.

## Notes

1. *Sanmin zhuyi* literally means "the three-*isms* (ideologies) of the People." Such a long expression will be shortened below into the single word *tridemism*, from the Greek *demos*, or *people*.

2. Since 1931 in Republican China, then in Taiwan after the central government withdrew from the island.

3. Such as high school, universities, professional schools.

4. Interview with the Yuan's secretariat director, Tsai Liang-wen, April 20, 1995, Taipei.

5. On the difference, see the *Handbook on the Statistics of the Examination Yuan, Republic of China* (in Chinese). Taipei: Examination Yuan, 1994.

6. Interview with Mrs. Chang Ting-chung at the Yuan, February 15, 1995.

7. Four years later, in March 1999, another step was taken in a meeting among the presidents of Taiwan universities, who decided outside the state-party nexus that the tests on the tridemism would be suppressed from the Joint Examination (the famous *liankao*) for entrance in universities. It had been discussed since the 1994–1995 reform.

8. Sun's official name inside the KMT.

9. Numerous events were organized, the presidential office was opened, students and teachers had to go to school (though it was a day off) to bow in front of his

portrait, and it was considered a good day for inaugurations, such as a civil organization (e.g., the China Youth Corps in 1952), a new type of train (Kuang-hua in 1966), a television station (Chinese Television in 1971), or a highway (the North-South Chungshan Highway in 1978). The stores often took this opportunity to grant discounts. Often, ministries or commissions tried to delay or move forward an important decision, to take it on that day, as a special gift to President Chiang, or to commemorate his birthday after his death.

10. Chiang Ching-kuo had always been thought to be Chiang Kai-shek's son, until General Chiang Wei-kuo, an adopted son of Chiang Kai-shek, declared before dying in Taipei in November 1997 that Chiang Ching-kuo had been borne by his mother Mao Fu-mei before being married to Chiang Kai-shek and that he was not Chiang's son. (Mao Fu-mei was Chiang's first wife, Chen Chieh-juh the second, Soong Mei-ling the third.)

11. I have written a long analysis of the process of ritualization of the cult of Chiang Kai-shek in Taiwan between 1988 and 1997, which is a fascinating phenomenon in Taiwan's complex identity transition under the KMT. Interested readers can read "Que reste-t-il de Chiang Kai-shek? Ritualisation d'une commémoration politique à Taiwan, 1988–1997," in *Études chinoises* (Paris) 16, no. 2 (spring 1997).

12. That surprising move could be explained by the need to appease the party stalwarts unable to accept seeing a Taiwanese preside over the destiny of the ROC.

13. Due to the official vision of a "divided China," the KMT has decided not to organize national funerals for Chiang Kai-shek in Taiwan, waiting for reunification. His heavy black marble coffin has consequently never been buried and lies on the ground in a mausoleum in Taoyuan County southwest of Taipei.

14. On January 8, 1996, the two asked Chen Shui-bian in the city council to take this decision to help their party reform itself.

15. Lu Hsiu-lien, like many others, sees Chiang as the person most responsible for the dramatic February 28 events (see chapter 2). Before being elected to Taoyuan County head, on March 16, 1997, she however went to his mausoleum in Tz'u-hu to plant her campaign flags in the garden, an action that she called the "strategy of the mausoleum of the two Chiangs" (*liang Jiang zongtong lingqin zhengci*). Heavily criticized by the KMT for her "political hypocrisy," she responded with irony that since the two Chiangs had been lying in Taiwan's soil for so long, they had been able to identify with it and, thus, were "the representatives of the new inhabitants." In other words: The Mainlanders (see chapters 5 and 8).

16. Chen Wan-chen is famous for her acts—for example, throwing paint on Chiang's statue, tearing up a picture of Chiang on the podium of the Legislative Yuan, or printing harsh criticism of him in various publications. During a March 1993 hearing in the Legislative Yuan on the "Law regulating the treatment of the 2-28 incident," she defended the idea of transforming every Chiang memorial on the island into a February 28 memorial.

17. In December 1994, Yu Cheng-hsien decided to remove all of Chiang Kai-shek's statues in his *xian*. But since the criminal code forbids "irreverent treatment of national symbols," mayors and heads of *xian* have always been careful to put them into storage rooms rather than destroy them. Yu Cheng-hsien chose a park, for a storage room might have been a little too small, in Fengshan district near Kaohsiung. Not without irony, he said, "The park will be a place where people can show their respect to all the statues at the same time."

18. It then adds that it also aimed at developing "autonomy spirit, civic virtues, health, sciences and intelligence to serve daily life."

19. *Zili zaobao* (Independence morning post), June 8, 1997.

20. *Ziyou shibao* (Liberty times), June 16, 1997.

21. For instance, in a May 26, 1996, speech in Tamshui, he declared that history books were ignoring that Taiwan had a "history of four hundred years" (Lee himself was forgetting the Aborigines' much longer history), calling on Taiwan to look at its national education with a "new thought" in order to nourish a feeling of "common destiny." Yet, by that time, Kuo Wei-fan's ministry had already started to prepare the reforms.

22. The committee soon initiated "a gradual opening" of the textbook edition to private companies. A few nonpolitical subjects (such as music and sport) were also reformed.

23. Ironically, the most ferocious opponent of reform in the tempest of June 1997, National Taiwan University history department professor Lee Ching-hua (son of former premier Lee Huan, former New Party president and now a member of the People First Party), was in charge of the educational committee in the Legislative Yuan; yet he was unaware of what was being prepared until the beginning of June, when, according to his own declaration, he was "informed by a high school teacher" (Lee 1997, 1).

24. Forty percent of the commission was composed of "specialists in courses," that is, specialists in required disciplines; 35 percent of active teachers; 10 percent of specialists in educational psychology and other fields of educational sciences; 5 percent of specialists in "media productions," since the production of textbooks was now open to the private sector; and, last, 10 percent of officials from the MOE and the National Institute of Editions and Translations.

25. Tu Cheng-sheng is now director of the National Palace Museum. As for the geography book, it did not provoke any comment from the conservative camp and has not been analyzed here.

26. See Chantal Zheng's *Les Austronésiens de Formose à travers les sources chinoises* (Taiwan's Austronesians as seen through Chinese sources) (1995). This fundamental contribution to Taiwan studies is a translation of seven ancient Chinese texts (mainly reports to the emperors about the situation in Taiwan and about its original inhabitants) showing the evolution and cultural prejudices, over seven centuries, of the Chinese dynasties on Taiwan and of the Aborigines.

27. *Zhongguo shibao* (China times [Taiwan]), June 6, 1997.

28. *Zhongshi wanbao* (China times express [Taiwan]), June 4, 1997.

29. Unpublished speech. Copy obtained from Kuo's office.

30. "'This is well said,' Candide replied. 'But we must cultivate our garden.'"

31. *Shankei Shimbun*, June 9, 1997.

32. The interview was published in Tokyo (weekly magazine of the *Asahi Shimbun*, May 5–13, 1994), then translated in Chinese by Taipei's *Independence Evening Post*. Lee Teng-hui's declarations to Shiba were made in Japanese. The Taiwanese president spoke of the sorrowful identity of Taiwanese; of the fact that the KMT, the party over which he was presiding, was originally foreign to Taiwan; and of the fact that until Taiwan's Retrocession, he was legally a Japanese citizen. The interview deeply shocked conservative prounification circles, usually anti-Japanese, and was regularly brandished by them as a proof of Lee Teng-hui's treacherous plans to promote Taiwan's independence. (See, for instance, Lei 1995, 75–92).

33. Here is a summary of the arguments of the most renowned intellectuals who

defended the reform: Lee Yuan-tse called on politicians to let historians write history. Tu Cheng-sheng complained that if Taiwan was regarded through Chinese Communist eyes, everything could be suspected as being proindependence, "even eating and sleeping." Huang Cheng-hsiu recalled that Japanese repression was also mentioned in the textbook. Renowned historian Huang Fu-san said that it was necessary to have consideration for Taiwan's Mainlanders' sensitivity concerning Japanese war atrocities in China, but that Taiwan and China's experiences were different at that time. Historian Chang Sheng-yen criticized China's traditional incapacity to learn from history, thinking that no other nation except Taiwan had been forbidden to learn its own language. Sociologist Chang Yen-hsien pleaded for giving back to Aboriginal people the status they deserved in historiography, and historian Cheng Jui-ming expressed the idea that it was normal for history textbooks to change regularly. For more information on the positions of these intellectuals and a detailed analysis of the symbolic meaning of the reform, the reader can see my paper on this 1997 event: "L'introspection Han à Formose. L'affaire des manuels *Connaître Taiwan, 1994–1997*," *Études Chinoises* 20, no. 1 (2001).

34. *Zhongguo shibao* (China times), June 5, 1997.

35. Wang Hsiao-po, ed. 1997. *Renshi Taiwan jiaoke shu* (The *Knowing Taiwan* textbooks). Taipei: Taiwan shi yanjiu hui.

36. Interview at the institute with Fang Chih-fang, July 24, 1997.

37. In 1996, Kuo Wei-fan, a native Taiwanese, was sent to Europe to represent Taipei. A Mainlander, Wu Ching, replaced him. Soon after Wu took over the ministry, he granted an interview to the magazine *Tianxia* (Commonwealth), in which he talked at length about educational reform in Taiwan and said he had "many dreams" about his new role (*Tianxia*, November 15, 1996). However, he did not mention even once the textbook reform that was conducted by the commission. Then, at the beginning of the June 1997 tempest, he spoke in support of the new program, but evoked personal doubts that the words used to designate the Japanese colonial period were accurate, a controversy provoked only by the conservative camp's ultrasensitivity on the matter. Tu Cheng-sheng estimated that the minister was showing that he refused to endorse the reform at a personal level (*Zhongshi wanbao* [China times express], June 5, 1997). The sixty-fifth anniversary of the institute, founded in Nanjing in 1932, occurred a few days later. No one was sent by the MOE to attend the ceremony, at a crucial moment when the institute was gravely embattled with the conservative camp.

38. *Lianhebao*, March 3, 1999.

## Bibliography

### In Chinese

Chou Yü-kou. 1993. *Li Denghui di yi qian tian* (The first thousand days of Lee Teng-hui). Taipei: Maitian.

———. 1996. *Li Denghui han ta shenbian di ren* (Lee Teng-hui and his supporters). Taipei: Maitian.

Lee Ching-hua. 1997. *Renshi Taiwan? Huo wujie Taiwan? Dui guozhong Renshi Taiwan jiaokeshu neirong di zhiyi* (Knowing Taiwan? Or misunderstanding Taiwan? About doubts concerning the quality of the content of the *Knowing Taiwan* textbooks). Taipei: Lee Ching-hua.

Lee Teng-hui. 1999. *Taiwan di zhuzhang*. Taipei: Yuanliu.
Lu Fei-yi. 1998. *Taiwan dianying: Zhengzhi, jingji, meixue, 1949–1994* (Taiwanese films: Politics, economy, and esthetism, 1949–1994). Taipei: Yuanliu.
Ministry of Education. 1995. *Guomin zhongxue kecheng biaozhun* (High school curricula reference). Taipei: Jiaoyu bu.
New Party. 1995. *Qinxiu neizheng ai Taiwan*; *Xindang gonggong zhengce baibishu* (Reforming quickly domestic politics, loving Taiwan: The New Party's white paper on collective political strategies). Taipei: Xindang.
Shih Chi-sheng, ed. 1993. *Yishi xingtai yu Taiwan jiaokeshu* (Ideology and Taiwan's textbooks). Taipei: Qianwei.
Taipei shili meishuguan. 1996. *1996 shuangnian zhan: Taiwan yishu zhutixing* (1996 bi-annual exhibition: Taking Taiwan arts as the center of the point of view). Taipei: Taipei shili meishuguan.

## In Engish

Gates, Hill. 1981. "Ethnicity and Social Class." In *The Anthropology of Taiwanese Society*. Ed. Emily Martin Ahern and Hill Gates. Stanford, CA: Stanford University Press.
Gillis, John, ed. 1994. *Commemorations: The Politics of National Identity*. Princeton, NJ: Princeton University Press.
Lei Ming (alias Tsai Chin-hsüan). 1995. *Waishengren mei de hun le?* (Do Mainlanders still have a future?). Taipei: Hansi chuban she.
Martin, Roberta. 1975. "The Socialization of Children in China and on Taiwan: An Analysis of Elementary School Textbooks." *China Quarterly* 62: 242–262.
Myers, Ramon H., and Linda Chao. 1998. *The First Chinese Democracy. Political Developments in the Republic of China on Taiwan*. Baltimore: Johns Hopkins University Press.
Nora, Pierre. 1989. Between Memory and History: *Les lieux de mémoire. Representations* 26: 7–25.
Wachman, Alan. 1994. *Taiwan: National Identity and Democratization*. Armonk: M.E. Sharpe.
Wilson, Richard W. 1970. *Learning to Be Chinese: Political Socialization in Taiwan*. Cambridge: The Massachussetts Institute of Technology Press.

## In French

Corcuff, Stéphane. 1997. "Que reste-t-il de Chiang Kai-shek? Ritualisation d'une commémoration politique à Taiwan (1988–1997)" (What remains of Chiang Kai-shek? Ritualization of a political commemoration in Taiwan, 1988–1997) *Études chinoises* 16, no. 2: 115–146.
——. 2001. "L'introspection Han à Formose. L'affaire des manuels scolaires *Connaître Taiwan* (1994–1997)" (Han introspection in Formosa: The question of *Knowing Taiwan* textbooks, 1994–1997) *Études chinoises* 20, no. 1–2.
Zheng, Chantal. 1995. *Les Austronesiens de Formose à travers les sources chinoises* (Taiwan's Austronesians as seen through Chinese sources). Paris: L'Harmattan.

# — 5 —

# Mirrors and Masks

## An Interpretative Study of Mainlanders' Identity Dilemma

### Kuang-chün Li

Examples of symbolic events, like those analyzed in chapter 4, are the two public marches organized on the streets of several major cities in Taiwan in the summer of 1995. The first marchers carried signs proclaiming "I am Taiwanese and Taiwan is not part of China." In about a week, the second march featured signs proclaiming "I am Chinese." These two marches not only reflect Taiwan's recent search for a new identity, but also dramatize the identity dilemma faced by the Mainlanders, who came to Taiwan as political refugees in the late 1940s. Though the two marches were reported by the media as a showdown leaving little room for reconciliation, I speculate that the issue of "I am Chinese" or "I am Taiwanese" is more than a matter of choosing sides, especially for the Mainlanders. I wonder, given the changing reality of the Taiwan–China relationship, how do Mainlanders cope with the increasing pressure for Taiwanization or localization, as illustrated in chapter 4? How would Mainlanders live with Taiwanese? Do the different generations of Mainlanders respond to "Taiwanese Ascendancy" (to the top political positions) in similar ways? Besides, how do Mainlanders position themselves, both politically and culturally, in relation to Taiwan and China? How would Mainlanders regard the Mainland hometowns while they continue to settle in Taiwan? Questions like these represent a sample of the concerns in this chapter.

My analysis focuses on how Mainlanders represent themselves in primary relationships (*mirror*) and in secondary relationships (*mask*). The analytical distinction between primary and secondary relationships[1] is based on the assumption that though identity is often characterized by unity and continuity, self-identification works as a situational improvisation, contingent upon the parties and situations involved. On the one hand, people experience emotional attachment to one another in primary relationships, real or perceived. Primary membership provides people with an intrinsic feeling of acceptance and belonging, and mirrors our self-identity. It is often seen in ritualistic participation in such as events as an anniversary ceremony or periodic social meetings. On the other hand, people control the impression they make in secondary relationships daily. Secondary membership emphasizes a calculation of consequences and often serves as a means to an end. Secondary interactions are usually based on covert regulations or preconceived stereotypes. Masking or impression management is often attempted.[2]

Another goal of this chapter is to pay due attention to the meaning of ethnic identity from the perspective of human actors. For a long time, the stress on the dissolution of ethnic differences as prescribed by assimilation theory overlooked the fact that human actors often employ ethnic identity strategically and are not just passively cast into an ethnic category. This chapter shows that given the extent of ethnic antagonism in Taiwan, some people can still manage identity experiences to their advantages through situations and careers. In the analyses that follow, I pay attention to the roles of generation, education, and ethnic marriage on Mainlanders' identity dilemma. In sequence, this chapter covers the following topics: 1. Nationalism and self-identity; 2. Collective memory; 3. Hometown and family; 4. Impression management; and 5. Life after the demise of *jiguan* (concept of provincial origin).

This study comprises thirty-two in-depth interviews of Mainlanders living in Taiwan; they were selected by stratified snowball sampling. The criteria for interviewee selection include generation (Taiwan-born vs. Mainland-born), education (college-educated vs. subcollege-educated), and ethnic marriage (exogamous vs. endogamous). The interview questionnaire design is semistructured and open-ended. Each interview lasted from one-and-a-half to three hours. Each interview was recorded and transcribed by the author for analysis.

## Nationalism and Self-Identity

One question in the 1992 *Taiwan Social Change Survey,* conducted by the Institute of Ethnology, Academia Sinica, asked, *Which of the following ways do you identify yourself?* 1. I am Taiwanese; 2. I am Chinese; 3. I am Taiwanese and Chinese; 4. I am Chinese and Taiwanese; and 5. Some other way.

The survey results by ethnicity are seen in Table 5.1.

Though a close-ended questionnaire like that shown above can provide a clearcut picture such as the percentage distribution of self-identity, it fails to provide information on the meaning behind a certain choice. Similar deci-

Table 5.1

**Percentage Distribution of Self-Reported Identity by Ethnicity**

|  | Taiwanese (%) | Taiwanese and Chinese (%) | Chinese and Taiwanese (%) | Chinese (%) | Others (%) | Number |
|---|---|---|---|---|---|---|
| Mainlanders first generation | 2.0 | 8.2 | 26.5 | 63.3 | 0.0 | 49 |
| Second generation | 6.7 | 12.5 | 31.7 | 47.5 | 1.7 | 120 |
| Subtotal | 5.3 | 11.2 | 30.2 | 52.1 | 1.2 | 169 |
| Taiwanese | 26.6 | 33.8 | 17.7 | 19.7 | 2.2 | 1,222 |
| Total | 24.0 | 31.1 | 19.2 | 23.7 | 2.1 | 1,391 |

*Source:* 1992 Academia Sinica Social Change Survey, Question II.

sions might be made on unlike grounds. Knowledge of the elaboration of these considerations and the thinking behind these choices is essential to understanding the dynamics involved in the Mainlander's identity dilemma. Therefore, I asked this survey question again in my interviews and tried to dig deeper into the dilemma that Mainlanders face in positioning themselves between Taiwan and Mainland China.

As shown in Table 5.1, 89.8 percent of Mainlanders pick Chinese-oriented identities (including "I am Chinese" and "I am Chinese and Taiwanese"), whereas the proportion of Taiwanese choosing these Chinese-oriented identities is only 37.4 percent. Furthermore, more than half of Mainlanders (52.1 percent) choose Chinese-only identity. The proportion of first-generation Mainlanders choosing Chinese-only identity is higher (63.3 percent). Conversely, only 19.7 percent of Taiwanese choose Chinese-only identity. However, I doubt that those Taiwanese who choose "I am Chinese" deny that they are Taiwanese. I wonder how they perceive themselves in relation to Taiwan and Taiwanese. Jeff (1YC3), a retired army colonel, explained his choice to me as follows:

> My choice is not too complicated. I am Chinese. And I am a person of the Republic of China. If we need to distinguish between Taiwan and the Mainland, I will emphasize that I am not from the People's Republic of China. The China I support is the Republic of China, which now takes refuge in Taiwan. The Republic of China is now confined to Taiwan due to the communist rebellion.

Q: Then do you consider yourself Taiwanese or not?

> Of course! I have been living here for more than forty years. It is prescribed by the law. You know the reason why I can have a vote here? It is because I live in Taiwan. It is a corollary. I think this question of considering me Taiwanese or not is superfluous. There is no need to discuss this.

Many of the people I interviewed responded like Jeff—unhesitatingly declaring themselves "Chinese" but not denying that they are Taiwanese. Perhaps partly influenced by recent political agitation in Taiwan, some of them would immediately add "Taiwan is part of China, there is no such thing as the Republic of Taiwan" (1YC2). Most Mainlanders, especially those of the first generation, thought that identifying themselves Chinese was sufficient and considered the identification "I am Taiwanese" to be redundant. Wayne (2YC1), a self-employed computer engineer, gave me an analogy while answering the self-identity question:

> I really doubt that I would introduce myself as "I am Chinese" to people in Taiwan. It is a very strange thing to call myself Chinese in Taiwan. The only time we will introduce ourselves as Chinese is when we have to meet someone who is not Chinese, such as an American or a Frenchman. There is no need to introduce yourself as a Chinese among Chinese. For example, it would be very odd to tell my family I am Mr. Chang. It will be very strange. Everyone in the family already knows my family name is Chang. Why do I have to mention this to them? I will address myself as Mr. Chang only when I visit our neighbor Mr. Lin, right? . . . Furthermore, I cannot figure out why I have to call myself Taiwanese in Taiwan. For example, since I live with my family under this roof, there is no reason for me to tell my family that I am the guy from the east-wing room or from the rear room. Would not that be strange?

The indoctrination of national identity is a major task for political socialization in many developing countries. Engineered by the ideology of nationalism, one primary goal of nationalist education is to cultivate "state loyalty" and "nationalist spirit." In general, the way Mainlanders perceive their relationship with Taiwan and Mainland China reflects the central doctrine of Chinese nationalism as promoted by the Kuomintang (KMT): "Taiwan is part of China and Taiwanese are Chinese." Mainlanders used to believe that with the imminent realization of Mainland Recovery from the rebellious Communists, they would soon return to their home province(s), which are part of Great China. For example, Shandongese anticipated returning to their hometowns, in accordance with the principles of Chinese nationalism: "Shandong is part of China and Shandongese are Chinese." This state-initiated national identity can be easily found in some Taiwan-born Mainlanders who were brought up and educated in Taiwan. Karl (2XH4), a personnel manager at a shopping mall in southern Taiwan, told me:

> I am Chinese. In fact, it doesn't matter if I call myself Taiwanese or Chinese. Originally we all migrated from Mainland China. I think as long as

you have yellow skin, whether you are Fujianese, Shandongese, or Cantonese, we are all Chinese. No matter what people think of me, I still consider myself Chinese. Even if I were in the United States, I would tell people I am Chinese, not Taiwanese.

Q: If someone considers you a Chinese from the Mainland, do you correct him?

No. If I am considered to be coming from the Mainland, it is OK. Because my *jiguan* is Shandong.

Q: What do you think of the idea that "Taiwanese are not Chinese"?

No comment. I wonder what criteria can be used to say "Taiwanese are not Chinese." In my opinion, this idea is just being circulated to make an issue. It tries to separate Taiwan from Mainland China. My rebuttal is "What is your evidence"? I am just a straight Chinese, one of the children of Yen Ti and Huang Ti, born yellow-skinned.[3]

The trademarks of modern nationalism are historical genealogy and cultural homogeneity. Karl's self-identification here exemplifies the defining belief of Chinese nationalism as indoctrinated by the KMT through the orchestration of school curricula in Taiwan, as Corcuff shows in chapter 4. According to the mythology of Chinese nationalism, Chinese are "the children of Yen Ti and Huang Ti, born yellow-skinned" (2XH4). The relationship between Taiwan and Mainland China is viewed as historically linked and inseparable because "Minnan-speaking people, Hakka-speaking people, and Mainlanders all migrated from the Mainland" (2XH2). Also, Eric (1YC1), a retired ocean liner shipmate emphasized his belief in the cultural homogeneity of Taiwanese and Mainlanders:

> The idea that Taiwanese are not Chinese is meaningless and irrational. Don't they know that all the religious practices and Taiwanese family names originated from the Mainland generations ago? Only the Aborigines are authentic Taiwanese.

Historically, what constitutes Chinese or Chinese culture has been controversial. It is not my purpose to argue about whether Yen Ti and Huang Ti are actually Chinese ancestors or how all the Han residents in Taiwan today migrated from the Mainland. Instead, my concern is to show how these cultural myths and immigration histories have been employed by the KMT as Chinese nationalist doctrines to underscore the future relationship between

Taiwan and Mainland China. According to Geertz (1973, 89), culture can be defined as "a historically transmitted pattern of meanings embodied in symbols, a system of inherited conceptions expressed in symbolic forms by means of which men communicate, perpetuate, and develop their knowledge about and attitudes toward life." In this sense, it can be argued that Chinese identity as a way of life has been brought to Taiwan by immigrants since the seventeenth century. On the other hand, there is certainly an element of modern nationalism behind the formation of the Mainlander's self-identity in Taiwan. For example, Mainlanders who were born in Taiwan and have no direct Mainland experience, such as Karl, would unhesitatingly answer, "I am Chinese," when asked their national identity. Therefore, an analytical distinction between the existence of Chinese culture as a system of meaning in the sense discussed by Geertz and the existence of Chinese culture as a political national identity promoted by the KMT state, is important when studying the nature of nationalistic confrontation in Taiwan. But does it suffice to say that Mainlanders' self-identity is merely a product of nationalist construction? Would people consider themselves Chinese simply because they were taught so in school? Is there any other way people can acquire this identity as a Chinese? The next section provides another perspective on Mainlanders' identity formation.

**Collective Memory**

Although the two generations of Mainlanders have overwhelmingly favored the identity choice of "I am Chinese," each generation might make this choice for different reasons. Taiwan-born Mainlanders might have chosen the Chinese-oriented identity because of school indoctrination or the influence of their parents. In contrast, the reason first-generation Mainlanders make this choice is because of their early life experiences, which closely paralleled the formation of modern China.

Individual self-identity has a temporal root in one's autobiography. For many first-generation Mainlanders, their identity as Chinese reflects the intersection of their personal life history with the formation of modern China in the twentieth century. When asked to name the most significant historical event of the last 100 years, overwhelmingly, almost all of my first-generation interviewees mentioned fighting the Japanese in the Second Sino-Japanese War (1937–1945). Rick (1XC2), a retired police officer, said:

> Of course it would be the invasion of China by Japan. Because this is what I personally went through. I was just in elementary school when the war occurred. I remembered clearly that my elder brothers and I participated in

an underground effort to sabotage the Japanese [in Beijing]. At that time, all the young people had a very strong anti-Japanese sentiment. The Japanese bullied us. We did not need guidance or assistance from the government. Our spirits were so high. We felt very proud about doing this even though it was in fact very dangerous.

Vivian (1YC5), a college professor, recalled with excitement:

After the victory over the Japanese, we stayed in the countryside for a while. My mother and other military dependents knitted some handkerchiefs for American soldiers to express our gratitude. China, the USA, the UK, and the USSR were the Four in Alliance. We students then practiced singing the national anthems of these four countries. I still know how to sing their national anthems today. I also know the Marseillaise of France [starts singing jubilantly].

Some Mainlanders carried this legacy of fighting the Japanese when they came to Taiwan. Kurt (1XH2), a retired taxi driver, told me his experience with the Japanese in Taiwan:

I will hate the Japanese until my death. I still do now. Let me tell you a story. When I was driving a taxi in Kaohsiung, I turned down Japanese tourists several times. Upon hearing them speaking Japanese, no way. I rolled down the windows, saw a note in Chinese reading, "Please take them to Pingtung." I guessed the note was prepared by their Chinese friends. I shook my head, pretending not to know the direction. I did not care about the business. You know why? Because there is a hatred against the Japanese in my heart. I believe because of Japan's invasion, China was hurt badly and was forced backward for at least more than fifty years. My house in the province of Jiangsu was burned down twice by the Japanese. Our young people were either killed or forced to work, worked to their death.

For many first-generation Mainlanders, fighting the Japanese stands out as an important historical index event. Their self-identity as Chinese was formed from their personal confrontation with the Japanese during the war. It was in opposition to Japanese (them) that Mainlanders' identity as Chinese (us) emerged.

However, from a long-term historical perspective, the war with Japan is not an isolated event, but a historic climax during China's collision with Western civilization. In the nineteenth century, the Western powers forced China to sign a series of unfair treaties. Many educated Mainlanders placed their identity as Chinese in a historical perspective that goes beyond fighting the Japanese. It is in China's contact with Western civilization that their Chinese identity emerged. Hank (1YC4), a professor, commented on what he believed was the most significant event in the last 100 years:

I think it should be the *baguo lianjun* [the invasion of the joint forces of eight foreign powers, which occupied Beijing in the wake of the Boxer Rebellion in 1900] because this represented the showdown between traditional Chinese values and Western ones. Before this incident, many Chinese intellectuals still believed that reforms should not deviate too much from traditional Chinese values. But after the incident of *baguo lianjun*, more and more people started to realize that there was no way to ignore or to resist the new reality emerging with the rise of modern Western civilization.

Wayne (2YC1), a self-employed computer engineer, had a similar comment:

The incident of *baguo lianjun* resulted in the signing of the Peace Treaty of 1901 with the foreign powers and an enormous amount of indemnities. I have often joked with my friends that we Chinese have been defeated forever since then. We still feel defeated today. Many of our countrymen still believe foreign-made products are better in quality than domestic-made. This loss of national pride is a result of the humiliating incident of *baguo lianjun* in 1900. . . . Even today, our countrymen often behave strangely as tourists. The unreasonable act of conspicuous consumption outside reflects a sense of inferiority deep inside our heart.[4]

The making of a national identity requires a recipe of historical ingredients. Today, some Mainlanders, especially the Mainland-born generation, still consider the competition between China and the West as an ongoing, unfinished task. Therefore, Taiwan's postwar "economic miracle" carries invaluable meaning to Mainlanders. For example, Hank (1YC4) said: "the significance of Taiwan is to prove that Chinese are also capable of achieving progress and modernization." That is, Taiwan exists as an epoch-making milestone on China's bumpy road to reach modernization. Taiwan's postwar development, though it is still a fledgling economy, represents a hard-earned achievement for Chinese and a restoration of national pride. But, all this restored Chinese pride will collapse in the event of Taiwan Independence; because Taiwanese are not Chinese and Taiwan is not part of China. For Mainlanders who personally participated in China's war with the Japanese, Taiwan Independence is the last thing they want. Taiwanese Independence becomes a funeral knell for Mainlanders' lifetime search for Chinese pride and national identity. Put differently, in view of the political reality of a divided China, Mainlanders would probably prefer a continued though untimed delay of reunification with China than an immediate declaration of Taiwan Independence. Mainlanders' identity as Chinese can still be kept intact under the umbrella concept of historical or cultural China. That is probably why most Mainlanders supported presidential candidate Lin Yang-kang in May 1996 for his proposal "Don't Hurry Reunification, No Independence." In a word, Mainlanders' identity as Chinese is oriented more toward historical continuity than to legal-political unity.

However, each individual's reading of historical events or figures differs according to his or her life experiences. While first-generation Mainlanders exhibit enormous emotion toward certain historical events such as the 1911 Revolution[5] or fighting the Japanese, the responses from Taiwan-born Mainlanders are somewhat lukewarm. Their comments on historical events lack the kind of passion commonly found in the first generation. During my interviews, some second-generation Mainlanders mentioned: "Fighting the Japanese is a must-do test question for history . . . now fewer people display the national flag on the National Day" (2XC2).[6] This generational difference on viewing the past can be illustrated by the comments of Vickie (2XC5), a high school fine arts teacher, as she recalled her father's schedule on the National Day:

> When it comes to the National Day, there has been a lot of difference before and after my father's death. When he was alive, he would always turn on the TV the first thing in the morning on that day and waited to see the televised military parade. I personally didn't really like it very much. After the parade, he would often bring me with him to see the folk show in front of the presidential office. In the evening, we would go to see the fireworks show. It was really exciting. After my father passed away, no one in the family would turn on the TV for the parade. It was so quiet. We just concentrated on our own work.

Other second-generation Mainlanders have similar responses. May (2XH3), a self-employed food vendor, said "There is really no big holiday around the year except the Lunar New Year. That is when all our family can get together. I do not think the National Day is very important. It is just a day off." Some younger second-generation Mainlanders have their own special holiday. Ellen (2YH4), a high school student, replied this way when I asked her which was the most meaningful day or holiday of the year for her:

> Of course I like Christmas.

Q: Why do you like Christmas?

I like the atmosphere of Christmas. You can hear Christmas music every-where you go. People exchange gifts and cards. People do these exchanges a lot in Taipei, but not in Chungli.[7] By the way, my birthday is around Christmas and New Year's Day is close too.

Q: Are you a Christian?

No.

Q: Do you know Christmas Day is also the Constitution Day of our country? Is it because of Christmas or because of Constitution Day that we have a day off?[8]

My father said it is because Madame Chiang [Soong Mei-ling] needed to go to church for Christmas Mass on that day. So that day has become a holiday [laughs a lot].

Q: Do you think the National Day is special for any reason?

No, it is just to remember the Revolution of 1911.

In my interviews, some second-generation Mainlanders have shown less passion toward the historical events once considered extremely sacred by their parents. Furthermore, while most first-generation Mainlanders regarded the KMT leaders, such as Chiang Kai-shek and his wife, with respect and piety, this sense of reverence was not observed in the comments of the sec-ond-generation Mainlanders. In fact, some younger Mainlanders had little difficulty joking about the KMT leaders as Ellen (2YH4) did.

The above discussion of generational variation in Mainlanders' percep-tion of the past highlights several things about being a Mainlander. First, especially for the first generation, being a Mainlander means the sharing of a collective memory more than the practice of a way of life. Commemoration of historical events such as the National Day serves as a reality-maintenance mechanism for Mainlanders to sustain their identity as Chinese. Though they do not all know one another personally, first-generation Mainlanders feel a sense of unity with one another because of the collective memories they share, which are reinforced through the annual memorial observance of his-torical events.

Second, the ethnicity of the Mainlander is a product of some unique his-torical circumstances. Mainlanderness is not a cultural given but a mentality embedded in historical contexts. Therefore, the property of Mainlanderness will not necessarily be transmitted from generation to generation. In other words, the identity formation of Taiwan-born Mainlanders has to be examined within their own life circumstances. The generational differences in the interpretations of certain historical events or figures reaffirm the role of circumstantial changes in identity formation. Another example is found in Mainlanders' reflections on hometown visits and family reunions.

## Hometown and Family

Human migration tests the strength of family bonds. Family is the foundation of immigrants' homeland connection. It is through family members that immigrants feel attached to the homeland and maintain their self-identity. However, the vitality of family bonds is subject to various circumstances of migration, such as migration duration and communication accessibility, for example. Due to the ongoing military confrontation over the Taiwan Strait, the connection between Mainlanders and their hometown families has been cut off for almost forty years. Even though the KMT's ban on home visits was lifted in 1987, would Mainlanders' ties to their hometown family be revived after a forty-year separation? Also, how would hometown visits and family reunions influence Mainlanders' self-identity?

In general, hometown visits help Mainlanders to consolidate their settler identity as Taiwanese, though they do not necessarily dissipate their self-identity as Chinese. According to my subjects, in the wake of their visits to Mainland hometowns, their impression of China today is characterized more by frustration than excitement, more by disappointment than satisfaction. It is important to note that while Taiwan's economic development took off in the 1960s, Mainland China was struggling against the destructive forces of the Cultural Revolution. Although the economic reforms since 1978 have certainly improved the living standard in China, the socioeconomic gap between Taiwan and China is still sizable. Therefore, Mainlanders' initial impression of their hometowns was poor and backward. "My impression of my Mainland hometown is from my father. It is very poor and low-income, and the facilities are ill-equipped, not as good as those in Taiwan" (2XH2).

However, in addition to the gap in living standard, some sociocultural differences regarding people's attitudes and values were of great concern to my subjects. For example, according to my interviewees, people in the Mainland have "very different thinking and values, they have no incentive to work hard" (2YH2). "People there struggled with each other during the cultural revolution. They are much deep-minded" (2YH3). "Their way of doing things is different. They have only top-down hierarchy relations, no horizontal friend-ship-based relations. Many of my high school classmates did not dare to contact each other" (1YC1). "Except for the blood, skin, and language, everything is different from what we have. Their education is different. Theirs is materialism" (2YC4). "The cultural revolution changed a lot of things there" (1XC1). One major sociocultural difference between Taiwan and China is elaborated by Wayne (2YC1), a self-employed computer engineer:

Q: What do you think accounts for the differences in people's attitudes and values in Taiwan and China?

> I think one difference is in the political system and way of doing things. . . . People in the Mainland do not believe in religion at all. They are atheists. In Taiwan, it is very hard to find an atheist. No matter what religion one has, he or she always believes in something. There are very few atheists in Taiwan. But it is very easy for you to meet people with atheistic ideas in the Mainland.

Q: Are these differences in attitudes toward religion significant to you?

> Well, for people who believe in religion, no matter what it is, their behaviors will be accountable. Isn't there a saying in Taiwan that "Heaven is watching over our behavior on the earth"? But for atheists, there is no constraint for their action. Anything is possible for them. That is the major difference between us and them.

Different from the general impression of socioeconomic conditions and social ethos in the Mainland, family reunions provide Mainlanders with an opportunity to experience their Chinese identity on a more personal level. According to the oriental tradition, family role is valued as the bedrock of social relationships. People have obligations to take care of their family members, and family bonds are considered to be enduring over time and space. Simply put, blood is thicker than water. However, after a forty-year separation, to what extent can the bond between Mainlanders and their hometown families be sustained? Can family ties survive such a long-term social vacuum? According to my subjects, the experiences of home visits and family reunions are exciting but somehow awkward. Jason (1XH4), a self-employed garment maker, mentioned his home visit experience:

> I do not think I will move back to my hometown in the Mainland, at least not now.

Q: Why?

Well, how should I put it? It seems there is not much there I can cling to. I was forced out of the hometown by the Communists at a very early age. Now when I see my original family members, I have little to talk to them about.

Q: Will you make another trip there?

Yes, I will make a future visit. I still have an uncle and several sisters there.

Currently, Jason (1XH4) owns a small-scale garment factory in Taiwan. He married a Taiwanese woman and is the father of two daughters. As Jason continues to establish himself socially and economically as a settler in Taiwan, his ties with the family in the Mainland are expected to weaken. Nevertheless, Jason's plans to visit his hometown in the future are more a ritualistic practice to fulfill cultural normative expectations than an effort to restore old family ties. In contrast, because of social displacement and isolation in Taiwan, some Mainlanders living alone were much more excited and had higher expectations of their home visits. But given the absence of regular interaction and knowledge about one another, their home visits put kinship bonds to the test. Millie (2XH3) told me what happened to some first-generation Mainlanders in her *juancun* village (the generic name of the old villages of Mainland soldiers and their families in Taiwan):

> They felt like moving back to their Mainland hometowns, but they didn't. Some of them could not get used to the life there. Some of them already had new families here.[9] Also some of them just couldn't tell if their children there are sincere or not. It seems little affection is involved. Some of them did sell out their property here to move back to Mainland hometowns. But after they ran out of the money, some of them came back here to check into the Home of Honorary Veterans.[10] If you asked them: "Why come back?" they would say their sons and daughters-in-law did not treat them well. It seems they are just *Taibao* [*Taiwan tongbao,* or Taiwan Compatriots][11] to bring money for expenses. When their money ran out, they had no choice but to come back here.

One cannot generalize Millie's anecdote to assume that all first-generation Mainlanders have been ill-treated by their families of origin—finding the truth of this is not my purpose here. My concern here is that what Mainlanders expect from their hometown visits is probably a function of their settlement in Taiwan. For those who have adapted themselves socially and economically in Taiwan, hometown visits serve to bring about a closure to their years of exile. This fulfills certain cultural expectations. Few Mainlanders move back to the Mainland because of home visits. Instead, they stay in Taiwan. But those who remained socially uprooted or economically deprived had nothing to lose by moving back to their homeland.

Anyway, although most first-generation Mainlanders did not move back to their Mainland hometowns, they are still concerned with the Mainland. While recognizing a sizable socioeconomic gap between Taiwan and Mainland China, most of them blame the backwardness on the Communist regime. They separate people from the regime. "What I am against is the Communist regime, not the people there" (1XC3). "We can try something to help people there, but there is no way to help the Communist regime" (1XH1).

By comparison, most second-generation Mainlanders do not have much emotional sentiment about the Mainland. Most of their feeling or attachment about the Mainland are symbolic. "I feel like going back to have a look around. That is my root. But I don't think I will move back. Neither would my father move back. He probably would go back to visit the relatives if he were alive" (2XC2). "It is quite unlikely that I would move back to the Mainland hometown because my father has passed away. Probably, I will just go back for a look" (2XC5).

In addition to a symbolic, root-seeking sentiment, however, I find in some second-generation Mainlanders a utilitarian attitude regarding Taiwan's future relationship with Mainland China. For them, Mainland China stands for a huge favorable market. Gary (2YH1), a self-taught businessman, stayed in Beijing for two years. He commented:

> I agree with the position of "no-hurry reunification." We need not set up a timetable for reunification. I am a Mainlander and I do not agree with either reunification or independence. You know, if we declare independence, we can never make money in the Mainland. Say if I go to Southeast Asia or the United States of America, I will not be accepted there. I can only go to the Mainland to make money, just to survive. . . . You know, being a businessman puts me in a very difficult position. If my business is based in Taiwan, it does not matter whether I support reunification or independence. But today the fact is that our best business opportunity is on the Mainland. A successful businessman has to be pragmatic. For the sake of business, we have to expect reunification with Mainland China. Reunification can promise good business opportunity and profit, lots of money. Businessmen have no nationality. Only money talks. Business rules. If we declare Taiwan Independence, the Communists will cut off your business.

You know the whole world is in line to do business on the Mainland, not to mention Taiwan. I know the socioeconomic gap between Taiwan and Mainland is sizable now. But now Mainland China is quickly coming from behind.

Although the mission of retaking the Mainland has never been achieved by the ideology-centered KMT leaders, a new offensive warfare is being launched by Taiwanese businessmen. This commercial warfare is certainly a logical consequence of Taiwan's economic prospects. In search of cheap labor for global competitiveness, Taiwan's business owners are shifting investments to Mainland China. But politically, it is hoped that a sustained economic development can eventually lead to a change in China. It is expected while Taiwanese merchants, including some second-generation Mainlanders such as Gary (2YH1), are engaging in business ventures in Mainland China, they will retain their roots in the Taiwan hometowns. To some extent, this is intriguing to Mainlander businessmen because of their difficulty in seeing their hometowns as being on the Mainland or in Taiwan. Furthermore, how do Mainlanders perceive their relationship with Taiwanese on a everyday base? That is the concern of the next section.

**Impression Management**

Impression management is characteristic of secondary relationships. Secondary interaction unfolds on overt stereotypes and some form of masking is often attempted. However, the success of impression management depends on whether people can distinguish one another in terms of social membership. The more difficulties people have in identifying one another's ethnic membership, the more likely impression management can be successful. The question for Mainlanders is "how do people distinguish a Taiwanese from a Mainlander?" According to my subjects, "to identify ethnic membership, the key is to tell from one's speaking accent" (2XH2). "When people find out your Taiwanese is kind of poor, they then will know you are a Mainlander" (2XC1). Therefore, it is fair to say that the key to Mainlanders' impression management hinges on language proficiency.

Obviously, because of their poor Taiwanese proficiency, first-generation Mainlanders are at a disadvantage in attempting impression management. "Whenever I start to talk, people will know I am a Mainlander" (1XH2). Therefore, first-generation Mainlanders' strategy for ethnic interaction is in general defensive. During the recent years of escalating ethnic antagonism, they either keep silent or just avoid social contact in public places. Edwin (1XC2), a retired high school teacher, speaking with a strong Shandong accent, told me his taxi experience:

I did not take taxi a lot. But if I did, I would take it with my wife. When I took the taxi with my wife, I told her: "Use your language to give directions, I don't want to talk. You talk in your Minnan language." I try my best not to talk. I cannot make myself very clear to the driver, nor can I understand the driver. I had very few experiences of social contact.[12]

Vivian (1YC5), a college professor, also shared her experience:

For example, it happens when I go to the beauty parlor for my hair. It is a Taiwanese-owned beauty parlor. She has many Taiwanese customers. If it was election time, you would see many people there giving their own opinions about certain candidates or parties. I feel I am a minority there. Their talking makes me feel uncomfortable.

Q: How do you deal with this kind of situation?

Well, I just keep silent. I try not to join their discussion. I don't even know them at all. The owner knows I am a Mainlander. Also, she might know I support the New Party. After I come in and sit down, she will stop her discussion.

The strategies used by the second-generation Mainlanders are more diverse. Thanks to their ethnic capital, such as language proficiency, family background, and so forth, some second-generation Mainlanders can put on masks for various situations. Earl (2YC4), a real estate agent, told me of his game of changing masks:

It depends on under what kind of circumstance this question is asked. As a salesman, I often say: "If he is a Mainlander, I am a Mainlander; if he is a Taiwanese, I am a Taiwanese." A salesman should not be confined to nationality. I once sold a house to a foreigner. We are all human beings, right? . . . But when confronted with this situation, I will be very careful to approach him or her, to organize or get an idea of who he or she is. Actually, I really do not care who he or she is. Not at all. It is OK for you to say I am Chinese. It is also OK for you to say I am Taiwanese. It is also OK for you to say I am a Mainlander. It all works for me.

Millie (2XH3), a politically active person, mentioned the way she talked to people in her electoral district:

As for language use, the gap exists only for first-generation Mainlanders, not for the second generation. When I am helping out for the rally in the election, if I heard he or she is speaking with a Mainlander accent, I will introduce myself as a Shandongese. If I hear a Taiwanese accent, I will talk to them in Taiwanese.

In general, language proficiency pays off. Sharing a language helps bring two strangers closer. Vickie mentioned her experience at the roadside market: "I add some Minnan dialects into my shopping, it makes people closer, especially for some senior Taiwanese" (2XC5).

However, there is a paradox with regard to a Mainlander's masking. If a person keeps wearing a certain mask for a long time and does not take it off, how can we tell whether the mask is part of this person's identity or not? Is a mask forever a mask? Or will a certain mask eventually become part of our identity? Though some Mainlanders' *jiguan* have been recorded as non-Taiwanese, they have self-ascribed themselves as Taiwanese. While some Mainlanders identify themselves as Mainlanders, they speak and live as "Taiwanese." It seems *jiguan*-based ethnic division can be transcended by both self-ascription and participation in social organization. This blurring between official ethnic categories and self-ascription becomes more obvious as *jiguan* as a system of social categorization continues to crumble.

## Life After the Demise of *Jiguan*

I have more Taiwanese friends than Mainlander friends because I can speak Taiwanese. After I started to work, I had even more Taiwanese friends. But sometimes if you said: "Oh, you are Taiwanese?" My friend would say: "No, I am a Mainlander." Because you cannot tell it from the appearance. Sometimes my friend would just forget he is a Mainlander. Because his parents died early. He has been working in the society for a long time. Only when you asked which *jiguan* is he of, does he say, "Jiangsu, my father is from Jiangsu, but he died a long time ago." My friend was born in Taiwan but he almost forgot he was a Mainlander. It would only occur to him when he needed to fill out some forms. He felt it strange too. My friend said it would be more correct to put his *jiguan* as Taiwanese because he did not feel like a Mainlander at all.          —Millie (2XH3)

Perhaps it is also true that many of the subjects I interviewed have rarely called themselves a Mainlander. It seems that the practice of *jiguan* as a system of social categorization has expired. Historically the KMT used the practice of *jiguan* to endorse its ruling legitimacy over the Mainland and Taiwan. There is an ideology of Chinese nationalism and a favorable geopolitical context behind the imposition of *jiguan*. But over the years, the legitimacy of *jiguan* has drained away as the myth of Mainland Recovery has collapsed. Not only has *jiguan* become alienated from the reality of people's life in Taiwan, but also it has become more and more difficult to distinguish people's ethnic membership by mere appearance.

With the withering of *jiguan*, when asked about the future of ethnic relations, most of my subjects have quite an optimistic view. First, it is well agreed that first-generation Mainlanders will soon die out. All the early ethnic distrust due to opposed historical experiences will soon disappear. Besides, Taiwan itself is becoming more open and diversified. This increasing pluralism in terms of social composition will weaken the significance of ethnic categories. The presence of multiple differences will prevent the converging of social confrontation along the lines of ethnic division. Hank believes:

> Ethnic relations are going to become more harmonious anyway. In the future, people in the Mainland will come to this island. Foreign labor will come too. As Taiwan becomes integrated into the global system, the original differences between Taiwanese and Mainlanders are going to be blurred and become less salient. What is more, easy identification is required for ethnic prejudice to be sustained. Today ethnic identification has become less and less obvious.

However, the declining significance of *jiguan* as a principle for social categorization does not necessarily spell an immediate end to the Mainlander's identity dilemma. In any rate, the differences between Taiwanese and Mainlanders are more than those of administrative record. As mentioned earlier, first-generation Mainlanders' identity as Chinese has a strong root in their life history and their connection to the hometown families will not disappear soon. In the near future, some of them, especially the more educated, will still be perplexed by a continued dispute about national identity or the reinterpretation of collective memory. This is a struggle about symbolic meaning. The Retrocession "incident" in 1995 provides an example of first-generation Mainlanders' symbolic identity dilemma.[13]

In contrast, second-generation Mainlanders' identity dilemma is more far-reaching than that of their parents. There is substantial socioeconomic consequence brought about by the ascendency of the Taiwanese (*Taiwan ren chu tou tian*). Most of all, for those socially ill-equipped for ethnic interaction, the challenge from the ascendency of the Taiwanese is more urgent than the need to reconstruct the meaning of being Chinese. Most second-generation Mainlanders are young or middle-aged and they are very eager for career achievement. Teresa, the daughter of Vivian (1YC5), compared her feelings with her mother's:

I care more about the use of language in everyday life. Because I have to face it every minute I work. My mother paid attention more to the changing meaning of ideas and values such as national identity. I was born here and grow up in Taiwan. I have less feeling for Mainland China.[14]

Unlike their parents, second-generation Mainlanders have to cope with anxiety over language use during their work every day. They are under pressure to attend Taiwanese language classes; otherwise they can only choose to avoid ethnic contact. Their perception of the threat from the ascendency of the Taiwanese is determined by their experiences of interethnic contact. It is believed that Mainlanders from endogamous families might feel more threatened than Mainlanders from exogamous families, mainly because of a lack of ethnic knowledge or Taiwanese language proficiency. In addition, perhaps Mainlanders who feel threatened are those who work in industries formerly dominated by Mainlanders, such as the media and press. They feel threatened because of the increasing competition from their Taiwanese cohorts. Daisy (2XC4) is a TV reporter. According to her, the news media have traditionally been the prime area for Mainlanders because it requires good Mandarin. But the situation is different today. She feels more pressure from her Taiwanese cohorts.

Besides, Taiwanese ascendancy promotes an overhaul of Taiwan's historical and cultural environment, which has significantly challenged the Mainlander's worldview and beliefs. As a result, it might neutralize the immunity provided by individual acquisition of ethnic capital such as Taiwanese language proficiency. It is obvious in the complaints from Chris (2YC5). When asked about his view on social issues, Chris, a painter, said:

> I worry about the future of our cultural activities, such as the confrontation between local complex and *Zhongyuan* complex [the central plain, a more neutral term for China].

Q: Do you speak from personal experience?

> It is from my personal work experience. My specialty is *shui-mo* painting [Chinese painting]. It originated from the central plain. After the rise of local consciousness, *shui-mo* painting has been losing favor for some unknown reason. Local painting styles, such as oil painting, are more appreciated by the market. It seems to me this market has been created politically on purpose. I remember in the early years, Huang Chun-pi and Chang Ta-chien were the masters. Their works were most favored. But now theirs are less favored.

Q: At that time, their paintings were called *guo hua* [national painting], right?

Yes, I feel very frustrated that my commitment to work on the modern transition for *shui-mo* painting has been dampened by the market.

Q: When did you start to have this feeling?

When? I felt this very strongly during my last joint exhibition with others. It was in 1990. When I had my exhibition in southern Taiwan, I was disappointed by the response in the market. You know, I speak very good Taiwanese, but those painters with better Taiwanese or local styles have all the advantages.

Chris is a fine-art painter, with specialty in *shui-mo* painting. He came from an exogamous family and grew up in southern Taiwan. According to Chris, he speaks Taiwanese very well and has many Taiwanese friends. Although he admitted no sense of crisis, his complaint about the changing taste of the painting market highlights something fundamental about the meaning of Taiwanese ascendancy. In fact, the downplay of traditional painting is part of the very definition of the ascendency of the Taiwanese, which is trying to create a culture of its own, including painting style. Chris's story shows how individual acquisition of ethnic capital can fail to guarantee immunity from an identity dilemma. The ascendency of the Taiwanese is thus a movement that extends beyond ethnic revival to nation building. While the ascendency of the Taiwanese has promoted a right to use the mother tongue, it also has attempted to establish its own historical and cultural perspective. This historical and cultural renaissance movement not only has perplexed the first-generation Mainlander's collective memory, but has brought second-generation Mainlanders an identity dilemma which carries profound socioeconomic consequences.

### Notes

1. Charles Cooley, *Social Organization* ( New York: Scribner, 1909).
2. Face-to-face interaction is not required for the formation of perceived primary relationships. Perceived members do not have to know each other personally. Vietnam veterans, the victims of an atomic bomb, or survivors of a disaster such as a war or an earthquake, constitute perceived primary members.
3. According to Chinese mythology, Yen Ti and Huang Ti were two of the earliest rulers of China.
4. There are reports that tourists from Taiwan often act more like shopping troops than sight-seeing travelers.
5. On October 10, 1911, the revolution led by Sun Yat-sen succeeded in over-

throwing the Manchu Qing dynasty. As a consequence, the Republic of China was founded with international recognition. Sun Yat-sen is remembered as the founding father of the Republic of China. The tenth of October is celebrated as the National Day (Double Ten Day).

6. The government used to urge citizens to display national flags to honor the National Day.

7. Chungli is a mid-size city, about twenty-five miles south of Taipei. Ellen (2YH4) lives in Chungli but goes to school in Taipei.

8. In Taiwan, December 25 is a holiday in honor of Constitution Day.

9. Some Mainlanders were married before they moved to Taiwan as refugees. However, some Mainlanders have remained unmarried throughout their lives in Taiwan.

10. The Home of Veterans was established by the government as a nursing center to take care of senior, unattended veterans, most of whom are refugees from the civil war on the Mainland.

11. Though some second-generation Mainlanders have business on the Mainland, the majority of Taiwan's businesses and investments on the Mainland are managed by Taiwanese. However, Communist China's official vocabulary of *Taishang* (Taiwanese merchants) or *Taibao* (compatriot from Taiwan) does not distinguish Mainlanders from Taiwanese.

12. Throughout my interview, Edwin kept writing his words on pieces of paper. It seemed he was afraid his strong accent would lose me.

13. In 1995, the debate over the words used concerning Taiwan's Retrocession to China (October 25, 1945) provides an example of how collective memory is politicized to reflect the heated debates of national identities. Traditionally, the Mainlander-dominated KMT's interpretation of the Retrocession of Taiwan to China and the end to Japan's colonial rule of the island, was that it resulted from the Japanese defeat by Mainland China. It meant Taiwanese were expected to be grateful for this and in return were to help Mainlanders recover the Mainland from the Communists. But after the Taipei mayoralty was won by the DPP's Chen Shui-bian, the celebration of Retrocession Day was defined as an "end to war" (*zhongzhan*) rather than a return to China. It has caused much social commotion among senior Mainlanders.

14. Teresa is Vivian's (1YC5) daughter. She accompanied her mother throughout the interview, and her timely comments have provided a great opportunity to understand Mainlanders' generational differences.

# — 6 —

# The Evolution of National Identity Issues in Democratizing Taiwan

## An Investigation of the Elite–Mass Linkage

*Tsong-jyi Lin*

National identity issues have been on Taiwan's political agenda for decades. In the early 1980s, the opposition raised the issues in election campaigns, asking the right of self-determination to decide Taiwan's status. When the island's democracy became more consolidated in the late 1990s, national identity issues remained hot issues on agendas. A variety of political outcomes, such as factional interactions within and among political parties, constitutional reforms, voter realignment, and foreign-policy making all were related to the debate over national identity (Chu and Lin 1996; Cheng and Hsu 1996; Hughes, 1997; Wachman 1994). Needless to say, the salience of national identity issues in Taiwan's political development is evident. With an emphasis on the elite–mass linkage, this chapter mainly investigates the evolution of national identity issues in the 1990s. The study begins with the review of related literature. Second, why and how political elites raise national identity issues will be discussed. Lastly, elite–mass interactions during the surge of the issues are the focus of the third section.

## Issue Dynamics and Elite–Mass Linkage

In any country, thousands of issues pushed by different actors can emerge both inside and outside the political system in a week. Only a few of these issues get the chance to appear on the formal agenda. A large literature has suggested that a successful setting of political issues is determined by the selective pressure of competition in an environment that is itself always in flux. That is, the development of issues can be explained in terms of conscious political forces and unconscious environmental ones. The political forces are the interests of politicians: Previous winners seek to maintain the status quo of issues on which they have won, while previous losers try to bring new issues on which they can win in the coming political struggle. But beyond the conscious manipulation of strategic politicians, there are a variety of environmental factors such as war, depression, terrorism, and other crises (Carmines and Stimson 1989, 5–9). In addition, Kingdon (1995) notes the effect of political processes, including vagaries of public opinion, election results, changes of administration, and turnover in Congress. Bosso (1987) points out that the success of an issue evolution may be hindered by "the structure of bias," that is, the prevailing social values that determine the legitimacy of some interests and screen out others. Undoubtedly, manipulations of elite actors in beneficial environments are the necessary and sufficient conditions for setting particular issues on political agendas. Both elements in fact are interdependent. International or domestic climates create the chance for elites, who might in turn reshape those climates for further political actions.

Like other environmental factors, mass opinion always interacts with elite manipulations during the process of issue evolution. Mass opinion is traditionally highlighted by previous research, because the elite–mass linkage is a crucial element in determining the fate of a political issue. Without mass support, an issue is unable to remain on political agendas for a long run. The interaction between elite and public could be illustrated by the theory of issue careers. As Cobb and Elder (1972) suggest, an issue must experience four major stages—initiation, specification, expansion, and entrance—before being put on a formal agenda. According to them, after the elite initiate the issue, it should be further specified into some concrete and persuasive appeals to attract potential supporters. By doing so, the elite can expand the issue to the public; the elite thus can engage in mass mobilization. Once an influential elite–mass linkage is established, a powerful pushing force behind the issue will appear. This issue therefore has the opportunity to be on the formal agenda. Apparently all stages of issue careers are primarily ignited by political elites. This elite-driven model, however, does not overlook the significance of mass opinion. The public does not respond to elite initiatives in a completely mechanical fashion; the elites' calculations always take mass opinion into account. As a political scientist highlights:

> [E]lites–always having some ideas that are autonomously their own, always potentially split among themselves along partisan lines and maneuvering for partisan advantage, and always looking over their shoulders to

see what the public is thinking and might think in the future—attempt to lead and to follow at the same time. Or, to put the point somewhat differently, the question is not whether elites lead or follow, but how much and which elites lead rather than follow mass opinion, and *under what circumstances* they do so. (Zaller 1992, 273) [emphasis in original]

These arguments of issue dynamics can be applied to examine the evolution of national identity issues in Taiwan. In the late 1970s, the fledgling opposition employed ethnic discrimination as the theme of national identity issues. After this phase of issue initiation, the dissidents further specified the issues into two distinct appeals. First, self-determination became the major platform for the opposition in 1983. Second, when the sentiment of Taiwanese nationalism was on the verge of a climax in 1991, the Democratic Progressive Party (DPP) voted the adoption of a "Taiwanese Independence Clause" in its constitution that enabled the party to start *formally urging* Taiwan's independence in its election campaigns. By specifying its appeals, the opposition elites simultaneously extended national identity issues to the public and attempted to mobilize mass support. Therefore, the stage of issue specification and expansion happened almost in the same time period (1983–1991). These developments of national identity issues in fact were shaped by the elite's tact in making calculations contingent upon favorable environments. We could investigate this thesis by taking the self-determination appeal of 1983 as an example. In the early 1980s, the ruling Nationalist Party, the Kuomintang (KMT), suffered from legitimacy crises abroad and at home. In 1982, the United States and China signed the 8/17 communiqué, implying that the United States's arms sales to Taiwan might gradually decrease in the future. This was another heavy strike at the KMT after the termination of U.S.–Taiwan official ties in 1979. Along with the United States's failing support, China reinforced its pressures on Taiwan for unification. In October 1981, Ye Jianying, the chairman of China's National People's Congress, articulated a nine-point statement, offering Taiwan a high degree of autonomy in unified China. In September 1982, Deng Xiaoping proposed a "one country, two systems" formula for incorporating Hong Kong and Taiwan. Despite these concessions, China unwaveringly claimed that, if necessary, it would exercise military force to complete unification. Domestically, the unprecedented triumph of the Tangwai, the predecessor of the DPP, in the 1980 national election clearly sent a crucial signal to the KMT, warning the ruling party not to overlook the power of the opposition's mobilization after the Kaohsiung Incident. Additionally, a series of events undermined the KMT's ruling base. On February 28, 1980, the mother and twin daughters of Lin Yi-hsiung were murdered at their residence. In July 1981, Chen Wen-chen, an outspoken advocate of the Taiwanese independence movement, was found dead on the campus of Taiwan University. Both cases seriously damaged the KMT's reputation.

These international and domestic environments together contributed to the emergence of the self-determination platform in 1983. The uncertainty of American promises and the active campaign of China for unification deepened the sense of insecurity on the island. Faced with an unpredictable future, the Taiwanese people had to find their own way out. This stimulated political elites to raise various political proposals, including some radical ones, such as self-determination. Most important, the crumbling legitimacy of the KMT regime and growing Tangwai electoral strength made the KMT hesitate to crack down the opposition. Once the self-determination issue was set on the agenda, it became a powerful appeal for the opposition to promote ethnic mobilizations in election campaigns. Increasing mass support for the opposition, which came mostly from the native Taiwanese, compelled the KMT to accelerate its political reforms. Based on these successes, the opposition then elevated other issues for more mobilizations. The whole process indicated that a successful setting of campaign issues by the opposition's political elite had created favorable environments for further political actions. It also revealed that the elite–mass connection was a reciprocal, not one-way, mobilization.

From the late 1970s to the early 1990s, national identity issues had rienced three stages of development: initiation, specification, and e Despite the opposition's effort, the ruling KMT, by its domination setting, had refused to put national identity issues on formal politica das. This consequence was not surprising because the KMT tradition regarded Chinese identity and Chinese unification as self-evident and unquestionable; there was no room for discussing an alternative such as the independence issue. The situation, however, has changed in recent years. Under internal and external pressures, the KMT was forced to loosen its grip. National identity issues eventually emerged on Taiwan's official agendas, completing their fourth and final stage: entrance. National identity issues were no longer unilaterally raised by the DPP. Instead, the issues became debatable topics attractive to various political forces. Moreover, many of the national identity issues of the 1990s were translated into concrete policies. When elite debates gradually focused on unification versus the independence alternative, related issues such as Taiwanese foreign policies and Taiwan–China relations were intertwined into political agendas. This chapter thus will adopt a broader definition. Namely, four interrelated subissues: Taiwanese/Chinese identities, unification/independence options, Taiwan–China relations, and Taiwanese foreign policies will be treated as national *dramatic?*

identity issues. In this study we argue that in the 1990s the entrance of national identity issues into Taiwan's formal agendas is due to the dramatic change of the KMT's official policies. This elite-driven development is based on the surge of Taiwanese public opinion for political reforms. The KMT's new policies soon aroused international reactions, which in turn required political elites of different parties to take further action in response to the emerging public opinion. The whole process shows that, in Taiwan's consolidating democracy, there is no huge gap between the elite–mass linkages in regard to national identity issues. To win electoral support, which is the primary base of legitimacy in a democracy, Taiwan's political elites became more sensitive to the voices of people in the 1990s.

## The KMT's Changing Stance on National Identity Issues

As mentioned, national identity issues in the 1980s were mainly promoted by the opposition party, at first shaped in terms of self-determination and later as part of the Taiwanese independence platform. In the 1990s, the ball was in the KMT's court. In addition to tolerating the independence issue, President Lee Teng-hui decided to make efforts to break Taiwan's diplomatic isolation, which had been a nightmare for the island since the 1970s. Before Lee's administration, the government of the Republic of China (ROC) espoused a "one China" policy, asserting that the ROC is the sole legitimate Chinese government. Unlike his predecessors, Lee insisted on the principle of pragmatic diplomacy. Lee argues that Taiwan must do its best to develop either official or unofficial relations with other countries, including those recognizing the People's Republic of China (PRC). Additionally, the government should make efforts to participate in international organizations. With regard to the future of Taiwan, Lee asserts that unification with China is the only resolution; nevertheless, reunification should be based on several preconditions: China must become a democracy and there must be no huge gap between the two sides' level of economic and social development. Before these preconditions emerge, Lee insists, Taiwan should have the right to participate in international organizations and be officially recognized by the international community. In other words, though Lee denies it, he indeed promotes a "two Chinas" policy that seeks final unification based on the German experience.

   Lee's pragmatic diplomacy is obviously an effort to moderate the pressure within Taiwanese society. With growing democratization and economic prosperity, the Taiwanese people are proud of their accomplishments, desiring others around the world to acknowledge their country's success. Voters support politicians who promise to secure such recognition. Since the early

1990s, the DPP had focused on raising issues related to Taiwanese foreign policy, asking the government to take action for extending international relations. By adopting these issues, the DPP gained increasing popular support. In September 1991, for instance, the DPP held a series of marches in several cities, demanding that the government apply for UN membership. These mass mobilizations received emotional responses from the society; tens of thousands of people islandwide joined the marches. These grassroots mobilizations exerted strong pressure on the KMT regime, because the ruling party was attempting to make itself more responsive in a democratizing Taiwan. In addition to the growing popular demands, the promotion of pragmatic diplomacy is linked to the issues of Taiwan's national security. To the extent that Taiwan can secure recognition of itself as a member of international society, the costs to Beijing of an attack on it will increase. China may still be willing to assume those costs, but it will have to face international opprobrium, and Taiwan will be less likely to stand alone.

The KMT's big turn pleases reform-minded people; nevertheless, any shift of the KMT's traditional foreign policy will unavoidably encounter internal and external challenges. The conservatives, who insist upon the "one China (ROC)" policy, will not accept pragmatic diplomacy. In regard to the PRC, it is also unwilling to see any shift of the ROC's "one China" policy. Any move away from the "one China" principle is interpreted by Beijing as an attempt to foster Taiwan's independence or create either "one China, one Taiwan" or "two Chinas." All of these outcomes are absolutely opposed by the PRC.

Accordingly, Lee applies various maneuvers to avoid strong opposition from any political force. On the one hand, Lee created a National Unification Council and announced the "Guidelines for National Unification" to show his determination for Chinese unification. On the other hand, Lee tolerated the passing of the Taiwanese Independence Clause by the DPP. Lee's manipulation is apparent when we investigate his political rhetoric. In addition to the term "ROC" or "Taiwan," Lee created "the ROC on Taiwan" as a name for the country he rules, attempting to satisfy both liberals and conservatives in Taiwan's political arena. For Lee, all these terms—the ROC, Taiwan, and the ROC on Taiwan—are transferable. Lee utilizes one or another on different occasions, depending on the background of his audience. Additionally, without claiming "two countries" or "two Chinas," Lee asserted that there exists "two political entities" across the Taiwan Straits. One is the ROC that has jurisdiction over Taiwan; another is the PRC that presently rules the Mainland. Taiwan is part of China, and the Mainland is part of China as well. Therefore these two political entities (neither two countries nor two Chinas) are "the ROC on Taiwan" and "the PRC on the Mainland."

To solve the controversy over national identities, Lee encourages mixing identities, combining both Taiwanese and Chinese. In fact, Lee intentionally avoids using the terms "Taiwanese identity" or "Chinese identity," because either one will infuriate individuals in different political camps. To find an appropriate terminology, Lee first used "ROC consciousness." He explained that "ROC consciousness is employed to transcend the concept of either unification or independence" (*Liberty Times*, June 15, 1991). Later he frequently adopted the term "a living community of shared destiny," which showed lofty ideas of being in the same boat or sharing the same fate. Lee obviously attempted to use this concept to replace any individual ethnic or national identity. His goal was to emphasize that all people in Taiwan shared the same destiny and should identify with the island. Faced with his two major competitors, the Chinese Communist Party (CCP) and the DPP, Lee defends his policy by condemning their extreme stances. On the one hand, Lee contends that the emergence of the Taiwanese independence movement resulted from China's diplomatic isolation and military intimidation. On the other hand, Lee contends that the promotion of Taiwan's independence will induce more antagonism from China and lead to disaster.

Lee's pragmatic diplomacy gains the consonance of most people in Taiwan (see the analysis of public opinion later in this chapter). In the past several years, Lee has successfully visited several countries that do not have official ties with Taiwan. Each visit arouses enormous support and excitement from Taiwanese society. Lee's popularity reached its apex in June 1995 when the American government, under congressional pressure, allowed Lee to conduct a six-day unofficial visit to the United States. In addition, since 1993 Lee has promoted a campaign to seek UN membership for Taiwan. This campaign has failed each year because of China's opposition. Taiwan has also tried to join other international organizations, such as the World Health Organization. All these efforts have been unsuccessful so far.

The KMT's new foreign policy eventually evoked military confrontations across the Taiwan Straits. Lee's unofficial visit to the United States in 1995 deeply irritated China and the latter decided to make some concrete warnings. In July 1995, China held missile exercises around the waters of Taiwan, approximately 85 miles off Taiwan's coasts. From August 15 to 25, China held another round of missile exercises in the East China Sea, which is eighty miles north of Taiwan. China reinforced its military threats the next year when Taiwan held its first-time-ever election for a popularly elected president. During the periods of March 8–15 and March 18–25, China again held two rounds of missile exercises near Taiwan's waters and assembled the largest military operation it had ever conducted. China's war games finally incited the response of the American government. On the eve of Taiwan's presidential election, the Clinton administration dispatched two U.S. aircraft carrier battle groups to the waters around Taiwan. As a result, China soon lessened its military intimidation.

American involvement indicates that the United States cannot simply be a bystander in the storm of Taiwan–China confrontations. It is evident that if the conflict expands, it will definitely jeopardize American interests in the region of East Asia. The Chinese missile exercises tested American commitment and forced the U.S. government to show its bottom line. As a result, everyone learned a lesson from the scrape. Taipei and Washington found out that Beijing would respond militarily to what it thought were Taiwan's tendencies toward independence. The Chinese government discovered that the United States would not let Taiwan be shoved around if it did nothing wrong. Finally, the U.S. government on the one hand demonstrated its determination to defend peace in the Taiwan Straits; on the other hand, the United States also indicated that it would not support Taiwan if the island unilaterally claims its *de jure* independence. This new policy became more explicit and concrete in June 1998 when President Clinton visited China. Though he did not express it in a formal document, under pressure from the Chinese government, President Clinton for the first time verbally stated America's "three no's" policy toward Taiwan. That is, the United States will not support "independence for Taiwan; 'two Chinas' or 'one Taiwan, one China'; or Taiwan's membership in any organization for which statehood is a requirement." The U.S. concession to China unquestionably struck Taiwan a heavy blow. The "three no's" policy clearly announced that neither the KMT's pragmatic diplomacy nor the DPP's proindependence stance will gain support from the U.S. government.

## Responsive Political Elites: Contending and Converging Stances

The KMT's pragmatic diplomacy ignites the tension among Taiwan, the United States, and China. The American and Chinese governments' responses in turn exert influence on Taiwan's domestic politics. The major political parties on the island have to make themselves more responsive, readjusting their stances to correspond with the interest and opinion of the majority of people. Faced with changing political climates, Taiwan's political elites have debated over Taiwan–China relations within and among political parties. The elite interactions subsequently sketch out the different parties' China policies and diplomatic strategies.

Under the shadow of the 1995 and 1996 missile games, the ruling KMT, on the one hand, reiterated its willingness to negotiate with the Chinese government and to accept the eventual goal of Chinese unification; on the other hand, the KMT still regarded its pragmatic diplomacy as the best weapon against China's pressures. China's military threats did not change Lee's determination. After winning his reelection by a majority of votes, Lee, in his inaugural speech, insisted,

> Patience on the part of the 21.3 million people [of Taiwan] is not tantamount to cowardice. Because we believe quiet tolerance is the only way to dispel enmity bred by confrontation. We will never negotiate under threat of attack, but we do not fear to negotiate. (*Central Daily News*, May 21, 1996)

Lee did not change his mind, even after the American government declared the "three no's" policy toward Taiwan. In a recent interview by the *New York Times*, Lee repeatedly complained about Taiwan's isolation in the world and said he will keep searching for ways to break through that isolation. By firmly sticking to his foreign policy, Lee made it clear that he was not thinking about concessions to the Mainland. Rejecting China's threat, Lee stressed that "Taiwan's destiny must be determined solely by the people of Taiwan" (*New York Times*, September 1, 1998). This assertion obviously echoes the DPP's traditional view. As a result, pragmatic diplomacy remains one of the priorities on the KMT's policy agenda while negotiation with China is another. Top officials of the government use every opportunity to contact other countries' political leaders. The government keeps urging participation in international organizations, though attempts at it rarely succeed.

A larger policy shift happened in the DPP. Many politicians, either outside or inside the DPP, attributed the party's loss in the 1991 election to its incorporation of the Taiwanese Independence Clause. According to them, the Taiwanese Independence Clause frightened most voters because such a campaign platform would definitely anger the Chinese government and evoke China's military threat. Within the party, the independence appeal was seen by some DPP leaders as poison for electoral competitiveness. Whether to amend the Taiwanese Independence Clause thus became a controversial issue within the party for several years. Although the DPP's elites finally reached a consensus to maintain the clause, the DPP has adapted its independence platform by a variety of approaches. In the Legislative Yuan election of 1992, for instance, the DPP no longer bluntly proposed the platform for independence; instead, the party devised the slogan "one Taiwan, one China" despite the fact that its allegiance to Taiwan's independence hdd not changed. In December 1994, the DPP's secretary-general, Su Cheng-chang, suggested that, to avoid misunderstanding by the public, the Taiwanese Independence Clause should be renamed the Plebiscite Clause. "Although the DPP advocated independence, the party argued that the proposal of claiming independence should be eventually decided by all people of Taiwan. . . . What the DPP emphasized was the right of self-determination for people" (*Central Daily News*, December 11, 1994).

China's missile games caused the DPP further to adjust its position on the independence issue. In September 1995, one month after China's missile exercises and three months before the year-end Legislative Yuan election, the DPP's chairman Shih Ming-teh maintained that his party "will not and will not have to declare Taiwan's independence in case that the DPP becomes the ruling party," because "Taiwan has been (*de facto*) independent for nearly half a century" (*Liberty Times*, September 16, 1995). Apparently, the DPP under the pressure of electoral competition has to respond to China's threats. Military confrontations across the straits thus drive the DPP to become more pragmatic than ideological. The reason for this outcome is evident. Having been an opposition party for more than a decade, the DPP has completed its traditional mission of promoting Taiwan's democracy. In the 1990s, the party's ambition is to win a majority of the votes and become the ruling power. To accomplish this goal, the DPP has to extend its electoral bases, moderating its issue position to please most of the electorate. In other words, after Taiwan accelerates its steps toward democratization, the DPP in the 1990s has gradually transformed itself from a missionary to a broker. As a result, faced with China's enmity, the DPP was compelled to change its rigid stance on the independence issue.

However, the DPP would like merely to modify its approaches to fostering independence rather than completely abandon them. This rationale also mainly comes from the calculation of electoral competitiveness. First, even to gain as many votes as possible, the DPP is surely unwilling to lose the supporters of the independence movement, who are traditionally a crucial part of the DPP's constituency. Second, it is unnecessary to give up the independence appeal to urge the support of the majority of the people. Although numerous polls have indicated that over 90 percent of Taiwanese currently prefer maintaining the status quo to moving toward immediate unification or independence, the polls also show that a large number of the people may potentially support independence in the future if political climates change (see further analysis in the next section). Therefore, like the KMT, the DPP presently emphasizes its intention to maintain the island's status quo. The DPP's platform for independence, just like the KMT's for unification, is a distant and ideal goal. The DPP will embrace the dream of independence, but not treat it as a priority in its current political agenda. As Hsu Hsin-liang repeatedly stated when he was the chairman of the DPP, "the Taiwanese Independence Clause will not be revised, because it has become a historical document" (*Liberty Times*, December 8, 1997, and July 2, 1998). The DPP's revised argument obviously echoes the KMT's proposition of unification, that is, that Chinese unification is the eventual destination, but currently the most crucial goal is to sustain the survival of Taiwan.

Consequently, to recruit the majority of voters who favor the status quo option, the DPP in the past several years has gradually shifted its blunt independence appeal; instead, the party has been proposing the maintenance of Taiwan's status quo without abandoning the ideal of independence. At present, the DPP has positioned itself as a party actively defending the status quo and passively promoting independence. Although the DPP insists that Taiwan's future should be decided by the island's people via a plebiscite, the party emphasizes that the timing of a plebiscite should be cautiously chosen. As Lin Yi-hsiung, the DPP chairman, stated,

> A plebiscite can be held only under the condition that there is no, or very low, risk of China's military attack. Taiwan has to wait for a favorable international atmosphere. By promoting exchanges with China, Taiwan must convince China that military means can not resolve the Taiwan problem. This is difficult, but not impossible. (*Liberty Times*, June 19, 1998)

This stance was further illustrated when the American government announced its "three no's" policy in the summer of 1998. In response to this policy, after reiterating the determination to defend Taiwan's *de facto* independence, the DPP declared that under current circumstances the DPP would not propose a plebiscite (*Liberty Times*, July 2, 1998).

In addition, the DPP continues to support Lee's pragmatic diplomacy, which was originally proposed by the DPP. With regard to cross-strait interactions, the DPP has changed its former policy opposing contact with the CCP. Instead, a new guideline concerning positive engagement in Taiwan–China relations was formed in the DPP's China Policy Symposium of early 1998. The DPP's elites reached the consensus that, to defend Taiwan's status quo, the government should promote cross-strait interactions and prepare to negotiate with China. Such a resolution indeed is similar to the KMT's China policy. A significant distinction is that the DPP sees Taiwan and China as two independent and separate countries; therefore the Taiwan–China relationship in the eyes of the DPP is international. In contrast, the KMT insists that on both sides of the Taiwan Straits are "two political entities." Based on this ambiguous definition, the KMT varies its interpretation on different occasions. Sometime Taiwan–China interactions are seen as domestic affairs; sometimes they are interpreted as international relations.

The positions of the New Party (NP), originally a splinter group of the KMT, on national identity issues are generally similar to the KMT's. The NP favors the eventual unification of Taiwan and the Mainland. Like the KMT, the NP argues that unification should be based on some preconditions, namely, that Mainland China must become a democracy and other social and economic conditions across the straits are convergent. In some official documents, the NP adds another condition, asserting that the cross-strait negotiations concerning unification should depend on "the support of the majority of people in Taiwan" (The New Party, 1995: 105) or that "unification should be based on the agreement between the people of the two sides" (Mainland Affairs Council, 1997: 16). However, unlike the DPP's proposal of holding a plebiscite, the NP never specifies by which means public opinion, either solely in Taiwan or both sides of the straits, can be investigated.

In addition, the NP echoes the KMT's idea of "one China, two political entities." Generally speaking, the NP also supports the official policy of pragmatic diplomacy. The difference between the NP and the KMT and DPP may be the NP's relatively softer attitude toward China. The NP stresses that Taiwan should avoid infuriating China when engaging in the pragmatic foreign policy; the ROC government should show its amity and willingness to negotiate with the PRC as best it can. To promote unification, the NP insists, the government also should do its best to undertake cross-strait interactions, including comprehensive exchanges in social, cultural, economic, and political spheres (The New Party 1995, 41–49, 105–108). Due to its softer position toward China, the NP is always seen as the most prounification of Taiwan's major parties.

## Public Opinion about National Identity Issues

As Taiwan consolidates its democracy, none of the policy makers in the island can simply overlook the flow of public opinion. Formerly in this chapter we have argued that the changing policies of political parties in Taiwan are mainly influenced by public opinion that responds to shifting environments. This section will show evidence for this argument, indicating the trend of public opinion about national identity issues in the past several years.[1]

### Taiwanese/Chinese Identity

Examining mass attitude on national identity is the first step to clarify the public opinion toward related issues. Table 6.1 shows the distribution of national identities among party identifiers during 1992–1997, the critical period of cross-Strait interactions and implementation of pragmatic diplomacy.

The table indicates several findings. First, except for the NP identifiers, increasing Taiwanese identity and decreasing Chinese identity are two sig-

Table 6.1    **Distribution of National Identities by Party Identification, 1992–1997**

Q: Some people identify themselves as "Taiwanese"; some identify themselves as "Chinese"; some identify themselves as "both Taiwanese and Chinese." Do you identify yourself as "Taiwanese," "Chinese," or "both"?

|  | Taiwanese (%) | Both Taiwanese and Chinese (%) | Chinese (%) | N |
|---|---|---|---|---|
| All identifiers | | | | |
| 1992 | 19.3 | 46.4 | 30.2 | 1,402 |
| 1994 | 25.5 | 47.3 | 23.5 | 1,236 |
| 1995 | 29.5 | 49.0 | 18.4 | 1,292 |
| 1996 | 32.3 | 46.4 | 17.3 | 1,256 |
| 1997 | 33.0 | 49.4 | 15.0 | 1,408 |
| KMT identifier | | | | |
| 1992 | 9.4 | 45.6 | 43.2 | 616 |
| 1994 | 17.1 | 49.1 | 31.6 | 497 |
| 1995 | 24.3 | 51.3 | 22.5 | 538 |
| 1996 | 29.5 | 45.9 | 21.4 | 584 |
| 1997 | 23.2 | 52.1 | 23.5 | 426 |
| DPP identifier | | | | |
| 1992 | 40.0 | 41.1 | 15.7 | 185 |
| 1994 | 52.7 | 36.7 | 9.7 | 207 |
| 1995 | 55.0 | 28.9 | 10.0 | 249 |
| 1996 | 63.4 | 27.2 | 7.7 | 235 |
| 1997 | 51.8 | 38.7 | 9.0 | 199 |
| NP identifier | | | | |
| 1994 | 11.7 | 49.2 | 35.8 | 120 |
| 1995 | 8.2 | 65.5 | 25.7 | 171 |
| 1996 | 6.2 | 58.5 | 33.1 | 130 |
| 1997 | 9.3 | 69.2 | 19.6 | 107 |
| Nonpartisan | | | | |
| 1992 | 23.1 | 48.8 | 21.3 | 601 |
| 1994 | 26.0 | 50.0 | 17.2 | 412 |
| 1995 | 29.6 | 51.8 | 14.4 | 334 |
| 1996 | 25.1 | 57.0 | 10.1 | 307 |
| 1997 | 37.0 | 47.9 | 10.8 | 676 |

*Sources:* Surveys of the 1992 Legislative Yuan election, the 1994 mayoral and gubernatorial election, the 1995 Legislative Yuan election, and the 1996 presidential election; 1997 survey on the Mainland policy and the cross-strait relations. Surveys are conducted by The Election Study Center, National Chengchi University.

*Note:* Numbers do not add up to 100 percent because percentages of other answers are not shown in the table.

nificant and general trends, although the growth in Taiwanese identity is relatively unstable from year to year. During this six-year period, for all respondents, Taiwanese identity increases 13.7 percent; in contrast, Chinese identity declines 15.2 percent. A similar situation happens in the KMT's and

DPP's identifiers, as well as a nonpartisan electorate. The largest variation occurs among the KMT's identifiers; Taiwanese identity rises 13.8 percent and Chinese identity drops by 19.7 percent. In regard to the NP partisans, the distribution of their Chinese identity also decreases; their Taiwanese identity however does not grow. Instead, the increase occurs in the mixed identity; expanding NP loyalists have seen themselves as both Taiwanese and Chinese. This finding is consistent with the stance of the NP elites, who, though reluctant to claim solely Taiwanese identity, instead acknowledge a mixed or Chinese identity. Second, among the three kinds of national identity, mixed identity is claimed by around 50 percent of all respondents. When we investigate the identifiers of the individual party, this situation is also true for the KMT partisans as well as nonpartisan respondents. The figure supporting mixed identity is even higher among the NP loyalists. These results explain why the KMT, a party making efforts to sustain its ruling position, has claimed a mixed identity rather than a merely Chinese identity in the past several years. With regard to the identifiers of the DPP, most of them embrace Taiwanese identity. This consequence reveals that the DPP identifiers' opinions on national identity correspond with the party elite's stance.

### Unification/Independence Alternative

Table 6.2 shows the opinion distribution on the unification/independence issue. There are several tendencies at the level of the general electorate. First, the prounification stances, including options 1 and 2, have steadily decreased. Second, despite a preference for different timings for resolving the unification/independence issue, maintaining Taiwan's current *de facto* independence (options 2–5) is the most favored choice of Taiwanese people; less than 5 percent of respondents asked for immediate independence or unification. Among options 2–5, support for the third alternative has been steadily growing and has become the dominant attitude of all respondents. This indicates that more Taiwanese people have chosen to leave the unification/independence problem open rather than presuppose any solution. Additionally, support for option 5, "maintaining the status quo, then claiming independence in the future," has also increased. Third, compared to national identity, the proportional change of opinion on the unification/independence issue is relatively moderate. The most dramatic difference is 6.7 percent, shown in option 3 (comparing the figure in 1993 and 1997), which is still far less than the changed figures for national identity shown in the preceding table. This implies that people become more realistic and cautious when faced with the unification/independence issue. Unlike national identity, which is merely an affective attachment, the choice of independence or unification may highly

Table 6.2    **Opinion Distribution of Unification/Independence Alternatives by Party Identification, 1993–1997**

Q: There are several options* regarding Taiwan–Mainland relations. Which one is the most favorable to you?

| | Option 1 (%) | Option 2 (%) | Option 3 (%) | Option 4 (%) | Option 5 (%) | Option 6 (%) | N |
|---|---|---|---|---|---|---|---|
| **All identifiers** | | | | | | | |
| 1993 | 4.6 | 24.6 | 33.8 | 11.3 | 7.7 | 3.0 | 1,278 |
| 1994 | 4.1 | 24.8 | 35.3 | 11.1 | 10.5 | 3.7 | 1,234 |
| 1995 | 3.9 | 22.1 | 33.1 | 15.3 | 10.9 | 3.3 | 1,288 |
| 1996 | 3.2 | 20.3 | 36.1 | 11.0 | 15.5 | 3.7 | 1,259 |
| 1997 | 2.3 | 18.7 | 40.5 | 11.4 | 14.3 | 4.8 | 1,407 |
| **KMT identifier** | | | | | | | |
| 1993 | 5.0 | 31.9 | 37.2 | 9.9 | 6.7 | 0.9 | 436 |
| 1994 | 5.6 | 35.7 | 30.9 | 11.2 | 6.0 | 2.2 | 498 |
| 1995 | 4.7 | 26.4 | 35.0 | 17.9 | 6.0 | 0.7 | 537 |
| 1996 | 4.3 | 24.1 | 35.1 | 12.8 | 12.8 | 1.5 | 584 |
| 1997 | 4.0 | 25.8 | 38.7 | 12.7 | 12.0 | 2.3 | 426 |
| **DPP identifier** | | | | | | | |
| 1993 | 4.7 | 17.4 | 31.6 | 10.0 | 16.8 | 11.1 | 190 |
| 1994 | 4.8 | 9.3 | 28.6 | 10.9 | 27.8 | 11.3 | 248 |
| 1995 | 5.4 | 10.2 | 30.6 | 11.9 | 29.7 | 12.2 | 230 |
| 1996 | 1.7 | 6.3 | 30.8 | 11.0 | 33.3 | 12.7 | 237 |
| 1997 | 2.5 | 11.1 | 31.8 | 9.1 | 31.3 | 10.1 | 198 |
| **NP identifier** | | | | | | | |
| 1993 | 5.6 | 39.4 | 35.2 | 2.8 | 15.5 | 0 | 71 |
| 1994 | 2.5 | 41.2 | 42.9 | 7.6 | 4.2 | 0 | 119 |
| 1995 | 4.7 | 38.2 | 38.8 | 7.6 | 7.1 | 1.8 | 170 |
| 1996 | 4.6 | 44.3 | 37.4 | 4.6 | 8.4 | 0 | 131 |
| 1997 | 2.8 | 35.5 | 42.1 | 5.6 | 9.3 | 2.8 | 107 |
| **Nonpartisan** | | | | | | | |
| 1993 | 4.1 | 19.8 | 31.8 | 13.8 | 4.6 | 2.2 | 581 |
| 1994 | 3.9 | 13.6 | 39.7 | 12.9 | 7.3 | 2.7 | 411 |
| 1995 | 1.5 | 16.5 | 30.3 | 18.3 | 8.1 | 2.1 | 333 |
| 1996 | 1.6 | 13.7 | 41.4 | 10.1 | 9.8 | 2.6 | 307 |
| 1997 | 1.2 | 13.9 | 44.1 | 12.4 | 10.9 | 5.0 | 676 |

*Sources:* Surveys of the 1993 county magistrate election, the 1994 mayoral and gubernatorial election, the 1995 Legislative Yuan election, and the 1996 presidential election; 1997 survey on the Mainland policy and the cross-strait relations. Surveys are conducted by The Election Study Center, National Chengchi University.

*Note:* Numbers do not add up to 100 percent because percentages of other answers are not shown in the table.

*Option 1. Taiwan unifies with China as soon as possible; Option 2. Taiwan maintains the status quo, and then unifies with China in the future; Option 3. Taiwan maintains the status quo. Unification or independence will rely on different conditions in the future; Option 4. Taiwan maintains the status quo forever; Option 5. Taiwan maintains the status quo, and then becomes independent in the future; Option 6. Taiwan claims independence as soon as possible.

influence people's future. The change of opinion on the latter issue thus is conservative.

Generally speaking, the above characteristics are also evident and stable among KMT's and NP's identifiers, as well as among the nonpartisan electorate. The DPP partisans however show a different picture. The mainstream opinions in this category are options 3 and 5. A large increase particularly happens in the fifth alternative, "maintaining the status quo, and then claiming independence in the future."

The elite–mass linkage within individual parties is worth noting. The KMT's official stance apparently is consistent with option 2. However, the supporting percentage for option 2 has decreased in the studied period; in 1996 and 1997, merely around a quarter of the KMT partisans saw the second as their preferred alternative. Instead, leaving the unification/independence issue open in the future (option 3) remains at 35 to 39 percent in most years. Additionally, option 4 and 5 together are favored by nearly 25 percent. At this point, a gap between the KMT's elite and mass levels has appeared; the KMT's official policy thus might not fulfill the expectation of its supporters. If the mass's support for the KMT's prounification policy continues to decrease, then the KMT as an electoral party must adjust its official pose to pursue its voters. As noted, Lee Teng-hui, in his latest interview in the *New York Times,* stated that "Taiwan's destiny must be determined solely by the people of Taiwan," an announcement similar to option 3. Whether the KMT will follow Lee's latest viewpoint and move toward a median position in the near future will strongly affect Taiwan's politics and cross-strait relations.

With regard to the DPP, the weakness of its radical supporters perhaps constitutes a crucial factor forcing the DPP to soften its original proposal for actively advocating independence. Support for option 6 is merely 10 to 13 percent; instead, options 3 and 5 have become the dominant opinions among the DPP partisans, as indicated in Table 6.2. In addition, as mentioned, the DPP has attempted to win ruling power by extending its constituency. This reason further demands that the DPP's elites seek a more moderate position to attract the voters with other partisanships. Therefore, it is not surprising that DPP's leaders have reiterated its moderate approaches in recent years. Sometime the party echoes option 5, that is, "maintaining the status quo, and claiming independence in the future." But more frequently, the DPP leaders have emphasized an open alternative: "Taiwan's future should be jointly determined by all inhabitants of the island." This argument is close to option 3, which has been the most popular among all respondents.

In the NP camp, although the prounification options (options 1 and 2) still occupy 38 to 50 percent in each year, support for option 3 has gradually increased among the party loyalists. Having perceived this changing attitude, some NP legislators in February 1998 asked the party to adjust its policy to a more moderate pose. This attempt was soon opposed by other NP senior elites. At present there is no any sign that the NP will lessen its prounification stance. The NP's unwillingness to shift its policy may also stem from its calculation for electoral competitiveness. Since its establishment, the NP has attempted to make itself a small but pivotal party, like the Free Democratic Party of Germany. Therefore, to pursue the prounification constituency, the NP may just stay at its original position. This rationale is plausible, particularly as the KMT, the NP's major competitor on the unification/independence issue, has moved toward a more modest position.

*Foreign Policy and Taiwan–China Relations*

The never-ending diplomatic strangulation imposed by the PRC over Taiwan has been a major factor in the increased alienation between the two parties across the Taiwan Straits. As mentioned, after achieving economic prosperity and democracy, the Taiwanese people are eager for recognition and respect from the international community. People's resentment of diplomatic isolation has been growing in recent years; this is the reason that all major political parties in Taiwan have argued the promotion of pragmatic diplomacy. The Taiwanese people's determination to win international recognition can be understood by comparing the attitude toward Taiwan–China interactions. According to Table 6.3, "developing Taiwan's diplomatic relations" has been the most popular choice of either all respondents or different partisan groups. Except for the NP identifier, the figures of those supporting this category are particularly high for 1995, the year China began its missile exercises.

This shows that Taiwanese people are inclined to become tougher when suffering higher pressure. In addition, "equally important" is always the second crucial alternative ranked by various categories of interviewees except the NP supporters. This outcome is consistent with the NP's official policy. The previous section has pointed out that, compared with other parties, the NP holds a relatively softer stance toward China. The NP elites insist that Taiwan should do its best to promote cross-strait exchange and avoid angering China when enforcing pragmatic foreign policy. In contrast, among proindependence's DPP identifiers, support for developing Taiwan–China interactions is lower when compared with that of general respondents or other partisan groups. Generally speaking, with regard to the priority of pragmatic diplomacy versus cross-strait interactions, the above data reveal that

Table 6.3    **Public Opinion Toward Foreign Policy and China Policy by Party Identification, 1994–1997**

Q: Which alternatives, "developing Taiwan–Mainland exchanges" or "developing Taiwan's diplomatic relations with other countries," should be the priority?

|  | Taiwan– Mainland exchanges (%) | Taiwan's diplomatic relations (%) | Equally important (%) | Don't know or refuse to answer (%) | N |
|---|---|---|---|---|---|
| All identifiers |  |  |  |  |  |
| 1994 | 20.7 | 31.9 | 26.7 | 20.7 | 1,311 |
| 1995 | 14.2 | 43.4 | 21.2 | 21.2 | 1,425 |
| 1997 | 21.7 | 40.6 | 23.1 | 14.6 | 1,410 |
| KMT identifier |  |  |  |  |  |
| 1994 | 24.9 | 33.3 | 26.5 | 15.3 | 366 |
| 1995 | 14.8 | 46.7 | 23.9 | 14.6 | 514 |
| 1997 | 24.6 | 43.8 | 20.8 | 10.8 | 427 |
| DPP identifier |  |  |  |  |  |
| 1994 | 23.8 | 34.4 | 28.7 | 13.1 | 122 |
| 1995 | 10.4 | 58.4 | 19.7 | 11.6 | 173 |
| 1997 | 21.2 | 49.0 | 23.2 | 6.6 | 198 |
| NP identifier |  |  |  |  |  |
| 1994 | 29.8 | 33.3 | 26.3 | 10.6 | 57 |
| 1995 | 36.7 | 35.6 | 21.1 | 6.6 | 90 |
| 1997 | 30.8 | 39.3 | 25.2 | 4.7 | 107 |
| Nonpartisan |  |  |  |  |  |
| 1994 | 17.5 | 30.7 | 26.5 | 25.3 | 766 |
| 1995 | 11.7 | 37.8 | 19.4 | 31.1 | 648 |
| 1997 | 18.9 | 36.0 | 24.0 | 21.1 | 678 |

*Sources:* 1994, 1995, and 1997 surveys on the Mainland policy and the cross-strait relations. Surveys are conducted by The Election Study Center, National Chengchi University.

there is no significant opinion gap between elite and mass levels in individual parties.

The Taiwanese people's determination to end diplomatic isolation is very clear when we examine the figures, in Table 6.4, from a poll conducted in 1997. In the category of general respondents, 71 percent of them agree that the government should keep developing diplomatic relations regardless of China's warnings. Other figures for the various partisan groups confirm the previous findings. DPP's identifiers are the strongest supporters for pragmatic diplomacy. Next in order is the KMT, and then the NP. It should be noted that nonpartisan voters, the majority of the electorate, have the lowest percentage of those supporting pragmatic diplomacy. This might cause Taiwan's political parties to seek a new balance between diplomatic relations and cross-strait interactions.

Table 6.4    **Public Opinion Toward Foreign Policy and China Policy by Party Identification, 1997**

Q1. Some people argue that our government's active promotion of diplomatic relations will lead to tension between the two sides across the straits. Do you agree with this assertion?

|  | Disagree (%) | Agree (%) | Don't know or no answer (%) | N |
|---|---|---|---|---|
| All identifiers | 42.4 | 41.9 | 15.7 | 1,410 |
| KMT identifier | 43.0 | 44.8 | 12.2 | 427 |
| DPP identifier | 56.5 | 34.1 | 9.4 | 199 |
| NP identifier | 38.2 | 58.1 | 3.7 | 107 |
| Nonpartisan | 38.2 | 40.1 | 21.7 | 677 |

Q2. If our government's active promotion of diplomatic relations leads to tension between the two sides across the straits, do you agree that the government should keep developing diplomatic relations?

|  | Disagree (%) | Agree (%) | Don't know or no answer (%) | N |
|---|---|---|---|---|
| All identifiers | 14.5 | 71.0 | 14.5 | 1,410 |
| KMT identifier | 12.3 | 77.1 | 10.6 | 427 |
| DPP identifier | 13.8 | 79.9 | 6.3 | 199 |
| NP identifier | 26.6 | 68.5 | 4.9 | 107 |
| Nonpartisan | 14.4 | 64.5 | 21.1 | 677 |

*Source:* 1997 survey on the Mainland policy and the cross-strait relations. Survey is conducted by The Election Study Center, National Chengchi University.

## Conclusion

Needless to say, Taiwan's democratization forces the ruling KMT to soften its rigid stance on national identity issues. This shift of official policies, though responding to the trend of Taiwanese public opinions, has encountered resistance from China and the United States. Faced with voices of the Taiwanese people and feedback from the international community, Taiwan's political elites of different parties have had to readjust their positions on national identity issues in order to pursue mass support in electoral competitions. During our studied period, the elite–mass interaction was a reciprocal one and there was no huge gap between the opinions of the elites and the masses. There are several findings from the analysis of mass-level data. First, around 50 percent of Taiwanese people identify themselves as both Taiwanese and Chinese. In addition, increasing Taiwanese identity and decreasing Chinese identity are two significant trends. Second, despite the preferences for different timings for resolving the unification/independence problem, the maintenance of Taiwan's current *de facto* independence is the favorite choice of the Taiwanese people; fewer than 5 percent of respondents ask for immediate independence or unification. Among different options for maintaining the status quo, increasing numbers of Taiwanese people have chosen to leave the unification/independence problem open in the future, rather than presuppose any solution. Additionally, compared with the change of opinion on the national identity issue, the proportional change of opinion on the unification/independence issue is relatively moderate. This implies that people become more realistic and cautious when faced with the unification/independence issue. Third, most Taiwanese people highly support pragmatic diplomacy. In the survey of 1997, around 70 percent of respondents supported promotion of pragmatic diplomacy, even if this would cause Taiwan–China tensions.

Taiwan's two major parties—the KMT and the DPP—undoubtedly follow the directions of public opinion. Both parties have emphasized their efforts in maintaining the island's status quo. Although the KMT and the DPP do not renounce their traditional goals—Chinese unification and Taiwan's independence, respectively—they have regarded the goals as a far and ideal dream. For the KMT and the DPP, currently it is unnecessary to take any concrete action to achieve the goals. With regard to the NP, there is no any sign that it will soon lessen its prounification stance or moderate its soft attitude toward the PRC. This study argues that the NP's unwillingness to shift its policy is mainly due to its calculation for electoral competitiveness. To pursue the prounification constituency, the NP may just hold to its original position. This rationale is credible, particularly when the KMT, the NP's major competitor, has hesitated to recommend concrete policies for Chinese unification.

## Note

1. Data analyzed below were collected by The Election Study Center, National Chengchi University, Taiwan. The author appreciates the assistance of the institute, but the views expressed herein are the author's own.

## Bibliography

Baumgartner, Frank R., and Bryan D. Jones. 1993. *Agendas and Instability in American Politics*. Chicago: University of Chicago Press.
Bosso, Christopher J. 1987. *Pesticides and Politics: The Life Cycle of a Public Issue*. Pittsburgh, PA: University of Pittsburgh Press.

Carmines, Edward G., and James A. Stimson. 1989. *Issue Evolution: Race and the Transformation of American Politics*. Princeton, NJ: Princeton University Press.

Cheng Tun-jen and Yung-ming Hsu. 1996. "Issue Structure, the DPP's Factionalism, and Party Realignment." In *Taiwan's Electoral Politics and Democratization: Riding the Third Wave*. Ed. Hung-mao Tien. Armonk: M.E. Sharpe, 137–173.

Chinese New Party. 1995. *The Policy White Paper of the Chinese New Party*. Taipei: Chinese New Party (in Chinese).

Chu, Yun-han, and Tse-min Lin. 1996. "The Process of Democratic Consolidation in Taiwan: Social Cleavage, Electoral Competition, and the Emerging Party System." In *Taiwan's Electoral Politics and Democratization: Riding the Third Wave*. Ed. Hung-mao Tien. Armonk: M.E. Sharpe, 79–104.

Cobb, Roger W., and Charles D. Elder. 1972. *Participation in American Politics: The Dynamics of Agenda-Building*. Baltimore, MD: Johns Hopkins University Press.

Democratic Progressive Party. 1993. *The Policy White Paper*. Taipei: Democratic Progressive Party (in Chinese).

———. 1995. *Giving Taiwan a Chance: The DPP's Platforms for the 1995 and 1996 Elections*. Taipei: Chieh Wei Press (in Chinese).

Hughes, Christopher. 1997. *Taiwan and Chinese Nationalism: National Identity and Status in International Society*. New York: Routledge.

Kingdon, John. 1995. *Agendas, Alternatives, and Public Policies*. 2d ed. Boston, MA: Little, Brown.

Mainland Affairs Council. 1997. *Consensus Formed at the National Development Conference on Cross-strait Relations*. Taipei: Mainland Affairs Council.

Wachman, Alan. 1994. *Taiwan: National Identity and Democratization*. Armonk: M.E. Sharpe.

Zaller, John R. 1992. *The Nature and Origins of Mass Opinion*. Cambridge: Cambridge University Press.

# 7

# National Identity and Ethnicity in Taiwan

## Some Trends in the 1990s

### Robert Marsh

This chapter argues that to analyze the future national identity of the people of Taiwan, two considerations are central: the will of the people and geopolitical constraints on Taiwan's independence. As for the first, politicians say "The future of Taiwan should be decided by the residents of Taiwan." But we cannot assume, as some political activists do, that "self-determination" necessarily means "Taiwan nationalism" and "Taiwan independence" (Shu 1997–98, 100). Survey research is a good tool for uncovering attitudes toward Taiwan independence, reunification with China, and other types of national identification.

Among the population of Taiwan, those who favor the establishment of an independent Republic of Taiwan face the reality constraint that the People's Republic of China (PRC) has not renounced the use of military force to prevent what, in Beijing's logic, is regarded as "the loss of Taiwan." Supporters of the opposite type of national identity—reunification of Taiwan with Mainland China—also face a reality constraint: the nondemocratic, economically less developed character of the PRC. Surveys of attitudes in Taiwan toward future national identity made a significant advance in 1992, when researchers began annually to use Wu Nai-teh's new formulation and to ask respondents,

1. If, after Taiwan announced its independence, it could maintain peaceful relations with the Chinese Communist government, then Taiwan should become an independent country. Do you agree?
2. If Mainland China and Taiwan were to become similar in economic, social, and political conditions, then the two sides of the strait should be united into one country. Do you agree?

Table 7.1 **National Identification Preferences of the People of Taiwan**

| Taiwan Independence if no military threat from China | Unification with China if China becomes similar to Taiwan in political, economic and social conditions | | |
|---|---|---|---|
|  | Agree | No answer | Disagree |
| Agree | Pragmatist |  | Taiwan nationalist |
| No answer |  |  |  |
| Disagree | China nationalist |  | Conservative |

*Source:* Adapted from Wu 1997, 4, table 1.

The second view is basically the position of President Lee Teng-hui, who stated in an address to the National Unification Council on July 22, 1998, "China must be reunified. However, this reunification must be under a system of democracy, freedom, and equitable prosperity. . . . The nation should by no means be unified under the proven failure of Communism or the so-called one country, two systems formula" (Taiwan Research Institute 1998, 5). Even the PRC regime is aware that China's present political institutions and economy are more alienating than appealing to Taiwan residents.

From answers to these two questions, Wu (1993, 1997) and Shen and Wu (1998) classified respondents according to four types of national identification preferences: Taiwan nationalists, China nationalists, pragmatists, and conservatives (see Table 7.1).

1. *Taiwan nationalists* favor Taiwan independence and oppose unification with China even if China becomes as democratic and economically developed as Taiwan.
2. *China nationalists* favor unification with the Mainland and oppose Taiwan independence even if Taiwan could have peaceful relations with the PRC after independence. These China nationalists oppose Taiwan independence not because this would threaten Taiwan's security, but because they see Taiwan independence as morally wrong.
3. Instead of favoring one and opposing the other of the two preceding alternatives concerning national identification, *pragmatists* favor Taiwan independence (providing that does not provoke a military attack from China), and *also* favor unification with the Mainland (if China catches up with the level of democracy and economic development in Taiwan). In real terms, of course, Taiwan independence and unification with China are mutually exclusive. Therefore, by implication, these people are saying, "Pragmatically, I'll accept whichever of the two outcomes occurs first. If China becomes as

Table 7.2   **Changes in Attitudes Toward National Identification in Taiwan, 1992–1996**

| National Identification Preference | February 1992 | | February 1993 | | July 1994 | | May 1996 | |
|---|---|---|---|---|---|---|---|---|
| | N | % | N | % | N | % | N | % |
| Taiwan Nationalist | 116 | 9.3 | 138 | 10.3 | 135 | 9.4 | 298 | 21.2 |
| Pragmatist | 311 | 25.0 | 341 | 25.4 | 346 | 24.1 | 548 | 39.0 |
| China Nationalist | 472 | 38.0 | 371 | 27.6 | 355 | 24.7 | 237 | 16.9 |
| Conservative | 137 | 11.0 | 100 | 7.4 | 85 | 5.9 | 40 | 2.8 |
| Other* | 207 | 16.7 | 393 | 29.3 | 516 | 35.9 | 283 | 20.1 |
| Total | 1,243 | 100.0 | 1,343 | 100.0 | 1,437 | 100.0 | 1,406 | 100.0 |

*Sources:* For 1992 and 1993, Wu 1997, 4, table 1; for 1994, Yi 1994; for 1996, Hu Fu's Presidential Election survey.
*N.A. to one or both questions.

democratic and economically developed as Taiwan *before* it renounces the use of force to prevent Taiwan independence, I'll agree to unification with China. But if China, still not as democratic or economically developed as Taiwan, renounces force as a means of preventing Taiwan independence, I'll favor Taiwan independence."

4. Conservatives reject both Taiwan independence and unification with Mainland China, even under the hypothetical ideal conditions posited by the two questions. They prefer the status quo in which Taiwan is and will remain the Republic of China (ROC), with some but not all the attributes of an internationally recognized sovereign nation. Neither a Republic of Taiwan nor the PRC appeals to them as a national identity.

**Trends in National Identification**

Let us first examine how these four types of national identification were distributed in "The Social Image" surveys done in Taiwan in 1992, 1993, and 1994 and in the Taiwan presidential election survey of 1996 (see Table 7.2).[1] Between the 1994 and 1996 surveys, the PRC fired missiles into waters near Taiwan's two largest ports, in effect blockading them for a while. Let us see if this military aggression affected national identification preferences in 1996.

Scholars and others who advocate Taiwan independence have emphasized that the proportion of respondents who were Taiwan nationalists, only 9 to 10 percent in 1992–1994, more than doubled to 21 percent in 1996, while China nationalists steadily declined, from 38 percent in 1992 to only 17 percent in 1996. Conservatives (who favor the status quo rather than independence or unification, even under the ideal conditions posed hypothetically in the questions) became an endangered species, declining from 11 percent in 1992 to only 3 percent in 1996. But previous analysts have not given sufficient attention to the rise of the pragmatists, from 25 percent in 1992 to 39 percent in 1996. Pragmatists were much more numerous than either Taiwan nationalists or China nationalists in 1996. Recall that pragmatists accept both Taiwan independence and unification with China, whichever first meets the ideal condition of either peaceful postindependence relations of Taiwan with the PRC or the PRC's "catching up" with Taiwan's level of democratic and economic development. Finally, we must note that in Table 7.2, a considerable minority in each sample—ranging from 17 percent to 36 percent—by refusing to answer one or both of the questions, rejected all four of the foregoing types of national identity.

**Effect of Ethnicity on National Identification**

Traditionally, ethnicity in Taiwan is the registration-based distinction between Taiwanese (*Benshengren*, including Minnan and Hakka) and Mainlanders (*Waishengren*). How closely related is ethnicity to national identification? (Chang 1993). Between 1992 and 1996, the trends already noted in the overall samples were also true for Taiwanese: Taiwan nationalists and pragmatists increased, while China nationalists decreased (see Table 7.3). But what earlier analysts have not remarked enough is that even after the 1996 missile firing, more Minnan and Hakka Taiwanese were pragmatists (39 percent) than Taiwan nationalists (23 percent). Among Mainlanders in Taiwan, the missile firing appears to have decreased the percentage who are China nationalists. But Mainlanders did not become Taiwan nationalists; rather, 38 percent had become pragmatists by 1996, and the absolutely largest group of Mainlanders (42 percent) continued to be China nationalists, even in 1996.

Going against proindependence feelings are the findings in Table 7.3 that, both before and after the provocative military aggression of the PRC in 1995 and 1996, Mainlanders in Taiwan were more likely to support unification with China (if and when it became as developed politically and economically as Taiwan) than were Minnan and Hakka respondents to support Taiwan independence (even assuming this could be achieved in the future without a war with China).

**Ethnic Consciousness**

The conventional classification of the population of Taiwan into *Benshengren* and *Waishengren* uses the social construct, *jiguan*, as the ba-

Table 7.3  **Changes in Attitudes Toward National Identification Among Taiwanese (Minnan and Hakka) and Mainlanders in Taiwan, 1992, 1993, and 1996**

| National Identification Preference | 1992 | | 1993 | | 1996 | |
|---|---|---|---|---|---|---|
| | N | % | N | % | N | % |
| | Minnan and Hakka | | | | | |
| Taiwan Nationalist | 112 | 10.4 | 131 | 11.3 | 286 | 23.2 |
| Pragmatist | 287 | 26.7 | 312 | 26.9 | 483 | 39.2 |
| China Nationalist | 372 | 34.6 | 238 | 20.6 | 166 | 13.5 |
| Other* | 305 | 28.3 | 477 | 41.2 | 298 | 24.1 |
| Total | 1,076 | 100.0 | 1,158 | 100.0 | 1,233 | 100.0 |
| | Mainlanders | | | | | |
| Taiwan Nationalist | 1 | 0.7 | 6 | 3.0 | 11 | 6.6 |
| Pragmatist | 24 | 15.8 | 25 | 12.6 | 63 | 37.7 |
| China Nationalist | 95 | 62.5 | 112 | 56.6 | 70 | 41.9 |
| Other* | 32 | 21.0 | 55 | 27.8 | 23 | 13.8 |
| Total | 152 | 100.0 | 198 | 100.0 | 167 | 100.0 |

*Sources:* For 1992, Wu 1993, 48, table 2; for 1993, Wu 1997, 8, table 2; and for 1996, Hu Fu's Presidential Election survey.

*"Other" combines Conservatives (see Table 7.1) and those who did not answer one or both of the questions. Given the data available, it is not possible to separate these two categories, as was done in Table 7.2.

sis for an administratively defined ethnicity (see the inquiry in chapter 8 into the historical construction of these new ethnic labels after the Retrocession). It classifies a person not by his or her subjective ethnic identification or ethnic consciousness, but by province of registration. The obvious question is: To what extent do *Benshengren* think of themselves as Taiwanese? To what extent do *Waishengren* (an increasing proportion of whom as respondents in these surveys are the children or grandchildren of late–1940s migrants from the Mainland to Taiwan, who themselves have never lived on the Mainland) think of themselves as *Zhongguoren* (Chinese)? Wu (1997) has suggested that subjective ethnic consciousness may be an important intervening variable, moderating the influence of bureaucratically defined ethnicity on national identification preferences. In other words, the hypotheses are

1. Ethnic self-identification as "Taiwanese" will strengthen the tendency of Taiwanese persons to be Taiwan nationalists
2. Ethnic self-identification as *Zhongguoren* will strengthen the likelihood that a *Waishengren* will be a China nationalist

3. Ethnic self-identification as both Taiwanese and Chinese will cause Taiwanese persons to favor Taiwan nationalism less than those referred to in hypothesis 1 and will make *Waishengren* favor China nationalism less than those referred to in hypothesis 2.

Before testing these hypotheses, let us see how subjective ethnicity (ethnic consciousness) has been measured and whether it has changed during the 1990s. In surveys conducted in 1992, 1994 and 1996 (Shen and Wu 1998:14, 15), respondents were asked, "If someone asks you whether you are Chinese or Taiwanese, what do you say?" The response categories were

1. Taiwanese
2. Taiwanese and also Chinese
3. Chinese and also Taiwanese
4. Chinese
5. other

Table 7.4a shows how the distribution of these types of ethnic self-identification changed among Taiwanese (*Benshengren*); Table 7.4b shows this distribution among Mainlanders (*Waishengren*). Among the Taiwanese, between 1992 and 1996, self-identification as Taiwanese increased from 29.4 percent to 44.1 percent, while identifying as Chinese decreased from 35 percent to 13.4 percent. Identification as both Taiwanese and Chinese (categories 2 and 3 in the responses to the above question) remained relatively constant between 35.6 percent and 42.4 percent. Thus, the trend of ethnic consciousness among Taiwanese has been for exclusively Taiwanese identity to be substituted for exclusively Chinese identity. But the 1996 survey also shows that even after the firing of the PRC missiles, almost as many *Benshengren* thought of themselves as both Taiwanese and Chinese (42.4 percent) as thought of themselves as exclusively Taiwanese (44.1 percent).

Looking next at the *Waishengren* respondents in Table 7.4b, we see that over the period from 1992 to 1996 there was a precipitous decline, from 77.3 percent to 36.4 percent, in the propensity to define oneself exclusively as Chinese. But the shift in Mainlanders' ethnic self-identification was not to Taiwanese, but to "I'm both Chinese and Taiwanese" (from 20 percent in 1992 to 55.9 percent in 1996). Note that this shift among Mainlanders from Chinese to both Chinese and Taiwanese cannot be explained simply by the shock of the PRC missile firing, as the trend was already under way between the 1992 and the 1994 surveys, before the missile incidents. The most that can be inferred about the effect of the missiles is that they pushed further a trend in ethnic self-identification already under way.

**Ethnicity, Ethnic Consciousness, and National Identification**

We can now test the hypotheses stated earlier about whether ethnic self-identification—ethnic consciousness—strengthens the effect of bureaucratically defined ethnicity upon national identification. The data are shown in Tables 7.4a and 7.4b. To test hypothesis 1 we compare (a) the percentage of *Benshengren* who were Taiwan nationalists with (b) how much this percentage increases when we know the *Benshengren* also had a Taiwanese ethnic self-identification, in each of the three survey years. To test hypothesis 2 we compare (a) the percentage of *Waishengren* who were China nationalists with (b) how much this percentage increases when we know the *Waishengren* also had a Chinese self-identification. For ease of comprehension, these comparisons are as follows:

|  | 1992 | 1994 | 1995 |
|---|---|---|---|
|  | % Taiwan nationalists | | |
| Among *Benshengren:* | | | |
| Bureaucratically defined Taiwanese | 18.4 | 19.9 | 30.8 |
| Bureaucratically defined Taiwanese who | | | |
| also think of themselves as Taiwanese | 32.9 | 29.7 | 46.9 |
|  | % China nationalists | | |
| Among *Waishengren:* | | | |
| Bureaucratically defined Mainlanders | 78.2 | 67.7 | 48.2 |
| Bureaucratically defined Mainlanders who | | | |
| also think of themselves as Chinese | 82.8 | 76.1 | 57.7 |

Hypotheses 1 and 2 are both supported. Knowing that a person's subjective ethnicity (ethnic self-identification) is *either* "Taiwanese" or "Chinese" enables us to predict his or her national identification preference better than when we know only that person's bureaucratically defined ethnicity. Note also that this increase based on ethnic self-identification is larger among *Benshengren* than among *Waishengren* in each of the three survey years.

Hypothesis 3 is also confirmed: Among people whose subjective ethnicity is both Chinese and Taiwanese, (a) bureaucratically defined Taiwanese favor Taiwan nationalism less than those referred to in hypothesis 1; and (b) bureaucratically defined Mainlanders favor China nationalism less than those referred to in hypothesis 2. Put another way: As hypothesis 3 states, people whose ethnic self-identification is "both Chinese and Taiwanese" are in the

Table 7.4a **Bureaucracy-Defined Ethnicity, Ethnic Self-Identification, and National Identification in Taiwan, 1992, 1994, and 1996** (Ethnicity: Taiwanese)

| | Ethnic Self-Identification | | | | | | | |
| | Zhongguoren | | Both Chinese and Taiwanese | | Taiwanese | | Total | |
| National Identification | N | % | N | % | N | % | N | % |
|---|---|---|---|---|---|---|---|---|
| | | | | 1992 | | | | |
| China Nationalist | 182 | 53.4 | 125 | 36.1 | 39 | 13.6 | 346 | 35.6 |
| Pragmatist | 119 | 34.9 | 176 | 50.9 | 153 | 53.5 | 448 | 46.0 |
| Taiwan Nationalist | 40 | 11.7 | 45 | 13.0 | 94 | 32.9 | 179 | 18.4 |
| Total | 341 | 100.0 | 346 | 100.0 | 286 | 100.0 | 973 | 100.0 |
| | | 35.0 | | 35.6 | | 29.4 | | 100.0 |
| | | | | 1994 | | | | |
| China Nationalist | 67 | 60.9 | 70 | 31.1 | 36 | 16.2 | 173 | 31.1 |
| Pragmatist | 33 | 30.0 | 120 | 53.3 | 120 | 54.1 | 273 | 49.0 |
| Taiwan Nationalist | 10 | 9.1 | 35 | 15.6 | 66 | 29.7 | 111 | 19.9 |
| Total | 110 | 100.0 | 225 | 100.0 | 222 | 100.0 | 557 | 100.0 |
| | | 19.7 | | 40.4 | | 39.9 | | 100.0 |
| | | | | 1996 | | | | |
| China Nationalist | 43 | 34.7 | 87 | 22.3 | 32 | 7.9 | 162 | 17.6 |
| Pragmatist | 70 | 56.4 | 221 | 56.7 | 183 | 45.2 | 474 | 51.6 |
| Taiwan Nationalist | 11 | 8.9 | 82 | 21.0 | 190 | 46.9 | 283 | 30.8 |
| Total | 124 | 100.0 | 390 | 100.0 | 405 | 100.0 | 919 | 100.0 |
| | | 13.4 | | 42.4 | | 44.1 | | 100.0 |

*Source:* Shen and Wu 1998, 14–15, tables 1 and 2 for 1992 and 1994; for 1996 data, Hu Fu's Presidential Election survey.

middle, are less likely to be Taiwan nationalists than those who think of themselves as only Taiwanese, and are less likely to be China nationalists than those who identify themselves as only Chinese.

One last question about the survey data: Are bureaucratically defined and subjective ethnicity the most important influences on attitudes toward national identification in Taiwan? What about the influence of gender, age, education, economic status, and social class? The 1996 presidential election survey data do indicate that ethnicity is more important than these other variables. Using tau-c as the statistical measure of strength of association between variables, respondents' ethnic self-identification (Taiwanese, Chinese, or both Taiwanese and Chinese) has the strongest relationship to national identification (.32***),[2] followed by bureaucratically defined ethnicity (father is *Benshengren* vs. Mainlander) with a tau-c of .18**), education (.09**), and marital status (.04*). Other variables, including age, gender, number of wage earners in one's household, household income, and social class identi-

Table 7.4b   **Bureaucracy-Defined Ethnicity, Ethnic Self-Identification, and National Identification in Taiwan, 1992, 1994, and 1996** (Ethnicity: Mainlander)

| | | | Ethnic Self-Identification | | | | | |
| | *Zhongguoren* | | Both Chinese and Taiwanese | | Taiwanese | | Total | |
| National Identification | N | % | N | % | N | % | N | % |
| --- | --- | --- | --- | --- | --- | --- | --- | --- |
| | | | | 1992 | | | | |
| China Nationalist | 144 | 82.8 | 30 | 66.7 | 2 | 33.3 | 176 | 78.2 |
| Pragmatist | 21 | 12.1 | 15 | 33.3 | 2 | 33.3 | 38 | 16.9 |
| Taiwan Nationalist | 9 | 5.2 | 0 | 0 | 2 | 33.3 | 11 | 4.9 |
| Total | 174 | 100.1 | 45 | 100.0 | 6 | 100.0 | 225 | 100.0 |
| | | 77.3 | | 20.0 | | 2.7 | | 100.0 |
| | | | | 1994 | | | | |
| China Nationalist | 102 | 76.1 | 51 | 63.8 | 8 | 33.3 | 161 | 67.7 |
| Pragmatist | 26 | 19.4 | 20 | 25.0 | 10 | 41.7 | 56 | 23.5 |
| Taiwan Nationalist | 6 | 4.5 | 9 | 11.3 | 6 | 25.0 | 21 | 8.8 |
| Total | 134 | 100.0 | 80 | 100.1 | 24 | 100.0 | 238 | 100.0 |
| | | 56.3 | | 33.6 | | 10.1 | | 100.0 |
| | | | | 1996 | | | | |
| China Nationalist | 30 | 57.7 | 36 | 45.0 | 3 | 27.3 | 69 | 48.2 |
| Pragmatist | 20 | 38.5 | 37 | 46.3 | 6 | 54.5 | 63 | 44.1 |
| Taiwan Nationalist | 2 | 3.8 | 7 | 8.8 | 2 | 18.2 | 11 | 7.7 |
| Total | 52 | 100.0 | 80 | 100.1 | 11 | 100.0 | 143 | 100.0 |
| | | 36.4 | | 55.9 | | 7.7 | | 100.0 |

*Source:* Shen and Wu 1998, 14–15, tables 1 and 2 for 1992 and 1994; for 1996 data, Hu Fu's Presidential Election survey.

fication had no significant relationship to whether one was a Taiwan nationalist, a China nationalist, a pragmatist or a conservative. Thus, researchers are on the right track when they focus on bureaucratically defined and subjective ethnicity as the key variables in understanding national identification. In other words, what divides people in Taiwan in their views on Taiwan independence versus unification with China has more to do with their ethnicity than with their education, age, gender, economic position, and social class identification.

**Geopolitical Constraints: Comparative Analysis**

I have been struck by the fact that advocates of Taiwan independence typically do not take into account what is known about the history of outcomes of secessionist movements in other times and places. Is the Taiwan/PRC case so atypical that the comparative record is irrelevant?

Without claiming to present an exhaustive analysis, let us use Hechter's (1992) classification of four types of outcomes of secessionist movements:

1. Pure secession
2. Successful secession from an ineffective state
3. Successful secession despite resistance from the predecessor state
4. Unsuccessful attempts at secession

The first type of outcome—pure secession—occurs when an effective state *permits* a secessionist territory to withdraw. In the twentieth century this has occurred only twice: when Norway left Sweden in 1905 and when Ireland left the United Kingdom in 1922 (Hechter 1992; Thomas 1994). The secession of Singapore from Malaysia in 1965 is a partial example of this type. Although the Malaysian State allowed the peaceful secession of Singapore, there was conflict involving actors other than the State. In the summer of 1965 there were serious ethnic riots in Singapore. But even before this unrest became manifest, the prime minister of Malaysia, the Tunku Abdul Rahman, had decided that Singapore's secession would be desirable because it would improve Malaysia's stability (Young 1994). Chinese-dominated Singapore was jettisoned by the Malays of Malaysia, who wanted to reduce the proportion of Chinese in their state (Thomas 1994).

The secession of Eritrea from Ethiopia is also a partial example of type 1. At first, successive Ethiopian governments fought civil wars to prevent Eritrea's independence. But in 1991 a government came to power in Ethiopia that was sympathetic to Eritrean national aspirations and permitted Eritrea to become independent (*Europa World Handbook* 1998, 1225). This first type of secession is impossible in Taiwan's case, since it is extremely unlikely the PRC would ever want to evict Taiwan or allow it to secede peacefully.

The second type, successful secession from an ineffective state, is illustrated by the several new states that emerged between 1991 and 1993 from the dissolution of the Soviet Union (Azerbaijan, Georgia, Kazakhstan, etc.), Yugoslavia (Bosnia and Herzegovina, Croatia and Macedonia), and Czechoslovakia (Czech Republic and Slovak Republic). Since the PRC shows no signs of dissolving as a state, this type of secession does not fit Taiwan's case.

The third type of outcome occurs when the secessionist movement is successful despite the resistance of the predecessor state. This type rarely occurs. The basic reason for this is that although the emergence of a secessionist movement is determined by internal, domestic politics, the success of the movement "is determined largely by international politics, by the balance of interests and forces that extend beyond the state" (Horowitz 1981, 167). Given that the state will normally resort to force to prevent secession, the few instances of successful independence movements are due to the support and intervention of foreign states. Two examples can be cited. When the American colonies declared independence from Great Britain in 1776, Britain went to war to prevent it. The Americans won that war only because Britain was distracted by its major war with France and the Americans gained the military support of France against Britain. The American victory at Yorktown, the final battle of that war, was due to a naval victory of the French fleet over the British fleet near Chesapeake Bay.

In the twentieth century many of the postcolonial "new states" were grotesquely artificial units, reflecting only the vagaries of the boundaries drawn by colonial administrators. Despite this, the central fact is that of all the attempted secession movements, only Bangladesh succeeded. East Pakistan rose in riots and strikes in 1971 after being denied victory at the polls. West Pakistan's armed attacks on the Bengalis of East Pakistan led to a war between India and Pakistan later that year. India's victory permitted the Bengalis to establish their own independent state, Bangladesh. The USSR also provided arms to India. By contrast, Pakistan's allies, notably the United States and the People's Republic of China, did not intervene to preempt or upset India's assistance (Heraclides 1990, 349). This suggests that unless one or more states is willing to go to war against China to help Taiwan achieve full independence, this type is also inapplicable to Taiwan.

The last type of outcome, by far the most common, is unsuccessful attempts at secession. These failures (thus far) include Katanga in Zaire, Biafra in Nigeria, the Sudds in Sudan, the Kurds in Iraq, and the Moro Muslims in the southern Philippines. The PRC crushed Tibetan separatism in the1950s and Indonesia suppressed the Timorese in the 1980s. Since independence, some ethnic groups in South Asia have passed through such stages as ethnic disaffection, autonomy demands, and finally insurgent separatist demands. "The last step has invariably provoked state violence to prevent separation" (Thomas 1994, 98).

Specialists on secession and independence movements have identified the structural reasons why successful secession in the face of state resistance is so unlikely. As a normative concept, the modern state has two universal properties, strongly supported by the international state system—territoriality and sovereignty. Sovereignty "is the untrammeled prerogative of the state to the exercise of authority within its territory and over the population contained within its frontiers" (Young 1976, 68). Each state is defined in terms of its territorial integrity: "The existing international regime favors the territorial integrity of states at any costs" (Heraclides 1990, 377).

Independence movement activists cite the principle of self-determination to justify their action. The UN principle of the right of self-determination was originally framed in the context of decolonization after World War II. Once independence from colonial rule had been achieved, the concept of self-determination was not thought to continue to apply to subunits seeking secession from those new states. Nixon (1972) has pointed out that "self-determination" as a UN principle was in conflict with another UN principle: "Any attempt aimed at the partial or total disruption of the national unit and the territorial integrity of a country is incompatible with the purposes and principles of the Charter of the United Nations" (Nixon 1972, 473–74). States are only too aware of the demonstration effect and fear that successful separatism in one nation will encourage separatist threats in other states (Islam 1985, 213). Another factor is that it is not always clear, in a given independence movement using the argument of "self-determination," who is the "self" in self-determination. And even when that "self" is defined, who within the designated community has the authority to make binding commitments for the whole? (Nixon 1972).

The conclusion of my comparative analysis is that, in Hechter's words, "If there is one constant in history . . . it is the reluctance of states to part with territory" (Hechter 1992, 277). "No matter how united secessionists are in their desire for independence, the central power holders opposed withdrawal with all the force they could muster" (Young 1976).

## Geopolitical Constraints and Taiwan

The DPP and other Taiwan independence activists claim Taiwan is *de facto* already a sovereign state. This is true in the sense that the ROC government exercises exclusive control over internal affairs within Taiwan. But it is not true in that the ROC lacks several key defining characteristics of a sovereign member of the international community: for example, diplomatic relations with all other nations, a seat in the UN and other international organizations, the ability of the ROC president to travel abroad in that formal role. This paper has argued that the problem of the future national identity of Taiwan should be analyzed in terms of two paramount considerations: the will of the people and geopolitical constraints.

Interpretation of the survey data in this paper is another instance of the question: Is the glass half-full or half-empty? Advocates of Taiwanese ethnic nationalism and the independence of Taiwan have stressed the trend: The proportion of the population who are Taiwan nationalists has undoubtedly been increasing, while support for unification with China has been declining. But the data can just as validly be interpreted as showing that even after the firing of missiles at Taiwan by the PRC, only one-fifth of the population favored Taiwan independence, even if this could be achieved without war with the PRC. The largest sentiment (39 percent) favored pragmatism—the acceptance of either unification or independence, depending upon which of the ideal conditions—peaceful relations between Taiwan and the PRC after independence, or China's "catching up" with Taiwan in its level of political and economic development—occurs first. And despite the trend, we have seen that in 1996, even after the missile crisis and even among Taiwanese who self-identified as Taiwanese (rather than Chinese or "both"), the percentage who were Taiwan nationalists (47 percent) had still not reached the halfway point.

In response to these realities, the DPP transformed its view of independence in more reformist terms. The goal of abolishing the ROC system and establishing an independent Republic of Taiwan "is to be pursued through democratic procedures such as referenda; until the majority of Taiwanese people agree to this platform, the DPP is willing to accept the name of ROC" (Shu 1997–98, 108). If the DPP waits until the majority of the population are Taiwan nationalists, it may have to wait some time. Much experience indicates that we cannot assume that a trend observed over a few years will continue in the same direction.

The hypothetical survey question asked in Taiwan since 1992—Do you favor Taiwan independence if Taiwan could continue to have peaceful relations with the Chinese Communist government?—is a powerful method of uncovering popular opinion. But it obviously begs the question of whether the PRC will ever allow this loss of territory, which would be so significant, both materially and symbolically. In July 1998, the PRC's State Council issued what it called its first public defense policy review in three years. The review asserted the PRC's right to "resort to force" against Taiwan (Taiwan Research Institute 1998, 1). Peking is obsessed with Taiwan: Because it was once lost to Japan, Taiwan is a vestige of national humiliation, and should never be lost to China again. But Peking also has strategic motives: Taiwan is centered in a chain of islands running from Indonesia and the Philippines to Japan and Russia's Kamchatka Peninsula, and control of this coastal zone is key to Peking's plans to become a dominant military power in the region (Halloran and Mehta 1998, 7).

If Peking has the intention to use military force to prevent Taiwan independence, it is also developing the capability to do this. The Chinese Communists are currently deploying missiles in Fujian and Jiangxi provinces across the strait from Taiwan. These are the same type the Mainland test-fired into waters near Taiwan in 1996. Peking is also developing its own cruise missiles and submarines, and its military textbooks use Taiwan as the hypothetical target in attack scenarios (*Free China Journal* 1998).

As to the other element in the geopolitical equation—the U.S. role—Washington has, since the 1972 Shanghai communiqué, "acknowledged" the rival claims of Taipei and Peking to sovereignty over Taiwan (Halloran and Mehta 1998, 7). The U.S. government has become increasingly firm in its refusal to support a Taiwan bid for independence and has informed the DPP of this in no uncertain terms (Shaw 1998, 7).

Since the majority in the 1996 survey are pragmatists, not Taiwan nationalists, let us follow out the implications of this. Pragmatists can be seen as swing voters. If the time comes when the PRC would accept Taiwan's independence, pragmatists could swing to join Taiwan nationalists and that group would become the majority (the 39 percent in Table 7.2 who were pragmatists in 1996 would join the 21.2 percent who were Taiwan nationalists, making a total of 60.2 percent who were Taiwan nationalists). But if China's democratization and economic development occur before this major change in the PRC's policy toward Taiwan independence, pragmatists in that event could swing to support unification with China, and then China nationalists would become the majority (39 percent + 16.9 percent = 55.9 percent in Table 7.2).

Pragmatists will accept either unification with the PRC or Taiwan independence, depending on which ideal condition is realized first, we must ask: Given everything we know about the relevant contextual factors, which condition is likely to occur first in the future:

—the PRC lets Taiwan declare independence and remains in peaceful relations with Taiwan;

—the PRC catches up with the level of democracy and economic development in Taiwan?

In my view, while neither outcome can be taken for granted, the first alternative is unlikely ever to happen, for the basic geopolitical reason identified earlier in our comparative analysis: Sovereign states do not countenance the loss of what they regard as their territory. Given this, Taiwan's independence could be accomplished, even temporarily, only at a time when the PRC is heavily distracted by an internal crisis and/or a foreign conflict with a nation or nations other than Taiwan.

Barring the first alternative, the second—the PRC becomes as democratic and economically developed as Taiwan—is the more likely to happen first. In this case, the conditions for unification with China would be more favorable. Note, however, that even if China at some future time becomes a democracy, it still would not accept Taiwan's independence peacefully. The generalization that "democracies do not fight wars against other democracies" may be valid *except* when one democracy faces a loss of its territorial integrity to another democracy. Again, it does not matter that the PRC has never in fact exercised sovereign control over Taiwan. It gained control over Mainland China by military force and to date has not achieved control over Taiwan by those means. What matters is that the PRC claims this control over Taiwan and has both the intention and, increasingly, the capability, of carrying it out.

## Conclusion

The survey data that reveal the will of the people and geopolitical considerations lead to the same conclusion. Although attitudes show a trend toward Taiwan independence and away from unification with China, an even stronger trend supports pragmatism. Pragmatists support Taiwan independence *if* the PRC accepts this and remains in peaceful relations with Taiwan. But pragmatists also favor reunification with Mainland China *if* the PRC catches up with the level of democracy and economic development in Taiwan. Whether Taiwan retains (or increases) or loses its present level of independence and sovereignty therefore depends upon which of these two scenarios is the more likely to occur first.

## Notes

1. There are two sources of data for this paper. The first is "The Social Image Survey in Taiwan" sponsored by the National Science Council, Republic of China (NSC83–0301–H001–050–B1), conducted in 1992, 1993, and 1994. This research project was carried out by the Sun Yat-sen Institute for Social Sciences and Philosophy of the Academia Sinica, and directed by Yi Chin-chun. The Office of Survey Research of Academia Sinica is responsible for the data distribution. My second source is the 1996 Taiwan Presidential Election survey conducted by a team led by Hu Fu of the Department of Political Science, National Taiwan University and the Workshop on Political Systems and Political Changes. Hu Fu and Hu Chin of Syracuse University kindly provided me with the data from the 1996 survey. Dr. Wu Nai-teh also gave me much useful information and help. I appreciate the assistance of these scholars and organizations. The views expressed herein are the author's own.

2. Asterisks (*) following the numbers in this sentence have the conventional statistical meaning. Each refers to the probability that the relationship between a given pair of variables could have occurred by chance. One asterisk indicates a .05 level of probability, two asterisks a .01 level, and three a .001 level. Thus, the .32*** tau-c means that a relationship as strong as .32 between respondents' ethnic self-identification and their national identification could have occurred by chance less than one in a thousand times (.001). In other words, it is a relationship that can be taken seriously as "real," rather than the product of random chance.

## Bibliography

Chang Mau-kuei. 1993. "Shengji wenti yu minzu zhuyi" (The ethnic problem and nationalism). In *Zuqun guanxi yu guojia rentong* (Ethnic relations and national identity). Ed. Chang Mau-kuei et al. Taipei: Yeqiang, 233–278.

*The Europa World Handbook 1998.* London: Europa Publications.

*Free China Journal,* October 2, 1998:1.

Halloran, Richard, and Manik Mehta. 1998. "Comments on Taiwan Ties by U.S. Leader Rankle Allies." *Free China Journal* (July 17): 7.

Hechter, Michael. 1992. "The Dynamics of Secession." *Acta Sociologica* 35:267–283.

Heraclides, Alexis. 1990. "Secessionist Minorities and External Involvement." *International Organization* 44:341–378.

Horowitz, Donald L. 1981. "Patterns of Ethnic Separatism." *Comparative Studies in Society and History* 23, no. 2 (April): 165–195.

Islam, M.R. 1985. "Secessionist Self-Determination: Some Lessons from Katanga, Biafra and Bangladesh." *Journal of Peace Research* 22:211–21.

Nixon, Charles R. 1972. "Self-Determination: The Nigeria/Biafra Case." *World Politics* 24:473–497.

Shaw Yu-ming. 1998. "New Political Trends Lead ROC Into Future." *Free China Journal* (July 24): 7.

Shen Hsiao-ch'i and Wu Nai-teh. 1998. "Waishengren de rentong: Taiwan minzu xincheng de liang chong lujing." (Mainlanders' identity: Two crossroads in the formation of Taiwan nationalism). Paper presented at the conference on Globalization's Challenge and Taiwan Society, Tungwu University Institute of Literature, Taipei, April 16–17, 1998.

Shu Wei-der. 1997–98. "The Emergence of Taiwanese Nationalism: A Preliminary Work on an Approach to Interactive Episodic Discourse." *Berkeley Journal of Sociology: A Critical Review* 42:73–121.

Taiwan Research Institute. 1998. "Stability in the Taiwan Strait Depends on Maintaining ROC's Defense Capability." *Taiwan Perspective* 1, no. 4 (August): 1–2.

————. 1998. "New Cross-Straits Talks to Begin, But Old Inhibitions Still Exist." *Taiwan Perspective* 1, no. 4 (August): 5.

Thomas, Raju G.C. 1994. "Secessionist Movements in South Asia." *Survival* 36, no. 2 (summer): 92–114.

Wu Nai-teh. 1993. "Shengji yishi, zhengzhi zhichi he guojia rentong" (Ethnic consciousness, political support and national identity). In *Zuqun guanxi yu guojia rentong* (Ethnic relations and national identity). Taipei: Yeqiang, 27–51.

————. 1997. "Re-Searching National Identities in Taiwan: Findings, Puzzles, and Agenda." Paper presented at the conference Social and Political Change in Postwar Taiwan, sponsored by the Joint Center for East Asian Studies, Washington University, St. Louis, and the University of Missouri, St. Louis, October 16–18.

Yi Chin-chun et al. 1994. *The Social Image Survey in Taiwan: The Regular Survey of August, 1994.* Taipei: Sun Yat-sen Institute for Social Sciences and Philosophy, Academia Sinica.

Young, Crawford. 1976. *The Politics of Cultural Pluralism.* Madison, WI: University of Wisconsin Press.

Young, Robert A. 1994. "How Do Peaceful Secessions Happen?" *Canadian Journal of Political Science.* 27, no. 4:773–792.

# Part III

## Perspectives on Ethnicity and Taiwanese Nationalism

# 8

# Taiwan's "Mainlanders," New Taiwanese?

*Stéphane Corcuff*

In recent years, the validity of the traditional distinction between *Waishengren* and *Benshengren* was so challenged that it is finally becoming more and more common to divide the Taiwanese population into four main groups: the *Austronesians*, the island's original inhabitants, forced to cohabit with the *Hakka* and *Holo* peoples arriving from Fujian and Guangdong provinces of China, particularly since the seventeenth century; and fourth, the *Mainlanders* coming to Taiwan during a final wave of Chinese migration from the Mainland during the watershed years 1945–1949. The Austronesians, labeled as *Shanbao* (compatriots from the mountains) as late as 1994, were then renamed more appropriately "Aborigines" and represented 1.7 percent of the total population in 1989.[1] The Holo (73.3 percent) and Hakka (12 percent) peoples, who have been on Taiwan for between one hundred and four hundred years, are the "native Taiwanese" who call themselves "Taiwanese" (*Taiwanren*), or "people of this land" (*Bendiren*). The last to arrive have, since 1945, been called *Waishengren* (people from outer provinces), and they numbered around 13 percent of the island's population in 1989 (Huang 1993).[2]

The Mainlanders ruled Taiwan from the top from 1945 until 1988. Even today, they retain a nonnegligible power of influence within the Taiwanese army, administration, diplomatic circles, media, and academic spheres. By dint of their background, many tend to see Taiwan as a part of China, temporarily separated from it for political reasons, before their wish for "national reunification" is fulfilled. But the twelve-year period that came to an end in May 2000 with the departure from office of President Lee Teng-hui have seen an uninterrupted series of shake-ups in Taiwan's "official" identity—the one the government tries to promote both domestically and internationally—that none would have dared to predict in 1988, so profound and generalized have they been. The accelerated pace of transformation of an island, formerly seen as an appendage of Han expansion on the maritime rim of China, into a national entity, has plunged the Mainlanders into an identity crisis that few have studied until today (see chapter 5). But their abiding influence within the state's institutions in Taiwan raises the question of their allegiance to a government clamoring for its Taiwaneseness for a decade. It is a rarely asked question, but one that is on many minds.[3]

### *"Waishengren"*: The Emergence of a New Ethnic Category

In order to get a better understanding of this, let us first try to find out what the term "Mainlanders" actually means, as it lacks clarity in English and is used here only for convenience. It is a spontaneous way to refer to those people in Taiwan who are called in Chinese "people from the outer provinces"—*Goa-seng-lang* in Taiwanese, *Waishengren* in Mandarin.[4] The term designates the Chinese migrants who fled to Taiwan at the end of the Chinese civil war. This migration can be seen as extending from October 1945 until February 1955. October 1945 was the month when Taiwan was handed back to Republican China after fifty years of Japanese colonization. February 1955 was the month of the last great evacuation to Taiwan of soldiers and civilians from a zone that was to fall under the control of Chinese Communists, the island of Dachen. The figures put forward to estimate the number of people transferred to Taiwan after the 1945 Retrocession range from 908,500[5] to over two million.[6] This latter figure is most likely grossly overestimated. It is difficult to know the truth, as the number of soldiers actually transferred to Taiwan has long been a sensitive issue for the government and the Ministry of Defense under the Kuomintang's (KMT) rule. Moreover, the troubled context of the time was not conducive to keeping exact records. I have addressed this complex counting question elsewhere (Corcuff 2000b, 47–55). Li Tung-ming, in a precise and relatively trustworthy study, estimated in 1969 that a little over one million *Waishengren* were present in Taiwan in 1956.[7] The total population in Taiwan was estimated at 6 million in 1946 and 7.87 million in 1951.

The term *"Waishengren"* is hardly used at all in China. It occurs only in official contexts, such as a statistical study focusing on one province, comparing the inhabitants of that province to those of the other provinces, taken collectively. The latter are then designated by the term *"Waishengren."* In everyday speech, people prefer to use the term *"waidiren"* to refer collectively to people who have come from other parts of China. As this term has pejorative overtones, it may be replaced by other, more precise expressions, such as "people from other cities" or "other *xiangs*" (a rural canton with a strong connotation of local identity) or one directly mentioning the individual's origin. We can therefore regard the term, as it will be analyzed here, as now being peculiar to Taiwan.

My first objective in this present chapter is to clarify how this ethnic category came into being. The term *"Waishengren"* was most likely used in the beginning by the new Nationalist officials sent to Taiwan by the Republican government in Nanjing. The words *"wai-sheng-ren"* explicitly refer to the status of Taiwan as a new province of (Republican) China. It is doubtful that the local Taiwanese and the Mainlanders themselves would spontaneously use this administrative concept of "people from the outer provinces." Naturally and logically, the local Taiwanese would first call them Mainlanders (*Daluren*). On their side, the Mainlanders would call themselves by the name of the province they came from: It was more natural for them to identify with their province of origin, or their familiar continental locale, than with this new, globalizing concept.

It is a good example of a designation of otherness through exteriorization (*wai*). This fundamental "Other" for the Taiwanese came from "outside." Such a definition of otherness through reference to exteriority was based in the beginning on a simple geographical criterion. But identifying the Other by an outsider status as flagrant as that imposed by Taiwan's insularity has fostered the construction of the otherness of Chinese migrants by the Taiwanese, the Nationalist government, and the *Waishengren* themselves. The definition of such outsiderness within a Taiwan-centered perspective has been produced in a context in which Taiwan, from 1895 on, gradually felt a distance, indeed isolation, with respect to China (see chapter 1). The events of February 1947, which led to the bloody crackdown against the Taiwanese elite by Chiang Kai-shek's troops, only served to intensify this feeling (see chapter 2). The geographical determinant in the definition of the otherness of the *Waishengren* has thus weighed particularly heavily since 1947, in the way the Taiwanese opposed to reunification with China have viewed the *Waishengren* and the Nationalist government—seeing the *Waishengren* as colonizers, who came from the outside to rule the island.[8] At the same time, despite the difference between "us" and "them" implied by the expression, the word *"sheng"* contained in *"Waishengren"* signifies "province" (of China) in the administrative sense of the term and hence implies the feeling of a common belonging to China, of which Taiwan is seen as a mere province. In order to understand this, we must situate the development of the expression on the island in the context of that period. Many accounts bear out the fact that at the time of the arrival of the first *Waishengren* there in 1945, and before the onset of corruption in the new administration, the Taiwanese were happy to return to the bosom of what they then considered to be their motherland.

The otherness–outsiderness of the *Waishengren* nevertheless became increasingly "real" in the eyes of the Taiwanese as some misunderstandings developed between the two communities from 1945 on. The corruption of the new Chinese administration set up in Taipei, the events of February–March 1947, the imposition of martial law, then the police repression of the 1950s, all after the Chinese Nationalist government had retreated to Formosa, quickly contributed an added layer of meaning to the term. The people associated with the geographical entity of Mainland China, were also associated with a regime, an army, a police force, but more important still, an ideology, a project for winning back the lost continent. At the outset the word did not designate the "Chinese" as opposed to the "Taiwanese," but later that became the meaning. A new ethnic category was in the process of being born, that of the *Waishengren*, who had not previously existed as a group sharing a homogeneous cultural identity.

Why identify the *Waishengren* in general with the new order, which was set up during the watershed years of 1945–1950, since, in point of fact, not all *Waishengren* belonged to the military? Nor did they all support the dictatorship, nor were they all privileged beneficiaries of the regime, at any rate not the soldiers who were stationed far from their home provinces and who led an unenviable existence in Taiwan. But it was natural for most of them to long for their forsaken plot of land and, believing what the government told them, to see the island of Taiwan as merely a place of temporary exile. For years, they lived in Taiwan with a "guest mentality" (*zuoke de xintai*).

Two main reasons explain the fact that the *Waishengren,* however, were on the whole mentally associated to the new ideological order imposed on the island after the withdrawal of the Nationalist government to Formosa in December 1949. On the one hand, the type of regime set up in Taiwan by Chiang Kai-shek did not make Taiwanese keen to draw a distinction between some "good" and some "bad" *Waishengren.* On the other hand, the inability of most of those Chinese migrants to converse with speakers of Holo (Taiwanized Minnan)[9] or Hakka, the two main languages of the islanders, rendered them incapable of knowing and appreciating this different culture, specific to the island, which had originated in Southeast China, but which had progressively indigenized. There ensued a generalized contempt on the part of the *Waishengren* for Taiwanese popular traditions and the Japanese cultural heritage of the island (at the same time, a Taiwanese elite formed under the Japanese was itself disdainful of the uncouth and uneducated *Waishengren*). This was made official in a government policy of cultural preference for linguistic and artistic forms of expression which had come from the Mainland with the *Waishengren*, something that was a source of deep frustration for the Taiwanese.

Powerful geographical and political factors thus led to an identity labeling in the sense of the assimilation into a single group of what was nothing other than a mosaic of Chinese provincials from all over China. A good number of the *waisheng* soldiers who had arrived in Taiwan did not necessarily communicate easily together, more often than not speaking provincial dialects. Many expressed themselves falteringly in the "national language" (*guoyu*), China's Northern dialect imposed in 1931 as the *lingua franca* by the Nationalists. They had learned it during a few years of schooling cut short by poverty, the Japanese invasion of China, and the civil war. Some did not even know *guoyu* and spoke only a local dialect, which did not help them think about learning Taiwanese: For many, the so-called national language was already another language to learn. In the 1930s, the sociologist Maurice Halbwachs, in his pioneering work on collective memory, showed that there exist as many memories as there are groups in a society, as long as their members stay in contact with one another—the requirement for keeping the collective memory alive (Halbwachs 1997). If the diversity of provincial China, suddenly reproduced in miniature in Taiwan, finally resulted in a view of the *Waishengren* as a group with a distinct cultural identity, it is only through a phenomenon that could be characterized as an "historico-optical illusion." Historical events determined the way an immediately perceptible diversity (the multiplicity of provincial backgrounds, and hence dialects, customs, and patronymics; the variety of social conditions and political sensitivities) was interpreted, namely as assimilation within a group seen as a homogeneous whole, or at least one welded by a certain number of basic political objectives (the reunification of Taiwan with the Chinese Mainland). Temporarily brought together on this small island, the *Waishengren* finally stayed there, politics and history turning them into actors, authors, or scapegoats—in any event bound in a common destiny. Among other factors, an illusion was able to play a significant role here in the incarnation of a new ethnic label.

A new ethnic category thus came into existence, a regular occurrence in the history of human societies. Anthropologist Arjun Guneratne points, for instance, to the fact that the Nepalese Tharus, made up of ethnic groups that saw themselves as separate until the nineteenth century, have come to think of themselves as a single ethnic group for purely historical and political reasons linked to the modernization of the "Nepalese State" in the twentieth century (Guneratne 1998). Ethnic borders are not fixed, and in order to understand this, we should not see ethnicity in terms of biological or cultural continuities between the members of a group, but rather in terms of the shared perception of an identity which is, or progressively becomes, common to them, both through the way in which others view them and their own self-perception. This question of ways of seeing underlies the definition of ethnicity given by Fredrik Barth as a form of social organization, admittedly territorialized, but one whose perspective takes no account at all of physical criteria, explicitly rejecting the traditional compilation of cultural signs for defining an ethnic label. Barth stresses the idea that an ethnic group can be differentiated by the definition it gives to its border with others (in other words, what are the diacritical factors that it chooses to promote in order to differentiate itself) more than through the "cultural stuff" particular to the group and upon which traditional anthropology largely drew (Barth 1969, 15). In this process of defining and maintaining the border, the question of "ascription" and "self-ascription," in Fredrik Barth's language, of a characteristic of identity or ethnic label, becomes crucial.

Which particular people's way of seeing should we then adopt in order to determine whether or not the *Waishengren* form a distinct ethnic group? Before speculating that the *Waishengren* might form such a group, we must ask ourselves whether those concerned see themselves thus. Indeed, what could be the legitimacy of an identity "label" that did not take into account the awareness of those concerned that they belong to the group in which they are classified? Now, the idea of the existence of an ethnic group of *Waishengren* is not something that they themselves accept universally. The *Waishengren* who most strongly reject the idea of a Republic of Taiwan are also the first to deny that there exists an ethnic or cultural identity group called *Waishengren*, and prefer to stress the idea that all Taiwan's inhabitants, apart from the Aborigines, are of Han ethnic ancestry. But more generally, as mentioned earlier, many first-generation *Waishengren* still identify with the province they come from. In data collected in Taiwan through a research questionnaire distributed in 1997 to *Waishengren*,[10] I found that the *Waishengren* do not all see themselves therefore as *Waishengren* (Table 8.1)

We could ask whether we are dealing with an "ethnic group" or a simple "social group with a common cultural identity" brought together by the vicissitudes of recent history, distinguished by nothing more than the twists of history, giving them a particular memory within the great Chinese nation? But these latter criteria are already adequate identity markers to create important distinctions between two populations, and most definitions of ethnicity call upon one or other of such cultural criteria. And even if Taiwan's *Waishengren* were all to deny *en bloc* that they are a separate group, would it yet be impossible to consider them as a distinct group, if the island's other ethnic groups in fact see them that way? For the Taiwanese, the question of the existence of a distinct Mainlander group is in no doubt at all; the overwhelming majority, if not indeed the entirety, of the population are convinced of the existence of such a specific group, different from themselves, particularly since the 1947 crackdown.

What viewpoint should one adopt in such circumstances? This is a difficult question, one that we may attempt to summarize in three points. First, several writers have emphasized the role played in self-definition by the defini-

Table 8.1 **Waishengren's Self-Ascription in a Two-Possibility Choice:**
**Waishengren or Taiwanese, 1997** (percent)

Q. In the two following choices, which would you choose to describe yourself?

| | Waishengren | Taiwanese | Checked both answers | Added their own answer (e.x., Chinese) | No answer |
|---|---|---|---|---|---|
| **Between 1945 and 1967** | | | | | |
| Mainland-born Waishengren | 59.4 | 10.1 | 11.6 | 1.4 | 17.4 |
| Taiwan-born Waishengren | 45.5 | 27.6 | 10.9 | 10.3 | 5.7 |
| **Between 1968 and 1981** | | | | | |
| Taiwan-born Waishengren | 40.7 | 42.9 | 8.2 | 4.1 | 4.1 |

*Source:* Author (data collected in a 1997 questionnaire; see endnote 10).
*Note:* Total of each line = 100% of the total number of a generation.

tion given by the Other, particularly if such Other constitutes a majority (for instance, Barth 1969, 15) But, second, it is morally necessary to respect the idea according to which a population cannot be arbitrarily classified as an ethnic group or included in a larger group without questioning whether this is the perception that it has itself. Finally, we must also bear in mind the fact that the question takes on another dimension when the groups under consideration interact within one and the same entity and do so peacefully. Being seen as different from the Taiwanese and never having been able or at least willing to make the effort to learn Holo, how could the *Waishengren* end up seeing themselves in fact as anything but different? In my 1997 data, I found that, indeed, a good part of the *Waishengren* population considered that being a *Waishengren* could make them "different" from the Taiwanese. Table 8.2 shows that on the theoretical question "Does being a *Waishengren* give you the feeling of being 'different'?" only 38.5 percent of the *Waishengren* respondents said "yes"; but later, when I asked in which respect they feel such a difference, 50 percent of the respondents chose one or more answers in the different fields proposed for an answer, where a difference can be felt. From Table 8.2, we can conclude that at least half of Taiwan's *Waishengren* openly stated that they consider themselves as different from the Taiwanese.

Unlike the South African regime at the time of apartheid, the Nationalist government in Taiwan during the years of dictatorship did not introduce

Table 8.2 **Waishengren's Feeling of Being "Different," 1997** (percent)

Q. Does being a *Waishengren* gives you the feeling of being "different"?

| Yes | No | No answer; Does not know |
|---|---|---|
| 38.5 | 46.2 | 15.3 |

*Source:* Same as Table 8.1.

systematic ethnic segregation that might have excluded a Taiwanese majority in favor of a Mainland minority. However, some elements suggest a segregation based on provincial origin. For one thing, the organs of civil and
military authority have been marked by an overrepresentation of the
*Waishengren* to the detriment of the Taiwanese between 1945 and the 1980s,
the Taiwanese majority having been ruled by a Mainland minority for more
than four decades. For another, a residential separation on the basis of ethnicity
was put in place by the system of *juncun* (the villages of military families),
of which the *Waishengren* who lived there ended up being the victims. Hill
Gates talks in this context of "*de facto* residential segregation" leading to
"segregated schools" with profound linguistic and social consequences (Gates
1981, 261–262). These villages, hurriedly built to house soldiers from the
Mainland, restricted their contacts with the local Taiwanese population. One
qualification, however, is in order here, and that is that the soldiers were
nonetheless obliged to go out in order to do their shopping, for instance. By
the same token, many of them married or remarried in Taiwan with Taiwanese women (and in some cases, Aboriginal women), opening their eyes to
the outside world, a situation of which Chen Kun-hou's 1983 film, *Xiao Bi
di gushi* (The story of little Bi), is a picturesque illustration. At the same
time, life in the *juncun* was forging an undeniable feeling of solidarity among
individuals from very different backgrounds, whatever the generation. A
number of so-called second generation *Waishengren* born in Taiwan still remember with emotion their childhood days in the *juncun*.

In this brief history of the emergence of the *Waishengren* ethnic category
in Taiwan, a final factor is worth our attention, that of the *jiguan*. Taiwan has
undergone a legal imagination of otherness through the use by the Nationalists of a system they had used on the Mainland, relating an individual's identity to his or her father's place of origin, the *jiguan*.[11] A social construct *par
excellence*, it has, however, become a fundamental identity marker for many
*Waishengren*, as if it had always existed and as if it provided the "true" origin
of a family and the individuals composing it.[12] The system lasted until 1992.
Finally, by 1997, a fair number of *Waishengren* had accepted the decision to
suppress the *jiguan* from all administrative documents, but a third of that
population were still opposed to the measure.

Table 8.3 **Waishengren's Position Regarding the 1992 Suppression of the "Jiguan," 1997** (percent)

Q. Do you think the 1992 decision to suppress the notion of "jiguan" in all administrative documents was a good one?

| Yes | No | No answer; Does not know |
|---|---|---|
| 41.6 | 33.5 | 24.9 |

*Source:* Same as Table 8.1.

Through the *jiguan*, an instrument was available for distinguishing between those whose *jiguan* was a province on the Mainland and those whose *jiguan* was the "Province of Taiwan"; the democratization movement naturally went against a tool of potential ethnic discrimination. The Taiwanese complain that when the *Waishengren* were present at all decision-making levels of government, they gave preference to other *Waishengren* when it came to hiring people for jobs in public administration. Such a policy was never official, nor was it ever enshrined in law. The scope of such segregation may have been exaggerated by some frustrated Taiwanese, but there is a strong presumption that there was indeed such a policy, given the great number of testimonies to the fact and the extent to which the system depended on such co-optation for its ideological survival. The system of the *jiguan*, which was abolished on July 1, 1992, served as an instrument of identity categorization by law in addition to the factors already mentioned as contributing to the emergence of a so-called Mainlander group with a specific, shared cultural identity. Consequently, whereas it was supposed to stress the provincial background of individuals, thereby rejecting the global concept of "*Waishengren*," it is highly likely that the system of *jiguan* also gave the impression that *Waishengren* globally benefited from a sort of special political status, having for a long time enjoyed a quasi-monopoly of power. Here, it was no longer a social illusion, but this time a legal imagination that helped shape and incarnate a new ethnic category. This vital role played by the state in the definition of ethnicity, and that Fredrik Barth had not taken into consideration in 1969, was the core of the criticism directed at him by the anthropologist Hill Gates (Gates 1981, 246–247). Barth redressed this point in his analysis of the influence exerted by national bureaucracies on ethnicity via their power of resource allocation (Barth 1994, 19–20), of which the case of the *Waishengren* and the *jiguan* is a good example.

**The *Waishengren*'s Mind-Set**

Because of this situation, the Taiwanese feel a deep sense of frustration, which is responsible for the fact that they usually do not know well the

*Waishengren*'s mind-set. Judgments they make about the Mainlanders are often laden with a variety of prejudices. First among them is *Waishengren* are regarded as a community unable to identify with Taiwan, bound together by their opposition to the Taiwanization of the island and the objective of reunification. Up until now, the efforts of proindependence thinkers or activists to integrate the *Waishengren* into a "Taiwanese community with a common destiny" have not been legion, but such efforts do exist. As for Taiwanese politicians, most show a limited knowledge of the *Waishengren* mind-set. Only the world of cinema has frankly explored this subject, mainly because many directors are of Mainlander origin and they have been concerned about the *Waishengren*'s growing identification problems in the 1980s and 1990s. Yet, an understanding of the *Waishengren* worldview is a prerequisite for understanding their reactions to the Taiwanization-of-Taiwan movement.

Who are the *Waishengren*? From 1945 on, several waves of people have settled in Taiwan arriving from China. Before the massive exodus of late 1949, different kinds of *Waishengren* had already established themselves in Taiwan. First, there were the people who arrived with Chen Yi to take Taiwan over from the Japanese. These were followed by all the people sent by the Kuomintang to establish civil and military authority. Then, some Chinese people left the Mainland to look for job opportunities in the island. Many left when the February 28 event occurred, but some stayed, either because they could not afford the expense of going back or because they had decided to stay, having no place to go back to or no job opportunity on the Mainland. As some testimony shows, those were not particularly obsessed by "returning to the Mainland," after Taiwan was cut off from China in 1949 (see, for instance, Ma 1995, 32). Though we do not know yet their exact number, those different categories were composed of "unusual" types of Mainlanders, and their small number allegedly decreased severely with the outbreak of the 1947 events.

The situation of the "forty-niners," as we could call the military and civilians who were evacuated from the Mainland between 1949 and 1955, was not the same. Totally different conditions shaped their mentality upon their arrival and during their early years in Taiwan. Those were refugees who had been evacuated from the Mainland, often in dramatic circumstances. They arrived on an island already experiencing tense ethnic relations, following the February 28 events and in a context of martial law imposed in Taiwan on May 19, 1949. They depended heavily on the government for their living and housing. They were told that their return would be imminent, and thus viewed themselves as temporary hosts in Taiwan. Last, they had no encouragement from the government to learn about the local culture. The forty-niners made up the biggest part of the *waisheng* population in the 1950s and 1960s, before the second-generation *Waishengren* were born. Conditioned by such a situation, their mind-set can be characterized with reference to three important dimensions of identification: identification with the ruling Kuomintang, identification with a Chinese province, and cultural prejudice. I speak here of "national identification" instead of the "national identity," because it seems to me that the expression "national identity" does not describe *feelings* shared by *individuals*. In my eyes, individuals as such do not have a "national identity" but rather share feelings of identification with one nation—or with more than one, and we would benefit from distinguishing more seriously both notions. Studying national identification is studying the cognitive dimension of national identity, a dimension that is too often eluded.

In 1949, all the conditions were ripe for these Chinese refugees to be encouraged to sacrifice for the Nationalist government, to identify with the latter, to feel a self-induced conviction that what it was doing was right, and to agree tacitly to a reprehensible political repression—at least for some. Deprived of their native land, removed to Taiwan in dramatic circumstances, mobilized by propaganda hiding from them the impossibility of returning to the Mainland, living in a traumatic situation, they joined their fate to that of the Nationalist government. If that government were to collapse, they would go down with it. For a long time they were convinced that they were going to be able to go back home to the Mainland and that only a strong Nationalist government was going to enable them to do so. In my 1997 data, I found that 76.8 percent of the Mainland-born *Waishengren* were or had been members of the Kuomintang (KMT). Forty-niners knew they were survivors of a collapsed regime that was revived on Taiwan by a man that most found charismatic, Chiang Kai-shek.[13] No wonder Alan Wachman could speak of a "sacred" dimension of this identification with the KMT and to the goal of reunifying China (Wachman 1994b, 25). Few in the West have an idea of how deeply this emotional identification with a political party and its goals has gone among elder *Waishengren*.

Identification with a Chinese province is the second evident dimension of the forty-niners' psyche. The question of identification often comes in times of crisis (Erickson 1968). The forty-niners had been uprooted. Cut off from their province, they had lost their land. At the same time, the government was telling them that they would go back and that they should not forget to *wish* to go back, as expressed, for instance, in the political motto *"Wu wang zai ju."*[14] They missed their wives, parents, and other relatives, and organized themselves in companionship guilds based on common local origin, the famous *tongxianghui*. As said above, most first-generation *Waishengren* identify strongly with a particular *xiang* of a particular province and present themselves as coming from that province, and many resented the government's decision to force them to learn the standard Mandarin (*biaozhun guoyu*). This is likely to be an important reason explaining why they have not seen in Taiwan anything else but another province of China. They did not see the point in studying the local dialect, just as they would not learn the other dialects of other *Waishengren* they met. But the state power tried to work and to a certain point successfully influenced this identification scheme. All the cultural and educational systems told them China was the only motherland, and the disparate *Waishengren* have all in all been, just like the Taiwanese, educated into identifying with a nation as a whole to which their initial identification may not have been so strong. Books conspicuously and deliberately emphasized the unity of China, with titles and a logic following the *"Women de Zhongguo"* (our China)-style rhetoric. School textbooks shaped the nation's history—as they always do. The aim was to foster national identification, a method that Hegel, comparing India and China in his 1820s *Lessons on the philosophy of History*, saw as a tradition in the latter, and that P. Duara has recently explored (Duara 1995). But as Kuang-chün Li emphasized in chapter 5, there was no reason for them to stress the fact that they were Chinese as long as their belief that Taiwan was part of China was unshaken. Once democratization had started to provide the antiunification movements with a forum of free expression, another reason prompted them to emphasize their being Chinese at the expense of, or in addition to, their former primordial identification with their native locality: In 1997, 79 percent of my first-generation *Waishengren* respondents said they agreed with the slogan "I am Chinese" of a 1995 march (on this march, see chapter 5).

Cutural prejudice is the third important dimension of the refugee generation's state of mind. As stated above, this socialization process partly explains why very few first-generation *Waishengren* have learned Taiwan's main local language, Holo, not to mention the others dialects or languages. The incapacity to understand the local language has prevented *Waishengren* from knowing and appreciating the local culture. *Waishengren* are beset by cultural prejudice, especially first-generation ones, and to a lesser extent, the second generation ones born in the 1950s and 1960s. Policies of cultural preference were implemented by the state in favor of forms of artistic expression imported to Taiwan in 1949. The state severely restricted the use of the Taiwanese language, and a severe competition came with the systematic promotion of a political, cultural, and linguistic invention, the "standard national language," based on the dialect of Hebei's Sanhe district, refined and codified by the KMT state's linguists in Taiwan. A series of questions, in the above-mentioned questionnaire distributed in 1997, tackled the question of cultural prejudice.

Table 8.2 showed the percentage of respondents to my 1997 survey who thought that being *Waishengren* gave them a feeling of difference (*yi zhong bu yiyang*). It was of course impossible to raise directly in the questionnaire

Table 8.4a **Waishengren's Feeling of Cultural Superiority, 1997** (percent)

Q. If you think being *Waishengren* makes you different, in which field do you feel this difference?

| Cultural background (*wenhua beijing*) | Cultural level (*wenhua shuizhun*) | In terms of language (*yuyan fangmian*) | Other |
|---|---|---|---|
| 42 | 37 | 61.5 | 3.5 |

*Source:* Same as Table 8.1.
*Note:* Percentages of the total number of respondents who chose one or more answer to this question. They represent 49 percent of the total sample.

Table 8.4b **Waishengren's Feeling of Cultural Superiority, 1997** (percent)

Q. Do you think this difference is a "plus" *(yi zhong youshi)?*

| Yes | No | No answer; Does not know |
|---|---|---|
| 51.3 | 48.7 | 24.9 |

*Source:* Same as Table 8.1.
*Note:* Percentages of the total number of respondents who answered this question. The number of respondents who said "yes" represent 20.2 percent of the total sample, meaning that in 1997, there was a fifth of the *Waishengren* considering that being *Waishengren* was a "plus" in Taiwan.

the idea of a feeling of cultural superiority. A detailed analysis of their answers (multiple choice possible) showed that 42 percent of them saw this difference in terms of "cultural background" (*wenhua beijing*), 37 percent in terms of "cultural level" (*wenhua shuizhun*), and 61.5 percent in terms of language. Then I asked whether this difference was "a plus" (*yi zhong youshi*). The number of respondents who answered was significantly lower, perhaps due to the sensitivity of this question. A little more than half of these respondents (51.3 percent) said "yes," and this group made up to 20.2 percent of the total sample, which means that after ten years of dramatic changes (1987–1997) in terms of national identity, no more than—or still—a fifth of *Waishengren* thought that their Mainland origin was a kind of plus in Taiwan (Table 8.4a and 8.4b).

In this exploration of cultural prejudice, I also tried to measure the *Waishengren*'s preconceived opinions toward native Taiwanese's "cultural level," often attributed to the *Waishengren*. Table 8.4c and 8.4d give a nuanced answer to this question. It is often said among *Waishengren* that Taiwanese are now rich, but that, to put things simply, "they have no culture." I tried to measure this judgment with two questions. In the first one (Table 8.4.c), I asked *Waishengren* whether they agree with the assertion, often heard among them, that the natives' cultural level has not risen as fast as their economic situation since the Retroces-

Table 8.4c  *Waishengren's* Feeling of Cultural Superiority, 1997 (percent)

Q. Do you think that during the fifty years since the Retrocession, native Taiwanese's cultural level has followed the increase in their economic well-being?

| Yes | No | No answer; Does not know |
|-----|-----|--------------------------|
| 68 | 20 | 12 |

*Source:* Same as Table 8.1.

Table 8.4d  *Waishengren's* Feeling of Cultural Superiority, 1997 (percent)

Q. Do you think that native Taiwanese are materialistic and neglect cultural matters?

| Yes | No | No answer; Does not know |
|-----|-----|--------------------------|
| 63 | 21 | 16 |

*Source:* Same as Table 8.1.

sion. A fifth of the respondents agreed, while a large majority did not. This shows a probable change in their positions after ten years, though we can only suppose that, since we do not have statistics on this question for earlier periods. However, when I asked whether they considered Taiwanese people to be materialistic, a large majority said "yes," which is a blatant expression of ethnic prejudice. One respondent protested: "I do not agree, because today, everyone on this island has become materialistic," [and not Taiwanese only].

Here, an explanation *must* be given for these cultural prejudices, for they have poisoned much of the postwar *Waishengren–*Taiwanese relations up to this day. The root of such a misperception is above all the very fact that *Waishengren* were, originally, a *displaced* people. Part of this people was, undeniably, the Republican China's cultural elite, which imposed on Taiwan its cultural canons and transmitted them to its offspring. This has caused a fundamental misunderstanding: The *Waishengren* live in a society which, *like every other*, contains well-educated elements and less-well-educated ones. The *Waishengren*, being unable to communicate in Holo and Hakka, have ignored, partly deliberately, the existence of an insular cultural elite. The February 28 repression might have accentuated this phenomenon, by suppressing part of Taiwan's elite. At the same time they were ignoring the local elite, the *Waishengren*, as a minority, focused on the vast majority of the people in Taiwan surrounding them, necessarily less-well-educated than its elite. Most *Waishengren*, trying to impose their cultural models, and proud of their cultural heritage, have thus consistently despised the Taiwanese culture, viewing it as a local culture without particular interest. At the same time, the Taiwanese have indeed enhanced their living at remarkable speed in five decades, and no one can blame them for concentrating for a long time on economic matters when the need for development was so urgent and at a time when the Nationalist government was erecting many barriers to the expression, development, innovation, and rejuvenation of Taiwan's local cultures.

In 1988, from the high horse of their cultural certainties, the *Waishengren* harbored very different feelings from those of the majority of the population on the identity of Taiwan and the objective of reunification. When profound changes occurred in terms of the regime's political objectives and symbols, following their fall from power, the shock for the first-generation *Waishengren* was full on. Their descendants have reacted better, however—a generational difference that can be explained by the fact that the development of *Waishengren* identity would have been simple had it stopped at the main features of the mind-set described in summary fashion above.

The growing consciousness of a *Waishengren* specificity has indeed been complemented, confused, and challenged—without ever being eradicated—by another movement, just as inevitable, that of their Taiwanization. While a majority of the middle-aged and older Mainlander generation still do not speak Holo, they have all been influenced by the Taiwanization of their "national language." After decades of acclimatization on Taiwan, the "standard national language" is increasingly giving room to a "Taiwanized national language" (*Taiwan guoyu*), which is technically a Taiwanized Chinese Northern dialect. It is no longer the same as the language they spoke fifty years ago, and even farther from that spoken today by Chinese on the Mainland. The *Waishengren* who do not speak Taiwanese sometimes readily point out their ability to assimilate linguistic expressions specific to Taiwan into Mandarin, or, again, expressions that have come straight from Holo and are pronounced in Mandarin, or even, in some cases, words pronounced directly in Holo.[15] For instance, a friend meeting me in Taipei in 1999 arrived at our meeting after going shopping with her aunt, who later appeared to me as being as prounification as her niece. The aunt, speaking in perfect Mandarin, handed me some pineapples she had just bought in a market and told me kindly, *in Mandarin*: "Take some! These are *ong-lai-so*." But "*ong-lai-so*" are Holo words inserted in her Mandarin sentence. She could simply have said "*fengli su*," the Mandarin equivalent. But she chose the Holo words and smiled at me when pronouncing them—had she chosen to use the Mandarin "*fengli*," it would be have been different from the Mainland Mandarin anyway, since Chinese in China call pineapple "*boluo*," and not "*fengli*." This is in part the work of illusionists, but each time the *Waishengren* play this role, they acculturate themselves a little further. Such Taiwanization of the *Waishengren* is undeniable, and how could it be otherwise after fifty years of life in the place and very limited contacts with the Mainland? The dilemma of time has played a considerable role here, virtually destroying the hopes of all those who might have wished for nothing to change, while awaiting a hypothetical reunification.

That is only one of many examples illustrating the inevitable Taiwanese tropism of the *Waishengren*. If most *Waishengren* still denied in 1997 Taiwan the quality of a nation-state (25.8 percent of my respondents thought that Taiwan could be seen as a nation-state, and 58 percent thought the opposite), their daily preoccupation has clearly Taiwan as its main focus, for it is the place where they live. In my questionnaire, I used a formula employed, for instance, by Lee Yuan-tse, the head of Academia Sinica, to help reticent *Waishengren* acknowledging that they are taking root in Taiwan. Sayings in Chinese culture seem to have in a tremendous power over minds, as one frequently hears a speaker describe reality with a simple saying or use a saying to avoid answering a question. Sayings have in the Chinese mentality a strong identification power, probably through their metaphoric meaning (Chang 1998). One of them concerns deeply the uprooted, first-generation *Waishengren*: "*luoye guigen,*" "when the leaf falls, it returns to the root." To escape the impasse created by the identification with this saying, often re-ferred to by older *Waishengren*, Lee Yuan-tse used a saying in 1996 that kept the same sonority and the main words of the original saying, in order to make more bearable a major semantic shift: the expression "*luo di sheng gen,*" the leaf "falls on the soil and takes root." I used this useful tool in my questionnaire and asked *Waishengren* "whether they felt this feeling once called *luo di sheng gen* by Lee Yuan-tse." Table 8.5 shows that even among first-generation, Mainland-born *Waishengren*, the majority acknowledge a feeling of having taken root, to some extent, in Taiwan. A total of 31.8 per-cent say they do not have this feeling at all or have it only partially. But 60.9 percent say they clearly have this feeling, and for some, it is strong.

Then, at the end of my questionnaire, I tried to place the *Waishengren*'s theoretical position on Taiwan's unification with China, which they most often support for the long term, in perspective with *political imperatives of immediately domestic nature* that the government has to deal with *in Taiwan*. The idea was to see whether the theoretical position on unification would be contradicted by a judgment on the order of priorities in their day-to-day life. I asked *Waishengren* to classify six policy items in the order of priority they would wish the government to implement them. Those six items were the following: unification, the extension of Taiwan's international visibility, the fight against corruption, administrative efficiency, environmental protection, and economic development. We can see here that one item explicitly con-cerns unification with China, another is closely linked to Taiwan's identity (the international visibility of the island), and the four others all concern more urgent domestic stakes. Table 8.6, 8.7a and 8.7b can show that the data

Table 8.5    First-Generation *Waishengren's* Feeling of Having "Taken
Root" in Taiwan, 1997 (percent)

Q. To what extent do you have the feeling described by Lee Yuan-tse that "When the
leave falls down, it takes root"?

| Absolutely not (*wanquan meiyou*) | Partly (*bu wanquan you*) | Somehow (*you yi dian*) | Strongly (*fei chang you*) | No answer; Does not know |
|---|---|---|---|---|
| 7.2 | 24.6 | 34.8 | 26.1 | 7.3 |

*Source:* Same as Table 8.1.
*Note:* Percentage of the first-generation respondents.

confirmed the intuition of a change in the order of priorities, depending on
the context (theoretical or pragmatic) in which the question of unification is
put into perspective. It seems that, perhaps for the first time, the Taiwanization
of the *Waishengren*'s values could be measured statistically. Table 8.6 shows
what could be called the *theoretical position* of Taiwan's *Waishengren* regarding unification. It shows, depending on what we want to stress: either
that already in 1997 a third of the Mainlanders who did not necessarily view
the unification with China a categorical imperative; or that a majority of
*Waishengren* still considered unification as a categorical imperative—in other
words, a priority with which the island's government cannot compromise
under any circumstance, "a question of principle."

What is interesting to see now is how this position varies when it is put in
perspective with domestic priorities. Tables 8.7a and 8.7b present the results
obtained when respondents were asked to choose among the six above-
mentioned political priorities and to classify their choices in order of importance. Table 8.7a shows that unification is the least often chosen item here,
whatever the rank, though it is still chosen by a vast majority of *Waishengren*.

But what is even more interesting is the rank attributed to each potential
political priority offered for classification by the respondents. As Table 8.7b
shows without ambiguity, the number of *Waishengren* who deliberately ranked
unification as the top priority, ahead of all other domestic policies proposed,
is a very small minority, and the largest part of those who chose it as a priority ranked it as their last and next-to-last choice.

Reunification was the first choice of only 5.4 percent of the total number
of respondents who chose this item (whatever rank they attributed to it). The
number of those who chose it as second, third, and fourth choice is even
more insignificant. But those who chose it as the next-to-last and last choice
are 30 percent and 55.6 percent, respectively. This means that for 85.6 per-

Table 8.6   **Waishengren's "Theoretical Position" Regarding the Unification with China, 1997** (percent)

Q. Do you think that unification is an objective with which the ROC government cannot compromise?

| | Yes | No | No answer; Does not know |
|---|---|---|---|
| Total sample | 50.3 | 33.6 | 16.1 |
| Waishengren born in Mainland | 78.3 | 15.9 | 5.8 |
| Waishengren born in Taiwan 1945–1967 | 41.7 | 37.2 | 21.2 |
| Waishengren born in Taiwan 1968–1981 | 34.7 | 51.0 | 14.3 |

Source: Same as Table 8.10.

Table 8.7a   **Waishengren's Classification of Six Political Priorities, Comparing Unification with Domestic Policies (1), 1997** (percent)

Q. Please rank the six following objectives that you think the government should implement soonest:

| Proposed policy item | Chosen by (without consideration of rank given) |
|---|---|
| Fighting against corruption | 92.6 |
| Enhancing administrative efficiency | 91.6 |
| Helping economic development | 91.6 |
| Protecting Taiwan's natural environment | 90.2 |
| Extending Taiwan's international visibility | 86 |
| Implementing national unification | 84.2 |
| Other | 2.8 |

Source: Same as Table 8.1.

cent of respondents who decided to put a rank to this policy item (some did not), unification with China is considered as the last priority of the six. On the contrary, other policy items concerning Taiwan's administrative reform, environment, and economic development are all considered more urgent priorities. The order of these items, classified by the number of people who chose them as first priority, is as follows: the fight against corruption (45.1 percent), improvement of administrative efficiency (23.4 percent), economic development (14.7 percent), environmental protection (8 percent), extension of Taiwan's international visibility (5.2 percent), unification with China (4.5 percent), and "other" (1.4 percent).[16] Again, this does not mean that the Waishengren consider unification as the least important political matter; they still consider it a priority. But very clearly, when compared to policies such as reforming the administration, or improving the economy, the vast majority of Waishengren remain pragmatic and local-oriented.

Table 8.7b **Waishengren's Classification of Six Political Priorities, Comparing Unification with Domestic Policies (2), 1997** (percent)

Q. Please rank the six following objectives that you think the government should implement soonest:

| Response chosen | First choice | Second choice | Third choice | Fourth choice | Fifth choice | Sixth choice | Seventh choice |
|---|---|---|---|---|---|---|---|
| Fighting corruption | **48.7** | **23.4** | 18.1 | 6.8 | 2.6 | 0.4 | 0 |
| Enhancing administrative efficiency | **25.6** | **43.9** | 16.4 | 9.2 | 5 | 0 | 0 |
| Helping economic development | 16 | 11.5 | **26** | **33.2** | 8 | 5.3 | 0 |
| Protecting Taiwan's natural environment | 8.9 | 12.8 | **29.8** | **31** | 12.8 | 4.7 | 0 |
| Expanding Taiwan's international visibility | 6.1 | 6.1 | 6.9 | 11.4 | **40.8** | 28.2 | 0.4 |
| Implementing national unification | 5.4 | 1.2 | 1.7 | 5.8 | **30** | **55.6** | 0.4 |
| Other | 50 | 25 | 0 | 0 | 12.5 | 12.5 | 0 |

*Source:* same as Table 8.1.

*Note:* Percentages of the total number of people who choose an item, and not of the total sample: Total of each line = 100% of the total number of persons who chose this item and gave it a rank. Total of each column > 100 if some respondents gave the same rank to more than one item.

By extension, could not this scheme be applied to the insular period of the KMT's history? The preparation of the ROC government for recovering the Mainland in the 1950s was largely psychological, and it was a tool for political socialization. Concretely, the government was forced to deal with day-to-day Taiwanese matters, and we can legitimately consider that from the very beginning, when the Nationalist government retreated to Taiwan and was totally cut off from the Mainland, the above-described process started and developed, finally to mature into the 1990s' largely indigenized KMT policy imposed from the top by Lee Teng-hui, probably differing from the KMT's preferred goals in the 1950s and 1960s, but likely with the party's awareness of what was going on.

## The Figuration of the *Waishengren*'s National Identification

One of the main political questions posed by the *Waishengren* in Taiwan is with which national object do these Chinese refugees and their descendants born in exile identify. To answer quite simply that it is "China" would be to oversimplify the question, ignoring the problems of defining what is "China" as well as the possibility of a pluralistic national identification. The central question that they force us to ponder concerns their process of national identification, after a decade of multidimensional changes in the order of political and identity symbols in Taiwan. Do they identify with China, and if so with what kind of China? Do they identify with Taiwan—as a part of China? Can one talk in this regard of a plurality of national allegiances? Behind such questions is above all to be found the transition of Taiwan's identity, which is moving from provincial status to one of national entity. This transition upsets the fundamental bearings of the *Waishengren* longing for national identification and for whom the basic cause of trauma, at least for the refugee generation, is the loss of national territory and emigration to a land that they hold deep down to be foreign to the Chinese heartland, but that they force themselves to define politically as an integral part of the "motherland" and where they have finally taken root.

In light of the situation described in this chapter, one can understand that the *Waishengren* of Taiwan have a pluralistic figuration of national identification, comprising two elements. On the one hand, an ethnic and cultural identification first and foremost with China, as the country where their province or local birth place is situated and with the ROC as long as it sticks to the official reunification line; this is complemented by the particular phenomenon of a sentiment of belonging to the subnational or quasi-national entity that is Taiwan-as-a-part-of-China. I will come back in the conclusion to the complex distribution of the *Waishengren*'s different identification feelings toward these two potential identification objects.

One way to measure that was to ask the *Waishengren* whether they would consider a Chinese attack on Taiwan to be as being an invasion, or a legitimate act to stop the division of China and prevent the island officially from adopting the "Republic of Taiwan" as its regime name *de jure*—what it already is *de facto*. My respondents were confronted with a very particular theoretical situation in which Taiwan would have provoked the Chinese attack: In other words, if Taiwan had been the *casus belli* after which the island is to be considered the troublemaker and is not to be helped to defend itself against a Chinese attack by the United States (Table 8.8a). I expected that this formulation would help me measure more properly the percentage of *Waishengren* who would support Taiwan in this case *anyway*. The results were very surprising, even while a good part of the respondents had earlier claimed that unification was necessary and that Taiwan's Chineseness was indisputable. Offered the choice of qualifying such an attack as "an invasion" or "an annihilation of the [independentist] traitor, but at the same time an invasion" or "an annihilation of the [independentist] traitor and a liberation of Taiwan,"[17] 39.1 percent of my respondents said such an attack would be an "invasion." The generational analysis shows that the younger the respondents were, the more likely they were to qualify a Chinese attack as an "invasion," even if, as stated, it was provoked after a declaration of independence (Table 8.8a).

The second answer, which expresses an ambivalent feeling, was the choice of 39.8 percent. Only 12.2 percent chose the third. Let us be clear: such a situation, in which Taiwan is attacked after declaring independence is, for several reasons, not likely to happen. My questionnaire was aimed only at measuring the figuration of Taiwan's *Waishengren*'s national identification. This required such theoretical questions to clarify the *Waishengren's* position in a time of relative peace. We will come back to this question again in conclusion. Table 8.8b shows a similar phenomenon: The younger the respondents are, the more important the Taiwan pole becomes in their pluralistic identification.

In fact, the national identification of Taiwan's *Waishengren* appears to the observer in various guises. The twin components, the Chinese pole and the Taiwanese pole are indeed interwoven in each individual—one could almost say apportioned—in a way that varies according to the degree of her or his Taiwanization. Indeed, within this mainstream of identity there exist older *Waishengren* who feel uncomfortable and not very Taiwanese, and *Waishengren* of the second or third generation born in Taiwan who regard the island as their homeland, yet without necessarily being proindependence. Every *Waishengren* feels in a personalized way the duality of such national identification. In this sense, the study of Taiwan's *Waishengren* strongly shows that theories of ethnicity should take much more into account the individual and particular history of the genesis of everyone's ethnicity.

Table 8.8a  *Waishengren's* **Theoretical Reaction to a Chinese Attack in Case of a Declaration of Independence (1), 1997** (percent)

Q.  If Taiwan declared its independence, or it was proved that the government was about to do it, and that it prompted China to unify Taiwan by force, which one of the following three expressions would you choose to qualify China's attack?

| | An invasion of Taiwan | An annihilation of the traitor but at the same time an invasion | An annihilation of the traitor and a liberation of Taiwan | No answer; Does not know |
|---|---|---|---|---|
| *Waishengren* born in China | 30.5 | 40.5 | 16 | 13 |
| *Waishengren* born in Taiwan (1945–1967) | 37.2 | 43 | 9.6 | 10.2 |
| *Waishengren* born in Taiwan (1968–1981) | 63.3 | 30.7 | 2 | 4 |

*Source:* same as Table 8.1.
*Note:* Total of each line = 100% of the total number of a generation.

Table 8.8b  *Waishengren's* **Theoretical Reaction to a Chinese Attack in Case of a Declaration of Independence (2), 1997** (percent)

Q.  If Taiwan declared its independence, or it was proved that the government was about to do it, and that it prompted China to unify Taiwan by force, what would be, in your eyes, the best reaction to have?

| | Resist | Accept | Emigrate | Discuss | No answer; Does not know |
|---|---|---|---|---|---|
| *Waishengren* born in China | 23.2 | 5.8 | 11.6 | 53.6 | 5.8 |
| *Waishengren* born in Taiwan (1945–1967) | 32.1 | 9 | 11.5 | 38.5 | 8.9 |
| *Waishengren* born in Taiwan (1968–1981) | 40.8 | 12.2 | 10.2 | 34.7 | 2.1 |

*Source:* Same as Table 8.1.
*Note:* Total of each line = 100% of the total number of a generation.

Outside of this Mainland identity mainstream, two extremes can still be found, each just as diverse. These are the *Waishengren* who are radically opposed to any show whatsoever of Taiwaneseness and the *Waishengren* who are militating for the island's independence in the *Waishengren* association for Taiwan independence (*Goa-seng-lang Taiwan duli xiejinhui*). The former, those *Waishengren* who are the most imbued with Chinese nationalism, are not, however, in as radical a break as one could claim from the mainstream of Taiwan's *Waishengren*. Even those attempting to track down, so as to (un)mask, the slightest demonstration of Taiwanization in their way of being, saying, or thinking, are themselves examples of *Taiwanese Waishengren*, if only through their political ideas or the type of Chinese they speak. They therefore find themselves much more in a cultural *continuum*—made up of variations that are sometimes marked, sometimes less so—than within a group that is clearly distinct from the majority. Conversely, the break is clearer among the *Waishengren* militating for Taiwan independence. This is a fine show of their own independence of mind with respect to the force of the teachings which have been inculcated into them, in the immersion in family culture, and through years of Chinese nationalist political socialization. People in this group are able to shake off the education to the national feeling they received, the supposed basis of the cohesion of nation-states throughout the world. Yet, it is no great surprise that they are a minority among the *Waishengren*. If I find that 17 percent of the *Waishengren* consider that independence could be "a positive thing for Taiwan," this figures drops to 2.8 percent for those who hold this position while believing at the same time that Taiwan's Chineseness is subject to debate *and* that Chinese and Taiwanese are two different ethnic groups. In 1999, according to surveys made by the Electoral Study Center of Chengchi University, 2.7 percent of the *Waishengren* favor immediate independence (4.6 percent for the entire population) and 5.9 percent give their preference to the *status quo* leading to independence on the long run.[18]

One interesting point shown by the data given above in this chapter is the generational factor in question of the *Waishengren*'s national identification. Among my respondents, those who consider themselves *"Waishengren"* compose 59.4 percent of the Mainland-born cohort, 45.5 percent of the first Taiwan-born cohort (born between 1945 and 1967), and 40.7 percent of the second Taiwan-born cohort (those born between 1968 and 1981). Obviously, members of this last generation have the least reason of the three to view themselves as "Mainlanders," and the fact that 40.7 percent of them still do so shows the power of ascription by others in ethnic identification, in addition to self-ascription. The same transgenerational change is perceptible in the answers to the question asking whether being *Waishengren* makes someone different (yes, 44.9 percent, 38 percent, and 34.6 percent, respectively) and whether this difference is a "plus" (26 percent, 20.5 percent, and 14.3 percent, respectively). Conversely, *Waishengren* born on Taiwan are more likely to "strongly" share the *"luo di sheng gen"* feeling (26.1 percent, 41 percent, and 49 percent). Wachman has taken seriously into account this generational phenomenon in his 1994 work on the national identity question (Wachman 1994), but at the time of his 1991 fieldwork, precise data were not available on this point.

### *Waishengren*? New Taiwanese? New Inhabitants?

How then could we call this population? We have seen that the refugee generation of *Waishengren* are more prompt to identify with their province of origin than with the general concept of *"Waishengren."* Many older second-generation *Waishengren*, born during what Hsiao Hsin-Huang calls Taiwan's "political period" (*zhengzhi qi*), the 1950s and 1960s, and who view China as their motherland but have grown up in Taiwan, often complain that after half a century, they are still viewed as "extraneous": The term *"Waishengren"* contains the word *"wai,"* or "external," "extraneous," "foreign" (See, for instance, Ma 1995, 75–91). Younger second-generation or third-generation *Waishengren* already have a stronger feeling of identification with Taiwan and have stopped calling themselves *Waishengren*. Proindependence *Waishengren* simply demarcate themselves from the *Waishengren* label, even if they cannot drop it: When they want to promote their cause, they have to state who they are to give credit to their arguments. Globally, only 47 percent of the respondents to my questionnaire call themselves *"Waishengren"* (others use *Zhongguoren* and some *Taiwanren*). So if important segments of the *Waishengren* population, in each of the three generations cohort, dislike being called "People from outer provinces," is it legitimate to go on using this word? Probably not, but the problem is to find something else, and this is a difficult issue. And finding a correct name that has no more administrative or political meaning could have a positive impact on Taiwan's interethnic relations.

In recent years, a new expression has surfaced, the "New Taiwanese" (*Xin Taiwanren*). Many observers outside Taiwan became aware of this concept through Lee Teng-hui's famous article in *Foreign Affairs* (Lee 1999b). But the history of this concept goes back to some time before. In August 1995, Lee Teng-hui used this concept in a speech to the KMT after being chosen as the Nationalist Party's candidate for the 1996 presidential election. Even if the conservative faction was far from being powerless at that time,[19] he had just been chosen as the KMT's candidate and could afford to immediately advance one more step toward the Taiwanization of the political rhetoric. He carefully worded the concept, that he called *"Xin Taiwanren guan"* (The "New Taiwanese" conception). For him, it meant, "abandoning divisions based on who arrived first or later" (*xian lai, hou dao*), and stressing instead "the love of Taiwan" and the "efforts made for Taiwan," but still, then, with the idea that Taiwanese were Chinese and that they "should not forget ultimate reunification." The following spring, Soong Chu-yu, the Mainlander who would become Lee's bitter foe inside the KMT after the 1997 constitutional reform, tried to ride the wave of this new concept, calling it pompously *"Xin Taiwanren zhuyi"* (New Taiwanism) in an April 2, 1996, speech in the Provincial Assembly. The press commented widely, forgetting he was not the first to speak about this. For Soong Chu-yu, it meant "ethnic harmony, not Taiwan independence."[20] In the following days, Hsieh Chang-ting, who had just lost the presidential election as DPP's vice-presidential candidate, protested Soong's claim of political paternity, saying he was the one who had authored the concept a long time before.[21] The concept received strong publicity once again on December 5, 1998, when Lee Teng-hui questioned in Holo Ma Ying-jeou (a *Waishengren*), the KMT candidate for Taipei mayoralty, "Ma Ying-jeou, where do you come from?" (*Ma Eng-kiu, li si to-ui e lang?*), to which this latter replied "spontaneously" in Holo.

> *Po-ko Li Chong-thong, goa si lim Tai-oan chui, chiah Tai-oan bi e sin Tai-oan-lang, Bang-kah chhut-si e chin-chian e Tai-pak lang* (Here's my report to President Lee: I am a new Taiwanese who grew up drinking Taiwan water and eating Taiwanese rice, a true Taipeinese born in Wanhua).

This sentence was widely commented on in the Taiwanese press, and the concept used was now called *Xin Taiwanren lun* (The debate on the New Taiwanese). This latter episode was an obvious political strategy, and Lee Teng-hui soon confirmed this in his May 1999 political testament (Lee 1999a: 262–263). For Ma Ying-jeou, it was a live and widely broadcast invention, since he was not born in Taipei's Wanhua district, but on the Mainland in Henan Province, Hengshan district, on July 13, 1950. Ma Ying-jeou is a moderate prounificationist, and since his election, has totally abandoned the "New Taiwanese" rhetoric until, perhaps, the next electoral campaign. However, for Lee Teng-hui, the 1998 use of the concept as a political strategy did not mean he was not otherwise deeply convinced of its interest. In his *Taiwan di zhuzhang*, published on May 19, 1999, Lee Teng-hui repeated the two elements stated in 1995, but added a new one.

> Taiwan was able to melt together ethnic cultures with different historical backgrounds, which produced a new ethnic group, radically different from that one on Mainland (*Xingcheng yige han dalu wanchuan bu tong de xin zuqun*) (Lee 1999a, 78).

This sentence was written by the president of the KMT, which remained a prounification party in spite of Lee Teng-hui's efforts to Taiwanize it. Present in the Japanese version dictated by Lee himself (Lee 1999b, 58), it is contained in the Chinese translation. But it has been omitted in the official English translation (Lee 1999c, 63), though the translation had been overseen by the Presidential Office itself. It was probably too openly pressing the world to acknowledge that Taiwan is becoming a nation-state. Again, in his *Yaxiya di zhilüe*, published in 2000, Lee insists several times on the concept.

The idea of a New Taiwanese people is definitely political. Any claim that this would *already* designate the new reality of Taiwan would be exaggerated, for ethnic divisions have not yet vanished. People take the *shengji wenti* (the question of provincial origin) much less into consideration than before, which shows that behind political slogans, the progressive emergence of a new ethnic consciousness is real. However, the current ethnic dividing lines have not yet disappeared, and it will take many more years for them to vanish and be replaced by another divide: "we," Taiwanese in Taiwan, and "they," Chinese in China. As Hsiao Hsin-huang says in the preface to a book by a *Waisheng* author comparing *Waishengren* to "butterflies" eaten by [Taiwanese] "tigers": "Today, the true 'tigers' are Chinese Communists on the other side of the straits" (Ma 1995, 7–8). The idea of "New Taiwanese" is today still more a goal to reach than an already palpable reality. It suits the claim of Lee Teng-hui's Taiwanese faction inside the KMT to have transformed Taiwan, but this transformation is not yet finished, as Lee acknowledges in a recent book (Lee 2000, 11). I did not ask any questions about this concept of "New Taiwanese" in my 1997 questionnaire. The concept was still too recent at that time for me to include it. Yet, we have already seen important data showing the extent—which also means the limits—of the *Waishengren*'s identification with Taiwan. Clearly, most refugee generation *Waishengren* are not a group that can be easily included in the concept of New Taiwanese, and most would not like to be. However, even this group shows a process of "indigenization" (*tuzhu hua*) in their manner, thoughts, language, and political values; what we may call the unavoidable Taiwanese "tropism" of the *Waishengren*.[22] Second- and third-generation *Waishengren* less and less deserve to be called Mainlanders or *Waishengren*, for their identification with the land on which they were born is obvious, and, in many cases, claimed.

True, we can also find among them young second- or third-generation *Waishengren* who have not established any distance from the political socialization of the past and who hold various prounification feelings from soft to extreme. As a thirty-two-year-old *Waishengren* said to me in 1999: "Communists can invade Taiwan. I welcome them. It will be still better than Taiwan independence!" (*Zhonggong keyi da. Wo huanying tamen. Bi Taidu hao de duo!*). But such opinions are very rare among young *Waishengren* today. Surveys show that *Waishengren* are globally still more inclined to reunification than other Taiwanese, yet we should not fail to take their progressive indigenization into account. I hope to have shown here that, maybe more for this population than for others in Taiwan, age is a fundamental variable. The *Waishengren* force us to ask the question: For how many generations and how long can we still consider refugees as being foreign? For how many generations and years can an ethnic group coming from outside maintain its ethnic specificity? The Jewish diaspora's culture is increasingly seen as disappearing from most countries in the West, being reduced to parts of cities like New York, while the Israeli state is seen by some Jews as monopolizing a different, poorer, and official Jewish identity. Tibetan refugees have been closely monitored by the Dalai Lama's government-in-exile, yet this latter finds it more and more difficul to keep alive the Tibetan consciousness and culture among younger generations born in India. After 1988, Taiwan's *Waishengren* lost the key political safeguard protecting their cultural specificity, their political illusions of being in a province of China that should ultimately be reunified and the superiority conferred by their ethnic status: a government composed at the top of people extracted from their own ethnic group. Pressure to Taiwanization is so strong today that it makes it difficult to reverse the course of history.

The issue of finding the correct name for the *Waishengren* is a difficult, sensitive, and emotional one. The *Waishengren*'s Taiwanese tropism is gradual, often hesitant, and the degree varies a lot from one generation to another, from one person to another, and even for the same person, with the situation considered. However, it is obvious that this population is in the process of becoming part of a new "people," itself being born gradually under our eyes. Furthermore, a part of the *Waishengren* population reject the ethnic label used to designate them. It should also be noted that this expression is connoted by a past that most wish now to forget. Last, but important the expression *Waishengren*, as mentioned in the beginning of this chapter, contains a word, *"sheng,"* which is more and more in contradiction with the aim of building Taiwan into a nation, reminding the island of its theoretical constitutional status as a province of the ROC. It may still be premature to include them unilaterally in a New Taiwanese community, but it is certain that the words *Wai-sheng-ren* are more inappropriate than ever. So perhaps we should simply call them, for the time being, Taiwan's "New Inhabitants" (*Xin zhumin*).

**Where Is the Nation?**

In this chapter, I have tried to explain who the New Inhabitants are by showing how the *Waishengren* ethnic label appeared in Taiwan and by trying to characterize their mind-set regarding important dimensions of national identification. This question of identification has been central to this chapter, as it is, in my eyes, to the study of national identity itself. We have seen that the particular historical experience and political position of the New Inhabitants has complicated their perception of these two potential objects of national identification: China and Taiwan, between which the relation can be of inclusiveness or separateness (seeing Taiwan as a part of China or not). This means at least four possible identification schemes are available to them: identifying with Mainland China and with Taiwan-as-a-part-of-China; identifying with China and denying any identification with Taiwan, considered as a part of China or not; identifying with China and with Taiwan, while considering that now, the two are distinct national entities; identifying with Taiwan only, considering that Taiwan is now a nation-state of its own and rejecting any identification with China. But more important, it is the nature of these identification feelings that we must analyze, and only this can help us see plurality where, otherwise, we would see paradoxes or contradictions. It seems to me that the New Inhabitants are experiencing at the same time four different types of identification with these two poles, China and Taiwan. One is ethnic identification. Most New Inhabitants identify themselves as being Han people, the Han group constituting the majority of the population in China. The myth of the "yellow emperor" among New Inhabitants is described in chapter 5. In addition to this, there is a distinct identification with China that is of a different nature, and it is an identification with cultural China, or if we prefer, a cultural identification with China. China is the country from which their language and cultural customs originate; this is the country whose history they learned at school. In addition, they view this country as the main cultural matrix of Taiwanese society (many tend to forget that it is so far the only one), and so living in Taiwan is not supposed to contradict this identification. Their ethnic and cultural identification with the Han and with China has been heavily reinforced by the decades of a nationalistic political socialization stressing the so-called majesty and greatness of the Han race (*Hanzu de weida*). But obviously, after decades of irrepressible localization, the New Inhabitants also have a local-personal identification with the place where they have spent such a long time: Taiwan. In this scheme, Taiwan is not yet viewed as a national entity. This identification is not ethnic. It is not purely cultural either: It is a question of personal history, it is the local and personal dimension of the multilayered identification with places in the human experience, that range from the tinest locality to the national level and beyond. This identification is clearly associated with the place of birth and places where the individual has spent a lot of time. For first-generation New Inhabitants, this identification is plural itself and composed both of their place of origin and of the place where they live in Taiwan. I added the word "personal" in this form of identification because its shape varies from one person to another, depending on her or his personal history. Last, there is the national identification dimension, which is the most problematic one and the most difficult to define, perhaps because it partially contains the other dimensions. It is hard to define the manifestation of this national identification because it is hard to define the nation for the New Inhabitants (and for many Taiwanese, too). For most, it is no longer Mainland China only, but not yet Taiwan only. This difficulty in indicating where the nation is stems from Taiwan's identity transition, and inside this transition movement, New Inhabitants's ongoing process of indigenization. As long as Taiwan is officially named the Republic of China and does not officially abandon the goal of reunification, it is clear that the "national" identification of the New Inhabitants is directed to this regime. Completing the local-personal dimension of identification, we could say that it is more a national-civic identification. But in this national-civic identification, the two poles, Chinese and Taiwanese, interact and occasionally conflict. For some, the national identification with the ROC on Taiwan is blurred by the ethnic identification with the Han race and the cultural identification with China. Their growing exasperation, provoked by Taiwan's nation-building movement, makes them associate and confuse more and more the Han race, Mainland China, and the PRC, resulting in an ambivalent allegiance to Taipei's ROC regime.

I tried to show that the question of the national identification of such a politically sensitive population in Taiwan must be serialized to let us, if not answer complex questions, at least be aware of this complexity. As there is a constant pressure to politicize identities, as shown above, then the question can be analyzed politically. It is threefold. First, it is important to know that the New Inhabitants have indeed Taiwanized and most of them include Taiwan in their identification scheme, at least to some extent. But second, this day-to-day, irrepressible and undeniable movement of Taiwan tropism is contradicted each time a political choice is necessary, and as Taiwan is now a well-developed democracy, expressing a position or making a choice such as a vote is frequent in Taiwan. The political choice crystallizes the positions, simplifies complexity, and negates the possibility of plurality. Just because politics requires action and that action needs mobilization, this Taiwanization of the New Inhabitants, which appears so strongly in their day-to-day activities, instantly vanishes in most of their political acts, from expressing their view of Taiwan's identity to choosing the nation's president. Their Taiwanization is thus sometimes reduced to nothing when a political logic forces them to make a choice. But, third, this does not mean that this Taiwanization does not exist. Consequently, the most central question regarding their national identification is, in the end, their political behavior and national allegiance to

Taiwan's government in case of a major political and military crisis in the straits. The common assumption is that in such a *situation-limite*,[23] many would side with China. If we use the division of identification feelings into the four above-mentioned categories, we can see that different factors might play a different role: Would the ethnic identification supplant and annihilate their local identification? Or would they distinguish, in a situation of emergency when a choice is required, between a cultural identification with China and a political allegiance and national identification with Taiwan, which are not incompatible? Let us hope that this question will remain a theoretical one.

## Notes

1. It was only on May 1, 1963, that an official body (the civil affairs department of the provincial government, or *sheng minzhengting*), recommended calling the Austronesians "compatriots from the mountains" (*shanbao*, or *shandi tongbao*) and no longer "mountain savages" (*shanfan*), a term then occasionally used. In 1994, the Austronesians succeeded in having the expression "Aborigines" (*Yuanzhumin*) written into the "additional articles" of the constitution, nos. 1, 4, and 10, and adopted in 1991 and amended on August 1, 1994 and July 18, 1997. But, contrary to their intention, the National Assembly made a distinction between "Aborigines of the plains" (*pingdi Yuanzhumin*) and "Aborigines from the mountains" (*shandi Yuanzhumin*). Articles 1 and 4 determine the number of representatives elected by the *Yuanzhumin* to the National Assembly, the upper chamber (*guomin dahui*), and to the Legislative Yuan, the lower chamber (*lifa yuan*). Article 10, in its new formulation since 1997, lays down the constitutional principle of the protection of Aboriginal culture in Taiwan.

2. The 1990 census put the population of *Waishengren* at 12.74 percent. The question of ancestral origin (*zuji*) was removed from the 1966 census, whereas that of provincial origin (*jiguan*), asked by all government organizations, survived until 1992, when it was officially suppressed by the Legislative Yuan. As a consequence, it has been difficult ever since to obtain accurate data on this subject.

3. Some paragraphs of the present chapter appeared in my article, "Taiwan Mainlanders: A New Ethnic Category" (Corcuff 2000a). They are reprinted here with authorization of the editor of *China Perspectives* (CEFC, Hong Kong).

4. It is probably due to the complexity of the Chinese term and the strong association of those designated by it, with China directly opposite Taiwan on the Asian continent, that caused the term *"Waishengren"* to be translated simply as "Mainlanders." We should note that the translation of the Chinese expression as "People from outside the province" (of Taiwan), which is sometimes found, is erroneous. It would then be *"Shengwairen,"* an expression with a significantly different meaning.

5. Estimate by Li Tung-ming for the period 1947 to 1964 in the journal *Taipei Archives* in 1969 (Li 1969, 215–249).

6. Estimate by Chiang Kai-shek's aide-de-camp and strategic advisor at the time, Konsin Shah, who thinks that the number included more than a million military personnel (interview with Konsin Shah in Taipei, July 18, 1997). K. Shah was born on September 17, 1919, in Shanghai, into a family from Zhejiang Province, Chiang Kai-shek's birthplace. In his capacity as the latter's aide-de-camp, he was responsible for transmitting Chiang's orders to the military High Command. He had the function of

strategic advisor from November 1945 to March 1951, then of secretary for confidential affairs from March 1951 to May 1953. His biography provides insight into the reasons for a possible massaging of the real statistics. Inflating the numbers of *Waishengren* who followed Chiang Kai-shek from 1949 to 1950 quite possibly helped in the relegitimization of the regime, and this likely exaggeration of the number of soldiers who followed the Nationalists to Formosa may have also served as a tool of military dissuasion in the face of the Communist armies.

7. Li 1969.

8. Lee Teng-hui acknowledged the fact in an often cited interview with Shiba Ryotaro; he spoke of the KMT as a "power arrived from outside" (*Guomindang ye shi wai lai zhengquan*) (Lee 1994).

9. The various languages spoken in Taiwan are the Minnan dialect (originally from Fujian Province), two Hakka dialects, several minority Austronesian languages, and, since Taiwan's handover to China, the so-called Mandarin. The Minnan dialect spoken in Taiwan is slightly different from that spoken in Fujian Province, owing to Taiwan's particular historical and geographical circumstances. Proindependence supporters do not talk of "Minnan people" and the "Minnan dialect," as this expression refers to geographically specific Mainland origins, and has been used by the ruling KMT. They prefer the expression "Holo" (in Taiwanese), written "Helao," "Heluo," or "Fulao" in Mandarin, with a preference for the first one ("Helao"; see "Holo" in the glossary). The term "Holo" seems to have been first used by Hakka people to speak of the Minnan people (See Shih 1997, 99, note 2). The transcription *Hok-lo* or *Hoklo* is also often found.

10. This research questionnaire was entitled *Waishengren yu guojia rentong di zhuanbian* (*Waishengren* and the national identity transition). It was written and distributed in Taiwan between February and December 1997. The fact that no existing directory, index, or government database details precisely and systematically who is *Waishengren*, added to the fact that the *jiguan* (see following note) was suppressed in 1992, means that there is no way to scientifically select a sample. Three methods have been used for distribution in greater Taipei, Chiayi, Kaohsiung, Hualien, and Kinmen: (1) the extensive use of *guanxi*, by far the only efficient method to distribute a questionnaire on a sensitive topic; (2) distribution in personal mailboxes in *Waishengren*-populated areas; (3) door-to-door distribution to people after a face-to-face explanation of the nature of the study. The questionnaire was distributed to 948 persons along with a stamped envelope. Two hundred ninety-eight questionnaires were returned, of which 286 were useful. The ratio between the number of useful questionnaires received and the total distribution is 30.17 percent. The survey contained 178 questions in 26 pages, which made it impossible to conduct telephone interviews.

11. The *jiguan* states the subject's province, district, and locality of origin.

12. The system being a patrilinear one, the father passes on this character trait to all the children.

13. It is interesting to note that since then, Chiang Kai-shek's image has lost its luster, and in 1997, only 14.5 percent of the first-generation *Waishengren* (the refugees) surveyed expressed opposition to abandoning the holiday commemorating Chiang's birthday on October 31, a decision made the same year by the government.

14. "*Do not forget* the time when you were in Ju," in other words, "*Do not forget* the sacred goal of reunification."

15. A first compilation of a few expressions of "Taiwan guoyu" was made by Tsao Ming-tsung in 1993 (Tsao 1993).

16. The total is greater than 100 percent because some respondents chose to rank two or more policy items as number one priority, obviously misunderstanding how I wanted them to answer.

17. In these two answers, "independence" has been personified to facilitate the expression of the notion and clarify the respondents' theoretical position on this matter.

18. In those surveys, *Waishengren* are still more favorable to immediate unification (4.8 percent compared with 2.4 percent for the whole population) or to unification in a more distant future (32.5 percent compared with 14.1 percent), but most of them are today also for the upholding of a permanent *status quo* (19.1 percent compared with 19.3 percent for the entire population) or an undetermined delay of a final decision regarding this very sensitive question (30.9 percent compared with 30.8 percent) (*Xuanju yanjiu zhongxin*, National Chengchi University, 1999).

19. To give an example, the number of persons who signed, at the same time, a declaration to institute a conservative "Committee to Save the Party" opposed to Lee and his faction, reached 8,000.

20. *Ziyou shibao* (Liberty times), April 3, 1996.

21. According to Wei-der Shu, Hsieh Chang-ting may indeed be the author of this concept, having expressed in 1985–1986 a concept close to the notion of interethnic "community." But Shu opines also that as early as the 1970s, the question was raised among exiled proindependence activists of what to do with the *Waishengren* once independence had been declared. According to him, there was far from a consensus on this point, as some voices were raised to include the Mainlanders in Taiwan's "community," as long as they identified with Taiwan

22. The word "tropism" precisely means the orientation of an organism toward a certain direction, under the effect of an external stimulus such as light, especially by growth rather than by movement.

23. See Introduction, note 1.

## Bibliography

### In Chinese

Huang Hsuan-fan. 1993. *Yuyan, shehui yu zuqun yishi—Taiwan yuyan shehuixue di yanjiu* (Language, society and ethnic consciousness—Research on the study of Taiwanese linguistic society). Taipei: Wenhe chubanshe.

Lee Teng-hui. 1999a (May). *Taiwan di zhuzhang* (Taiwan's point of view). Taipei: Yuanliu.

——. 2000. *Yaxiya di zhilüe* (Asia's wisdom). Taipei: Yuanliu.

Li Tung-ming. 1969. *Guangfu hou Taiwan renkou shehui zengjia zhi tantao* (Investigation of the social increase of Taiwan's population after the Kuang-fu [Retrocession]). *Taipei wenxian* (November–December): 215–249.

Ma Yi-kung. 1995. *Laohu chi hudie* (Tigers eat butterflies). Taipei: Shangzhou wenhua.

Shih Cheng-feng. 1997. "Taiwan di zuqun zhengzhi." In *Zuqun zhengzhi yu zhengci* (Ethnic politics and strategy) Ed. Shih Cheng-feng. Taipei: Qianwei.

Tsao Ming-tsung. 1993. *Taiwan guoyu* (Taiwanese Mandarin). Taipei: Lianjing.

### In English

Barth, Fredrik. 1969. "Introduction." In *Ethnic Groups and Boundaries: The Social Organization of Culture Difference*. Ed. Fredrik Barth. Bergen: Universitetsforlaget; London: Allen and Unwin.

————. 1994. "Enduring and Emerging Issues in the Analysis of Ethnicity." In *The Anthropology of Ethnicity*. Ed. Hans Vermeulen and Cora Govers. Amsterdam: Het Spinuis.

Chang Hui-ching. 1998. "From 'Orphan of Asia' to 'Moses Out of Egypt': A Metaphorical Analysis of the Transformation of Taiwan's Political Identity." Working paper, University of Illinois at Chicago.

Corcuff, Stéphane. 2000a. "Taiwan's Mainlanders, a New Ethnic Category." *China Perspectives* no. 28 (March–April 2000):71–81.

Duara, Prasenjit. 1995. *Rescuing History from the Nation. Questioning Narratives in Contemporary China*. Chicago: University of Chicago Press.

Erickson, Erik H. 1968. *Identity, Youth and Crisis*. New York: Norton.

Gates, Hill. 1981. "Ethnicity and Social Class." In *The Anthropology of Taiwanese Society*. Ed. Emily Martin Ahern and Hill Gates. Stanford, CA: Stanford University Press.

Guneratne, Arjun. 1998. "Modernization, the State, and the Construction of a Tharu Identity in Nepal." *Journal of Asian Studies* 57, no. 3 (August): 749–773.

Lee Teng-hui. 1999c (September). *The Road to Democracy. Taiwan's Pursuit of identity*. Tokyo: PHP.

Lee Teng-hui. 1999d (November–December). "Understanding Taiwan. Bridging the Perception Gap," *Foreign Affairs*.

Wachman, Alan M. 1994a. *Taiwan, National Identity and Democratization*. Armonk: M.E. Sharpe.

————. 1994b. "Competing Identities in Taiwan." In *The Other Taiwan. 1945 to the Present*. Ed. Murray A. Rubinstein. Armonk: M.E. Sharpe.

**In French**

Corcuff, Stéphane. 2000b. *Une identification nationale plurielle. Les Waishengren et la transition identitaire à Taiwan, 1988–1997* (A pluralistic national identification. *Waishengren* and the identity transition in Taiwan, 1988–1997). Ph.D. thesis, Paris Institute of Political Studies, 821 p.

Halbwachs, Maurice. 1997 [1950]. *La mémoire collective* (Collective memory). Paris: Albin Michel.

**In Japanese**

Lee Teng-hui. 1994. Interview with a reporter from the *Asahi Shimbun*. Weekly magazine of *Asahi Shimbun*, Tokyo, May 5–13, 1994.

Lee Teng-hui. 1999b (June). *Taiwan no sucho* (Taiwan's point of view). Tokyo: PHP.

# — 9 —

# Toward a Pragmatic Nationalism

## Democratization and Taiwan's Passive Revolution

### *Rwei-Ren Wu*

The thesis alone in fact develops to the full its potential for struggle, up to the point where it absorbs even the so-called representatives of the antithesis: it is precisely in this that the passive revolution or revolution/restoration consists. The problem of the political struggle's transition from a "war of maneuver" to a "war of position" certainly needs to be considered at this juncture.

—Antonio Gramsci, *Selection from Prison Notebooks*

What on earth is the goal of Taiwan's democratization? Simply put, it is to "nativize Taiwan."

—Lee Teng-hui, *Strategic Wisdom for Asia*

## Introduction

This chapter studies the politics of contemporary Taiwanese nationalism. It argues that Taiwan's democratization in the decade 1988–1997, which resulted in the consolidation of President Lee Teng-hui's hegemony and the total political ascendancy of native Taiwanese can be understood as a particular form of decolonization through which a nativized state similar to a nation-state was formed. Following Antonio Gramsci's thesis of passive revolution, this paper identifies two contrary but mutually indispensable tendencies within this historical process, the moderate line led by Lee Teng-hui and his nativized Kuomintang (KMT) and the radical line led by the opposition Democratic Progressive Party (DPP). It posits that it was the final victory of Lee's moderate line in the struggle against the DPP that determined the reformist *du-Tai* (literally, independent Taiwan)[1] nature of the new regime and created the hegemony of the theory and practice of a pragmatic Taiwanese nationalism.

This is a project with limited ambition. It focuses its analysis on the relationship between two major players, the nativized KMT and the DPP. It does not deal with the exiled Taiwanese Independence Movement, which was crucial in articulating the early discourse of Taiwanese nationalism in the postwar era (see chapter 3) but played only a limited role in the later democratic movement within the island. It treats the New Party (NP) merely as a background factor because it is hard to interpret the NP's Chinese nationalism as any version of Taiwanese nationalism, at least during the period covered by this study.[2] The complicated relationship between the NP's increasingly pragmatic notion of Chinese nationalism and Taiwanese nationalism, while indispensable to grasping the whole dynamics of contemporary Taiwanese politics, must wait for a larger project.

### "Passive Revolution" and Nation-State Formation

Nationalism, as John Breuilly (1982) argues, is above all a form of politics. More specifically, it is mainly a form of opposition politics that seeks ultimately to seize state power. In accordance with this reasoning, we may well consider the process of any nationalist politics that succeeds in seizing state power as one of the formations of a particular type of state, that is, the nation-state.[3] If this formulation has merit, a crucial theoretical question then arises: How do we account for this process? Is there an observable pattern in the political dynamics of this process of nation-state formation?

Antonio Gramsci (1971, 180–185), the great political theorist of the Italian Communist Party in the early twentieth century, formulated an idea of "passive revolution" to characterize the political dynamics of the *Risorgimento* from which the modern Italian nation-state was born. To begin with, he indicated that three factors prevented a French style of revolution from taking place in Italy in the later half of the nineteenth century. First, on the level of "objective structure," the low level of material productivity, the agrarian economy, and the existence of powerful old ruling classes revealed the relative weakness of the bourgeoisie. Second, on the level of "relation of political forces," the hegemony of the bourgeoisie over the whole society was incomplete and fragmented. Third, on the level of "relation of military forces," there was no effective political–military leadership opposed to the occupying Austria. Combined, these three factors forced the bourgeoisie to give up any attempt at frontal assault, which he terms "war of maneuver," on the *ancien regime* as their French counterpart had done in 1789. They could only resort to an alternative strategy, one of gradual, protracted, and many-fronted struggle, a "war of position." They sought to neutralize most of the old ruling elite, attacked only a selected few, and co-opted some into a new ruling coalition so that a well-monitored, piecemeal, limited reform could be set into motion. It was a "passive" revolution because it was a revolution from above and largely bypassed the masses in the process.

Gramsci then depicts a more textured picture of the internal dynamics of the *Risorgimento*. He identifies two contrary tendencies within the movement: one of gradualism, moderate reform controlled from above, represented by Camillo di Cavour, the prime minister of Piedmont, and the other of popular initiative and radical challenge of the old order, represented by the nationalist visionary Giuseppe Mazzini and his radical Action Party. It was the reformist but shrewdly realistic Cavour and his Moderate Party that successfully appropriated Mazzini's popular line in an overall strategy of "war of position," took over the leadership of the *Risorgimento*, and ultimately defined the conservative and royalist nature of the new Italian nation-state. At the core of Gramsci's analysis is political leadership: According to Gramsci, the key lies in Cavour's ability—and of course, Mazzini's inability—to understand both the moderates' and the radicals' roles in the historical process of Italian nationalism. It was this ability to grasp the dialectics of antithetical forces in history that enabled Cavour to appropriate Mazzini's radicalism so effectively (Gramsci 1971, 106–114).

Gramsci does not pretend to propose a general theory of nation-state formation; nevertheless, he does intend to propose, through his dissection of the *Risorgimento,* an "interpretative criterion of molecular changes" for similar historical situations, such as India under the British Raj (114). As the theorist of subaltern studies, Partha Chatterjee (1993) points out that implicit in Gramsci's analysis of the *Risorgimento* is a claim that the aforementioned two tendencies, that is, war of position and war of maneuver, indeed constitute a general pattern of the political dynamics of similar movements that sought to create a state of their own from the nineteenth century on. Chatterjee cautions us, however, that for Gramsci the equilibrium that would result from the struggle between these tendencies was by no means predetermined; rather, it depended "on the particular moments of the relation of forces, especially on the relative quality of the subjective forces which provided political-ideological leadership to each tendency" (1993, 46).

Gramsci's thesis of "passive revolution" provides a useful interpretative framework for analyzing what Roger Brubaker calls "polity-seeking nationalisms" (1996, 79). Chatterjee himself, taking the cue from Gramsci's suggestion that Gandhism embodied in the Indian case an example of "war of position," goes so far as to argue that passive revolution is actually the general form of the transition from colonial to postcolonial nation-states. Such a bold claim is surely yet to be substantiated by further comparative studies, but Chatterjee's following remarks do offer heuristic guidelines for any study of nationalism that attempts to go along with the Gramscian argument:

> If we are to apply this "interpretative criterion of molecular changes" to anti-colonial movements in the non-European parts of the world, movements seeking to replace colonial rule with a modern national state structure, we would be led into identifying at the level of the overall political-ideological strategy the two conflicting and yet mutually indispensable tendencies. The specific organizational forms in which the two tendencies appear in particular national movements, the manner in which the struggle takes place between them, the particular form of resolution of the struggle—all of these could be documented and analyzed in order to provide a more varied and comprehensive treatment of the problem of the formation of national states in recent history. (1993, 46)

## The Case of Taiwan

### Settler State and Democratization/Decolonization

The KMT regime on Taiwan, from 1949 until the late 1980s, had been a special form of authoritarian regime. It was, first of all, a settler state[4]—an ethnically stratified political structure in which the émigré Mainlander settlers, a minority group, dominated the native Taiwanese who constituted an absolute majority of the total population (see the percentages per group given in the previous chapter).[5] Secondly, a systematic clientelistic structure was devised to incorporate the native Taiwanese elite into the political establishment, although mostly in subordinate positions (Wu Nai-teh 1987). Such an "ethnic authoritarianism" or "settler colonialism"[6] brought about a number of significant social outcomes. First, this institutionalized "cultural division of labor," to borrow Michael Hechter's term (1975), highly politicized the ethnic cleavage. Ethnicity—manifested in the official social classification based upon the provincial origins (*shengji*) of the population—which mainly differentiated the natives from the post-1949 immigrants from Mainland China, became the most salient social cleavage and thus carried the highest potential for political mobilization. Second, under this system of minority rule full democratization practically means nativization of the state. As a corollary, third, this system created a common interest for all native elite in democratizing and nativizing the state power. Fourth, however, the clientelist arrangement, by dividing the native elite into two groups, one co-opted into the KMT regime and one not co-opted, helped forge two different strategic lines to attain this common goal: the moderate line of the those co-opted into the KMT and the radical line of those who formed the core of political opposition outside the KMT establishment.

Structurally speaking, what the KMT system of rule created was a quasi, if not a classical, colonial situation.[7] It is surely no accident that under this system political opposition consisted predominantly of the native Taiwanese. It is no more an accident that this native elite in the opposition should have started to couch their ideology of opposition explicitly in a discourse of Taiwanese nationalism in the 1980s once the KMT's gradual liberalization began to allow for more political space. The articulation of this ideology of Taiwanese nationalism is less a false consciousness invented by a few shrewd political entrepreneurs than a structural necessity of the KMT's form of minority rule. Inasmuch as it was perceived by the native elite as an opposition to a state imposed from without and inasmuch as its goal was to nativize or indigenize (*bentuhua*) the state power, the struggle for democracy in Taiwan inevitably took on an outlook of an anticolonial national movement. Therefore, it is not so far-fetched to understand certain aspects of the process of Taiwan's democratization as, at least in a strictly political sense, a special form of decolonization and to compare the native-dominated state, emerging as a result of democratization, with a newly formed, independent, postcolonial nation-state.[8]

Still, it should always be borne in mind that the KMT's system of clientelism also divided the native elite into two groups, one inside the KMT and the other outside of it. Differentially situated in the structure of power game, these two groups developed, for all their common interest in nativizing the state, different interests and thus different preferences as to how to achieve this goal. The moderates, having chosen to collaborate with the KMT, although only as junior partners, clearly had an interest in maintaining the integrity of the KMT regime as long as they had a chance to take over the party power. For them, the shortest route to state power was party power. To nativize the state, therefore, was above all to nativize the party. There was no need to disturb the Republic of China (ROC) system as long as the natives came to dominate the state. In other words, their best strategy was to *ethnicize* politics without explicitly nationalizing it. The radicals, represented by the earlier *dangwai* (literally, outside the [KMT] party) movement in the late 1970s and early 1980s, and the DPP since 1986, on the contrary, preferred to overthrow the KMT regime and build a brand-new, native-dominated government both in reality and in name. For the elite who were marginalized by the KMT-ROC system, only a fundamental restructuring of the political order can bring about meaningful redistribution of power and plenty. Given the political salience of the ethnic cleavage, it was almost inevitable that these radicals should have framed their ideology of opposition in terms of Taiwanese nationalism, that is, the construction of not only a native-dominated state, but also a new and independent Republic of Taiwan. In other words, the radicals' best strategy was to *nationalize* politics.

These two tendencies were imbedded in the KMT system of domination. They were gradually articulated and developed along with the process of President Chiang Ching-kuo's (CCK) policies of liberalization since the mid-1980s. However, they did not mature into two well-defined political lines of a single historical movement through which a nativized state was formed until Lee Teng-hui assumed the presidency and started to launch his policies of democratization from above in 1988. The native elite within the KMT, led by Lee Teng-hui himself, may well be said to have stood for a line of "war of position," whereas those in the opposition, led by the DPP, represented a line of "war of maneuver." Eventually, it was Lee and his entourage that came to dominate the process of this historical movement and successfully create a native-dominated but symbolically eclectic "Republic of China on Taiwan."

It should be noted that the two terms "moderate" and "radical" used here are purely analytical and relative. They refer not to two politico-ideological programs such as liberalism and socialism or right and left, but to the two major strategic positions in the Gramscian analytical framework of passive revolution. Therefore the DPP is radical in relation to the KMT in terms of how to capture state power. Whether the DPP is necessarily more radical than the KMT in a purely ideological sense is beyond the scope of this study.

### Structural Passivity of Taiwan's Political Transformation

Why did Lee and his moderates within the KMT, instead of the radical DPP, come to dominate the process of democratization/decolonization? If we examine, as Gramsci does in his analysis of the *Risorgimento*, the structural constraints confronting the native elite in 1988, we will find that these constraints strongly favored Lee and his moderate line.

First of all, the highly politicized ethnic cleavage created by the KMT's minority rule gave the title "the first native president," no matter who assumed it, a high degree of legitimacy—or a political "halo," as many Taiwanese journalists like to call it. Judging from Chiang Ching-kuo's preemptive strategy of co-opting more native elites into the higher positions within the

KMT, especially that of vice-presidency, we should not be totally amazed to see that, whether as a result of sheer contingency or CCK's calculation, eventually a native collaborator, Lee Teng-hui, instead of a native dissident, should have become the first native president. The high symbolic legitimacy Lee enjoyed as the first native president, from the very beginning, substantially determined the asymmetric relation between the two lines of the native elite.

Second, the dark shadow of a formidable external threat, that is, the gigantic PRC, was haunting the island of Taiwan on the eve of her democratization. The paramount concern of national security, one comparable to what Gramsci calls the limit of the "objective structure," placed a severe constraint upon the feasible set of choices for action of all native elite. At least, it directly posed a thorny question to the DPP radicals: how to persuade the Taiwanese people that, given the threat of a nationalistic PRC, their program of establishing an independent Republic of Taiwan was not only legitimate, but also practicable?

Third, but no less important, was the factor of Mainlanders. The existence of a significant minority who were likely to perceive any drastic political change as ethnic collective disenfranchisement posed a real concern for domestic stability. This was a real concern because the Mainlanders were in fact a powerful minority group not unlike the Afrikaaners in democratized South Africa: On the eve of democratization they controlled not only the key coercive state apparatus, the military, but also a substantial portion of ideological apparatuses and civilian media. In other words, neither did the native elite enjoy a complete ideological hegemony over the whole society nor could they exercise effective control over the military. It was apparent that, given the external threat of the PRC, Taiwan could not afford any serious internal division. That is to say, the native elite would have to democratize/nativize the state without alienating the Mainlanders. They were therefore faced with two tasks at the same time: democratization/nativization and political integration. Simply put, democracy and stability had to come as a package. If nativizing the state in the name of democracy was inevitable, enlisting cooperation from the Mainlander elite, or at least to neutralize them, was imperative. Which group of the native elite, then, was situated in a better strategic position to strike a bargain with the Mainlander elite, the moderate "comrades" within the KMT, or those "extremists" of the DPP? The answer is transparent.

### The Political Dialectics of Two Lines

It is now public knowledge that Lee's moderate line dominated the whole process of democratization/decolonization and won the ultimate victory manifested in his landslide in the presidential election of March 1996. It is true that the structural conditions had put Lee's moderate line in an advantageous position. However, as Chaterjee reminds us, the outcome of the struggle between these two lines were never predetermined. Favorable macrostructural conditions did not guarantee the ultimate victory of the moderates. We still have to examine, in the words of Chatterjee, "the relative quality of the 'subjective forces' which provided political-ideological leadership to each tendency" (1986, 46). To be sure, this paper cannot give a detailed historical account of the vicissitudes of these two lines during the past decade. What it can do, nevertheless, is to demonstrate schematically that the dialectical interactions—the struggle within unity—between the "subjective forces" of these two lines is indeed characteristic of a passive revolution.

**Thesis: Lee and the Taiwanese KMT**

It was Lee Teng-hui's shrewd "political-ideological leadership" that enabled his moderates, that is, the so-called Taiwanese KMT, to exploit the favorable conditions effectively and thoroughly, dominate the course of democratization, and ultimately consolidate a reformist regime. Lee is reform-minded, but he is no revolutionary. Both by temperament and by conviction, he is a gradualist reformer.[9] The whole story of his rise to power is still yet to be known, but the series of strategies he employed in his fight for power and glory were, beyond any shadow of a doubt, those of a classical "war of position."

*Politics*

When he succeeded CCK as the president in January of 1988, Lee was confronted with challenges from two sides: real and potential resistance from the conservative Mainlander elite within the KMT *ancien régime* to democratic reforms and the mounting popular pressure for democratization outside the party, especially from the newly formed DPP. As a moderate who preferred piecemeal reform monitored from above, he apparently needed to consolidate his power within the KMT regime before he could initiate any meaningful reform, which means he would have to deal with the intraparty opposition first. It is clear, at least from hindsight, that Lee had adopted a classical strategy of *divide et impera* to eliminate intraparty resistance. By building a series of long-term or temporary alliances with the more reformed-minded or opportunistic members of the old ruling elite and by exploiting the internal division of the Mainlander-dominated military, he effectively fragmented the old Mainlander ruling class.[10] At some points, moreover, he even built tacit alliances with popular forces such as the DPP and the rising social movements, thereby deftly using popular pressures (the so-called DPP card or public opinion card) to force some conservative old guards from the power core of the KMT.[11]

Lee tackled the challenge of the DPP mainly by appropriating most of the latter's central platforms, such as democracy, nativism, and social welfare. This strategy of preemption proved to be most effective, and thus most harmful to the DPP, when Lee also started to play the card of nativism or "Taiwanese consciousness" and even dared to flirt with some ideas of Taiwanese nationalism, such as "the sadness of Taiwanese" and "the Taiwanese exodus," which had long been the core of the native opposition's self-identity.[12] In fact, Lee's nativism had appeared rather credible to many long-time supporters or even some leaders of the DPP, not only because he was the first native Taiwanese to become president, but also because he actually was doing what those in the opposition had been longing to do; that is, to nativize, both politically and symbolically, the state imposed from without a half century ago. What is more, while Lee did appropriate the DPP's nativism, he claimed his position was a milder and more pragmatic line that would not irritate the PRC and thus should be distinguished from the DPP's irresponsible radicalism of Taiwanese independence. This no-less-powerful "card of peace and stability," together with the strategy of preemption, especially of the card of nativism, successfully contained the DPP's electoral expansion during the process of democratization in the 1990s. This point will become even clearer when we turn to his ideological strategy.

*Ideology*

What was Lee's ideological strategy? Although Lee had never explicitly used the language of Taiwanese nationalism, he shared with the explicit Taiwanese nationalism of the DPP a common goal of creating on the island of Taiwan a new, sovereign, native-dominated democratic state. Indeed, it was above all this ideological "kinship," so to speak, with the proindependence DPP that made Lee's appropriation of nativism possible and credible, if not compelling. If we examine the ideology of Lee and his Taiwanese KMT, we shall find that, in spite of the high rhetoric of "Reunification of China" or "Chinese people," what it sought to articulate in reality was very close to a variant of Taiwanese national identity.

From a close examination of some major texts publicized by the end of 1996, the author identifies seven key elements of Lee's official "Republic of China on Taiwan" discourse.[13]

1. *Unique subjectivity of Taiwan.* The philosophical premise of Lee's "ROC on Taiwan" ideology. The 400 years of external rule gave the locus (*basho*) of Taiwan a unique meaning. Self-identity starts from recognizing the difference between "self" and "other." The uniqueness of the locus of Taiwan constitutes the starting point of a unique self-identity.[14]

2. *Community of life.* Taiwan has become, after half a century of common effort on the part of all 2.1 million people since the end of World War II, an organic "national community of life" (*guojia shengming gongtongti*). We have all become "new Taiwanese."[15]

3. *The ROC on Taiwan is an independent sovereign state.* The Republic of China on Taiwan is an independent sovereign state. It has enjoyed unbroken and continuous independent sovereignty since 1912, although the territory under its effective jurisdiction since 1949 has been substantially contracted and limited to Taiwan, the Pescadores, Kinmen, and Matsu.[16]

4. *Democratization as the beginning of a new history in Taiwan.*[17]

5. *Rhetorical reunification.* There is one and only one China, and Taiwan is a part of China. There is no doubt that eventually Taiwan will be reunified with Mainland China. However, reunification must be on equal terms. More specifically, we insist on reunification under the condition that Taiwan maintains her sovereignty. The confederation model of European Union is worthy of our attention.[18]

6. *A purely cultural conception of China.* Taiwan, with a history of only 400 years and a concomitant lack of cultural resources, cannot break up with Chinese culture. Located at the interface of ocean and continent civilizations, she has the best chance to become a new center of Chinese culture (*xin zhongyuan*) by creatively merging these two great civilizations.[19]

7. *Straw-man definition of Taiwanese independence.* The Republic of China on Taiwan is an independent, sovereign state. Why do we have to bother to declare independence? However, the Republic of China on Taiwan is not to be confused with Taiwanese independence, because Taiwanese independence means changing the official name of our country to the Republic of Taiwan. That will bring us disaster.[20]

Apparently Lee is, as everybody suspects, advocating a so-called ROC-style Taiwanese independence or independent Taiwan (*du-Tai*). While recognizing the cultural affinity with China, he nonetheless insists on a unique and separate Taiwanese identity. His idea of reunification is at best rhetorical because there is little chance for the CCP, at least for some time to come, to accept Lee's insistence on "a form of reunification under which Taiwan maintains her sovereignty,"[21] meaning a certain form of confederation, given the absolute asymmetry in size and status in international law between Taiwan and China.[22] To set up such a stern condition for unification is none other than to postpone its realization indefinitely. Why, then, did Lee favor the ambiguous name the "ROC on Taiwan"? Why bother to merge two conflicting nationalist discourses into one?

The ambiguous rhetoric of "Lee-ism," so to speak, indeed revealed the "revolution/restoration" nature of his coalition within the KMT and its necessary eclecticism or centrism. What may be more important, nonetheless, is that it revealed Lee's anxiety over the reality of divided national identities in Taiwan and an attempt to reconcile them, at least on a discursive level. The discourse of a "community of life" of the "new Taiwanese" with an "independent sovereign state" called the "ROC on Taiwan" was clearly invented with a view to integrating all the people in Taiwan divided by two conflicting national identities into one tightly knit entity. Later in 1999, while reflecting upon this controversial discursive strategy, Lee straightforwardly confessed that what he had had in mind then was to create a solid "Taiwan identity" inclusive enough to subsume both Chinese and Taiwanese nationalisms.[23] To do so, the more exclusive notion of Taiwaneseness conceived in the traditional discourse of Taiwanese nationalism must be broadened and "diluted" so as to allow a decent space for political and cultural ideas of Chineseness.

This eclectic discourse was also invented to legitimate the new Lee regime: Domestically it sought to claim legitimacy over both those with Taiwanese identity and those with Chinese identity; internationally it sought to justify Taiwan's *de jure* sovereign statehood by appropriating, or "borrowing," the sovereignty of the ROC. Finally, in the eyes of Lee and his protégés, the discourse of the ROC on Taiwan, with a rhetorical insistence of reunification, was probably the only form of Taiwanese sovereignty least provocative to the PRC and thus the safest for Taiwan. All in all, the ideology of "Lee-ism" had everything to do with his overall strategy of "war of position."

## Antithesis: DPP

Judging from his crafty and realistic political and ideological maneuvering, it seems apparent that Lee was not only aware that structurally the advantage had been asymmetrically on his side from the very beginning, but, imitating Cavour, he was also conscious of what roles both his moderate line and the DPP's radicalism could play in the process of forming a nativized state. How did the DPP respond to both an unfavorable initial situation and the challenge of a dexterous political enemy-friend?

*Politics*

Unlike the Italian "visionary apostle" Mazzini, the secularistic DPP leaders were not unaware of Lee's double roles both as opponent and ally, enemy and friend. Throughout the process of democratization, they had to engage in two games at the same time: Whereas they had to compete with Lee in the game of winning state power through elections, they also had to ally, at least tacitly, with Lee in the struggle against the conservative Mainlander elite. Forced into such a relation of "union and struggle" with the much more resourceful Lee and his KMT, the young DPP had to walk a tightrope. To prevail, they needed will, concentration, and perseverance. In political terms, they needed strong leadership and solid organizational capacity. These requirements, unfortunately, proved to be too much for the DPP.

This does not mean that the DPP did not try to cope with their austere situation. It is fair to say that as early as 1990, the tactics of the "general line of election" devised by Hsu Hsin-liang, the two-time DPP leader known for his relentless pragmatism and strategic thinking, had quietly become the consensus of all leaders of the DPP once haunted by the bitter but misleading struggle between "mass line" and "parliament line." Under the guidance of these tactics, the seizure of the government through election became a necessary step to achieving the ultimate goal of establishing a new, independent Taiwanese state. Unified at least in this common desire for state power, the DPP actually managed to launch a series of electoral "frontal assaults" on the Lee regime from 1991 on. In these "election wars," the DPP leaders did come up with some counter strategies to deal with Lee's preemptive strikes mentioned in the previous section. To break the "native card," they turned to a more radical position of explicit Taiwanese independence in the 1991 National Assemblymen's election. Although the DPP secured a solid 30 percent in the first national election of the Legislative Yuan in 1992, their radical brand of "native card" seemed to have reached its limit in mobilizing votes. Sensing the poverty of a purely nativist-nationalist platform, in the local election of 1993 they shifted to certain improvised and ill-conceived social-policy appeals, mainly concerning senior citizens' pensions. When Lee endorsed his top Mainlander client, James Soong, in the gubernatorial election in 1994, some DPP elite also did not hesitate to mobilize ethnic sentiments for votes.

Although the DPP had indeed made some inroads in both national and local elections, it still remained an opposition party. Its stagnant electoral growth seemed to suggest that, faced with Lee Teng-hui, Hsu's "general line of election" was no less a rocky and protracted path to power. The DPP's failure to gain the national regime in the 1990s surely had everything to do with extremely unfavorable initial conditions, but it also had much to do with its inability to create a unified and strong party leadership and solid grassroots organizations. To wage effective electoral warfare against an opponent as resourceful as the Lee regime, they would have needed a well-organized party with a strong leadership able to solve all kinds of collective-action problems, ranging from allocating electoral resources (nomination, etc.) and creating public goods (search for appealing platforms) to disciplining free riders. To compete for votes with Lee, who inherited an extensive clientelistic system with tremendous mobilizing capacity, they would also have needed a solid organizational base on the grassroots level. Both conditions were absent in the case of the DPP, which was essentially structured as a loose coalition of various factions. The DPP elite in all factions knew they had to come up with feasible platforms other than nativism and nationalism, but none had any incentive to search for answers on their own. They knew strong local organizations were necessary for the party to penetrate the grass roots, but few were patient enough to cultivate the soil.

As Gramsci once commented, the counting of votes is only the final ritual of a long process;[24] that is, a long process of organization, education, research, and propaganda. From this point of view, it seems pretty clear that there was much to be desired in the DPP's political effort to accumulate votes before they could happily count them.

*Ideology*

At the core of the DPP's official ideology was of course Taiwanese nationalism, but it had undergone a subtle transformation in the process of the party's battle with Lee. At the moment the consensus of "the general line of election" was formed, a process of redefining the quasi-revolutionary political movement into a radical party in a parliamentary democracy was set in motion. The idea of Taiwan independence, of which the meaning had been extremely vague due to lack of either consensus or discussion among the party elite, was redefined or finally clarified, by the transformed DPP in reformist terms: The goal of abolishing the ROC system and establishing an independent Republic of Taiwan now was to be pursued through the democratic procedure of referendum. The introduction of the idea of referendum implied that until the majority of Taiwanese people agreed to this platform, the DPP was willing to settle for the name ROC. This position was officially adopted by the DPP in its program in the party's fifth national convention in November 1991. In a sense, we may well say that the subversive, unruly, and emotionally charged quest for Taiwanese independence was thus transformed into a rational and domesticated "parliamentary nationalism," to paraphrase the political theorist Ralph Miliband's term of "parliamentary socialism."

A parliamentary nationalism, insofar as its goal was to change the name and symbols of the state, was still revolutionary, but what it advocated was now a revolution with what Przeworski and Sprague call "paper stones," that is, votes.[25] The DPP, now a parliamentary nationalist party like the Parti Québécois or the Scottish Nationalist Party, had recast its Taiwanese nationalism as a liberal and civic nationalism. Such a liberal reframing of Taiwanese nationalism, being an integral part of the DPP's self-transformation, was surely aimed at attracting more moderate voters and thereby broadening its power base. Although there was no clear evidence to prove that even this moderate nationalism did any damage to the DPP's elections, it was almost certain that its effect in swinging moderate voters away from Lee Teng-hui's camp was limited. In other words, the DPP's parliamentary Taiwanese nationalism was still no match for Lee's ambiguous, catchall, and, above all, safe-looking, ideology of the "ROC on Taiwan." However, the conditional acceptance of the name "ROC" by the DPP did suggest the possibility of negotiating a common ground with other political forces.

## Synthesis: A New Historical Bloc?

Lee Teng-hui's landslide in the presidential election of 1996 temporarily concluded the struggle between two lines within the movement of forming a nativized state in Taiwan. Toward the end of this struggle, however, we also witness a gradual coming close of these two lines. On the one hand, constrained by the pressure of winning votes from moderate voters, the DPP slowly but progressively downplayed the significance of its Taiwanese independence platform and allowed more and more flexibility in interpreting its meaning or meanings. On the other hand, under the increasing hostility of the PRC against Lee's pragmatic diplomacy, Lee also gradually toned down his reunification rhetoric and put more and more emphasis on the subjectivity and sovereignty of Taiwan. These trends suggested first the rise of pragmatism within the DPP and second the rise of a hostile and aggressive the PRC as the most immediate common enemy, the quintessential Other, of the Taiwanese people. It is fair to argue that well before the 1996 presidential election, most, DPP elite had acquiesced Lee's pragmatic line of *du-Tai*.

Lee's victory in the 1996 presidential election put a finishing touch to the nativization of the KMT regime, thereby signifying the birth of the first native sovereign state in Taiwan. More interestingly, in this election the votes obtained by Lee (54 percent) and by the DPP's candidate Peng Ming-min (21 percent) accounted for three-fourths of the popular vote. This fact was widely interpreted as the emergence of a new consensus, or, in Hsu Hsin-liang's words, a new "mainstream value," on the issue of national identity: In spite of the name ROC, a national consensus of "Taiwan Sovereignty," or more simply, a "new Taiwanese consciousness," with the PRC as its Other, was formed.[26] This interpretation is actually a prevailing opinion within both the KMT and the DPP, with some partisan nuances in the specific wording by each party.

The elated Lee, in one of his gratitude speeches, claimed that after this election, there was no longer any ethnic division, because "a new Taiwan was born." He hoped that "new Taiwanese [would] join together to create new Taiwanese history."[27] James Soong, then governor of Taiwan Province and a popular Mainlander politician, even attributed Lee's landslide to a "new Formosanism." Although he clarified that "new Formosanism" was not Taiwanese nationalism because its essence was a quest only for economic freedom and political democracy, he nevertheless warned that if the CCP continued to "distort" the efforts of Taiwanese aspiration for democracy and freedom, it would "further alienate Taiwan."[28]

Within the DPP, younger party cadres began to articulate a discourse of "new Taiwanese independence" or "pragmatic Taiwanese independence." This position was most clearly expressed in the "New Generation's Program for Taiwanese Independence" drafted shortly after the 1996 election. The text proposed to understand Taiwanese independence as a national goal because "after March 1996, the Taiwanese Independence movement is no longer an opposition movement. To maintain Taiwan's independence has become the national goal under which all political forces work together to resist China's annexation." Those who voted for Lee, these Young Turks argued, did so not to support unification but to protest against China. "If Taiwanese people judge that Lee is one of the protectors of Taiwan's independence," they pointed out, "The DPP should stop labeling Lee as a unionist." In their eyes, the election result proved that Taiwanese independence had become a mainstream opinion, and "this is a success of Taiwanese independence at this stage." Thus, they stressed that Taiwanese independence did not need to be realized in the hands of the DPP or other "orthodox" proindependence groups. They also maintained that since the top priority of Taiwanese independence was to strengthen the collective identity of all Taiwanese people, the name of the country was of only secondary concern. If the risk of changing the official name of the ROC should prove too high, due to either internal or external resistance, all proindependence groups should temporarily accept the status quo.[29] In a way, this program pretty much summed up the opinions of many "mainstream" elite of the DPP after the 1996 presidential election.[30]

It was clear that a pragmatic discourse of Taiwanese nationalism shared by the "mainstream" elite of both the KMT and the DPP had actually been in the making. Politically, too, a subtle process of convergence had been under way since the summer of 1996. After the presidential election, almost all important party leaders, most of them holders of public office, had publicly agreed on a more pragmatic position on the issue of Taiwanese independence.[31] The disagreement now lay not in Taiwanese independence but in whether the DPP should have formed a coalition with the KMT. On the one hand, the Machiavellian Hsu Hsin-liang, convinced that a "stable majority" was indispensable for Taiwan's political stability, proposed to form a Japanese Liberal Democratic Party–style ruling coalition by merging the DPP with the KMT into a dominant "Taiwan Party." The popular mayor of Taipei City, Chen Shui-bian, on the other hand, insisted that the DPP not rush into any coalition with the KMT since, after three years, the post-Lee KMT he forecast would be no match for the DPP. Despite this disagreement, nonetheless, no one really opposed the idea of cooperating, or even allying, with Lee on certain key issues so that the hard-earned native supremacy could be further institutionalized and consolidated.

Constrained by the fragile majority of the KMT in both the Legislative Yuan and the National Assembly, Lee actually needed the DPP's support to accomplish his project of constitutional revision. The active cooperation between the two parties at the Conference on National Development held at the end of 1996 revealed vividly a common effort on both sides to cement the political hegemony of native Taiwanese: The "freezing" of Taiwan Province, no matter how it was interpreted, would further shed the residue of a defunct Chinese organization, and the abolition of local elections on the levels of villages and townships would no doubt deal a deadly blow to any attempt by the prounification New Party to reach into the countryside and thereby keep it indefinitely an urban-based Mainlander and, for that matter, minority party. All these formal and informal alliances between Lee's KMT and the DPP pointed to the formation of a hegemonic *historical bloc*, albeit without organizational forms, unified by a common interest of maintaining native supremacy and Taiwanese sovereignty, as well as a common pragmatism in dealing with the PRC.

## Conclusion: The New Dialectics of Taiwanese Nationalism?

The historical journey through which the native Taiwanese, long dominated by an émigré Mainlander regime, managed to seize the regime and establish the hegemony of Taiwan supremacy indeed reminds one of an anticolonial national movement. However, what the native Taiwanese had to face was settler colonialism, that is, a colonialism without mother country. Decolonization in this situation meant not only to democratize and nativize the state power but also to reintegrate the settler group into this newly structured and nativized state. In other words, decolonization involved a complex and painstaking process of democratization and national integration. From the perspective of the native elite, democratizing amounted to building the nation, but the nation could be built only through democratic procedures. What they sought to carry out was a democratic nation-building: a political engineering that was inevitably constrained and undermined by compromises, contingencies, and uncertainties arising from the democratic processes; hence the ultimate convergence of a domesticated Taiwanese nationalism and the symbolic Republic of China on the territorial space of Formosa in late the 1990s. The passivity of Taiwan's revolution consisted of the beautiful historical dialectics that made Taiwan and the ROC one and indivisible, dignified with a sense of sovereignty renewed not by the stern public international laws but through the daily plebiscite of the people.

And yet the Taiwanese passive revolution during the 1990s was largely an internal process of democratization and state formation. What it accomplished ideologically is a solid domestic consensus on the sovereignty of Taiwan-ROC and the democratic right of Taiwanese people to determine their own future. Or more precisely, the passive revolution managed to construct among Taiwanese people a firm belief in the sovereignty of Taiwan-ROC and their right to self-determination regardless of the harsh reality of international politics.[32] However, no sooner did this democratically domesticated discourse on Taiwanese nationalism secure its domestic hegemony than it had to face an external and ever daunting Other: China. A new historical dialectic, this time between Taiwan and China, came to the fore immediately after Taiwan's political elite had finally managed to forge a domestic common ground. Lee Teng-hui's much maligned public utterance of the "two-state thesis" in July of 1999 in fact signified the first official outward turn of the newly born Taiwanese pragmatic nationalism to face up to China's irredentist nationalism. It was an agenda-setting move to preempt China's aggressive downgrading of Taiwan's international status by declaring Taiwan-ROC's parity with the PRC. The first strike of pragmatic Taiwanese nationalism was actually more defensive than it first appeared in that the "two-state thesis," short of declaring formal independence, was primarily a strategic move to break China's tightening diplomatic siege of Taiwan.[33] By publicly uttering the bold "two-state thesis," Lee, with his paramount domestic prestige and authority, also managed to define once and for all the terms of a new game for his successors: to defend Taiwan's sovereignty through actively engaging China in a new round of "war of position."

Ideologically speaking, the victory of Chen Shui-bian, the quintessential native son of Taiwan, in the presidential election of 2000 extends the rule of the very native KMT–DPP historical bloc that emerged during Lee's reign, even though the power relation between the two partners has now been reversed. Lacking Lee's unsurpassable power and resources and suffering profoundly from a fragmentation of power caused by the DPP's parliamentary minority and ill-conceived constitutional revisions, the popular president Chen nevertheless benefits tremendously from the preexisting domestic consensus on Taiwan-ROC's sovereignty. Indeed, the democratically formed discourse of Taiwan-ROC's sovereignty has already gained a status of what Gramsci (1971, 57) calls "moral and intellectual leadership" in the Taiwanese society from which almost no serious political contender can afford to deviate. Beneath the deafening cacophony and bitter partisanship in the post-Lee Taiwanese politics is a stable common identification with Taiwan-ROC as a sovereign state. This pragmatic Taiwanese nationalism is indeed the best the Taiwanese passive revolution in the 1990s could hope to achieve. Perhaps it will also be the only politically feasible form of Taiwanese independence for some time to come. But this pragmatic nationalism, which imagines a sovereign political community of Taiwan-ROC, was forged through a protracted yet bloodless process of democratization: It is therefore civic, liberal, and, above all, pacifist. In the ongoing engagement with an authoritarian and nationalistic China so haunted by a historical sense of *ressentiment* and so eager to redeem its hurt pride through claiming Taiwan, this liberal, pacifist, and quite flexible nationalism may prove to be the very shield most able to defend Taiwan's sovereignty.

The history of Taiwan's passive revolution continues, and it continues on a track yet to be beaten by the will—the "daily plebiscite"—of the Taiwanese people, even with the specter of Chinese nationalism looming ever larger over the tiny island. The final destination of this journey cannot be foretold, for, as Adam Przeworski reminds us, "under democracy, outcomes are determined by the strategies of competing political forces and are thus inevitably uncertain *ex ante*" (1991, 32). But maybe one thing is certain enough: These Taiwanese people will have to, in Ernest Renan's words, "bear the scorn of the powerful with patience" for a long time (Renan 1990, 20). But what would this collective bearing of "the scorn of the powerful," this collective experiencing of the hubris of *Realpolitik*, this collective waiting with patience bring about eventually? The tragic yet magical fact of "having suffered and hoped together" (ibid., 19) that further deepens the Taiwanese sense of nation? The ultimate absorption of this unruly "renegade province" into the motherland? Or a new dialectic synthesis that reconciles the mutually antagonistic Chinese and Taiwanese nationalisms into a union with separate sovereignties? History has yet to reach dusk, and Minerva's owl will have to wait.

# Notes

1. This term was first coined by ideologues of the PRC to describe the political position, usually associated with Lee Teng-hui, which advocated *de facto* Taiwanese independence under the name of ROC.

2. In February of 1998, some NP politicians, represented by Yao Li-ming, a former member of the Legislative Yuan, did propose changing the prounification platform into an explicit "One China, two states." However, the party hard-liners soon forced them to withdraw this proposal, even though the party had actually been following this pragmatic line in practice since 1996. Still, this recent pragmatic turn of the NP toward *de facto* Taiwanese independence is more an effect brought about by Taiwan's democratization.

3. "Nation-state" here refers to a general form of state in the modern international system which observes the norm of "one nation, one state." It goes without saying that few actually existing nation-states in this system really live up to the ideal set by this norm.

4. In Ronald Weitzer's succinct formulation, "settler societies are founded by migrant groups who assume a superordinate position vis-à-vis native inhabitants and build self-sustaining states that are *de jure* or *de facto* independent from the mother country and organized around the settlers' political domination over the indigenous population. . . . To constitute a settler state, the descendants of settlers must remain politically dominant over natives, who present at least a latent threat to the settlers' supremacy." Examples of settler state can be found in South Africa, Rhodesia, Liberia, Northern Ireland, Israel, and Taiwan (see Weitzer 1990, 25–26).

5. The term "native" used in this paper refers to inhabitants of Taiwan prior to the inflow of political refugees from Mainland China around 1949, including Aborigines, Hoklos, and Hakkas. To be sure, the dichotomy between native Taiwanese and Mainlanders cannot begin to illustrate the rich sociological complexities of ethnic relations in Taiwan. It is nevertheless a useful tool for analyzing the central political logic of Taiwan's ethnic relations, at least up until the 1990s, in that such structure of binary ethnic opposition was indeed created by the KMT regime itself in order to maintain its autonomy while dealing with the native population.

6. Heribert Adam uses the term "settler colonialism" to describe the apartheid system of South Africa: "South Africa represents both metropolis and colony in geographical unity and inseparable economic interdependence. . . . The key social feature of this 'settler colonialism'—as compared with a mere territorial exploitation by a distant metropolis—is the unique relationship of domination that develops from simultaneously living together and maintaining extreme social distance" (see Adam 1972).

7. *La situation coloniale* was a concept originally suggested by French sociologist Georges Balandier. According to Hechter's reformulation, a typical *situation coloniale* involves "domination by a 'racially' and culturally different foreign conquering group, imposed in the name of a dogmatically asserted racial, ethnic, or cultural superiority, on a materially inferior indigenous people. There is contact between the different cultures. The dominant society is condemned to an instrumental role by the metropolis. Finally, there is a recourse not only to force, to maintain political stability, but also to a complex of racial or cultural stereotypes, to legitimate metropolitan superordination" (see Hechter 1975, 30). It goes without saying that "race,"

"culture," and "ethnicity" here should be understood not as reified entities but as social constructs delimiting group boundaries. The cultural differences between the newly arrived Mainlanders and the native Taiwanese in early 1950s were indeed easily recognizable. The cultural dimension of Taiwan's colonial situation was, and still is, intriguing, complicated,and extremely important; but the present study has to confines its analysis to the purely political dimension of it.

8. The history of Taiwanese nationalism is surely much more protracted and complicated than this misleadingly brief statement. Long before the KMT took over Taiwan in 1945, an ideology of Taiwanese nationalism had emerged under the Japanese colonial rule in the 1920s. An extremely complicated and subtle process of adaptation, adjustment, and conversion of political attitudes and identity on the part of Taiwanese took place after Taiwan had been handed to Chiang Kai-shek through a unilateral decision of the Allied Powers. The prewar discourse of Taiwanese nationalism was accordingly submerged during this process. Nonetheless, the KMT misrule and the outbreak of the February 28 Incident in 1947 seriously undermined the newly acquired Chinese identity of the Taiwanese and thus revived the idea of Taiwanese nationalism, this time in opposition to the new Chinese Other. The ruthless crackdown of the KMT on the native dissidents in the aftermath of the incident and the imposition of military rule after KMT's retreat to Taiwan in 1949 forced the discourse on Taiwanese nationalism out of, or at least effectively contained its spread within, the island. After 1949, the idea of Taiwanese independence became largely an exile discourse. However, while KMT had just managed to crush a burgeoning anti-Chinese Taiwanese nationalism, it ironically reproduced a colonial situation conducive to inducing a national imagining on the part of Taiwanese. From the early 1950s on, when KMT began to allow local-level elections, the quest for civil rights and democracy among those few Taiwanese dissidents had invariably carried an undertone of ethnic resentment against the Mainlander rulers. Throughout the 1950s, 1960s and early 1970s, such simmering ethnic *ressentiment* had in fact kept the idea of Taiwanese nationalism alive within this island under martial rule, albeit in the form of an underground discourse. Later it took the successive diplomatic crises of the 1970s to bring this underground opposition discourse to the surface. For the history of Taiwanese nationalism under the Japanese colonial rule, see Rwei-Ren Wu 1999 and 2000. For a discussion of the complicated identity change in the immediate post–World War II Taiwan, see Rwei-Ren Wu 1994.

9. See Lee 1994, 351–365.

10. The most representative example of Lee's *divide et impera* was his appointment of Hau Pei-tsun, a Mainlander military strongman, as prime minister in April, 1990, thereby dissolving a potentially formidable coalition of the KMT old guards.

11. The unprecedented student demonstration of March 1990 against the "Ten-thousand-year Congress," meaning those members of the Legislative Yuan who had been elected in China in 1947 and thereafter enjoyed life-long tenure as legislators to keep the facade of ROC's legitimacy over the whole China after 1949, presented a most typical situation for Lee to play the DPP card and the "public opinion card" against the old guard. (See Chou 1993, 205–210.)

12. See his famous conversation with Japanese writer Shiba Ryotaro in Lee (1994, 469–83).

13. Lee's ideology of Taiwanese nationalism presents an extremely interesting yet thorny question to the study of modern Taiwanese political history and political thought.

The analysis of Lee's ideology has been an ongoing project for the author for some time. The schematic discussions in this section are only tentative observations intended to illustrate the overarching argument of the present study.

14. See Fukada (1996) and Lee's conversation with Shiba Ryotaro, in Lee (1994). Lee borrowed the philosophical term *basho* (the Japanese translation of the Greek *topos*, meaning locus) as the source of self-identity from the great prewar Japanese philosopher of Kyoto University, Nishida Kitaro.

15. The idea of "community of life" was first mentioned in Lee, 1996. It appears that he first coined the idea of "new Taiwanese" in 1995.

16. See the Chinese text of CNN's interview with Lee on May 18, 1996, in *Shijie ribao* (World journal), May 18, 1996.

17. See Lee Teng-hui, "The Beginning of a New Era," in Lee (1996, 99–102). Lee's idea of Taiwanese history starting anew after democratization and nativization is closely associated with his religious metaphor of a Taiwanese exodus (see Lee 1994, 471).

18. Interview with Lee Teng-hui by Andrea Koppel, CNN Beijing Bureau Chief, May 17, 1996.

19. *Lianhebao* (The united daily news), January 8, 1995; *Ziyou shibao* (Liberty times), April 14, 1994.

20. Interview with Lee Teng-Hui by Andrea Koppel, CNN Beijing Bureau Chief, May 17, 1996.

21. Ibid.; These are the exact words of Lee's answer to the CNN interviewer's question about the best form of reunification.

22. Murray Forsyth has succinctly summarized the nature of equal partnership of confederation: "A confederation is formed by a treaty or pact between partners who recognize one another as being equal in status, the status being that of 'statehood.' If there is no recognition of equal status the basis for a confederation is missing" (see Forsyth 1994, 63). Lee's insistence on Taiwanese statehood set a high threshold for the centralizing and nationalistic PRC, which has intended mainly to absorb Taiwan into her "one country, two systems" form of union.

23. Lee (1999, 77).

24. Przeworski and Sprague (1986).

25. Ibid.

26. See, for example, *Zili zhoubao* (Independence weekly), May 24, 1996.

27. *Ziyou shibao*, March 30, 1996.

28. *Zhongguo shibao* (China times), March 27, 1996.

29. DDP 1996.

30. Chen Wen-chien's comments in a DPP symposium on the practice of Taiwanese independence. See *Zili zhoubao*, May 24, 1996. To be sure, Shih Ming-teh, as early as 1980, has openly advocated his famous "ROC-style Taiwanese independence" in the trial of the Kaoshiung Incident. Hsu Hsin-liang said in an interview with *Xin xinwen* (The journalist) in 1988: "The meaning of TI is to prevent others from intervening in Taiwan's business, that's all. TI is essentially solved." (See Hua 1989, 316.) Also see Yang and Li (1993, 62). Of course, Hsu only expressed an long-time position of the Formosa faction. Yao Chia-wen also proposed dropping the traditional TI view of Taiwan's legal status as "uncertain" in the late 1980s. Instead, he affirmed the legal status of Taiwan as an independent sovereign state. It should be noted that authors of the "new generation program" were ideologically or organizationally close to The Movement faction—the once die-hard TI advocates.

31. However, this agreement did not become official until the May 1999 in the form of "DPP's resolution concerning the future of Taiwan."
32. The experience of Taiwan's state-formation thus is a telling illustration of the constructivist argument that sovereignty is essentially a discourse and a social construct (see Biersteker and Weber 1996).
33. Lee has made it clear that the "two-state thesis" was mainly intended to break the PRC's tightening diplomatic siege of Taiwan and to set the terms for the coming round of negotiation with Wang Daohan, the leading Chinese negotiator on cross-straits affairs, in November 1999 (see Lee 2000).

## Bibliography

### In Chinese

Chou, Yu-kou. 1993. *Li Denghui di yi qian tian* (The [first] thousand days of Lee Teng-hui). Taipei: Maitian.

*CNN zhuanfang Li Denghui zongtong quanwen* (The full text of CNN's special Interview with President Lee Teng-hui). *Shijie ribao* (World journal), May 18, 1999.

Democratic Progressive Party (DPP). 1996. "Taiwan duli yundong di xin shidai gangling" (The new generation's program of the Taiwanese independence movement). Unpublished manuscript.

Hua, Yi-wen. 1989. "Ruguo wo chuangguo le Feilubin zhe yi guan" (If I can come through this plight in the Philippines). In *Jubian shidai–Xin xinwen duihua lu* (Age of sea change: Interviews of the Journalist). Ed. the publication department of *Xin xinwen* (The journalist). Taipei: Xin xinwen, 310–19.

Lee Teng-hui. 1994. *Jingying da Taiwan* (Managing the Great Taiwan). Taipei: Yuanliu.

———. 1999. *Taiwan di zhuzhang* (Taiwan's point of view). Taipei: Yuanliu.

———. 2000. *"Yaxiya di zhilue" shuzhai* (Excerpts from *The Strategic Wisdom for Asia*). Taipei: Ziyou shibao.

Wu, Rwei-ren. 1994. "San ge zuguo: Taiwan zhanhou chuqi (1945–50) guojia rentong di jingzheng yu xingcheng" (Three motherlands: The competition and formation of national identities in early postwar Taiwan, 1945–1950). Paper presented at the First Annual Conference of the Taiwanese Political Science Association at National Taiwan University, December.

———. 2000. "Fu-er-mo-sha yishi xingtai: shilun Riben zhimin tongzhi xia Taiwan minzu yundong 'minzu wenhua' lunshu de xingcheng" (Formosan ideology: A tentative study on the formation of a discourse on "National Culture" of the Taiwanese national movement under Japanese colonialism ). Paper presented at the Annual Conference of Japan Association for Taiwan Studies (JATS) at Tokyo University, June 3.

———. 2001. "Taiwan fei shi Taiwanren di Taiwan bu ke: fan zhimin douzheng yu Taiwanren minzu guojia de lunshu, 1919–1931" (Formosa must be Formosans' Formosa: Anticolonial struggle and the discourse on the Taiwanese Nation-state, 1919–1931). In *Minzu zhuyi yu lingnan guanxi* (Nationalism and the relations across the straits). Ed. Lin Chia-lung and Cheng Yung-nian. Taipei: Xin ziran zhuyi, 43–110.

Yang Ai-li and Li Ming-hsüen. 1993. "Xu Xinliang: wo zhi zaihu ziji, zaihu lishi diwei" (Hsu Hsin-liang: The only thing that I care about is myself and my position in history). *Tianxia zazhi* (The commonwealth), no. 149 (October 1).

## In English

Adam, Heribert. 1972. *Modernizing Racial Domination: The Dynamics of South African Politics.* Berkeley, Los Angeles, and London: University of California Press.

Biersteker, Thomas J., and Cynthia Weber. 1996. *State Sovereignty as Social Construct.* Cambridge: Cambridge University Press.

Breuilly, John. 1982. *Nationalism and the State.* Chicago: University of Chicago Press.

Brubaker, Rogers. 1996. *Nationalism Reframed: Nationhood and the National Question in the New Europe.* Cambridge: University of Cambridge Press.

Chatterjee, Partha. 1993. *Nationalist Thought and Colonial World: A Derivative Discourse.* Minneapolis: University of Minnesota Press.

Forsyth, Murray. 1995. "Towards a New Concept of Confederation." In *The Modern Concept of Confederation.* Ed. European Commission for Democracy Through Law. Germany: Council of Europe Publishing, 59–67.

Gramsci, Antonio. 1971. *Selection from the Prison Notebooks.* New York: International Publishers.

Hechter, Michael. 1975. *Internal Colonialism: The Celtic Fringe in British National Development, 1536–1966.* Berkeley and Los Angeles: University of California Press.

Lee Teng-hui. 1996. *Peace Through Democratic Reforms.* Taipei: Wen Ying Tang Press.

Przeworski, Adam. 1991. *Democracy and the Market: Political and Economic Reforms in Eastern Europe and Latin America.* Cambridge: Cambridge University Press.

Przeworski, Adam, and John Sprague. 1986. *Paper Stones: A History of Electoral Socialism.* Chicago: University of Chicago Press.

Renan, Ernest. 1990. "What Is a Nation?" In *Nation and Narration.* Ed. Homi K. Bhabha, trans. Martin Thom. London and New York: Routledge, 8–22.

Weitzer, Ronald. 1990. *Transforming Settler States: Communal Conflict and Internal Security in Northern Ireland and Zimbabwe.* Berkeley and Los Angeles: University of California Press.

Wu, Nai-teh. 1987. "The Politics of a Regime Patronage System: Mobilization and Control Within an Authoritarian Regime." Ph.D. dissertation, University of Chicago.

## In Japanese

Fukada, Yusuke. 1996. "Wareware wa 'Hong Kong' wo gyoshisuru: Litoki soto tokubetsu indaviu" (We are watching Hong Kong: A special interview with President Lee Teng-hui). *Bungei shunju* (Chronicle of art and literature), August: 162–76.

# —— 10 ——

# The Political Formation of Taiwanese Nationalism

*Chia-lung Lin*

Being an ethnically divided society that is constantly under foreign threat, Taiwan has to face challenges related to nationalism in its transition to and consolidation of democracy. Accompanying democratization in Taiwan are the awakening of a long-suppressed Taiwanese consciousness, the society's quest for international recognition, and the surfacing of domestic disputes between Taiwanese nationalists and Chinese nationalists on the statehood issue. This paper aims to analyze the dynamic relations between Taiwan's democracy building, state making, and nation formation. The questions to be addressed here are why the Taiwanese identity surges so quickly and what the implication is for Taiwan's political future.

It will be argued that national identity is not inborn, but a socially and politically constructed sentiment that is subject to change, especially when under the intensive mobilization of political elites at times of regime transition. More specifically, the electoral process was opened to previously excluded Taiwanese people into national politics and induced the opposition (mainly, the Democratic Progressive Party [DPP]) to cultivate their social base in terms of ethnic and national identities. As a response, the incumbent party, the Kuomintang (KMT), was driven to indigenize its ideology and power structure to abate the impact of the opposition's ethnic and nationalist mobilization. President Lee Teng-hui's redirection of Taiwan's foreign and Mainland policies, as reflected in "pragmatic diplomacy" and "special state-to-state relations," respectively, nonetheless irritated the Chinese Communist regime, which claims Taiwan as an inalienable part of holy China. The Chinese Communist regime's increasing hostility during Taiwan's transition to democracy has given rise to a sense of common suffering among the people of Taiwan, who, regardless of their ethnic backgrounds, are forming a new political identity that is civic in nature. While the emerging of a tional identity in an ethnically divided society like Taiwan is a plus for its democratic consolidation, the rising cross-strait tensions have put Taiwan's national security in a more vulnerable situation, which, if not well managed, may endanger the stability of this new democracy.

This paper begins by clarifying some nationalism-related concepts and examining how the Taiwanese people's national identity and position on the statehood issue have changed during the democratization process. It then investigates how the terms "Taiwanese" and "Chinese" are perceived and points out that, for most people, Taiwanese identity is not only an ethnic identity, but also a citizen-based political identity and that a significant portion of the population actually have multiple identities, claiming to be politically Taiwanese and culturally Chinese. On the issue of identity transformation, this paper argues that political democratization and foreign threat are the two most critical explanatory factors in shaping the nature of Taiwanese nationalism.

### Nationalism-Related Concepts

Nationalism is a widely used term that has no agreed-on definition. Discussions on nationalism are difficult and at times confusing because three vaguely defined terms, namely, nationhood, statehood, and nation-state, have frequently been used interchangeably.

In a more precise definition, *nationalism* should be a political principle that calls for the building of a nation-state or the congruence of nationhood and statehood. Nationalism demands that a nation have its own political state and a state comprising a homogeneous national or ethnic group; or, simply put, nationalism demands one nation, one state.[1] *Nationhood,* or national identity, is a sense of identity shared among people who believe in their belonging to the same nation but do not necessarily demand that the nation build a sovereign state. And statehood refers to a sovereign state whose people can be of different ethnic and/or national origins. Contrary to nationalism, which demands "one nation, one state," the concepts of nationhood and statehood allow for the existence of "one nation, multiple states" and "one state, multiple nations," respectively.

Nationalist movements may present themselves in many forms. For instance, some uphold *expansionism* to incorporate their national population in other states; some pursue *separatism,* striving to control the destiny of their nations; and still, there is *irredentism,* where a minority national group(s) in a state seeks to unite themselves with group members in other states. In Taiwan's case, we see a group of people pursuing Taiwan independence, believing that Taiwan and China are two different nations, and another group

Table 10.1 **Typology for Distinguishing Nationalists and Non-Nationalists**

| Stateness Preference/ National Identity | Taiwan Independence | Status Quo | Chinese Unification | No Opinion |
|---|---|---|---|---|
| Taiwanese | *Taiwanese Nationalist* | *Realist* | *Unificationist* | *Passivist* |
| Taiwanese & Chinese | *Independentist* | | | |
| Chinese | | | *Chinese Nationalist* | |

*Note:* Two survey questions are used to build this typology. The question on national identity was worded as such: "In our society, some people regard themselves as Taiwanese and some regard themselves as Chinese. Do you think you are Taiwanese or Chinese?" The question on the stateness preference was worded as follows: "Some people in our society advocate that Taiwan should be an independent country and some advocate that Taiwan should unite with the Mainland. Do you support Taiwan independence or Chinese unification?"

pushing for the reunification of the Chinese nation. Nationalism is of course not the only reason why people support Taiwan independence (TI) or Chinese unification (CU). For instance, some support TI because they are concerned about the huge socioeconomic and political differences between the two sides of the Taiwan Strait and some support CU, not for ideological reasons, but for the security and economic benefits associated with unification.

To tell the nationalists from the nonnationalists in the population, a typology of six categories was constructed based on the people's national identity and their attitudes toward the statehood issue (see Table 10.1). There are two categories of nationalist: *Taiwanese nationalists* are those who self-identify as Taiwanese and support TI, and *Chinese nationalists* are those self-identifying as Chinese and support CU. Those who support TI but have some degree of Chinese identification fall into the category of *Independentists,* and those who support CU but have some degree of Taiwanese identification are classified as *Unificationists.* And we define those who, regardless of their national identities, advocate maintaining the status quo as *Realists.* And finally, *Passivists* are those without opinions on the stateness issue or those who find all three situations (TI, CU, and status quo) acceptable.

Table 10.2 exhibits changes of the people's national identity, stateness preference and attitude toward nation-state building in the 1990s and compares these data with those of the political elite (legislators). Over the past decade, those with a sense of Taiwanese self-identification rose sharply from 16 percent in 1989 to 36 percent in 1996, while Chinese identity quickly lost

Table 10.2   **Changes of National Identity, Stateness Preference, and Attitudes on Nation-State Building over Time, Mass, and Elite Compared**

| | Mass (%) | | | | Elite (%) | |
|---|---|---|---|---|---|---|
| | 1989 | 1992 | 1993 | 1996 | 1999 | 1995–1996 |
| National Identity | | | | | | |
| Taiwanese | 16 | | 27 | 36 | 33 | 59 |
| Chinese | 52 | | 33 | 21 | 12 | 11 |
| Taiwanese and Chinese | 26 | | 34 | 41 | 52 | 30 |
| Stateness Preference | | | | | | |
| Taiwan Independence | 6 | 8 | 13 | 18 | 23 | 35 |
| Chinese Unification | 55 | 40 | 39 | 23 | 17 | 17 |
| Status Quo | | 18 | 11 | 41 | 44 | 49 |
| Attitudes on Nation-State Building | | | | | | |
| Taiwanese nationalist | | | 7 | 12 | 14 | 35 |
| Independentist | | | 6 | 6 | 8 | 0 |
| Realist | | | 11 | 41 | 43 | 49 |
| Unificationist | | | 17 | 13 | 12 | 11 |
| Chinese nationalist | | | 22 | 10 | 5 | 6 |
| Passivist | | | 37 | 18 | 18 | 0 |

*Source:* Data in the 1992, 1993, 1996, and 1999 columns were provided by Workshop on Electoral Studies, Department of Political Science, National Taiwan University. These four face-to-face interviews were conducted after the 1991 National Assembly election, and the 1992, 1995, and 1998 Legislative election, with the effective cases being 1,384, 1,398, 1,376, and 1,356, respectively. Data in the 1989 column came from a telephone survey conducted by *The United Daily* (see *The World Journal,* July 4, 1997). Data in the elite column are based on the author's interviews with sixty-six legislators during January 1995 and April 1996 (Chia-lung Lin, 1998, Appendixes 1, 2, 3).

*Note:* Percentages in each category may not add to 100 percent because some interviewees either gave answers that are not listed in this table or they declined to answer.

its popularity, declining from 52 percent in 1989 to 21 percent in 1996, and to 12 percent in 1999; and there continues to be a significant portion of people who consider themselves both Taiwanese and Chinese (26 percent in 1989 and 52 percent in 1999). In terms of the shift in the people's statehood preference, we also find a general trend of increasing support for TI (from 6 percent in 1989 to 23 percent in 1999) and a sharp drop in the support for CU (from 55 percent in 1989 to 16 percent in 1999). At the same time, support for the status quo also rose quickly from 18 percent in 1992 to 49 percent in 1999. One reason for the increasing popularity of multiple identities and the status quo is that, during democratization, many of those who grew up with an education that strongly emphasized Chinese nationalism have gradually come to regard themselves as "both Chinese and Taiwanese" and to accept

Table 10.3  **Changes of Attitudes on Nation-State Building over Time, by Ethnicity** (percent)

| | Native Taiwanese | | | | | | Mainlander | | |
| | Holo | | | Hakka | | | Mainlander | | |
| | 1993 | 1996 | 1999 | 1993 | 1996 | 1999 | 1993 | 1996 | 1999 |
|---|---|---|---|---|---|---|---|---|---|
| Taiwanese nationalist | 9 | 16 | 17 | 5 | 5 | 9 | 0 | 2 | 2 |
| Independentist | 7 | 7 | 9 | 7 | 3 | 10 | 3 | 3 | 4 |
| Realist | 12 | 40 | 43 | 11 | 52 | 43 | 5 | 40 | 52 |
| Unificationist | 18 | 11 | 11 | 17 | 15 | 13 | 14 | 22 | 17 |
| Chinese nationalist | 15 | 7 | 3 | 21 | 9 | 6 | 60 | 23 | 15 |
| Passivist | 39 | 20 | 17 | 40 | 17 | 18 | 19 | 11 | 10 |

*Source:* Same as Table 10.2.

the reality that CU might not be as good a choice for Taiwan as the status quo, although they still feel it uncomfortable to self-identify as Taiwanese and embrace TI.

By combining responses to the two questions on national identity and statehood preference (see note in Table 10.1), we can place each interviewee in our six-category typology of nationalists versus nonnationalists. Table 8.2 shows that, between 1993 and 1999, Taiwanese nationalists rose from 7 percent to 14 percent while Chinese nationalists dropped from 22 percent to 5 percent. The most dramatic change occurred in the Realist category, which increased from 11 percent to 43 percent during the same years. Overall, in the late 1990s, roughly one-fifth of the population fell into our two categories of nationalist.

Compared to the mass, a higher percentage of the elite self-identified as Taiwanese and support TI (roughly 20 percent higher). The 1996 data showed that while only 12 percent of the mass could be classified as Taiwanese nationalists, 35 percent of the interviewed elites were Taiwanese nationalists. This finding seems to support the arguments that the political elite are generally more concerned with national identity and that the sudden rise of Taiwanese identity is to a certain extent the result of elite mobilization.[2]

Table 10.3 breaks down the data in Table 10.2 by the interviewee's ethnicity. Not surprisingly, we find a high correlation between one's ethnicity and his or her attitude on nation-state building. When compared to Mainlanders, native Taiwanese (including Hoklo and Hakka) tend to have a clearer sense of Taiwanese identity and are more likely to support TI. And, most

Taiwanese nationalists are native Taiwanese (especially the Holo people) and most Chinese nationalists are Mainlanders. It is interesting to note that the sharp decline in the support for Chinese nationalism was a common phenomenon both among the native Taiwanese and among the Mainlanders, whose Chinese nationalists dropped from 60 percent in 1993 to only 15 percent in 1999. However, only very few of these former Chinese nationalists turned to endorse TI; most of them found it more comfortable, at least for the time being, to support the status quo and remain Realists (whose percentage increased from 5 percent of the population in 1993 to 52 percent in 1999).

## Taiwanese Identity Versus Chinese Identity

The awakening of Taiwanese consciousness among the native Taiwanese and the Mainlanders' deepening sense of crisis have made identity politics the most salient issue on Taiwan's political agenda since the onset of democratization. To find out whether the identity issue will endanger Taiwan's democratic stability, we must first probe the nature of the two identities and examine whether they are competitive or complementary.

People in Taiwan, especially politicians, are increasingly using the words "Taiwanese" and "Chinese," as political weapons for distinguishing between "us" and "them" in the promotion of group consciousness. There is a tendency to assume that one's ethnic identity is congruent with his or her national identity. However, as data in Table 10.3 demonstrates, although there is a high correlation between the two, one should not equate ethnic identity with national identity. In other words, not all Mainlanders lack Taiwanese consciousness and not all native Taiwanese embrace Taiwanese identity. In addition, we should also be aware that the terms "Taiwanese" or "Chinese" may have different meanings for different people and may change their meanings when the contexts change.

Tables 10.4 and 10.5 give us a better understanding of how the terms "Taiwanese" and "Chinese" are perceived, respectively. A general finding is that people tend to define "Taiwanese" with territorial/political and subjective/psychological criteria and "Chinese" with primordial/cultural criteria. For most people, the term "Taiwanese" is quite loosely defined; 55 percent thought that "Taiwanese" refers to those born or resident in Taiwan, and 55 percent and 39 percent, respectively, thought that one qualifies to be a Taiwanese as long as he or she has a strong sense of Taiwanese identity or self-identifies as a Taiwanese. However, there is also a significant portion of the population who apply a narrower, thus more exclusive, set of criteria to the definition of "Taiwanese." For instance, 38 percent thought that provincial origin should be the criteria, 22 percent thought that the ability to speak

Table 10.4  **Meaning of Being Taiwanese** (percent)

| | Mass (1996) N=1,031 | Elite (1995–1996) N=66 |
|---|---|---|
| Q. Many people in our society say "we are Taiwanese." What does "Taiwanese" mean to you? | Multiple Choice | Multiple Choice (Top Choice) |
| I. Primordial/Cultural Criteria | | |
| (1) those with common blood and lineage | — | 3 (0) |
| (2) those who speak Taiwanese (e.g., Minnan or Hakka language) | 22 | 6 (2) |
| (3) those with common historical or cultural background | 38* | 18 (5) |
| II. Territorial/Political Criteria | | |
| (4) those born, live or work in Taiwan | 55† | 64 (40) |
| (5) those with Taiwan's citizenship | 16‡ | 29 (9) |
| III. Subjective/Psychological Criteria | | |
| (6) those who self-identify as Taiwanese | 39 | 32 (28) |
| (7) those with a strong sense of Taiwanese consciousness | 55 | 17 (17) |

*Source:* The mass data were based on a telephone survey conducted by *Yuanjian* magazine between May 16–18, 1996 (see *Yuanjian*, June 15, 1996). For elite data, see Table 10.2.

*Note:* In the mass survey, interviewees were allowed to have multiple answers to the question. For the elite interviews, the author asked the elites to name and rank their answers to the question. The percentages in parentheses were compiled based on their top choice.

*For the mass survey, this choice was worded as: "Taiwanese are those with Taiwan provincial origin."

† In the mass survey, this question was actually divided into two parts. While 55 percent considered those born in Taiwan as Taiwanese, 49 percent thought that just living in Taiwan qualified one to be a Taiwanese.

‡ For the mass survey, the choice was worded: "Taiwanese are those who consider Taiwan an independent country."

Taiwanese (whether Hoklo or Hakka language) is a must, and 16 percent thought that Taiwanese are those who recognize Taiwan as an independent state.

Table 10.4 also shows how the elite and the mass differ in their definitions of "Taiwanese." The most significant difference is that a much lower percentage of the elite used the narrower, more exclusive, primordial/cultural criteria for defining Taiwanese. For instance, when asked a multiple-choice question, only 6 percent of the interviewed elite answered that the ability to speak Taiwanese should be a criterion (compared with 22 percent of the mass) and 18 percent of the elite thought that common historical or cultural

Table 10.5  **Meaning of Being Chinese** (percent)

| Q. Many people in our society say "we are Chinese." What does "Chinese" mean to you? | Elite (1995–96) N=66 Multiple Choice (Top Choice) |
|---|---|
| I. Primordial/Cultural Criteria | |
| (1) those with common blood and lineage (i.e., the Han nation) | 33 (20) |
| (2) those who speak Chinese (i.e., Mandarin) | 6 (0) |
| (3) those with common historical or cultural background (i.e., the Hua Jen) | 50 (32) |
| II. Territorial/Political Criteria | |
| (4) those live and work in China | 8 (3) |
| (5) those with the PRC (China) citizenship | 41 (26) |
| III. Subjective/Psychological Criteria | |
| (6) those who self-identify as Chinese | 17 (12) |
| (7) those with a strong sense of Chinese consciousness | 9 (8) |

*Source:* The mass data were based on a telephone survey conducted by *Yuanjian* magazine between May 16–18, 1996 (see *Yuanjian*, June 15, 1996). For elite data, see Table 10.2.
*Note:* Same as Table 10.1.

background was a must (compared with 38 percent of the mass). When given as a single-choice question, only 6 percent of the elite adopted primordial/ cultural criteria in defining "Taiwanese." The rest either adopted territorial/ political criteria (49 percent) or subjective/psychological criteria (46 percent).

Walker Connor (1994, 75) has reminded us that "it is not *what is*, but *what people believe is* that has behavioral consequences." One's national identity is, for the most part, also a matter of perception. Whatever constitutes "Taiwanese" and "Chinese," it is how the differences are conceptualized and whether they are considered compatible or irreconcilable that actually determines people's reactions to nationalism-related issues.

One way to reconcile the differences between the two identities and minimize their potential conflicts is for one to treat his or her Chinese identity as a cultural expression (*Hua ren*) or an ethnic origin (*Han ren*) and to treat his or her Taiwanese identity as a political identity, one shared by a group of people living in the same political territory with a common citizenship. As long as those self-identifying as Chinese do not deny Taiwan as a sovereign political entity, whether an independent state or a geographical territory, whether under the name "Republic of China" or "Republic of Taiwan," and as long as those self-identifying as Taiwanese do not deny the fact that the

Chinese culture and the Han people have constituted a large portion of the Taiwanese culture and the Taiwanese people, then the surge of Taiwanese identity may not necessarily exacerbate ethnic confrontations and bring about political instability. We may even argue that, as long as the nature of the newly formed Taiwanese identity remains politically inclusive, liberal, and civic, the rising of Taiwanese nationalism is not only compatible with, but also conducive to, the consolidation of democracy in Taiwan.

## Political Democratization and Common Glory

National identities are not inborn, they are socially and politically constructed sentiments that are subject to change. While it is natural for people tend to develop a sense of group consciousness after a long period of social integration and territorial isolation, any sudden change of group identity nonetheless calls for a political explanation.[3]

### Democratization and "Everyday Plebiscite"

The impact of democratization on Taiwan's nation building can be examined at both the mass and elite levels. At the mass level, political democratization, especially electoral opening, acts like a swirl, involving everyone in the political process through campaigning, voting, mass-media reporting, participating in political parties and social movements, and discussing public affairs among families and friends. The practice of democracy gradually accustomed people to participating in the deliberation and decision making of "national" affairs and made them implicitly or explicitly accept the island as the legitimate boundary of the deliberations and decision making. Democratization not only provides a public sphere for people to communicate and understand each other, but also broadens and deepens the people's daily interactions by absorbing different groups and interests into the political system. Constant political participation has gradually formed a collective consciousness among the people, transforming the term "Taiwan" from a geographic location to a political society and the term "Taiwanese" from an ethnic term for "native Taiwanese" to a civic term for "citizens of Taiwan."

If a nation is what Benedict Anderson (1991) calls an "imagined" community, then the community imagined by the people of Taiwan is most likely to comprise those on the island, not those on the Mainland, because the boundaries of their daily social, economic, and political activities coincide with the physical boundary of the island. According to the author's personal interviews in the mid-1990s, 80 percent of Taiwan's legislators agreed that if the government continues to be formed via democratic procedures, then all citizens, regardless of their ethnicity and political beliefs, will eventually internalize a sense of national loyalty (for source, see Table 10.1). This expectation was indeed supported by a general survey conducted after the 1996 presidential election, which found that most people thought that the first direct presidential election had a very positive influence on Taiwan's political development.[4] About 70 to 80 percent of the interviewees thought that the election helped to push Taiwan's democracy forward, strengthen the people's sovereignty consciousness, enhance the government's ruling legitimacy, and increase international support for Taiwan. Most important, even the Chinese nationalists and unificationists at large also agreed that this election helped improve Taiwan's democracy, sovereignty consciousness, international support, and the government's ruling legitimacy.

Taiwan's complete transition to democracy has a profound impact on its domestic politics and foreign relations. As a democratic polity whose government draws its ruling legitimacy from the electorate on the island alone, Taiwan is no longer able to claim its sovereignty over the Mainland. And what inevitably accompanies democratization is the trend to Taiwanization. Although the official name of Taiwan is still the Republic of China, the exercise of democracy on the island, especially its direct presidential election, may be seen as a form of self-determination and is indeed an act that proves Taiwan's independent sovereignty. The successful rooting of democracy in Taiwan has made it increasingly difficult for Chinese nationalists at home to deny Taiwan as a sovereign state and to promote Chinese identity at the expense of Taiwanese identity. At the same time, democracy and self-determination also provide a more legitimate base for Taiwan to appeal for international recognition, especially for sympathy from Western liberal democracies, and to subvert the position of the Beijing government, which derives its claim of sovereignty over Taiwan not through the consent of the Taiwanese people but through a revolutionary triumph over the KMT government in the Chinese Civil War five decades ago.

### Elections and Elite Settlement

Because "politicians are specialists in the mobilization of hopes and grievances," to quote the words of Juan Linz and Alfred Stepan (1996), one cannot afford not to examine the attitudes and strategies of political elites in accounting for people's identity formation and transformation. In the early stage of democratization, opposition elites were able to use ethnic and nationalism mobilization to help consolidate their social bases. However, when this type of mobilization ran into a bottleneck at a later stage of democratization, opposition elites turned to modify their nationalist appeals, hold cross-party dialogues, and build various strategic coalitions for securing majority popular support.[5] Why were Taiwan's political elites so flexible? The democratization provided opportunity structure of ethnic and nationalist mobilization and the elite's cost-benefit calculations on electoral gains can provide some answers.

1. *Opportunity Structure for Nationalism Mobilization.* The first challenge nationalist elites faced in promoting ethnic nationalism was the fact that a significant portion of the population has dual identities and prefers that the cross-strait relations maintain the status quo. And, given the social and political conditions at the time of transition, ethnic mobilization, though powerful at the initial stage, also quickly reached its limits. To attract the support of median voters, the opposition DPP and NP (New Party) were induced to modify their nationalist appeals and soften their ideological stances.

For the NP, an explicit ethnic and nationalism mobilization is certainly not a good approach and may even have serious consequences, mainly because Mainlanders account for only 15 percent of the population and roughly half of the party's supporters are native Taiwanese.[6] On the other hand, intensive ethnic mobilization also became less attractive to the DPP in the late stage of the democratic transition in part because the KMT had already indigenized, hence greatly alleviating the ethnic tension, and partly because ethnic mobilization could actually hinder the pursuit of Taiwan independence. After nearly five decades of social integration, mostly through intermarriage, work, and school, most native Taiwanese have Mainlander friends, in-laws, or neighbors, making it very difficult for the DPP to pursue the building of a Taiwanese state on the island that excludes all Mainlanders. The logic is political. As pointed out by Juan Linz (1984, 203–53), in a heterogeneous society where people of various ethnic backgrounds are mixed-living, because the building of a nation-state based solely on primordial ties is nearly impossible, and if not, too costly, most nationalist elites who promote separatism are eventually forced to put more emphasis on territoriality and less on primordial characteristics, even though primordial mobilization is important in the initial development stage.

2. *Emergence of Multiple and Crosscutting Issues.* The second challenge to ethnic and nationalism mobilization is the emergence since democratization of multiple and crosscutting political issues. The surface of various social and economic issues and their crosscutting with ethnicity and nationalism issues have constrained the elite's ethnic and nationalism mobilization capacity and provided them with a strong incentive to broaden their electoral base via cultivating social and economic reform issues such as social redistribution, anticorruption, environmental protection, gender equality, and others. With each party having its own comparative advantages on certain issues

and a chance to form winning majority coalitions with others, politics in Taiwan has turned into a non-zero-sum game.[7]

As David Truman (1951) and Seymour Lipset (1960) point out, whenever crosscutting social cleavages emerge or cross-issue party coalitions are formed in a society, people tend to moderate their political views and exhibit greater political tolerance because they are psychologically confronted with cross-pressures from their own multiple identities and conflicting interests. Arend Lijphart (1977, 71–87) and Giovanni Sartori (1987, 223–27) further argue that both the existence of crosscutting cleavages and the forming of multiparty coalitions based on crosscutting issues are favorable conditions for democratic stability. Anthony Downs (1957, 51–74) and William Riker (1982), who hold a similar view from the rational-choice perspective, argue that in a multidimensional setting, if nonincumbent parties can strategically form a "coalition of minorities," then nearly all of the incumbent's platform can be defeated by some other platforms in a majority vote. Overall, the rise of multiple and crosscutting issues on Taiwan's political agenda, the existence of diverse issue concerns that are of differing interests and priorities to different groups, and the constant building and shifting of political coalitions among parties, all serve to constrain the degree of ethnic and nationalist mobilization and induce nationalist elites to modify and broaden their political appeals.

3. *Election-Driven Party Adaptation.* The third challenge both Taiwanese and Chinese nationalists faced was the ruling party's exceptional organizational adaptability. Because the KMT under Lee Teng-hui's leadership was able to indigenize itself and pragmatically stress the compatibility of Taiwanese and Chinese identities and the *de facto* independent status of the "Republic of China on Taiwan," the long-existing political tension among different ethnic groups gradually abated and potential conflicts were prevented. By asking the people of Taiwan to treasure their own cultural heritage, overlook their ethnicity differences, and maintain a political loyalty to the newly democratizing state called "ROC on Taiwan," Lee has innovated a new set of political rhetoric and policy that seems acceptable to most people in Taiwan.[8]

As the KMT moved toward the center of the political spectrum, the more radical Taiwanese and Chinese nationalists were gradually isolated. Unwilling to be marginalized by the KMT and punished by voters in elections, the DPP and the NP both moved to soften their nationalist stances. When visiting the United States in September 1995, three months before a legislative election, Shih Ming-teh, the DPP's chairman at the time, announced that "the DPP will not and will not have to declare Taiwan independence after becoming the ruling party because Taiwan has been independent for nearly half a century."[9] Two weeks later, Dr. Peng Ming-min, long a Taiwan independence advocate and the DPP's nominee for the 1996 presidential election, followed by saying: "Taiwan has been independent for decades; therefore, supporting the status quo is supporting Taiwan independence; it is unification that will change the status quo, not Taiwan independence."[10] At the end of 1997, after the DPP triumphed in the local elections, its party chairman Hsu Hsin-liang even said that the DPP's Taiwan Independence Charter is a historical document that states the ideal of the DPP, not a policy to be carried out immediately.[11] A more dramatic change happened during the 2000 presidential election. To win over the support of middle-class median voters, the DPP officially passed a resolution on Taiwan's political future, recognizing that the national name of Taiwan is the Republic of China. After his election as president of the ROC, Chen Shui-bian announced in his inaugural address that as long as the Chinese Communists do intend to invade Taiwan, he would not declare Taiwan independent during his four-year term.

The calculations behind the DPP's modification of its nationalist position, or at least of its rhetoric, are partly based on its understanding of Taiwan's current situation and its expectation of Taiwan's future development. To most DPP elites, the pursuit of *de jure* independence does not seem very pressing for the following reasons. First, to the DPP and most people, Taiwan has *de facto* enjoyed its independent sovereignty, and unification is just a view and an option. Second, the DPP is now less concerned that unificationists might betray Taiwan, partly because the KMT has indigenized and partly because the NP's nationalist appeal has gradually lost its popularity. The third and probably most important reason why the DPP is not rushing to push for *de jure* independence lies in its optimistic expectation of Taiwan's political development. In the DPP's calculation, there is no need to announce Taiwan independence immediately because its winning of the national election has to a great extent confirmed the people's support for Taiwan independence, or at least, rejection of unification with the Chinese Mainland.

## Enduring Rivalries and Common Suffering

War-making facilitates state-making by mobilizing resources to the state and homogenizing people's loyalty to the state. In the words of Charles Tilly (1975), states make war, and war makes states. In fact, what history has witnessed is that war not only makes states, it makes nations. The constant threat from the People's Republic of China has been a very important element in Taiwan's recent state building and nation building. Ever since the late 1940s, the specter of the Chinese Communist regime has dominated

Taiwan's political stage. Although Taiwan began to normalize its relations with the PRC in the early 1990s, the cross-strait tension has not subsided as a result. Rather, increasing cross-strait people-to-people and government-to-government contacts only make the differences between the two sides stand out even more, both culturally and politically.

Taiwan's Mainland policy has changed quite dramatically in the last decade from the initial "no contacts" to allowing for cross-strait family visits and trade activities, to terminating the wartime mobilization system, and to holding various quasi-official talks. However, due to the huge difference in social and political systems as well as the lack of consensus and trust, trivial frictions between the two societies can easily escalate into serious problems. Viewing Taiwan's democratization, prolonged separation from China, and efforts to gain international recognition all as moves toward independence, the PRC has taken active measures to contain Taiwan, trying to force Taiwan into negotiation talks on its terms. The increasing animosity from the Chinese Mainland has raised the Taiwanese people's concern over their national security and national identity. Indeed, cross-strait interactions in the last decade have made a profound impact on Taiwan's nation-state formation, which can be seen clearly from the rising number of people who self-identify as Taiwanese and support Taiwan independence.

### Awakening of Taiwanese Consciousness

Changes in public opinions reveal a positive correlation between the rise in cross-strait tension and people's self-identification as Taiwanese and support for Taiwanese independence. Telephone surveys conducted by the *United Daily* between 1989 and 1997 indicated that whenever the animosity from China increased, Taiwan consciousness also rose as a result.[12]

1. *Public Opinions between 1989 and 1993.* Surveys show that, at the early stage of democratization (late 1989 and early 1990), when promoting Taiwan independence was still taboo, less than 10 percent of the population supported independence and less than 20 percent self-identified as Taiwanese. From 1991 to 1993, the people's sense of being Taiwanese and support for independence climbed 10 percent following the normalization of cross-strait relations (e.g., the KMT government's adopting of the *Guidelines for National Unification*, abolishing of the Period of Mobilization for the Suppression of Communist Rebellion, and holding of the Koo-Wang Talks) and the PRC's accentuating moves to isolate Taiwan in the international community (e.g., through forcing South Korea to withdraw its recognition of the ROC government, announcing a hostile *PRC's Principles on the Taiwan Issue*, and boycotting Taiwan's efforts to seek UN membership).

2. *Impact of the Thousand Island Lake Incident.* After the Thousand Island Lake Incident on March 31, 1994, the people's support for independence and Taiwanese identity reached a historic high. For the first time,
supporters of independence and those self-identified as Taiwanese constituted 33 percent and 41 percent of Taiwan's population, respectively. In this
incident, twenty-four Taiwanese tourists were robbed and killed during their
visit to Thousand Island Lake on the Mainland. Mounting evidence suggested that the Chinese People's Liberation Army were heavily involved in
the murder, but the Beijing government was quick to put a lid on the investigation and even decided to burn the bodies to destroy the physical evidence.
This incident enraged the Taiwanese people and took the newly established
cross-strait cultural and economic links several steps back.

According to a popular survey conducted two weeks after the incident, 70
percent of the interviewees believed that the incident had hurt the people's
feeling toward the Chinese Mainland and 57 percent thought that the PRC's
attitude toward Taiwan was hostile; only 20 percent of the population did not
think that the incident had influenced their feeling toward the Mainland and
8 percent thought that the PRC's attitude toward Taiwan was friendly.[13] This
incident was very critical to the rise of Taiwanese nationalism for two reasons. First, it demonstrated the fundamental differences between the two
societies in terms of respect for human rights and the rule of law and provided a sharp contrast between a civic culture and an uncivil one. Second, it
enhanced a sense of common suffering and imprinted a collective memory
among the people of Taiwan because many people suddenly realized that,
whether they are native Taiwanese or Mainlanders in Taiwan, in the eyes of
the Chinese on the Mainland, they are all "Taiwanese fellows" and that both
ethnic groups share Taiwan's destiny when Taiwan is in conflict with China.

President Lee Teng-hui spoke quite critically of this incident, even calling
the PRC a bandit regime. In an interview with a well-known Japanese writer
after the incident, Lee spoke of "the misery of being a Taiwanese," implying
that Taiwan has, for hundreds of years, been ruled by different foreign regimes and never got a chance to determine its own fate. In another interview
on April 14, 1994, Lee talked about his afterthoughts on the incident, highlighting the cross-strait differences:

> The shock and anger that the Thousand Island Lake Incident invoked in
> Taiwan are universal and [felt] across parties; the PRC government has
> probably not realized its significance. It has also cast a deep shadow over
> our cross-strait exchanges. Our people are angry because a civil society
> would never allow things like this to happen. What makes it even more
> serious is that a modernized government would never behave as irrespon-

sibly as the PRC authority, and act so slowly and clumsily in critical events like this when human lives are involved.

I speak in such strong words because the PRC does not seem to me a civilized country. Taiwan is a civilized country; we wake up every morning expecting to have our newspapers and milk delivered to our doors on time. [In Taiwan,] everything is on track and has an order. It is not like this on the Mainland. . . . The basic point is that sovereignty should be put in the hands of the people. The Chinese Communists say that Taiwan is a province of the PRC; this is ridiculous. They have never received a dime of tax from Taiwan and never ruled Taiwan for even one day; also their government is not elected by the people of Taiwan. So where did their sovereignty over Taiwan come from? [14]

Lee's talks irritated the PRC government, who began to view him as an independence advocate. The tension between Taiwan and China continued to escalate and climaxed when Lee successfully broke the PRC's diplomatic blockade and visited the United States in June of 1995 to receive an honorary degree at his alma mater, Cornell University. The PRC interpreted Lee's foreign visits, especially that to the United States, as an intentional move toward *de jure* independence. In the ensuing months, Beijing retaliated with a series of military exercises and missile launches targeting Taiwan and started bashing Lee, calling him a "national traitor," "schemer," "double dealer," "lackey of the United States," with "ties to the underworld," and a "sinner of a thousand millennia" who should be "tossed into the dustbin of history." Despite the PRC's character assassination, Lee continued to implement his pragmatic foreign policy and to work on normalization of Taiwan's relations with the PRC.

3. *Confrontations in the 1996 Presidential Election.* As Taiwan began to count down its days to the first direct presidential election, Beijing initiated a new wave of verbal attacks and military threats. During the election period, the PRC launched a series of large-scale military exercises and missile tests around Taiwan, some as close as twenty or thirty miles from the coasts of Taiwan. Although the PRC claimed that the military exercises were just for training purposes, few people doubted that the major motivation behind these tests was political. Besides demonstrating to the international community its resolution and capacity to take over Taiwan by force should Taiwan declare independence, Beijing also tried to intimidate Taiwan's voters and undermine their support for Lee with these military exercises.

But, contrary to what the PRC had intended, Lee won the presidential race with 54 percent of the popular vote. Because the PRC insisted that Lee was taking Taiwan toward independence, if we add the 54 percent supporting Lee to the 21 percent who voted for the DPP's presidential candidate, then three-fourths of the population in Taiwan actually voted against unification, a rather humiliating result for Beijing.

The cross-strait tension did not subside after the presidential election. The PRC's subsequent moves to shut off the quasi-official cross-strait dialogue channels, encourage the international community to recognize its sovereignty over Taiwan, and isolate Taiwan from international participation (e.g., forcing South Africa to withdraw its recognition of the ROC government, bullying other countries out of supporting Taiwan's bids for UN membership and membership in other international organizations, and boycotting countries that tried to extend invitations to Taiwan's government officials), all serve to raise animosity and mistrust on the two sides of the strait. Popular surveys in the past few years repeatedly found a much higher percentage of people who think the PRC is hostile toward Taiwan (around 50 percent) than friendly (less than 20 percent).[15] A survey conducted by the *United Daily News* in mid-1997 showed that 43 percent of the interviewees supported independence and 55 percent self-identified as Taiwanese; both figures were historically high.

*Effects of the PRC's Military Threats*

Even though the PRC's military intimidation may make the Taiwanese people more cautious in pursuing *de jure* independence, the rise of Taiwanese nationalism has never slowed down as a result. A general survey conducted after the 1996 presidential election found that 21 percent of the population said that they were proud of being a Taiwanese and not a Chinese, compared to only 6 percent of the population who were proud only of being a Chinese and not a Taiwanese (see Table 10.6). When examining the data by self-identification, we find that only 19 percent of those who self-identify as Chinese said that they were only proud of being Chinese and not Taiwanese, but 43 percent of those who self-identify as Taiwanese said that they are proud only of being Taiwanese and not Chinese.

Question 1 in Table 10.7 asked whether the PRC's military exercises would strengthen or weaken the people's wish to unify with China. Responses showed that the majority of people across national identities said that it would weaken (62 percent) rather than strengthen (11 percent) the desire. In the same survey, only 7 percent of the people said that the PRC's military exercises had made them rethink their choice of presidential candidate, while 88 percent said that their choice would not be influenced. Although the military exercises did have a negative effect on commercial confidence, causing a big plunge in the stock market and a run on foreign exchange holdings, most people on the island did not feel panicky. In fact, only 2 percent and 12 percent of the people felt very panicky and somewhat panicky, respectively;

Table 10.6  **Taiwanese Pride vs. Chinese Pride** (percent)

| | Self-identification | | | |
| --- | --- | --- | --- | --- |
| | Taiwanese N=557 | Taiwanese and Chinese N=605 | Chinese N=208 | Total N=1,406 |
| Only proud of being a Taiwanese* | 43 | 8 | 4 | 21 |
| Only proud of being a Chinese | 1 | 6 | 19 | 6 |
| Proud of both identities | 29 | 62 | 60 | 48 |
| Not proud of either identity | 15 | 17 | 8 | 15 |

*Source:* Same as Table 10.1.
*Note:* Column percentages do not add up to 100 because those who had answers not listed here, had no opinion, or declined to answer were not included.
*The author combined two questions, namely, "Are you proud of being a Taiwanese?" and "Are you proud of being a Chinese?" to produce these four categories of answer.

Table 10.7  **People's Reactions to China's Military Intimidation During the 1996 Election** (percent)

| | Self-identification | | | |
| --- | --- | --- | --- | --- |
| | Taiwanese N=379 | Taiwanese and Chinese N=368 | Chinese N=298 | Total N=1,045 |
| Q1. Based on your judgment, do you think the recent military exercises of the PRC will strengthen or weaken the Taiwanese people's wish to unify with China? | | | | |
| (1) Strengthen | 9 | 9 | 15 | 11 |
| (2) Weaken | 62 | 59 | 66 | 62 |
| (3) Will have no significant change | 6 | 10 | 7 | 8 |
| Q2. How panicky are the people about the PRC's military exercises and missile tests off the coasts of Keelung and Kaohsiung? | | | | |
| (1) Very panicky | 1 | 2 | 2 | 2 |
| (2) Somewhat panicky | 9 | 9 | 19 | 12 |
| (3) Not very panicky | 26 | 30 | 27 | 28 |
| (4) Not panicky at all | 62 | 55 | 51 | 57 |
| Q3. Some people say "with the situations so tense between Taiwan and the Mainland, I would consider emigrating too if I had the money or the ability to do so." Suppose you had enough money and the ability to do so now, would you emigrate? | | | | |
| (1) Very likely | 5 | 8 | 11 | 8 |
| (2) Somewhat likely | 10 | 10 | 17 | 12 |
| (3) Somewhat unlikely | 17 | 19 | 14 | 17 |
| (4) Very unlikely | 64 | 60 | 54 | 60 |

*(Continued)*

Table 10.6 *(continued)*

| | Taiwanese N=379 | Taiwanese and Chinese N=368 | Chinese N=298 | Total N=1,045 |
|---|---|---|---|---|
| Q4. If the PRC continues its military threat toward Taiwan, trying to force Taiwan into accepting its "one China, two systems" principle and becoming its local government, do you think the people of Taiwan should accept the proposal or fight to the end? | | | | |
| (1) We should accept becoming a local government. | 2 | 3 | 8 | 4 |
| (2) We should fight to the end to protect Taiwan. | 78 | 72 | 70 | 74 |
| (3) Hard to say | 4 | 7 | 6 | 6 |
| Q5. Facing the PRC's military threat, some people say, "Taiwan had better stop all kinds of efforts to raise its international status, such as joining the UN, so as not to provoke the PRC." Do you agree with this view? | | | | |
| (1) Strongly agree | 6 | 7 | 11 | 8 |
| (2) Somewhat agree | 13 | 14 | 19 | 15 |
| (3) Somewhat disagree | 25 | 24 | 25 | 25 |
| (4) Strongly disagree | 40 | 36 | 34 | 37 |
| Q6. If the PRC does invade Taiwan, how likely do you think the people on Taiwan would be to set aside their partisan differences and different positions on the stateness issue to jointly protect Taiwan? | | | | |
| (1) Very likely | 35 | 29 | 33 | 32 |
| (2) Somewhat likely | 29 | 35 | 40 | 34 |
| (3) Not very likely | 15 | 16 | 12 | 14 |
| (4) Very unlikely | 2 | 3 | 4 | 3 |
| Q7. Generally speaking, does the PRC's repeated military exercises make you feel pessimistic about Taiwan's future? | | | | |
| (1) Pessimistic | 21 | 21 | 28 | 23 |
| (2) Not pessimistic | 70 | 75 | 70 | 72 |
| (3) Hard to say | 4 | 2 | 2 | 3 |

*Source:* Data were provided by the DPP's Public Opinion Survey Center. This telephone survey was conducted on March 9–10, 1996.

*Note:* The percentages in each question category do not add up to 100 because those who did not have an opinion or declined to answer were not included.

and interestingly, those who self-identified as Chinese somewhat seemed to sense more panic around them than those self-identified as Taiwanese (see question 2). Question 3 shows that 20 percent of the people said that they would consider emigrating if they had the money and ability to do so. Similarly, those with Chinese identity seemed more inclined to considering emigration (28 percent) than those with Taiwanese identity (15 percent). But overall, the majority (60 percent) of all ethnic identities said that they would not (or were very unlikely to) consider emigration even if they had the money and ability to do so.

Question 4 asked, "If the PRC continues its military threats toward Taiwan, trying to force Taiwan into accepting its 'one China, two systems' principle and accepting the PRC as its local government, do you think the Taiwanese people should accept the proposal or fight it to the end." A surprisingly high percentage of the population (74 percent) insisted that the people should protect Taiwan to the end, and only 4 percent thought that the proposal should be accepted. Similarly, responses to question 5 also show that most people (62 percent) disagreed with the view that Taiwan should stop all efforts to raise its international status (e.g., joining the UN) so as not to provoke China.

Questions 6 and 7 further revealed the people's optimism about the future even in the face of the PRC's military threats. Nearly 70 percent of the interviewees thought that if China does invade Taiwan, the people of Taiwan would very likely set aside their partisan and identity differences to jointly protect Taiwan. And 72 percent said that China's repeated military threats did not make them feel pessimistic about Taiwan's future.

## Conclusion

Highlighting the importance of political factors in explaining the transformation of national identity, this paper has argued that political democratization on the island and threats from the Mainland are the two most critical forces that have contributed to the sudden growth of a civic national identity among the people of Taiwan during the last decade of political transition. The dynamism can be summarized as follows.

On the one hand, democratization serves as a pulling force, drawing people together through the process of political participation, which not only creates in them a sense of loyalty to the political system, but generates multiple issues that are of interest to different groups and provides them with an incentive to form various cross-cutting issue coalitions, with no groups or interests able to permanently dominate other groups or interests. If the existence of a nation has to be demonstrated in what the nineteenth-century French historian Ernest Renan called in 1882 the "everyday plebiscite,"[16] then the practice of democracy in Taiwan is definitely the most important "everyday plebiscite" that has been nurturing the sense of belonging to a common nation among the people of Taiwan.

On the other hand, the Chinese Communist regime's increasing hostility toward the democratizing Taiwan has served as a pushing force. The long-existing and ever-growing threat from China is fostering a sense of common suffering among all people of Taiwan regardless of ethnicity. To protect their hard-earned civic rights against the Chinese Communist regime, the people on the island are being forced to overlook their differences and recognize one another as an indispensable part of this new democratic community that is under threat. Again, drawing on Renan, having suffered together actually weighs more in the formation of a nation than the sharing of triumph because suffering imposes obligations and demands common efforts, which later become a collective memory that is part of each individual's life. Together, the pulling and pushing forces have interacted to lead the people of Taiwan, who are in search of a collective identity, to develop an embracing civic identity that looks forward to what the new democracy must be, rather than backward to the unrealized ideal of building a Chinese nation-state.

## Notes

1. Ernest Gellner (1983, 1) points out that nationalism is primarily a political principle, which holds that the political and the national units should be congruent. According to Gellner, nationalism as a sentiment or as a movement can best be defined as such: nationalist *sentiment* is the feeling of anger aroused by the violation of this principle or the feeling of satisfaction aroused by its fulfillment; and a nationalist movement is one actuated by a sentiment of this kind.

2. For the rise of Taiwanese identity and support for Taiwan independence as a result of elite competition and mobilization, see Chia-lung Lin (1989), Fu-chang Wang (1996), Tun-jen Cheng and Yung-ming Hsu (1996), Tse-min Lin, Yun-han Chu, and Melvin Hinich (1996), and Yun-han Chu and Tse-min Lin (1996).

3. See Paul Brass (1991), John Breuilly (1993), Mark Thompson (1993), Rogers Brubaker (1996), and Juan Linz and Alfred Stepan (1996).

4. The general survey was conducted immediately after the 1996 presidential election by Soochow University. Data were provided by the Workshop on Electoral Studies, Department of Political Science, National Taiwan University.

5. For details, see Chia-lung Lin (2000a).

6. For the ethnic and social composition of Taiwan's political parties, see Chia-lung Lin (2000).

7. Tse-min Lin, Yun-han Chu, and Melvin Hinich (1996); Chia-lung Lin (2000a).

8. For an analysis of Lee Teng-hui's leadership of the KMT in constructing a mixed and inclusive national identity as well as counterbalancing proindependence and prounification pressures, see Chia-lung Lin (2000b).

9. *China Times*, September 15, 1995.

10. *World Journal*, October 1, 1995.

11. *China Times*, December 12, 1997.

12. Surveys sponsored by Taiwan's Mainland Affairs Council also show a similar correlation between the rise in cross-strait tension and the people's self-identification as Taiwanese and support for Taiwanese independence.

13. *United Daily*, April 18, 1994.

14. Government Information Office, ed. (1995, 387–88).

15. Those who believe the PRC is hostile increased from 35 percent in January 1995 (immediately after President Jiang Zemin announced his somewhat friendly "Eight Point Proposal" for conducting cross-strait relations) to 56 percent after Taiwan's 1996 presidential election and has remained at around 50 percent ever since (see the *World Journal,* January 30, 1996; September 15, 1996; January 30, 1997).

16. See John Hutchinson and Anthony Smith (1994, 17–18).

# Bibliography

Anderson, Benedict. 1991. *Imagined Communities: Reflections on the Origin and Spread of Nationalism*. London and New York: Verso.

Brass, Paul R. 1991. *Ethnicity and Nationalism: Theory and Comparison*. New Delhi: Sage.

Breuilly, John. 1993. *Nationalism and the State*. Chicago: University of Chicago Press.

Brubaker, Rogers. 1996. *Nationalism Reframed: Nationhood and the National Question in the New Europe*. Cambridge: Cambridge University Press

Cheng Tun-jen and Hsu Yun-ming. 1996. "Issue Structure, the DPP's Factionalism and Pary Realignment." In *Taiwan's Electoral Politics and Democratic Transition: Riding the Third Wave*. Ed. Hung-mao Tien. Armonk: M.E. Sharpe, 137–73.

Chu Yun-han and Tse-min Lin. 1996. "The Process of Democratic Consolidation in Taiwan: Social Cleavage, Electoral Competition, and the Emerging Party System." In *Taiwan's Electoral Politics and Democratic Transition: Riding the Third Wave*. Ed. Hung-Mao Tien. Armonk: M.E. Sharpe, 79–104.

Conner, Walker. 1994. *Ethnonationalism: The Question for Understanding*. Princeton: Princeton University Press.

Downs, Anthony. 1957. *An Economic Theory of Democracy*. New York: Harper and Row.

Gellner, Ernest. 1983. *Nations and Nationalism*. Ithaca, NY: Cornell University Press.

Government Information Office of the Executive Yuan, ed. 1994. *Sacrifice and Hard Work: A Collection of the Speeches of President Lee Teng-hui*. Taipei: Government Information Office (in Chinese).

Hutchinson, John, and Anthony Smith, eds. 1994. *Nationalism*. Oxford: Oxford University Press.

Lijphart, Arend. 1997. *Democracy in Plural Societies: A Comparative Exploration*. New Haven: Yale University Press.

Lin Chia-lung. 1989. "The Opposition Movement under an Authoritarian-Clientelist Regime: Political Explanations of the Social Base of the Democratic Progressive party in Taiwan." *Taiwan Research Quarterly* 2, no. 1: 117–43 (in Chinese).

———. 1998. "Paths to Democracy: Taiwan in Comparative Perspective." Ph.D. diss., Yale University.

———. 2000a. "Taiwan's Democratization and the Change of Party System." *Taiwanese Political Science Review*, no. 5 (in Chinese).

———. 2000b. "Political Leadership and Democratization: On Lee Teng-hui's Reform Strategy and Outcomes." Paper presented at the conference on Lee Teng-hui's Twelve-year Ruling and Taiwan's Achievements, held by the Taiwan Research Institute, May 18, Taipei (in Chinese).

Lin, Tse-min, Yun-han Chu, and Melvin J. Hinich. 1996. "Conflict Displacement and Regime Transition in Taiwan: A Spatial Analysis." *World Politics* 48 (July): 453–81.

Linz, Juan J. 1984. "From Primordialism to Nationalism." In *New Nationalisms of the Developed West*. Ed. Edward A. Tryakian and Ronald Rogowski. Boston: Allen and Unwin, 203–53.

Linz, Juan J., and Alfred Stepan. 1996. *Problems of Democratic Transition and Consolidation: Southern Europe, South America and Postcommunist Europe*. Baltimore: Johns Hopkins University Press.

Lipset, Seymour M. [1960] 1983. *Political Man: The Social Bases of Politics*, expanded and updated ed. London: Heinemann.

Riker, William H. 1982. *Liberalism against Populism: A Confrontation Between the Theory of Democracy and the Theory of Social Choice*. Prospect Heights, IL: Waveland.

Sartori, Giovanni. 1987. *The Theory of Democracy Revisited*. Chatham, NJ: Chatham House.

Thompson, Mark R. 1993. "Ethnofederalism and Democratization: The Role of Elites in Yugoslavia and the Soviet Union." Presented at the American Sociological Association meeting, Miami Beach, FL, August 13–17.

Tilly, Charles, ed. 1975. *The Formation of National States in Western Europe*. Princeton: Princeton University Press.

Truman, David B. 1951. *The Governmental Process*. New York: Knopf.

Wang Fu-chang. 1996. "Consensus Mobilization of the Political Opposition in Taiwan: Comparing Two Waves of Challenges, 1979–1989." *Taiwanese Political Science Review* 1: 129–209 (in Chinese).

# Conclusion

## History, the Memories of the Future

### Stéphane Corcuff

The ten essays that compose this collective book have addressed a very complex question: the transition of national identity in Taiwan. Never having been ruled by Communist China since the PRC's foundation in 1949, the island views itself as already *de facto* independent. However, China views Taiwan as a renegade province that must be prevented from declaring formal independence. The debate reveals two interesting questions regarding China's insertion into the current international system: the role of memory and the perception of what "identity" is.

### Memory

The Chinese Communist Party has not always claimed Taiwan was "an inalienable part of China." In the 1930s, the CCP pronounced itself in favor of the independence of Taiwan from the Japanese Empire. Everyone in China, including the Nationalists, has traditionally considered Taiwan as an insular, remote land that used to belong to the Qing Empire, but was certainly not strategically important to China proper, a continental power. Even today, some prounification "New Inhabitants" in Taiwan that I interviewed recall the time, before the Nationalists were forced to retreat to Taiwan in 1949, when they, like everyone else, used to consider Taiwan as far beyond the symbolic frontier of the Central Plain. Subsequent events can explain why the CCP is now saying that China is an inalienable part of China and why the Kuomintang (KMT) for decades tried to suppress, until the 1990s, the discourse on Taiwan's specific identity and tried to impress on Taiwanese minds the idea that their inalienable nation was China, continental China.

Memory has held an important stake in the Taiwan question since 1943, when a simple declaration during the Cairo Conference expressed the idea that Taiwan should be retroceded to the Republic of China (ROC) after the war was won against the Japanese. After the war against Japan, the civil war between the Nationalists and the Communists started again in 1946. When the People's Republic of China was founded in Beijing on October 1, 1949, the Nationalist regime was already in dire straits, and Chiang Kai-shek finally retreated to Taiwan in December. Taiwan instantly became the sanctuary of the Communists' enemy, Chiang Kai-shek's last refuge that was to be "liberated from its oppression." The situation has persisted, and Taiwan became for the Communist an enduring symbol that the civil war was not entirely won, that Chiang Kai-shek was still alive, that the Republic of China, the PRC's predecessor state, had not totally vanished from the earth and been turned into history.

This incomplete victory is a central explanation of why Taiwan has suddenly been transformed from an unimportant maritime province to one of tremendous political importance for the Communists. At the same time, the Nationalists had seen their regime reduced only to that of its province, Taiwan, and if Taiwan's status changed to an independent state, it would mean the total disappearance of the Republic of China. Aiming at recovering the lost continent, Chiang Kai-shek had to suppress every dissenting voice expressing, especially after a 1947 rebellion, the idea that Taiwan should be an independent nation. The two regimes have cohabited since, and neither disappeared. For decades, without fear of rewriting Taiwan's history, the People's Republic of China has convinced itself that Taiwan had been part of China since ancestral times. Not only was the ROC still existing somewhere, but moreover, it was surviving on what was now unanimously considered Chinese soil.

This evolution is an indication of the politicization of the nation's memory in China. Since the 1990s, the policy toward Taiwan has officially become a top priority on the Mainland. And as the debate heats up, it raises fundamental questions: Is regularly menacing Taiwan a risky game for civilian leaders in China, who might one day end up trapped in the military leaders' logic, one day finding it difficult to resist their pressure for action? Is the propaganda in favor of Taiwan's unification with China really affecting common people, who indeed seem today more concerned by the question that they used to be, but who are, before all, concerned with improving their economic condition? Is the intensification of this policy linked to Taiwan's political developments only since Lee Teng-hui rose to power in 1988, or is it also linked to China's domestic political situation? But is mobilizing the Chinese population—even with limited success and only for domestic goals—against Taiwan's independence totally harmless? Perhaps we should consider the impact such a mobilization has on the perception that common Chinese have about the way the international community deals with their nation, and realize the frustration they accumulate toward anyone defending the right of Taiwan's population to determine its own future. This may be detrimental for China's inclusion in the world community. And this is without mentioning the ongoing arms race in the Taiwan Straits: Pressed by military leaders and confronted by their failure to get the "one country, two systems" solution accepted by Taiwan, the civilian leaders have to agree to a military buildup against the island as the only way to protect the chances of seeing Taiwan unified one day with China.

## Identity

This problem is intimately linked to a second one: the perception of what "identity" is. In this process, China's official stance regarding Taiwan indicates a perception of the nature of identity that has long been contested in social sciences as being primordialist and politicized and believed not to reflect the true nature of what is the self, including the national one. China, it seems, is overwhelmingly viewing identity as a primordial, univocal, and fixed given. In contemporary social sciences, identity is increasingly considered pluralistic, constructed, and evolutive. Taiwan is ethnically diverse, has experienced several foreign rules, has been separated from China between 1895 and 1945 and again since 1949. Chinese culture is the main matrix of Taiwanese culture; however, it is not the only one. Taiwan was integrated late into the Chinese Empire. The gradual process began in 1683 and culminated in Taiwan's formal elevation to the status of a Chinese province in 1887. And after welcoming the Nationalist troops in 1945, the Taiwanese were horrified by the corruption of the Chinese, their inability to govern them, and their bloody suppression of the rebellion. Such historical events naturally had an impact on the Taiwanese psyche and on the identification the Taiwanese have with the so-called Han race, and finally led to a sentiment of severe difference from Chinese on the Mainland and deep mistrust of the regime in China. China's denial that these events can have played a role reveals a tendency on the Mainland to view identity as a fixed and immutable.

Increasingly, progressive intellectuals in Taiwan defend a new perception of identity, which enables the island to envision a new destiny for itself, but does not necessarily mean negating or rejecting its Chinese roots. What should be noticed here is that the frontier between prounificationists who have a traditional view of identity and those who view identity as pluralistic, evolutive, and constructed, does not go through the Taiwan Straits, opposing China on one side, and Taiwan on the other. The frontier goes through the Taiwanese society itself, and as stated earlier, not all Taiwanese yet identify with Taiwan as a separate nation, for several complex reasons. But what is clear is that more and more people do have a pluralistic identity in Taiwan: Is there a hope that this new vision of identity can gain momentum in China? We can hope so. China has more to gain from a Taiwan included voluntarily in a federal structure where the island keeps a maximum degree of freedom, or even from a friendly, cooperative independent neighbor, than from a structure in which Taiwan has been reluctantly unified with the Mainland, demotivated, and in rebellion against continental authority. If unification comes first, it might one day lead to full independence, but in this case, let us hope that it would not be after a terrible war of independence. Forcing Taiwan reluctantly into a political system in which the island would lose its sovereignty would be a counterproductive political folly, economical mistake, and a leap backward for both Taiwan and China. Should China consider the idea of negotiating on an equal basis with Taiwan, the island would probably have no other choice than stepping in immediately. However, what China fears, probably wrongly, is that Taiwan would understand this moderation as a weakness and would immediately declare formal independence, in other words, change its regime name. Such a position is visibly held by some military leaders in China. They obviously misread the complexity of the identity question in Taiwanese society.

**Nation**

Interestingly, Taiwan is, in a certain respect, already in a postnational phase. Undoubtedly it is experiencing a nation-building process. The current Taiwanese state has existed as a sovereign political entity since 1949, and though Chiang Kai-shek's aim was not at all to support the emergence of a Taiwanese nation, his policy ironically gave a strong impulse to it. First, it was under his direct orders that the 1947 antirebellion repression was launched. It is at this juncture of history that Taiwan's destiny radically changed orientation. Then, it was his failure on the Mainland and his retreat to Taiwan that totally cut the island from any official contact with the continent until the late eighties. Last, his authoritarian regime and his repression of the proindependence activists confirmed to the exiled militants that the only solution for Taiwan was now to declare independence from the Republic of China on Taiwan, meaning founding a Republic of Taiwan. Against his will, Chiang Kai-shek did much to stimulate the idea of an independent Taiwan.

Since Lee Teng-hui reached the supreme echelon of political power in the island, the affirmation of Taiwan's independence has been progressive, the slowness of this process being caused in part by the legal complexity of the matter. There is no doubt that the Republic of China is an independent and sovereign regime, both *de facto* and *de jure*. It is obvious that Taiwan is an island independent from the PRC regime, since Beijing exerts no sovereignty whatsoever on Taiwan. This fact can be ignored, but it can't be denied. Yet, "Taiwan" as such has no independent and sovereign regime called "The Republic of Taiwan," and the existing "Republic of China" was founded on the Mainland so that, constitutionally, it still views itself as a Chinese regime of which Taiwan is only one province—even if only prounification forces use this rhetoric today. Much argumentation has been made around this legal constraint on how to state Taiwan's *de facto* independence without changing the constitution and the name of the regime, something that would have been politically impossible to achieve in Taiwan and might have created a *casus belli* for war with China. In the meantime, important reforms have been made, many in the realm of national identity-related symbols, which have dramatically reshaped the Taiwanese polity.

However, constraints are too still strong for reformers to go much further than the achievements of the Lee Teng-hui era. First is the external factor, China. Second are domestic factors, among which are Taiwan's "New Inhabitants," who still have an important political influence in the island, even after Chen Shui-bian's election. Other domestic factors are also very influential: the effect of decades of Nationalist socialization; the youthfulness of the independence movement; the pragmatism of the Taiwanese, who do not all want to risk their wealth on an adventure called nation building or the Republic of Taiwan. This means that Taiwan, for the moment, can hardly envision a future other than the present *status quo* equivalent to independence or possibly a form of association with China. After Lee Teng-hui's reforms, during which Taiwanese pride and autonomy were highly publicized internationally, the new leaders have now to manage to find a way to cooperate with China, and the Taiwanese are debating more than ever about the form of association that could work and maintain respect for Taiwanese freedom and prosperity.

This means that Taiwan is at the same time going through a nation-building movement and thinking about a postnational form of association with China—such complex examples are rare in today's world, and this case is worth studying. One of the most interesting examples of this intertwining of nation building and postnational movements was presented in this volume, and it is the theory of concentric spheres of identification—elaborated between 1994 and 1997—which encompasses the local (Taiwan), the cultural (the Chinese world), and the global (the World) as three concentric horizons of identification to be cultivated by Taiwanese youth through new high school textbooks on history, geography, and social questions.

**Ethnicity**

As one can imagine, such reforms have caused considerable opposition from the prounification camp in Taiwan. The New Inhabitants still hold important positions in Taiwan and their pervasive ideology of Taiwan's Chineseness and fate to reunification is still present in Taiwan, but the very transition that deprived them of their power is causing an introspection that leads some Taiwanese to realize today that New Inhabitants must also be understood. Pluralization has meant listening to dissenting voices, which finally helped a proindependence party to win the presidency. But it also means listening to and respecting the voices of the New Inhabitants, even while they are considered by many to be a factor slowing down the nation-building process— and since the March 2000 political change, the conservative Mainlander politicians have been more vociferous than they were during the very last years of Lee's presidency. In January 2000, an exhibition about the New Inhabitants' history was held in the February 28 Peace Memorial Museum, a temple to the memory of the 1947 massacre. Such an event should catch our attention. The deep meaning of this surprising exhibition was to facilitate the psychological transition of the New Inhabitants, a population that is in a process of indigenization. Giving back the New Inhabitants their pride, while their political influence has not yet vanished, was not a symptom of weakness from the antiunification camp, but rather a sign of confidence. Showing the New Inhabitants that the Taiwanese majority respected them was an attempt to ease their way into a new community under formation that could ultimately lead to the appearance of a "New Taiwanese People." The history of this concept and its political significance was analyzed in chapter 8. Trying to go beyond ethnicity and ethnic misunderstanding is now an important dimension of Taiwan's nation-building process, which prompts Taiwan to think about building a model multicultural society in which differences are appreciated and tolerated. The tendency toward an integrated multicultural society is so necessary and so strong that even the prounification, anti-Lee Teng-hui New Party claimed it was its goal in a 1995 White Paper.

Giving back pride to minority groups does not, however, concern only the New Inhabitants, but also Hakkas and Aborigines. If Hakkas' demands for respect for their cultural differences are less mediated, the importance of Aborigine politics in Taiwan has been widely noted in recent years. Started in 1984, the movement has grown successfully and it is fair to say that today a respectable portion of Taiwanese society now accepts the idea that Aborigines are the first Taiwanese, that Han Chinese have wrongfully despised them for centuries, and that a fairer share of Taiwan's wealth must be available to them. If most Aborigines still remain marginalized in Taiwan's development, their culture and their specificity have now become an integral part of the Taiwanese discourse on a global, distinct insular identity.

The Aboriginal factor is very important in this respect. Taiwanese intellectuals who question the traditional Han reading of Taiwan's history are operating a deconstruction of the Taiwanese identity. Traditionally, Taiwan has been considered a historical place since Han people started colonizing the island. For centuries, Chinese had considered Aboriginal people savages, as either "raw" (*sheng*) or "cooked" (*shou*), depending on their degree of Sinicization. Taiwanese intellectuals have started to show that the multiplicity of Taiwanese historical experiences invalidates a linear history of the island viewed through the Han Chinese prism. This sort of deconstruction of history is a process also taking place in other Asian countries, such as Japan, Vietnam, or China. However, what is striking in the case of Taiwan is that it is being carried out by Taiwanese intellectuals, not foreign scholars, and that this deconstruction/reconstruction was accepted in national textbooks as early as 1997. This far-reaching reform, the numerous debates on a possible association with China, the theory of concentric circles of identification, as well as the irrepressible process of Taiwanization of the New Inhabitants or the debate on the New Taiwanese all show that the island has become, in a decade, a fascinating identity laboratory, where a new nation is being born under the shadow of the continent, where new definitions of Chineseness are proposed, where the fluidity of identity is openly discussed, where we can increasingly find a pluralistic figuration of national identification among each ethnic group of the island, including the generally prounification New Inhabitants.

## History and the Future

It is necessary to look into history to understand this plurality. It is probably legitimate to say that no history textbook can be objective, as objectivity in history does not exist. History, as a process, is too complex to be described exhaustively. As a human discourse, it is by nature a construction. However, returning to history can also help diffuse previous politicization of the national narratives. History is often used to nurture national identity and emulate national identification. This could encourage Taiwanese to read history and learn what can help them to better understand the present and to construct a new future. In Taiwan, the 1997 textbook affair has shown to what degree history had been politicized under the Nationalists and to what extent it had become a stake in the contemporary movement of nation building in Taiwan. It is a complex debate since the progressive intellectuals who are currently rewriting Taiwanese history by adopting a Taiwanese point of view are considered, by those who caution about previous excesses, to be working on the island's history to make a national narrative for Taiwan's future as an independent entity. But is this reform unacceptable for all that? Obviously not. Interestingly, both prounification forces and nation-building forces in Taiwan invoke history to legitimize their respective interpretation of what Taiwan's identity is and what Taiwan's future relationship with China should be. The first, usually Chinese nationalists, consider that history "proves" that Taiwan is an inalienable part of China, because, basically, "Taiwan has been Chinese," so "it can but remain Chinese." In this scheme, history is haunting the present, just as ethnicity prevails, for them, on civic identification. On the opposite side, proponents of the Taiwanese nation increasingly consider that, to be brief, "Taiwan has been Chinese," and that "It might be desirable to claim this part of Taiwan's identity," but that in any case, "it does not prevent Taiwan from becoming something else": to keep the blood metaphor that many Chinese like, and that most social scientists dislike, it is not because brothers share common blood and grow up together that they must live under the same roof. When such a question becomes politicized, it is virtually impossible to resolve it rationally.

This book has made a few references to the historical roots of the question, though its primary goal was to deal with contemporary issues. It is an old debate to know whether history repeats itself or not. But history probably teaches us a few lessons. Perhaps because the island's very special geographical nature (an island) and situation (in the strategic Taiwan Straits) put Taiwan at the confluence of several cultural and political influences in the region, Taiwanese history sometimes gives the impression of repeating itself. The island was Cheng Cheng-kung's retreat base from which he tried to overthrow the new Qing dynasty. It became Chiang Kai-shek's shelter to prepare his Reconquista and to plan to drive away the new PRC regime. Continental troops sent by Beijing at the end of the nineteenth century were not sincerely committed to Taiwan's defense and finally looted Taipei before fleeing back to the Mainland. The new government sent by Nanjing at the end of the Second World War was a bunch of corrupt officials, the first of which, Chen Yi, owed his nomination to Chang Kai-shek's desire to thank him for his services during the war against Japan. Chiang offered him Taiwan as a reward; his government's behavior caused the February 28 events. Again, Chinese troops sent to the island roamed and killed. Could China, a continental empire, possibly have a true commitment to Taiwan's development? The Taiwanese doubt it, simply because China will never—this is simple political and geographical logic—look at Taiwan from a Taiwanese point of view. As long as China regards Taiwan as a province, and there is little reason why it should not do so, any true commitment will be hard to envision. Taiwan never will be better defended than by people originating from the island: as the Chinese expression says, *tui yi bu, ji wu si suo*: [when] you have no place to die if you step backward, [you fight until your death]. Even with Taiwan's separation from China, the necessity for Chiang Kai-shek to relegitimize his defeated regime, and the fact that the Mainlanders were a small minority imposing their power on the Taiwanese majority, if the two Chiangs' KMT had been able to go back to the Mainland, any true commitment to Taiwan would probably soon have vanished. China-Taiwan politics can easily give us the intuition of such a "Continental complex" of the prounification forces, both on the Mainland and in Taiwan.

History can also give us some perspective about the declaration of independence in the hope of international recognition of the island's sovereignty. In 1895, it was aimed at discouraging Taiwan's invasion by Japan. It was a very modern thought—the idea that Taiwan had proclaimed its independence, and that popular sovereignty, expressed through the republican form of the regime, would prompt the Powers to defend Taiwan. In some ways, this is the same logic that Lee Teng-hui followed: Without formally adopting "the Republic of Taiwan" as regime name (*guohao*), Lee has nevertheless proclaimed Taiwan's independence step-by-step, the last one being his July 1999 declaration about the "special nation-to-nation, or at least state-to-state relationship" *(guojia yu guojia, zhi shao shi teshu de guo yu guo de guanxi)*.[1] In 1895, the declaration of independence was aimed at protecting Taiwan from occupation by Japan. In the 1990s, it was aimed at rallying international support in the face of an irredentist China. In 1895, as we saw, it failed. But the situation is not the same today. Once while visiting America, President Jiang Zemin declared that the United States had fought a civil war, and that China could do the same; President William Clinton reminded him that Taiwan had been separated from Mainland for a long time already and that the comparison with the American civil war was invalid. Moreover, today international opinion plays a far more important role than it did a century ago. In 1895, only a few newspapers, such as those in Paris, supported the Taiwanese Republic in the light of a Japanese landing. However, today, it is not difficult to measure how critical the international press is of China's political system, human rights record, and, to a lesser extent, diplomatic strangulation of Taiwan. International opinion is a factor that now counts and on which Taiwan knows how to play. Both China and foreign ministries of other countries should take it more into account. In the last few years, the knowledge about Taiwan in the world has changed dramatically, and many now know that, as people say, "Taiwan is not China," that it has a different regime and a different identity. If China did not care about the international impact of an attack on Taiwan, one can wonder why then Beijing would have waited so long to act. And though China can threaten Taiwan, it cannot force people who know what Taiwan is to change positions and go back to a former understanding of the situation. The Taiwanese case confirms that force and law are no longer the only important factors in defining an international relationship such as that between China and Taiwan and that international opinion is an important new dimension. By its very lack of "normal" international relations, Taiwan has long been accustomed to developing this dimension and leaving the narrow frame of "diplomatic relations" to plead its cause and let other countries know about its political transformation by other means.

Therefore, if history can only give intuitions, perhaps the combination of history and geography sends more clear signals, especially when the geographical determinant is as obvious as insularity, as in the Taiwan case. Without any knowledge of what would happen more than a century later, Hegel probably gave us a simple, and fundamental, remark about the role geographical factors play in identity formation, in his 1820s lessons on the *Philosophy of History*:

> The sea gives us the representation of the indeterminate, of the unlimited and of infinity; and Man, in this infinity, feels encouraged to go beyond what is limited; the Sea incites him to conquer, to rob, but also to gain and acquire; the continent, the plains and valleys fix Man on the land; he engages himself in countless servitudes, but the sea enables him to leave these confined spheres. . . . In Asia, the magnificent State edifices, like those in China, do not have this thrust away from the continent that the sea provokes. For them, the sea is simply the place where the land stops, they do not have with them a positive relation. The activity to which the sea invites is very particular; that is why it happens that, later, coastal countries in general always separate from countries from inside the land.

**Note**

1. Presidential Office Press Release, July 9, 1999, p. 1.

# About the Editor and Contributors

**Stéphane Corcuff** received his Ph.D. in political science from the Institute of Political Studies in Paris. He specializes in the study of identity politics in Taiwan and the relations across the strait. He has published several papers, both in French and English, on those subjects. A former head of the Press division of the French Institute in Taiwan, he is presently lecturer in Asian politics and Chinese language at the Université de la Rochelle, France.

**Robert Edmondson** is a Ph.D. candidate in the department of anthropology at Michigan State University. He has studied aspects of social memory and nationalism in Taiwan and is now working on research that explores national and ethnic identity issues among transmigrant Taiwanese in the United States.

**Kuang-chün Li** received his Ph.D. degree in sociology from the University of Texas at Austin. He is currently an assistant professor at the Center for General Education of Chang Gung University, Taiwan. His academic interests include ethnic studies, family and marriage, and medical sociology. He is now working on a project that studies names and naming patterns in postwar Taiwan.

**Chia-lung Lin** received a Ph.D. from Yale University and is currently Assistant Professor of Political Science at National Chung Cheng University in Taiwan. He has edited several books, including *Party–State Transformation and Democratic Reform in Taiwan and China* (1999) as well as *Nationalism and Cross-Strait Relations* (2000), and *Paths to Democracy* (2001).

**Tsong-Jyi Lin** received his Ph.D. in political science from Purdue University. He is currently an assistant professor of public administration at Tamkang University in Taiwan. His research interests focus on political parties, voting behaviors, and media politics.

**Robert Marsh** is a professor of sociology at Brown University. He earned his Ph.D. in sociology and Chinese studies from Columbia University (1959). He has also taught at the University of Michigan, Cornell, and Duke. His teaching and research have centered upon societal modernization and development, with special reference to East Asia. He has been visiting professor at National Tsing Hua University in Taiwan and Kyoto University and Kwansei Gakuin University in Japan. He has been a Guggenheim Foundation Fellow, a fellow of the Ford Foundation and the Social Science Research Council, and of the Chiang Ching-kuo Foundation and the National Science Council, Republic of China. Marsh conducted research in Taiwan in 1957–58, 1963, 1981, 1991–92, and presented his findings during a visit to Taiwan in 1996. Among his publications is his 1996 book *The Great Transformation: Social Change in Taipei, Taiwan Since the 1960s* (M.E. Sharpe).

**Andrew Morris** is Assistant Professor of History at California Polytechnic State University, San Luis Obispo. He received his Ph.D. in modern Chinese history from the University of California, San Diego, in 1998 and has also taught at the University of Oregon and Colgate University. He has published articles on several different elements of modern Chinese and Taiwanese history. His foremost research interest is the origins and formation of modern sports and physical culture in twentieth-century China and Taiwan.

**Wei-Der Shu** is a Ph.D. candidate in the department of sociology at Syracuse University. His areas of scholarly interest include political psychology, social movements, political sociology, and nationalism. One of his research papers about Taiwanese nationalism was honored with the Distinguished Graduate Student Paper Award by the Section of Political Sociology, American Sociological Association, in 1995. Combining the literature of political socialization and collective identity, he is currently working on his dissertation about the life histories of activists affiliated with the Taiwan independence movement in the United States.

**Rwei-Ren Wu** is a Ph.D. candidate in the department of political science at the University of Chicago. His major fields of study include comparative politics (comparative study of nationalism, colonialism, and ethnic politics) and political philosophy (democracy and the idea of political community). He has published several papers in Chinese on the political and intellectual histories of Taiwanese nationalism in both colonial and post–World War II periods and on modern Western and Japanese political thought. His Chinese translation of Benedict Anderson's *Imagined Communities* was published in Taiwan in 1999. Currently he is writing his dissertation on the ideological formation of colonial Taiwanese nationalism under Japanese rule.

# Glossary

## Place Names

| | |
|---|---|
| Aoti | 奧底 |
| Jieshou lu | 介壽路 |
| Juifang | 瑞芳 |
| Kaohsiung | 高雄 |
| Keelung | 基隆 |
| Kinmen | 金門 |
| Matsu | 媽祖 |
| Meilidao | 美麗島 |
| Menchia/Bangka | 艋舺 |
| Patu | 八堵 |
| Penghu | 澎湖 |
| Santiaoling | 三貂嶺 |
| Shichiuling | 獅球嶺 |
| Tamshui | 淡水 |
| Tainanfu | 臺南府 |
| Tataocheng | 大稻埕 |
| Takou | 打狗 |
| Taipei | 臺北 |
| Yenping | 延平 |
| yuanhuan | 圓環 |

## Names

| | |
|---|---|
| Bao Ganchen | 包幹臣 |
| Chang Hsiao-yen | 章孝嚴 |
| Chang Mau-kuei | 張茂圭 |
| Chang Sheng-yen | 張勝彥 |
| Chang Yen-hsien | 張炎憲 |
| Chang Ta-chien | 張大千 |
| Chao Li-yun | 趙麗雲 |
| Chen Chi-mai | 陳其邁 |
| Chen Fa | 陳法 |
| Chen Shui-bian | 陳水扁 |
| Chen Yi | 陳儀 |
| Chen Wan-chen | 陳婉貞 |
| Cheng Jui-ming | 鄭瑞明 |
| Chiang Ching-kuo | 蔣經國 |
| Chiang Kai-shek | 蔣介石 |
| Chiu Chuang-huan | 邱創煥 |
| Fang Yuanliang | 方元良 |
| Hau Pei-tsun | 郝伯村 |
| Hsieh Chang-ting | 謝長廷 |
| Hsu Hsin-liang | 許信良 |
| Hu Fo | 胡佛 |
| Huang Chun-pi | 黃君璧 |
| Huang Fu-san | 黃富三 |
| Huang Hsiu-cheng | 黃秀政 |
| Huang Yide | 黃翼德 |
| Ito Hirobumi | 伊藤博文 |
| Jiang Zemin | 江澤民 |
| Kabayama Sukenori | 樺山資紀 |
| Ke Yuan-fen | 柯遠芬 |
| Koo Hsien-jung | 辜顯榮 |
| Konsin Shah | 夏功權 |
| Kuo Wei-fan | 郭爲藩 |
| Kung Chao-yuan | 龔照瑗 |
| Lee Ching-hua | 李淸華 |
| Lee Huan | 李煥 |
| Lee Teng-hui | 李登輝 |
| Lee Yuan-tse | 李遠哲 |

| | | | |
|---|---|---|---|
| Lien Chan | 連戰 | Shi Ming-teh | 施明德 |
| Li Hongzhang | 李鴻章 | Shiba Ryotaro | 司馬遼太郎 |
| Li Wenkui | 李文奎 | Soong Mei-ling | 宋美齡 |
| Liao Wen-I | 廖文毅 | Su Chen-chang | 蘇貞昌 |
| Lin Wei-yuan | 林維源 | Sun Yat-sen | 孫逸仙 |
| Lin Yang-kang | 林洋港 | Tang Jingsong | 唐景崧 |
| Lin Yi-hsiung | 林義雄 | Tu Cheng-sheng | 杜政勝 |
| Liu Mingchuan | 劉銘傳 | Wu Ching | 吳京 |
| Liu Yongfu | 劉永福 | Wu Guohua | 吳國華 |
| Lu Fei-yi | 盧非易 | Wu Nai-teh | 吳乃德 |
| Lu Hsiu-lien | 呂秀蓮 | Yang Qizhen | 楊岐珍 |
| Mao Zedong | 毛澤東 | Yu Cheng-hsien | 余成憲 |
| Peng Meng-chi | 彭孟緝 | Yu Mingzhen | 俞明震 |
| Peng Ming-min | 彭明敏 | Zeng Xizhao | 曾喜照 |
| Shao Youlian | 邵友濂 | Zhang Zhidong | 張之洞 |
| Shen Baozhen | 沈葆楨 | Zhou Zhenbang | 周振邦 |
| Shi Ming/Su Bing | 史明 | Yao Chia-wen | 姚嘉文 |

## Notions, Expressions, Names of Organizations

| | |
|---|---|
| baguo lianjun | 八國聯軍 |
| buchang | 補償 |
| beiju | 悲劇 |
| beitong | 悲痛 |
| Bensheng ren | 本省人 |
| Bendi ren | 本地人 |
| Bentuhua | 本土化 |
| biaozhun guoyu | 標準國語 |
| bo-li-xi-tian-de | 伯里璽天德 |
| Dalu ren | 大陸人 |
| Daotai | 道臺 |
| Dangwai | 黨外 |
| Datusha | 大屠殺 |
| du-Tai (duli Taiwan) | 獨臺 |
| er-er-ba shijian | 二二八事件 |
| fei zhuliu pai | 非主流派 |
| gezhou zhouxiu er-ri | 隔週週休二日 |
| Goa-seng-lang | 外省人 |

Goa-seng-lang Taiwan
    duli xiejin hui               外省人臺灣獨立協進會
guo hua                           國畫
guoli bianyi guan            國立編譯館
guo hao                         國號
teshu de guo yu
    guo de guanxi           特殊的國與國的關係
guojia shengming
    gongtongti              國家生命共同體
Guomin dahui              國民大會
Guomindang ye shi
    wailai zhengquan       國民黨也是外來政權
guo shi guan                 國史館
guoyu                              國語
heixiang zuoye             黑箱作業
Hakka                           客家
Han ren                       漢人
Holo                           鶴佬，福佬，河落
Hua ren                      華人
Huai                           淮
Lifa Yuan                   立法院
jiguan                        籍貫
jinian er-er-ba,
    bu zuo
    Zhongguo ren           紀念二二八，不作中國人
liangguo lun               兩國論
juancun                     眷村
liang Jiang zongtong
    lingqin zhengci        兩蔣總統陵寢政策
liankao                      聯考
luoye guigen               落葉歸根
luodi shenggen             落地生根
Meilidao                  美麗島
Minnan                    閩南
ong-lai-sou/fengli su       鳳梨酥
peichang                   賠償
pingdi Yuanzhumin       平地原住民
renshi Taiwan             認識臺灣
sanmin zhuyi de
    mofan sheng           三民主義的模範省

| | |
|---|---|
| Shanbao (Shandi tongbao) | 山胞（山地同胞） |
| shandi Yuanzhumin | 山地原住民 |
| Shanfan | 山番 |
| shengji wenti | 省籍問題 |
| sheng minzhengting | 省民政廳 |
| shenwairen | 省外人 |
| shuimo | 水墨 |
| suijing | 綏靖 |
| Quan-Mei Taiwan duli lianmeng | 全美臺灣獨立聯盟 |
| Taibei dianying xiehui | 臺北電影協會 |
| Taimin | 臺民 |
| Tairen | 臺人 |
| Taishang (Taiwan shangren) | 臺商（臺灣商人） |
| Taiwan duli lianmeng | 臺灣獨立聯盟 |
| Taiwan duli jianguo lianmeng | 臺灣獨立建國聯盟 |
| Taiwan gongchandang | 臺灣共產黨 |
| Taiwan gongheguo linshi zhengfu | 臺灣共和國臨時政府 |
| Taiwan guoyu | 臺灣國語 |
| Taiwan hun | 臺灣魂 |
| Taiwan minzhuguo | 臺灣民主國 |
| Taiwan qingnian she | 臺灣青年社 |
| Taiwan qingnian hui | 臺灣青年會 |
| Taiwan qingnian duli lianmeng | 臺灣青年獨立聯盟 |
| Taiwan ren | 臺灣人 |
| Taiwan ren chu tou tian | 臺灣人出頭天 |
| Taiwan ren de ziyou Taiwan | 臺灣人的自由臺灣 |
| Taiwan renquan weiyuanhui | 臺灣人權委員會 |
| Taiwan tongbao | 臺灣同胞 |
| Taiwan wenti yanjiuhui | 臺灣問題研究會 |
| Taiwan zhumin zijue lianmeng | 臺灣住民自覺聯盟 |
| tongxiang | 同鄉 |
| tongxiang hui | 同鄉會 |

| | |
|---|---|
| tongxin yuan | 同心圓 |
| tui yi bu, ji wu si suo | 退一步即無死所 |
| tuzhu hua | 土著化 |
| Waishengren | 外省人 |
| Women de Zhongguo | 我們的中國 |
| wenhua beijing | 文化背景 |
| wenhua shuizhun | 文化水準 |
| wu wang zai Ju | 毋忘在莒 |
| xian lai hou dao | 先來後到 |
| xiang | 鄉 |
| Xin Taiwan ren | 新臺灣人 |
| Xin Taiwan ren guan | 新臺灣人觀 |
| Xin Taiwan ren lun | 新臺灣人論 |
| Xin Taiwan ren zhuyi | 新臺灣人主義 |
| Xin Zhongyuan | 新中原 |
| Xin zhumin | 新住民 |
| xiucai | 秀才 |
| yizhong bu yiyang | 一種不一樣 |
| yizhong youshi | 一種優勢 |
| youmin | 游民 |
| Yue | 粵 |
| Yuanzhumin | 原住民 |
| zhengzhi qi | 政治期 |
| Zhongguo ren | 中國人 |
| Zhongyuan | 中原 |
| Zhongzhan | 終戰 |
| zizhu | 自主 |
| zongtong | 總統 |
| zongli | 總裡 |
| zuji | 祖籍 |
| zuoke de xintai | 做客的心態 |

# Index

National identification preference
  conservative *(continued)*
    characteristics, 145, 146
    status quo preference, 145, 146
  considerations
    attitude, 144–52, 155–58
    geopolitical constraints, 144, 152–58
  ethnic consciousness impact
    attitude survey (1992/1994/1996),
      147–49, 151*t*, 152*t*
    Chinese/*Zhongguoren*, 147–49, 151*t*, 152*t*
    *jiguan* system, 147–48
    Mainlander/*Waishengren*, 147–49, 151*t*,
      152*t*
    Taiwanese/*Benshengren*, 147–49, 151*t*,
      152*t*
  ethnicity impact
    Mainlander/*Waishengren*, 147, 148*t*
    Taiwanese/*Benshengren*, 147, 148*t*
  Lee Teng-hui, 145
  overview, xviii-xix
  pragmatist
    attitude increase (1992–96), 147
    attitude survey (1992), 144–46
    attitude survey (1992–96), 146–47
    characteristics, 145–46
    Mainlander/*Waishengren* increase
      (1992–96), 147
    preference stipulations, 145–46
    Taiwanese/*Benshengren* increase
      (1992–96), 147
  research study
    data sources, 158n.1
    implications, 155–58
    methodology, 144
    objectives, 144
    summarization, 158
  secessionist movement analysis, 152–55
    pure secession characteristics, 153
    pure secession examples, 153
    self-determination, 154–55
    successful/ineffective state examples, 153
    successful/state resistance characteristics,
      153–54
    successful/state resistance examples, 154
    successful/state resistance rationale,
      154–55
    unsuccessful examples, 154
  Taiwan nationalist
    attitude increase (1992–96), 146, 147
    attitude survey (1992), 144–46
    attitude survey (1992–96), 146–47

National identification preference
  Taiwan nationalist *(continued)*
    characteristics, 145
    independence proponents, 145
    Taiwanese/*Benshengren* (1992/1994/
      1995), 150–52
    Taiwanese/*Benshengren* increase
      (1992–96), 147
  Wu Nai-teh, 144
National Institute of Editions and Translations
  (NIET), 84, 85–86, 88, 90
National radio, 28
National Unification Council, 128
Nation-Building Forum (1997), 40–41, 43n.9
New Inhabitants
  international relations
    ethnicity impact, 247–48, 249
    memory impact, 243
    nation-building impact, 247
  Mainlander/*Waishengren* identity, 189
New Party (NP)
  elite-mass linkage
    elite manipulation, 133–34
    mass opinion, 134–35, 136, 138–41
    reunification vs. independence, 133–34,
      138–39, 142
    Taiwan-China relations, 134, 139–41
    Taiwanese/Chinese identity, 133,
      134–35, 136
    Taiwan foreign policy, 140–41
  history textbooks, 85–86, 89, 99n.23
  international relations, 248
  passive revolution, 197, 211
  political identity construction, 229,
    230–31
New Taiwanese
  February 28 Incident (1947)
    civic nationalism, 37
    ethnic identity, 37–38
    narrative interpretation, 37–38, 42
    oceanic nationalism, 37
    political opposition, 38
    state identity, 37
  Mainlander/*Waishengren* identity
    the debate on the New Taiwanese, 187–88
    generational factor, 186, 188–89
    New Inhabitants, 189
    the New Taiwanese conception, 186–87
    New Taiwanism, 187
    origination, 186–87, 194n.21
    political factor, 188–89
    *sheng* signification, 189